# Economic History
## of the South

PRENTICE-HALL HISTORY SERIES
CARL WITTKE, Ph.D., EDITOR

# Economic History
## *of the*
# South

*by*

### Emory Q. Hawk, Ph.D.
*Professor of Economics*
*Birmingham-Southern College*

### FOREWORD

*by*

### Tipton R. Snavely, Ph.D.
*Professor of Economics*
*University of Virginia*

## GREENWOOD PRESS, PUBLISHERS
### WESTPORT, CONNECTICUT

Library of Congress Cataloging in Publication Data

Hawk, Emory Quinter, 1892–
    Economic history of the South.

    Reprint of the 1934 ed. published by Prentice-Hall,
New York, issued in series:   Prentice-Hall history
series.
    Includes bibliographical references.
    1.  Southern States—Economic conditions.
I.  Title.
    HC107.A13H3   1973          330.9'75          75-136535
    ISBN 0–8371–5456–1

Originally published in 1934 by Prentice-Hall, Inc., New York

Reprinted by Greenwood Press, Inc.

First Greenwood reprinting 1973
Second Greenwood reprinting 1977

Library of Congress catalog card number 75-136535

ISBN 0-8371-5456-1

Printed in the United States of America

TO

THOMAS WALKER PAGE

# Acknowledgments

THE writer wishes to express his deep appreciation to all those who have taken an interest in the preparation of this study. He is indebted particularly to President Guy E. Snavely, of Birmingham-Southern College, for encouragement in this undertaking; to Professor Carl Wittke, of the Ohio State University, for invaluable suggestions; and to Professor T. R. Snavely, of the University of Virginia, for sympathetic aid. Grateful acknowledgment is made to Professor W. D. Perry, of the English Department of Birmingham-Southern College, who read the entire manuscript; to Mr. E. C. Denne, of the Engineering Staff of the United States Steel Corporation's plants in Birmingham, who prepared all the graphs and maps reproduced in this book; and to the editorial department of Prentice-Hall, Inc., for many helpful suggestions and painstaking care in reading manuscript and proofs. In gathering material, the writer was especially aided by Miss Lillian Gregory, Librarian of Birmingham-Southern College; by Mr. James A. McMillen, Librarian of the Louisiana State University; and by his colleagues in the Department of Economics at Birmingham-Southern College: Messrs. Thomas Debnam and Perry W. Woodham. Finally, grateful acknowledgment is to be made to his wife, who gave unfailing aid in securing clarity of thought and expression in the work, and who typed the entire manuscript.

E. Q. H.

# Table of Contents

# Foreword

SINCE the beginning of the present century it has become increasingly necessary to examine the basic economic factors of our civilization. At first glance this statement may seem paradoxical, inasmuch as there has been, during this period, a significant growth in wealth and income, and in the general standard of living. The fact is, however, that the economic system of today is more tenuous, and far more intricate and sensitive, than any that has yet been evolved. Furthermore, one can scarcely hope to achieve in the future the same rapid progress in wealth and income that has been realized during the past several decades. This progress has resulted in large measure from the abundance of natural resources and the momentum of our natural environment. If it remains true that the arts, religion, and learning "have meaning and vitality only in relation to their economic sub-structure," we can ill afford to preserve the calm indifference of the past toward precise thinking about economic policy.

The observation has frequently been made that the problems arising as an aftermath of the World War have been too vast and too complex for any human mind to grasp. The subnormal economic situation has penetrated to nearly every region of the earth. The difficulty of maintaining a harmonious adjustment of the delicate parts of the economic machine has led to an insistent demand for radical changes in government and social organization. Fundamental economic forces themselves are being challenged as though they may be readily controlled or altered by mere human fiat. Despite prevailing assertions, however, it seems clear that the stage has by no means been reached

when mere changes in governmental organization or a re-
distribution of income will result in a satisfactory level of
economic welfare.  We are still far from the goal of an ideal
standard of living.

It is not for naught, therefore, that we have turned to
the field of economic history for guidance in the solution
of economic problems.  Until recent years comparatively
little emphasis has been placed on the economic aspects of
history.  It has been the vogue to regard history as a chronicle of political events or religious movements; as a por-
trayal of battles and military leaders.  While political and
religious history need not be minimized, it should be remembered that "the work of exploiting nature, if it has
also its sordid side, has called forth the finest intellectual
efforts and the finest qualities of character in men."  Nor
is economic history itself a simple narration of facts, without analysis and interpretation.

Professor Hawk has written, I believe, the first general
treatise to appear, covering the entire period of the economic evolution of the South.  Existing volumes on American economic history have given correlative treatment to
the Southern States.  In recent decades numerous mono-
graphs of high merit have been published.  For the most part
these works have dealt with specific phases of the South's
economic development.  Professor Hawk's objective has
been to prepare for the Southern region a treatise similar
in character to the standard works which have been written for the United States as a whole.  The justification for
such a regional study lies in the homogeneity of certain
factors of geography and climate in the South and, from
the time of the early settlements, in a certain mutuality of
economic interests.

The primary aim which Professor Hawk has held in mind
has been the preparation of a satisfactory textbook for use
in colleges and universities.  It is my belief that he has
succeeded admirably in this task and that the volume will
prove unusually stimulating and informative.  He has

sought only to discover the truth and to disclose the truth
as he found it. The book is characterized by a nicety of
balance and symmetry of structure. From a medley of
facts, conflicting motives, and confused actions, Professor
Hawk has endeavored to develop a synthesis which would
portray the dominant tendencies and movements of each
period. He has not been oblivious of the theory that economics is concerned not so much with "any particular set
of economic facts" as with a "particular point of view upon
almost all human activities." In short, he has attempted
to give, first, a clear perspective of the forest and, afterwards, to offer such an inspection of the individual trees
as has been found practicable.

It should be said that, while Professor Hawk makes no
particular claim to originality of sources of material, he has
read widely in remote places and has found many quarries
to which reference has not previously been made. He has
had access, for example, to manuscripts embodying a plantation diary written during the Civil War. Probably more
emphasis has been placed on public finance than is to be
found in any general work on economic history. In this
field he has examined a considerable amount of material
which has not hitherto been made accessible. An illuminating and critical bibliography has been placed at the end
of each chapter. Finally, if the root of originality consists
of keen insight into essentials, the volume should take high
rank as a permanent contribution in the supremely important field of economic history.

TIPTON R. SNAVELY

# Economic History of the South

## CHAPTER I

## The South

WHAT is the *South?* The term has long been used and variously defined.

In the colonial period, the South comprised five colonies: Maryland, Virginia, the Carolinas, and Georgia. These lay along the Atlantic seaboard and stretched westward through the Piedmont to the Appalachian frontier. In 1790, the South definitely embraced 405,365 square miles, or about half the area of the new nation. Seventy years later, when Florida, Louisiana, and Texas had been added and when the frontier had shifted to the Far West, the South included the thirteen slaveholding states below the Mason and Dixon Line. During the Civil War, eleven of these states were collectively termed the *Southern Confederacy.* Today, no line sharply divides the South from the North; in fact, each section merges into the other almost imperceptibly, for the border states—Maryland, West Virginia, Kentucky, and Missouri—have characteristics of both sections. Nevertheless, for the purpose of this study, the South is considered basically a homogeneous economic section comprised of the following states: Maryland, Virginia, West Virginia, North Carolina, South Carolina, Georgia, Florida, Alabama, Mississippi, Louisiana, Texas, Arkansas, Oklahoma, Missouri, Kentucky, and Tennessee.

To obtain a clear understanding of the economic history of this section, popularly termed the *South*, it is necessary not only to visualize a chronological series of economic events beginning over three hundred years ago, but, what is even more important, to realize the influence of certain factors and forces in determining the course of economic development.

## Physiographic Factors and Natural Resources

It is well, therefore, to begin with a discussion of the physiographic factors, for at every step the economic development of the South shows their far-reaching influence. Originally the contour of the coast determined the places of early settlement: the river valleys, the dividing ridges, and the mountain gaps pointed the routes westward; while climate and soil determined the kinds of crops and made cotton king. Likewise the natural resources, though dependent for use upon the progress of technology, have, because of availability, practically localized Southern industry within narrow areas. Indeed, all these factors—topography, climate, and natural resources—basically limit Southern economy to a degree not generally appreciated either by those who herald the rise of industrialism in this section, or by those who lament the alleged passing of an agrarian economy.

### TOPOGRAPHY AND SOILS OF THE SOUTH

The land area of the South includes 945,025 square miles, or 31.7 per cent of the national area, and as a whole is broadly divisible into six physiographic provinces. These are: an extensive low-lying coastal plain on the east and the south; the deep embayment of the lower Mississippi and its tributaries; the elevated plains of the Piedmont Plateau on the east; the Appalachian Highland region to the west; the outliers of the Appalachians, better known as the Ozark Plateau and the Ouachita Mountains; and finally, the Great Plains of western Oklahoma and Texas.

The *Atlantic Coastal Plain* extends the full length of the seaboard. In width it varies from less than 50 miles to more than 200, but averages about 150. Rising very gently from the swampy shores and estuaries on the coast, it reaches an elevation at its inner margin of about 200 or 300 feet, and ranges from less than 100 feet in Maryland to more than 600 feet in Mississippi. However, as a whole the surface of the Coastal Plain is practically level or gently rolling.

For the most part the soils of this plain are composed of sand and light sand loams, with some scattered deposits of silts and heavy clays. Except for the river bottoms, these soils are residual from underlying strata of either sandstone, limestone, or shale. The lighter sandy soils are found not only along the seacoast but sometimes far inland. Thus, the greater part of Florida, where there are no swamps such as the Everglades, is covered with this kind of soil. Much of the hinterland of several coastal cities—as for example, St. Augustine, Pensacola, and Wilmington—was in its natural state entirely too sandy for the production of ordinary grains and vegetables; and there are at the present time extensive areas which are practically covered with pine forests, the pine apparently being well adapted to such soil. Usually these areas are called *pine barrens* and are to be classified with the poorer areas of the South.

In contrast with these sandy soils, heavy clays are located near the inner margin of the plain. Silts, silty clays, and black calcareous soils are found, particularly in the rice-producing sections of Louisiana and Texas, which, according to the United States Bureau of Soils, have no equivalent in the Atlantic division. There are even more fertile soils in those areas where the soil rests upon limestone beds. The two most notable of these areas are: (1) The *Black Belt* of Alabama, so called from the color of its soil and not on account of its 87 per cent negro population, and (2) the *Black Waxie* of Texas. The former area extends in crescent shape from Montgomery to Tuscaloosa; the latter, from north of Dallas to south of Austin. These areas comprise two of the most productive cotton sections of America. Finally, there are very fertile alluvial strips which border all the larger rivers flowing through the Coastal Plain. Some of these—for example, the one along the James River in Virginia—have been seed beds for Southern culture.

It must be especially noted that to the early colonists the Coastal Plain was the whole of the South and that, as will appear hereafter, its topography, soil, and climate were predominating determinant factors in the establishment of the plantation system.

The *Mississippi embayment*, embracing the lower part of the Mississippi Valley, bisects the belt of the Coastal Plain and extends 500 miles from the tip of the delta to the mouth of the Ohio River. From east to west this province includes all of Mississippi and Louisiana, eastern Arkansas and western Alabama, and western Tennessee and western Kentucky. According to geologists, this whole area was inundated by the Gulf during the Tertiary and Cenozoic Ages. Then sands, clays, gravels, marls, and limestones, derived largely from the erosion of the continental mass, were deposited and spread out into broad flood plains. Along the Mississippi River from Cairo to the Gulf is a strip of alluvial soil from 75 to 100 miles wide. This strip is, perhaps, as fertile as the famous Nile Valley. In the rest of the Mississippi embayment, the soils, when well drained, are generally productive of cotton and truck. But always, especially along the Mississippi River, floods and malaria have hindered the free and effective utilization of great areas of this territory.

The *Piedmont Plateau* lies between the Fall Line of the Coastal Plain and the eastern base of the Appalachian Mountains. In length, it extends all the way from Maryland, through Virginia and the Carolinas, into Georgia. In width, it varies from 20 miles in Maryland and 50 miles in Virginia to more than 150 miles in North Carolina. If viewed from a point of advantage, it appears as a broad, rolling plain with here and there a few round hills, and is deeply trenched with many small streams and a few larger ones, such as the Potomac, the James, the Roanoke, the Savannah, and the Chattahoochee.

The surface of this plateau is covered with sandy loams, clay loams, and clays, the type of soil depending primarily upon the kind of bedrock from which it is residual. Usually the clays are bright red in color because of the oxidation of the iron oxides. Although the subsoil is generally much more compact than the surface soil, the susceptibility to erosion is one of the chief drawbacks of the entire area. Nevertheless, the degree of fertility of this plateaù is nearly everywhere sufficient to support hardwood forests and productive farms.

The *Appalachian Highland region* lies immediately west of the Piedmont Plateau and extends from the Mason and Dixon Line southward into Alabama. This region consists of three parallel belts: on the east, the Blue Ridge and Unaka Mountains, with their foothills in Georgia and Alabama; on the west, the Allegheny-Cumberland Plateau; and between these truly highland areas, a large central depression, scientifically termed the *Great Appalachian Valley*.

The *Blue Ridge belt* may roughly be compared to a narrow, lance-shaped leaf. In Maryland, it extends only about 10 miles in width, and less than 2,000 feet in elevation; but near the headwaters of the Roanoke it begins to rise and spread out until, in North Carolina, it reaches a maximum width of 70 miles, and in Mount Mitchell an elevation of nearly 7,000 feet. Then southward, in Georgia, it becomes irregular and loses itself in the Piedmont Plateau.

Although the Unakas, west of the Blue Ridge proper, reach their highest altitude in this belt, on the Blue Ridge proper is located the main divide between the streams flowing into the Atlantic and those flowing into the Gulf. On the eastern side of the divide, the slopes are very precipitous, and the streams dash down to the Piedmont Plateau in a series of high cascades and deep gorges. On its western side, the slopes are much more gradual; and, after flowing through broad valleys, narrow mountain gorges, and the Great Valley, the streams eventually go to join the Mississippi.

These rugged and picturesque mountain ranges, the Blue Ridge and the Unakas, are formed of crystalline rocks similar to those in the Piedmont Plateau. Ages ago they were probably the first areas on the continent to emerge from the primordial sea. Now they are covered with residual soils, consisting principally of red or yellow clays and clay loams. In many places, especially on the steeper slopes, the soil is not only stony but very susceptible to erosion. The coves and frequently the upland ridges, however, are very fertile and are excelled in the production of grass and grain by few other regions in the South.

Along the northwestern border of the Great Valley and facing the Blue Ridge, like a great wall, rises the escarpment of the Allegheny-Cumberland Plateau. This plateau extends to the loessal and bottom lands of the Mississippi. The surface as a whole is rolling, often hilly and rugged, and occasionally mountainous. The soils are formed from sandstones and shales, and, except in a few isolated areas, are of very low productive value.

In Maryland and West Virginia, this plateau is locally known as the *Allegheny Plateau;* in eastern Kentucky and central Tennessee, it is termed the *Cumberland Plateau.* The latter area is the very heart of a Southern district of human isolation, where early populations stranded, perpetuated their archaic customs and language traits, and became almost fossilized. However, in recent decades the region has become economically significant on account of abundant mineral resources, and the agencies of education and technology are establishing a closer relationship between it and the modern world.

Within this plateau, moreover, there are two extraordinarily fertile and progressive areas, the Lexington and the Nashville Basins. When Daniel Boone and other pioneers passed through the Cumberland Gap, they followed an Indian trail into central Kentucky. There they found the floor of a great basin walled around by the sandstone hills of a plateau. This basin, scientifically known as the *Lexington Basin,* is famous in history and in literature as the land of the Kentucky Blue Grass. The pioneers who followed the Tennessee River likewise came upon a somewhat similar basin in middle Tennessee, known later as the *Nashville Basin.* This latter area, while not so extensive as the Lexington Basin, includes approximately 5,500 square miles of very fertile land, partly level and partly rolling. Both areas are highly productive agriculturally; perhaps nowhere in America can be seen better examples of the influence of soils upon economic development. In each basin there is a thriving and populous city surrounded by prosperous farms, while upon the rim of the plateau there is poor sandy soil furnishing a meager subsistence for a sparse population.

Between the Allegheny-Cumberland Plateau on the west and the Blue Ridge on the east extends the Great Appalachian Valley. This central trough is 75 miles wide, though sunk several hundred feet below the highland borders, and is itself an upland region varying from less than 500 to more than 1,000—even 1,700—feet in elevation. To the geographer, technically it is a physiographic unit extending all the way from New York to the southern tip of the Appalachian Highlands. Through human use, however, it has been broken into sections; and in the South it is now severally named: the Hagerstown Valley, the Valley of Virginia, the Valley of East Tennessee, and the Valley of the Coosa River.

The floor of the whole Appalachian Valley is often hill-studded and is sometimes cut into parts by long, high residual ridges. In the Virginias, this valley is a series of lesser valleys taking their names from their rivers; as, the Shenandoah, the James, the Roanoke, the Kanawha, and the New. Likewise in Tennessee and further southward where the main valley appears more unified, there are prominent ridges, numerous hills, and vales of various size and arrangement.

Throughout the Appalachian Valley the prevailing soils fall into three classes: in the lower valleys and hills, brown and red clay soils formed from the underlying limestones; on the higher ridges, shallow and often gravelly and stony soils formed from the underlying shales, sandstones, and impure limestones; and in the lower Tennessee Valley and on through upper Alabama, the alluvial soils. Hence, the uses of the land in this valley are diverse. In every section there are agricultural lands, forest lands, and waste lands. The scenic beauty of this Great Valley diverts attention from its several isolated spots of poverty and backwardness. The Valley of Virginia, especially—with its green fields, dark cedars, fragrant apple orchards, and autumn floods of color against a background of hazy mountains—is one of the beauty spots of America and challenges many an imagination with its history and its possibilities.

The Appalachian Highland region has had a peculiar influence upon the economic history of the South. That this region in colonial times was a "trackless wilderness" and an "impassable barrier" is doubtless only a cherished figment of the imagination; for, when the time came, pioneers blazed trails and found gaps pointing the way westward. Nevertheless, until practically all the good lands of the Atlantic Coastal Plain and the Piedmont had been preëmpted, this vast region remained an unsettled frontier, little known and less wanted. Yet, finally, when population trekked westward, this region became—what perhaps it shall ever be—a kind of dividing line between two types of economic development in the South.

West of the Mississippi River there are two upland regions—the Ozark Plateau and the Ouachita Mountains—

termed by physiographers the *outliers of the Appalachians.*
The Ozark Plateau covers most of Missouri south of the
Missouri River and extends into northern Arkansas. The
Ouachita Mountains, a low range south of the Arkansas
River, extend from central Arkansas into Oklahoma.
These regions presumably were formed by the reappear-
ance of the strata of the Appalachian System and, therefore, have characteristics somewhat similar to those of the
Allegheny-Cumberland Plateau. In the upland districts
the soil is usually poor, while in the lower lands the soil
is richer and more productive. As a whole, however, these
regions are rather sparsely settled, and have had little economic importance, except as a source for some mineral
wealth.

The last physiographic province of the South consists of
a section of the *Great Plains,* which sweep southward from
the Canadian border to the Coastal Plain, and rises in
elevation from a few hundred feet on the east until it
reaches over 4,000 feet at the foot of the Rocky Mountains.
Topographically its surface is divided into three distinct
belts: to the east, the Low Plains; the central belt or High
Plains, called in Texas the *Llano Estacado,* or *Staked
Plain;* and, finally, the Pecos Valley of western Texas.
Most of this plain area appears as a flat and treeless ex-
panse. In soil and in climate these plains constitute a
transition zone between a humid east and an arid west.
The eastern portion is well adapted to farming and grazing,
the one supplementing the other; while the western portion is predominantly grazing land. These plains comprise
a land of sparse population, few cities, clear skies, and
great open spaces, where it is still possible to live relatively
free from the mechanization and sophistication of modern
civilization.

## CLIMATE OF THE SOUTH

According to climatologists, the South can be divided
into three general climatic provinces: the Gulf province,

which is a long irregular belt including Florida and stretching from the lower boundary of South Carolina to the Rio Grande; second, the Southern Plains province, which includes the Great Plains of Oklahoma and Texas; and the remaining area of the South, which lies within the eastern climatic province of the United States. Each province, however, is a somewhat arbitrary division, for, in reality, traveling from the north to the Gulf coast, or from the east to the west, one encounters no sudden changes in climate. In fact, even the differences between the southern and northern climates of the United States frequently have been exaggerated.

In the provinces of the South, moreover, the least difference occurs in midsummer, when the change experienced as one travels from the north southward is not over one degree in temperature per latitude degree. The greatest difference is in midwinter, when the average monthly temperature increases at the rate of about 1.5 degrees for every 40 or 50 miles traveled southward. To be noted, also, is the fact that each of these provinces is capable of much subdivision on account of local climatic variations, caused generally by differences in altitude. In each province there appear common factors, however—such as, length of the growing season, rainfall, and temperature—which, when compared, give a fair estimate of climates in the South.

For the Eastern province, the growing season in the border states averages about six months, and that in the states comprising the Gulf province, about seven months. The summer temperature varies ordinarily between 70 and 80 degrees. The days are usually hot, and the nights cool, especially in the Highland region. Droughts are seldom general; the average rainfall ranges from about 40 inches in the border states to over 50 inches in the states farther south. During the winter the snowfall is seldom over 10 inches and remains scarcely longer than one to ten days, except on the plateaus and mountains.

During the winter months cold rains with sleet are common. The atmosphere remains damp, and the temperature is more keenly felt than in somewhat colder climates where there is less humidity. On the whole, though, the climate in this region affords few sudden changes or violent contrasts and thus, perhaps, approaches the optimum more nearly than any other extensive section of the United States.

As compared with the Eastern province, the Gulf province has higher temperatures, much milder winters, and hotter summers. The growing season extends over a period of two hundred and forty days, and the rainfall averages more than 60 inches. Snow is a rarity, and the Peninsula of Florida has a genuine subtropical climate. Unfortunately, however, this province sometimes has unexpected, killing frosts that cause considerable economic loss; but on the whole it is a kind of hothouse area for the inhabitants of the northeastern part of the United States.

Between the Southern Plains province and the Eastern province there are practically no important differences in average mean temperatures. The mean winter temperature of the Southern Plains is generally over 40 degrees, and the summer temperature averages between 70 and 80 degrees. The growing season ranges from about six months along the northern border to over eight months in southern Texas. The essential difference between the two provinces is one of rainfall. The climate of the Southern Plains is, of course, continental; but, unlike the Eastern province, this area is remote from the Atlantic and Gulf winds, and to the west the Rockies rise to block the clouds rising from the Pacific Ocean. Hence, the Plains province is more arid, and evaporation is more rapid. The eastern portion of this province has an average rainfall of about 20 inches; the western portion, not more than 15 inches. Between these two portions is a line of demarcation between agriculture and grazing. As an old proverb declares: "East of it lies success; west of it, failure. Look out for the 'dead line.' "

Perhaps the worst climatic feature of this province is the so-called Texas *norther*. As described by Dr. Robert D. Ward, of Harvard University:[1] "It comes as a rushing blast from the northwest or north and brings a sudden drop of temperature of maybe 25 degrees or more in an hour, and over 50 degrees or more in two or three hours in winter. The wild sweep of the norther over the open plains is dreaded by all who are outdoors and exposed to its chilly fury. Shelter is sought when possible. Indoors, huge fires are quickly lighted, windows are closed, and the passing of the tempest is impatiently awaited. The sudden fall in temperature is especially disagreeable to human beings and injurious to stock and crops because of the warmth and mugginess which precede it." However, despite such drawbacks, it is only fair to say that most of the time the climate of the Plains province is unusually healthful and stimulating.

Although each of the three provinces, as here sketched, has its climatic faults—such as, excessive humidity, killing frosts, northers, and the like—nevertheless, no section of the United States is more generally favored in climate than is the South. More than three fourths of this vast area receives 40 or more inches of rain each year, and not more than 120,000 square miles can be classed as semiarid. The growing season varies from six months to that of the subtropical region along the Gulf coast. The temperature ranges from the invigorating coolness of the Highland region to the intense heat of the Mississippi embayment. In fact, in the territory embraced within the Coastal Plain, the Piedmont, the Highland region, and the Great Plains beyond the Mississippi, there is almost every variety of climate that man may desire.

From the economic viewpoint climate is basically important for two reasons: (1) It directly affects both agricul-

---

[1] *Climates of North America* (1925), p. 378. Reprinted by permission of Ginn & Co., Boston.

ture and industry by setting limits to the kind of crops that can be grown and by influencing consumer demand for manufactured goods. For example, cotton cannot be grown in a cold climate, nor will there be any appreciable demand for woolen clothes in a warm one. (2) It influences the productivity of human labor by stimulating or retarding physical and mental vigor. Therefore, because of the nature of the climate of the South, it is necessary at all times to reckon with its economic influence.

One of the chief reasons that the South for the most part has been a highly specialized agricultural region is climate. Cotton requires an average temperature of at least 77 degrees for three months (June, July, and August) and an average period of not less than two hundred days between the last killing frost of spring and the first killing frost of autumn. These climatic conditions are confined to the region south of the 37th parallel and extending westward to the territory in which the mean annual rainfall drops to 23 inches. Within this area, which extends 1,600 miles in length and from 125 to 500 miles in width, cotton is the chief crop. It is literally the *Cotton Belt;* for, aside from the growing of a little corn here and there, diversification has made scarcely any headway, and will not do so unless there is a prolonged cessation of demand for cotton, or the boll weevil makes its growing costs prohibitive. Tobacco, though less restricted by soil and climate, is also a Southern crop. In fact, 90 per cent of the tobacco produced in the United States comes from the South. This production, presumably, is due to climatic conditions, which give the leaves a distinct and desirable aroma and flavor. The areas utilized mainly for the growing of the tobacco plant are: northern and western Kentucky; the southern Piedmont of Virginia; and, in former times, the James River Valley down to the coast, the Piedmont and Coastal Plain of North Carolina; and the eastern part of the Coastal Plain of South Carolina.

In the Gulf province, the climate is well adapted to the

growing of citrus fruits, sugar cane, and rice. There is an important center of the citrus fruit industry on the Florida Peninsula. Sugar cane is produced on a commercial scale on the lower delta of the Mississippi River; and three fourths of the rice produced in the United States grows on the warm and well-watered Gulf Coastal Plain of Louisiana and Texas.

Aside from these major belts of agricultural products— cotton, tobacco, subtropical fruits, grains, and sugar cane— there is some diversification of farming in practically every section and especially in the Highland region. Here cattle raising is carried on extensively, but it is even more important as an industry on the Great Plains. It appears, then, that by the very nature of the case a large part of the South has been limited to a rather definite and highly specialized agrarian economy.

As to the effect of Southern climate upon physical and mental vigor, much has been written. Some writers declare that Southern climate is unhealthful; still others actually bewail "Southern languor." Nevertheless, such generalizations have frequently been made without foundation in facts. Several localities in the South are unhealthful; however, many are the most healthful in America. Some inhabitants, especially among the negroes and poor whites, do lack energy, and in the lower South the climate obviously does reduce human energy. But, as a matter of fact, there are no comparable statistics available anywhere showing the alleged differences between the efficiency of labor in the North and in the South.[2]

---

[2] Professor Ellesworth Huntington, who has studied the effect of climate upon physical and mental activity, by a method of *sampling* has arrived at the following conclusion: "A mean temperature of 64 degrees (Fahrenheit), a mean humidity of about 80 per cent and frequent changes of temperature are the most desirable conditions for purely physical health. . . . For purely mental work the conditions of humidity and variability should apparently be about the same but the mean temperature should be much lower, perhaps 40 degrees."—*World Power and Evolution*, p. 8.

### Mineral Resources of the South

In mineral resources—iron, coal, petroleum, and many minor minerals—the South is richly endowed, but the availability of these resources has been contingent upon the scope of contemporary scientific knowledge and technology. During the periods prior to the Civil War, the existence of many of these Southern deposits was unknown and the utilization of the known supplies was very limited. Later, needs and knowledge brought to light the existence of these rich sources and increased their exploitation to the extent that localities around the mines sometimes became highly urbanized—as for example, in the section around Birmingham, Alabama.

**Iron.** Deposits of iron ores are found distributed from Virginia on the northeast to Texas on the southwest. These ores belong to several groups: hematite, brown ores, magnetite, and iron carbonate. Of these the most abundant and the most important commercially are the Clinton hematite ores. Such ores occur throughout the Appalachian region from Virginia to Alabama. In the Tennessee-Virginia region, they occur sparsely and are worked only in a few localities. In the Chattanooga-Attalla region, they are more important and are worked at several points. In the Birmingham district, which is the iron and steel center of the South, they reach their maximum thickness and availability.

Next in importance to the hematite group are the several grades and classes of brown ores. The so-called "mountain-and-valley" brown ores are distributed along the eastern border of the Appalachian belt, and are perhaps most important in the Blue Ridge and the New River sections of Virginia. Although these ores were the basis of the first iron developments in the South, they have gradually come to be less and less exploited both on account of the labor cost and the scattered and fragmentary nature of the deposits.

Of more commercial importance are the Oriskany brown ores. These occur in varying thickness and purity at several points on the western side of the Appalachian region from western Virginia, through West Virginia, Kentucky, and Tennessee, to Alabama. In the Ozark Mountains of Missouri, there are somewhat similar deposits. but they are of slight commercial value. In northeastern Texas, there are extensive beds of brown ore, totaling about 1,000 square miles and varying in thickness from one to three feet. But these, like the deposits in the Ozark Mountains have never been very profitably or extensively exploited. Finally, scattered here and there are deposits of magnetite and iron carbonates of different grades and extent. Some occur in the Appalachian Valley of Virginia, Georgia, and Alabama, and in the Piedmont from Virginia to Georgia; and still others occur in central Missouri and in Llano County, Texas. Except for the magnetite deposits in North Carolina, scarcely any of these have been commercialized.

Unfortunately, many of the Southern iron ore deposits are of slight economic importance. There are various reasons for this condition, such as, low grade, meager size, and inaccessible location geologically or geographically. On the other hand, conservative estimates indicate that the South probably has half of the commercially valuable iron ores in the United States. Or, to be more specific. according to an estimate of an eminent authority, Edwin C. Eckel,[3] the South in 1913 had at least 2,600,000,000 tons, whereas the United States had a minimum total of about 5,200,000,000 tons. Also to be noted is the fact that in many localities coal is found in abundance near these iron ores; thus together, the two could form the basis of what might be an extensive iron and steel industry. But, strange to say, outside of a few localities, the chief of which is the Birmingham district, there never has been

[3] Edwin C. Eckel, *Iron Ores, Their Occurrence, Valuation and Control,* p. 245.

in the South an extensive exploitation of these iron ores.
Statistics of production show that the iron industry in the
South has not only failed to keep pace with the general
development of that industry in the United States, but

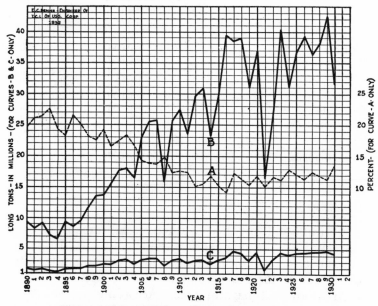

CURVE - A = PERCENT OF SOUTHERN PIG IRON PRODUCTION TO TOTAL
            UNITED STATES   PRODUCTION.
CURVE - B = PIG IRON  PRODUCTION  IN  UNITED STATES.
CURVE - C = PIG IRON  PRODUCTION  IN  SOUTHERN STATES.

Comparison of Pig Iron Production in the United States and in the
Southern States, 1890–1930

has actually declined in its relative position from that of
forty years ago.

**Coal.**  As estimated by the United States Geological
Survey,[4] the South has probably as much as 530,002,000,-
000 tons of coal reserves (see table, p. 18).  These occur
in varying amounts in twelve states, but the greater deposits lie within the southern part of the Appalachian coal

---

[4] U. S. Geological Survey, Professional Paper 100A; U. S. Bureau of
Mines, *Mineral Resources of the United States* (1929), pp. 673–858.

field, which extends from northeastern Pennsylvania into Alabama.

COAL IN THE SOUTH, BY STATES[a]

| State | Estimated Reserves (Tons) | Production (Tons—1929) |
|---|---|---|
| West Virginia | 149,026,000,000 | 138,519,000 |
| Kentucky | 103,771,000,000 | 60,463,000 |
| Alabama | 68,572,000,000 | 17,944,000 |
| Virginia | 22,380,000,000 | 12,748,000 |
| Tennessee | 25,499,000,000 | 5,405,000 |
| Missouri | 39,833,000,000 | 4,030,000 |
| Oklahoma | 79,201,000,000 | 3,774,000 |
| Maryland | 7,795,000,000 | 2,649,000 |
| Arkansas | 1,839,000,000 | 1,695,000 |
| Texas | 30,967,000,000 | 1,101,000 |
| Georgia | 920,000,000 | [b] |
| North Carolina | 199,000,000 | [b] |
| TOTAL | 530,002,000,000 | 248,328,000 |

[a] Arranged in order of commercial importance for 1929.
[b] Practically no production during last two or three decades.

Practically all of this Southern coal, except a little anthracite in Virginia and some lignite in Texas, is bituminous, or semibituminous, and is suitable either for coking coal or for general manufacturing uses.

**Petroleum and natural gas.** According to estimates, in 1922, the South contained more than 5,000,000,000 barrels of oil reserves, or 55 per cent of the total oil reserves of the United States. During recent years, oil has been obtained in eight Southern States: Arkansas, Kentucky, Tennessee, Louisiana, Missouri, Oklahoma, Texas, and West Virginia. Although the quantities produced in Tennessee and Missouri have been of practically no commercial importance, extensive oil operations have been carried on in the other six states, and the production of oil in Oklahoma and Texas has ranked second only to that of California.

The South has approximately 2,500 square miles of natural-gas producing areas, the most important of which are in Texas, Oklahoma, Louisiana, and West Virginia.

Of these the Panhandle field of Texas is the most extensive and is said to contain the largest gas reserve in the United States.

Before the Civil War, there was little knowledge of and need for these mysterious and hidden treasures of oil and gas. But during the second half of the nineteenth century, when petroleum had become an important item of commerce, sporadic wells were drilled in West Virginia and Kentucky. By 1900, oil was being obtained from both Louisiana and Texas, and the total annual yield for the South had reached more than 17,000,000 barrels. Thereafter, production increased at an extraordinary rate until, in 1929, it reached a peak of 610,719,000 barrels, or over 60 per cent of the Nation's aggregate for that year. Inevitably, therefore, such extensive exploitation of this rich resource has been of the greatest consequence in the material development of the region concerned.

**Other minerals.** Of other mineral resources the South has at least fifty classifications, ranging down the alphabet from asbestos to zinc. Some of these have had comparatively little commercial value, because of lack of quantity or quality, or both. Others have been available for extensive and profitable exploitation. Thus, copper occurs in considerable quantities in the Ducktown Basin of Tennessee and is worked by one large company. Zinc and lead have been mined in appreciable tonnage in Virginia, Louisiana, and Texas. In several localities there is an abundance of excellent granite, marble, and other building stones. Practically every state in the South, except Louisiana, has varying amounts and qualities of ceramic clays. Furthermore, the South has virtually a monopoly of bauxite, sulphur, and phosphate rock. Arkansas alone furnishes approximately 90 per cent of the bauxite required by the aluminum industry of the United States; Texas in recent years has produced nearly all of the sulphur consumed in this country; and Tennessee, Florida, and South Carolina have produced about 99 per cent of the phosphate rock. Throughout the South there are many other minor minerals, both metallic and non-metallic, which occur in sufficient quantity and satisfactory quality to be the bases of small local industries. As will appear hereafter, the development of such industries has been limited by factors other than the supply of minerals.

### TIMBER RESOURCES OF THE SOUTH

Of all the South's natural resources perhaps none has been so rapidly diminished as timber. Originally the entire section, except a few isolated spots and the semiarid parts of Oklahoma and Texas, was covered with trees. Experts of the United States Forest Service have estimated that this virgin forest in the Southern States probably covered as much as 601,680,000 acres. In the Appalachian Mountain region were found dense spruce and balsam forests and such hardwoods as red and white oak, yellow poplar, chestnut, hickory, maple, basswood, ash, cherry, and walnut. In the Piedmont were found mixed forests of hardwoods and softwoods. In the Eastern province were vast forests of yellow pine—long leaf, loblolly, and short-leaf, with here and there a sprinkling of cypress and tupelos. Today the total area of forests lands in the South, inclusive of idle land once forested, is only about 223,-813,000 acres, or 37 per cent of the original area.

This great diminution of Southern forests has been effected by two methods: (1) by clearing for settlements and crops; and (2) by lumbering as an industry.

To the first settlers, trees were an obstacle and a hindrance. They not only furnished dark haunts for savage animals and treacherous Indians, but they shaded the ground and prevented the cultivation of crops. Hence, it was necessary for the settlers to use the axe and the burning heap if they were to survive upon the new lands. Of course, this destruction was not a true economic waste —that is to say, it was not a willful ejection of material for which there existed a valuable use. In some regions,

however, extensive wasting of timber began with the cultivation of tobacco, since this plant quickly exhausted the
soil and required the overhasty extension of clearings to
obtain new acreage for further profitable production. As
the population gradually increased, the forests, through
cutting and fire, were still further depleted. Then trees
took on an increased valuation for commercial purposes.
During the late eighties of the last century, lumber production in the South began on an extensive scale; by 1920,
the section was furnishing 37 per cent of the lumber cut
in the United States. In spite of this vast devastation of
forests in the past, there are still adequate timber resources
for the future, if properly conserved.

## WATER POWER OF THE SOUTH

Until the Civil War, water wheels were the chief source
of industrial power in the South. Along various streams
were located grist mills, flour mills, saw mills, paper mills
and textile mills, all of which were driven by these cumbersome and noisy devices. Then, from the Civil War until
about 1900, steam gradually replaced water power, and
industries were often established in localities far distant
from water power sites. During the last three decades,
however, hydroelectric power plants have made it possible
to harness many of the streams and to transmit their energy to distant places. Indeed, this modern utilization
makes water power in the South a natural resource of great
value and promises even greater possibilities for the future.
In 1931, the installed capacity of water wheels in the
South was estimated to be 4,367,069 horse power, or about
29 per cent of the installed capacity of power plants in
the United States. The figures for 1933 would be practically the same. In other words, the hydroelectric power
plants of the South today could furnish, if used exclusively
in industry, nearly half the power required to operate
Southern factories. Besides sources already developed,
there are in the section many more streams which have,

all together, an estimated potential water power of about 4,873,000 horse power available 90 per cent of the time and about 8,572,000 horse power available 50 per cent of the time.

These water power resources, both potential and utilized, are distributed in varying proportions throughout the South. In each Southern State, except Mississippi and Louisiana, there are now in operation one or more hydro-electric plants. By far the most extensive developments have been made in the Appalachian Highland region. This is not at all surprising, for, as an eminent authority on hydraulic engineering has pointed out: [5] "The Southern Appalachian Region is more favored than any other part of the United States in having a topography adapted to the construction of dams, and a relatively high rainfall, well distributed throughout the year. The result is that both large fall and high stream flow make water power particularly attractive."

Many of these water power developments, though of recent origin, have already played a conspicuous part in the industrial expansion of certain Southern States. An analysis of their effect upon the general economic welfare of the South belongs to a later chapter, in which public utility companies are discussed.

## Localization of Industry

This brief sketch of the physiography and natural resources of the South will suffice to show that this section of the United States is, in many respects, well suited to be the home of an industrious people. By means of the beneficent distribution of resources, Nature has inevitably divided the economic development of the Southern States into two systems—namely, agrarian and industrial. In the Highland region and the Piedmont is found the larger portion of the South's resources of commercially usable

---

[5] Thorndike Serville, "The Power Situation in the South," in *Annals of the American Academy,* Vol. 153, p. 99.

coal, iron, water power, and hardwood forests. Hence, industry has become relatively more important in these regions than in the rest of the South. On the other hand, in the Coastal Plain, in the Mississippi embayment, and beyond in the Great Plains are vast areas of available land, which, together with a favorable climate, have made these regions predominantly agricultural. The division, however, cannot be marked by hard and fast lines; for, in many localities in the Highland region and the Piedmont, agriculture is practically the sole form of economic activity, while in the other regions there are several industries of varying size and kind. Nevertheless, if industrialism in the South should ever approach in extent anything like its predicted possibilities, it would, presumably, be localized mainly in the Highland and Piedmont regions and not in the other regions, which by their very nature are suitable primarily for agriculture.

### Bibliographical Note

The most complete statements that we have of the effect of physical influences on American history are: Ellen Churchill Semple's *American History and Its Geographic Conditions* (Boston, 1903); and Albert Perry Brigham's *Geographic Influences in American History* (Boston, 1903). The former work brings out the effect of mountain barriers, coast lines, and easy routes, but it has very little on the more subtle relationships between man and the climate, plants, and animals which form dominant features of his environment. The latter work is the effort of a geologist to interpret American history; it places emphasis primarily upon the influence of physiographic features.

In an article entitled "Physiographic Divisions of the United States," published in the *Annals of the Association of American Geographers*, December 1928, Nevin M. Fenneman designates the physiographic divisions agreed upon by geographers and traces their boundaries. But, for the most accurate description of the geographic areas of the United States, see Isaiah Bowman's *Forest Physiography* (New York, 1911). J. Russel Smith's *North America* (New York, 1925) contains some interesting descriptions of the South, although the author sometimes sacrifices accuracy of statement for literary effect. In 1921, Hugh Hammond Bennett published his text *Soils and Agriculture of the Southern States* (New York); and in 1930, A. B. Hulbert wrote *Soil and Its Influence on the History of the United States* (New Haven). In this latter work special attention has been given to the influence of the soils in Virginia on the westward movement. For an authoritative discussion of the climate of the South, see Robert De Courcy Ward's *Climates of the United States* (Boston, 1925).

Before the Civil War, systematic studies of natural resources were conducted by geological surveys in nine of the Southern States. In recent years, this work has been extended into every Southern State. These geological reports are the best available source of information on the natural resources of the South. Besides the state publications, special studies have been made of the natural resources of several of the Southern States. William Bullock Clark, *Geography of Maryland* (Baltimore, 1918); Ephriam Noble Lowe, *Economic Geography of Mississippi* (Jackson, 1928); Earl C. Case, *Valley of East Tennessee, The Adjustment of Industry to Natural Environment* (Nashville, 1925); Harriet Smith and Darthuld Walker, *Geography of Texas* (Chicago, 1923)—all of these are specialized studies which give facts and figures in an impartial manner. *The South's Development* (1924), published by the *Manufacturers Record*, Baltimore, Maryland, contains much statistical material; but the interpretation of the data must be accepted with reservations, as the purpose of the work was primarily commercial. In 1927, the United States Department of Commerce published a *Commercial Survey of the Southeast*, which contains a sketch of the climate and resources of the region covering North Carolina, South Carolina, Georgia, Florida, Alabama, and eastern Tennessee. Also, the *Annals of the American Academy of Political and Social Science*, Volume 153, which is devoted entirely to the industrialization of the South, contains some valuable information on the forest, mineral, and water power resources of the Southeastern States.

# CHAPTER II

# The Southern Colonies

THE economic background of the Southern colonists was predominantly English, because colonial expansion had become apparently an economic necessity for England at the time.

## English Background

By the close of the sixteenth century, England was beginning to develop an economic order marked by greater personal freedom. The old manorial system of agriculture, which had virtually bound the lower classes to the soil and had made them almost helplessly immobile, had practically broken down. In the towns and cities the guilds were rapidly disintegrating and giving way before the growth of urban freedom. While there was yet no marked measure of self-government in national affairs, the hold of the feudal nobility as a ruling class was definitely broken. Local government, moreover, was rapidly coming into the hands of the lower orders. With the breakdown of feudalism in England, class distinctions had become less rigid and were shifting, with the rise of the bourgeoisie, to new economic bases. On the Continent, however, the medieval systems of agriculture and trade still survived, the masses were still bound to the soil, and despotism prevailed generally. In comparison, the English had more opportunity to use personal energy and initiative; and this fact, in a broad sense, may have given the English their somewhat more individualistic and self-reliant character.

During the century previous to the settlement of

America, there was a noticeable increase in the number and prosperity of English manufactures. Considerable progress was made in cloth making. The cutlery and hardware industries; paper making; the production of wire, brimstone, salt, starch, and shipbuilding were developing rapidly. No doubt their development had been hastened to a large extent by the influx of religious and political fugitives from the Continent. Nevertheless, the processes of these industries were crude and were carried on mainly by hand labor, for it must be remembered that the spinning jenny was not invented until 1767; the steam engine, until 1769; the power loom, until 1787; and the Bessemer process of making steel, until 1856.

In agriculture there had set in a trend toward capitalistic farming, in order to raise wool for the growing woolen industry. At first, in the reign of Queen Elizabeth, this had worked great hardships on the peasant classes, because of the enclosures. However, the raising of sheep brought the landlords an income which greatly increased the total capital of the country.

Commerce, both internal and foreign, made new strides. Internal commerce was facilitated by the removal of medieval shackles, and national economy began to rise in the place of the self-sufficient town economy. There was a transition from a purely passive to an active foreign commerce. Thus, at one time during the reign of Henry VIII, there were as many as three thousand foreign traders in England. The *Hanseatic League* had been the leading commercial organization and had quarters in the steelyard of London. But, by the middle of the fifteenth century, the power of these German cities began to wane and in their stead arose the *Merchant Adventurers*—an English group—to carry on the foreign commerce of England. Furthermore, fifty or sixty trading companies were organized for the purpose of making profits from foreign commerce. Of these companies the most important were: the Muscovy, established in 1554 for the purpose of trading with Russia through the port of Archangel; the Prussian Company, established in 1576; and, a little later on, the Turkey Company, the Morocco Company, and, greatest of all, the East India Company. In the words of Woodrow Wilson:[1] "England had become a commercial nation, quickened in every seaport by a bold spirit of individual enterprise that would dare anything for success. The Tudor monarchs had, it is true, established a political absolutism; but they had, nevertheless, somehow deeply stirred individual initiative in their subjects in the process."

Comforts were increasing for those who could afford them. Houses, for the most part, were still made of wood, though stone was gradually coming into use. Chimneys had been introduced into homes at the close of Queen Elizabeth's reign. Pillows were in general use instead of blocks of wood that were used in previous centuries. Carpets were being introduced. Pewter and even silverware were taking the place of wooden trenchers. Glass was sometimes used in windows, and furniture was relatively more elaborate. Clothing was made of either wool or linen. The upper classes ate various kinds of meat and drank wine.

Capital was accumulating; the lure of gain had spread to such an extent that, when the time came to plant settlements in America, it was not necessary to "beg a pittance" from the Royal Treasury in order to "launch epoch-making expeditions."

On the other hand, many of the lower classes were being driven into pauperism. In 1600, the total population of England and Wales was approximately 5,000,000. This was a mean density of about 87 persons per square mile, or 2.1 times the 1930 density of the United States. Hence, from the point of view of the total production made possible at that time by limited technology, wages at best were necessarily low. During the same period, prices were

---

[1] *History of the American People,* Vol. I, p. 22.

rising, mainly perhaps because of the influx of gold, which had entered through southern Europe from the New World or had been seized by the English on the Atlantic. At any rate, the laborer was worse off than in the preceding century. Thus, for example, at Rutland in 1610, wages were about the same as in 1564, but the price of food was about 75 per cent higher. Wage statistics show that, during the sixteenth century, wages increased only slightly over those of the fifteenth century, but the cost of living increased almost 300 per cent. Thorold Rogers says: [2] "If we suppose the ordinary laborer to get 3s. 6d. a week throughout the year, by adding his harvest allowance to his winter wages, it would have taken him more than forty weeks to earn the provisions which in 1495 he could have got with fifteen weeks' labour, while the artisan would be obliged to have given thirty-two weeks' work for the same result."

The English Government in 1563 had set up a system, under the administration of the employers, for the adjustment of wages; but, as would be expected, practically nothing beneficial for the laborers resulted from this arrangement. Instead, the gaols were filled with debtors. The church, although free from the dead hand of Rome, was still an institution primarily for the promulgation of theological dogma and gave little attention, if any, to the social gospel.

Fundamentally, however, England had reached a critical point in her economic evolution. During the twelfth century, the country had been covered with virgin forests, broken only occasionally by fields and villages. But by the end of the Tudor period, five centuries later, the forests —on account of the population, the extension of agriculture, and the increased use of wood—had been so denuded that England could no longer look for prosperity from her old industries: shipbuilding, which required timber and naval stores; the manufacture of woolens, which called for

---

[2] *Six Centuries*, p. 390.

a supply of potash; and smelting, which was still dependent upon wood for fuel.

England sought relief from this situation through foreign commerce. At the beginning of the seventeenth century, she was importing from southern Europe large quantities of wine, silk, salt, sugar, and dried fruit; and from the Far East, dyes, saltpetre, and spices. Moreover, from the countries bordering the Baltic—Sweden, Russia, Poland, and Germany—she was purchasing the potash which she needed in the woolen industry, and the naval stores upon which depended her merchant marine and, consequently, her national security.

However, this dependence upon foreign trade was unsatisfactory to England. Not only was the trade balance often against her, but in case of war among the nations around the Baltic, her essential trade might be cut off. The effects of such action would mean severe damage to her merchant marine and the strangulation of her woolen industry. As the author of *A True Declaration* said: [3] "The merchant knoweth that through the troubles in Poland and Muscovy, (whose eternall warres are like the Antipathy of the Dragon & Elephant) all their traffique for Masts, Deales, Pitch, Tarre, Flax, Hempe, and Cordage, are every day more and more indangered." Likewise, the trade with the dominions of the King of Spain was carried on with great difficulty; and during the closing years of the sixteenth century, commerce with France greatly declined.

Thus, at the beginning of the seventeenth century, the English had more capital and a higher standard of living, but at the same time more unemployed and paupers. They were more dependent upon foreign trade than ever before in their history. Under these circumstances many English economists thought that a crisis had been reached and that

---

[3] Peter Force, *A True Declaration* (Vol. III of TRACTS AND OTHER PAPERS), p. 23.

disaster could be prevented only by establishing colonies in the New World.

Enmeshed with the economic situation was the problem of national rivalry. No doubt Dean W. R. Inge is correct in saying: [4] "No deep laid schemes of founding an empire were ever made in this country [England]." Nevertheless, the exigencies of national rivalry as early as the reign of Queen Elizabeth caused several leading Englishmen to urge the establishment of colonies in America as a possible means of counteracting the power of Spain. Thus, in 1583, Sir George Peakman declared that it was time for Englishmen to awaken "out of that drowsie dream" and set about colonizing the New World. Hakluyt, Raleigh, and, still later, the founders of Georgia emphasized similar views, for it was generally believed that by means of colonies Englishmen could enrich themselves from the New World's treasures of precious metals, as the Spaniards were doing, and at the same time establish a new and strong naval position against Spanish fleets and pirates.

## Establishment of Southern Colonies

Before judicious English merchants would invest in speculative schemes for establishing colonies beyond the unknown sea, someone fearing no risk of fortune had to take the initiative and blaze the way. This man was Sir Walter Raleigh, "who saw in his dreams the American wilderness subdued by the people of his native land."

### RALEIGH'S EXPERIMENTS

In March 1584, Sir Walter Raleigh secured permission from Queen Elizabeth to establish English colonies in North America. As specified in the letters patent, he was to have the right during a period of six years to transport subjects from England and to establish one or more colonies within the region he discovered. He was privileged to

---

[4] *England*, p. 90.

grant land and to control trade within the territory encompassing the place of settlement on all sides to a distance of two hundred leagues. Furthermore, he, his heirs, and assigns were empowered to provide such governments for the colony or colonies as were in harmony with the English constitution. In return for these rights and privileges, he was to pay the Queen one fifth of the gold and silver ore found in the soil.

Having secured this patent, Raleigh forthwith sent out two explorers, Amadas and Barlow, to select a site for a colony. In July 1584, they entered Albemarle Sound and landed on Roanoke Island. Barlow has left an almost Virgilian description of this island, in which he says: "This land lay stretching itself to the west, which after wee found to bee but an Island of twentie miles long, and not above sixe miles broade. Vnder the banke or hill whereon we stoode, we behelde the valleys replenished with goodly cedar trees, and having discharged our harquebuz—shot, such a flocke of cranes (the most part white) arose vnder vs, with such a cry redoubled by many ecchoes, as if an armie of men had shouted all together." Here, they decided, would be a suitable place for a colony, not only because of the attractiveness of the island, but especially because they had found the Indians friendly, and had seen crops of peas and maize and an abundance of game. Hence, upon their return to England these explorers gave to a credulous group such a glowing report that it almost rivals modern advertising copy. Even Queen Elizabeth, it is said, was so impressed that she decided to name the new country in honor of herself, the Virgin Queen; she called it "Virginia."

This course of events was precisely what Raleigh had hoped for, and he now proceeded to secure men, ships, and a commander to send to the new land. Such a task, apparently, was not difficult, for soon a complete outfit was ready to sail. It consisted of seven small ships and supplies of the usual sort—food and weapons—and one hundred seven colonists. Fourteen of these colonists bore the title of "master"; others were "gentlemen"; one was an Oxford graduate; and another was an artist. Sir Richard Grenville, famous fighter and sea rover, was commander of the fleet; Ralph Lane, presumably a "deputy" under Grenville, was to become governor of the colony.

The last of July 1585, this colony landed on Roanoke Island, and near the northeast corner established a camp about forty yards square. Although Raleigh, it is said, had granted a landed estate of five hundred acres or more to each colonist, there is no evidence that such estates were ever laid out. Instead, it appears that this settlement, at least theoretically, was to serve merely as a kind of outpost from which to conduct exploration parties; for Lane, aping the Spaniards, desired above all things to discover gold and a route to the "South Sea." Consequently, for an interim, the colonists "spun out their days in cursed thirst for gold" and relied for their food upon the ships' supplies and whatever fish, maize, and fruit could be had from the Indians.

It was not long, however, until two dangers presented themselves: Indian treachery and starvation. To meet the first danger was relatively easy, for the colonists were equipped with superior weapons and used tactics of warfare unfamiliar to the Indians. To obtain food became the paramount problem. The former sources of supply ceased to be available. The friendly Indians, who before had aided them, became aggressively hostile. The supply ships from England did not arrive, nor could it be predicted, on account of the hazards of storms and the pirates from Spain, when they would. In this predicament the colonists were compelled to break their group into small parties and to disperse these in search of food within the circle of their explorations. Each week from sixteen to twenty men had to be sent to the mainland opposite the island to live on oysters and whatever else might be available. Finally, in the spring of 1586, the colonists decided it would be best to raise their own crops, and forthwith they adopted a kind of collective method of agriculture which, presumably, would have yielded an abundance of produce. In fact, we are told that "they sowed, planted, and set such things as were necessary for their relief in so plentiful a manner as might have sufficed them two years without further labor." But, in June, before the corn was ready for harvest, Drake happened to be passing by with his fleet and, at the request of Lane, took the whole colony back to England.

Within less than a month after this colony had left Roanoke Island, three ships, under the direction of Grenville, arrived with supplies and more settlers. Surprised at the deserted camp, he set about searching for the settlers and exploring the immediate territory. Of course, he found no one, but rather than lose what had been done, he decided to leave fifteen men to guard the camp. He supplied them with provisions and arms sufficient for two years, and sailed away to the West Indies to recoup part of the expenses of the voyage. What became of these fifteen men historians are not certain; it is generally supposed that they were killed by the Croatan Indians.

Despite the failure of this first colony, which caused the Queen to refuse further aid and impaired his own private fortune, Raleigh, the next year (1587), sent out another colony to settle somewhere in the region of Chesapeake Bay.

The organization of this colony differed somewhat from that of Lane's. To raise the necessary capital, Raleigh associated with himself in the enterprise several influential men of London. Among these were nineteen merchants and thirteen "gentlemen." By the terms of the charter of incorporation, John White, the artist, was made governor, and the "gentlemen" who proposed to settle in the colony were to be his assistants. The colony consisted of one hundred twenty-one people, of whom seventeen were women and nine were children.

Instructions were given that the colony should be planted on Chesapeake Bay, and that the colonists should stop at Roanoke Island only long enough to pick up the fifteen men left there the previous year. However, on reaching Roanoke, the commander of the fleet, Simon Ferdinand—presumably a Spaniard—refused to sail farther. Therefore White was forced to disobey Raleigh's order and to try to reëstablish the colony of Roanoke.

Finding the luckless camp of Lane's colony still standing, the new settlers repaired the houses and set things in order. Then Ferdinand's fleet sailed away. Soon troubles began. In the first place, as Lane had found out and Raleigh had warned, Roanoke Island, on account of its natural characteristics, was not suitable for a small colony in a strange land. It was not long until the colonists were at war with the Indians, though it is recorded that one of the chiefs, Manteo by name, remained friendly. In a few weeks, White, against his better judgment, returned to England for supplies. His action was especially unfortunate for the colony, because, on arriving in England, White found the nation mustering all forces against a threatened invasion by Spain. Such circumstances, inevitably, detained him and blocked his attempts to send supplies to the colonies. Three years later, when he did arrive again at Roanoke, he found nothing but the empty houses of the colonists and the word "Croatoan" carved on a tree. Thus, the English had for the second time failed to realize that a colony, in order to exist in the New World, must be, not a mere outpost from which to conduct exploration parties, but essentially a producing unit.

After these failures Raleigh leased his patent to a company of merchants, and for nearly eighteen years no further effort was made to establish a colony on Chesapeake Bay. Yet Raleigh, in spite of the fact that he had spent no

less than £40,000 in an attempt to plant a new colony and
to locate the lost colony, never despaired of seeing Virginia
settled by the English.  Indeed, after all his unfortunate
attempts, he declared, with the obstinacy characteristic of
his countrymen: "I shall yet live to see it an Inglishe
Nation."  And before his death on the scaffold, a permanent colony was actually established in Virginia.

## VIRGINIA

Backing the first permanent English settlement in the
South was the financial support of a joint-stock company
instead of that of an individual.  Behind the joint-stock
company was a background of commercial capitalism that
made possible this advanced form of business organization.

In 1606, James I divided that part of the North American Continent which lies between latitudes 34 and 45 degrees into two zones and assigned the southern to the
London Company, which consisted of "certain Knights,
Gentlemen, Merchants, and other Adventurers, of our city
of London and elsewhere" who purposed to establish a
colony in Virginia.

Broadly speaking, the charter of this company embodied
four provisions of great economic importance.  (1) It provided for a *council,* which, with the approval of the King,
was to establish a government in Virginia.  Among other
provisions, the right was granted to settlers to hold land
and to have trial by jury, and only five offenses were to
be punishable by death—murder, manslaughter, incest,
rape, and adultery.  (2) The Church of England was to
be established, and Christianity was to be preached among
the colonists and natives.  (3) A kind of communistic
regime was to be established.  As explained by Doyle: [5]
"The colony was to be a vast joint-stock farm, or collection of farms, worked by servants who were to receive in
return for their labor, all their necessaries, and a share in

---

[5] *English Colonies in America,* Vol. 1, p. 128.

the proceeds of the undertaking." Moreover, all trade in the export products of the colony or in commodities from England was to be placed in the *magazine* under the control of a *cape merchant* and his two clerical assistants. The supplies which arrived in the colony were to be issued by the cape merchant for the maintenance of the settlers; the products which the settlers raised were to be transported from the magazine to England, and the proceeds from their sale were to provide profits for the shareholders. (4) The *patentees* were given the right to trade with the colonists, though not in a strict monopolistic form. Instead, they were permitted to exact a duty of 2.5 per cent from English subjects and 5 per cent from all foreigners trading with the colony.

Under this charter, three small ships, hired from the Muscovy Company, were equipped; and one hundred four colonists, including fifty-five gentlemen, a London tailor, a barber, and a perfumer, were sent to Virginia by the London Company. On April 26, 1607, they effected a landing at Cape Henry; then, several days later, they sailed up the James River for about forty miles and anchored off a low-lying peninsula. Here, they decided, was a suitable "seating place," and they hastened to establish the new settlement. As described by Captain John Smith in his *General Historie of Virginia:* "Now falleth every man to worke, the Councell contrive the Fort, the rest cut downe trees to make place to pitch their tents; some provide clapboards to relode the ships, some make gardens, some nets, etc." The fort which they built was a triangular, palisaded enclosure. Two of its sides were three hundred feet long, and the side adjacent to the river was four hundred twenty feet long. Within were erected tents and a few log huts. This was the beginning of Jamestown, the first permanent English settlement in America.

During the first three years of its existence, the colony was a total loss as a business venture. The London Company in return for its expenditures had received only a shipload of yellow sand, a few clapboards, and some sassafras roots; and the colony had served merely as a drain upon the resources of the company. It became necessary to reorganize the company upon a broader basis, if the colony was to be further sustained and developed. Consequently, in 1609, a new charter was drawn, making the company a great corporation that received the formal title of "Treasurer and Company of Adventurers and Planters of the City of London, for the First Colony in Virginia." Six hundred fifty-nine distinguished men of England and some fifty-six guilds of London—such as, the Salters, Vinters, Drapers, Goldsmiths, Haberdashers, Skinners, Mercers, Grocers, Fishmongers, Merchant Tailors, Ironmongers, Clothworkers, and Stationers—took shares in the reorganized company. Its prerogatives were enlarged and made more flexible, and the boundaries of Virginia were defined to be two hundred miles south and two hundred miles north of Old Point Comfort and to run "up into the land from sea to sea, west and northwest." Three years later, the charter was again modified, giving the council, or governing body of the colony, considerably more power.

The company tried hard to make the colony a success. The wealth of the new land was systematically advertised both in the press and in the pulpit. From time to time the company sent over supplies and additional settlers. But the colonists from the beginning were confronted with three handicaps: the difficulty of obtaining food, the hostility of the Indians, and the ravages of disease.

There were three possible methods of obtaining food: by producing it locally; by traffic with the Indians; and by relying upon shipments from England. However, during the early years of the colony, no one method alone was sufficient, and each was used to supplement the other two.

At the outset, the officers at Jamestown required a part

of the labor force to plant wheat and a few vegetable seeds (brought from England) on an area of about four acres, which had been cleared of trees in order to build the fort. The next year, more land was cleared and more wheat was sown. But the supply of food thus derived was inadequate to meet the demand, and the colonists had to supplement their meager supplies with maize, for which they traded with the Indians—a source of supply that proved to be very precarious.

Supplies were received periodically from England. During the first three years at Jamestown, three such shipments arrived. Unfortunately, because of the climate, these supplies often spoiled before they could be used. Nor did they always arrive during the periods of greatest need. This was especially true of the winter of 1609–1610, known as the "starving time." In fact, so intense was the famine during these months that not only was every horse, cow, and hog slaughtered and eaten, but the colonists ate dogs, rats, and even an Indian who had been killed. Furthermore, in its enthusiasm to develop the colony, the company sometimes sent over hundreds of colonists, without proper provision for their food. In regard to this policy, Governor George Yeardley, in 1620, wrote to Sir Edwin Sandys as follows: [6] "I pray think it not strange I should write thus to send victuals with your people for you may be pleased well to conceive that if such numbers of people come upon me unexpected, and that at an unhealthful season and too late to set corn I cannot then be able to feed them out of others' labors, what I can and am able to do if you will have patience I will from time to time inform you—but both you and I must give leave to time."

As time went on, however, the colonists so increased their production, not only of maize, but also of many vegetables indigenous to this country, that they became more and

---

[6] Letter from Yeardley to Sandys, June 7, 1620, in *Ferrar Papers*.

more self-supporting as their total number permanently increased.

There were about five thousand Indians within sixty miles of Jamestown. At first they were hostile to the new settlers, perhaps because of rumors of the relationship of the Croatans to Raleigh's first colony. However, through the diplomacy of Captain John Smith and, in no small measure, because of the marriage of Pocahontas to John Rolfe, their friendship was obtained and kept until the death of Chief Powhatan. Opecancanough then became the ruler of Powhatan's people, and, incensed at the encroachment of his lands by the whites, he urged his people to stop further English settlement. Consequently, in the spring of 1622, there occurred a sudden and unexpected Indian attack which resulted in the destruction of the town of Henriopolis and several smaller settlements, and in the death of three hundred forty-seven settlers, or about a quarter of all the white inhabitants in Virginia.

The greatest obstacle to success, however, was disease. Within a short time after the first settlers landed at Jamestown, the visitation of some terrible disease, probably malarial fever, swept away more than fifty of them. "If there were conscience in men," declared Captain George Percy, in describing the misery of the first summer, "it would make their hearts bleed to heare the pitiful murmurings and outcries of our sick men without reliefe, every night and day for the space of sixe weekes; in the morning their bodies being trailed out of their cabines like Dogges, to be buried." In 1609, five hundred additional immigrants, including one hundred women and children, were sent over from England. On reaching Virginia, the survivors (about one hundred having perished on the voyage) were planted in settlements as far up the James River as Richmond; but, after a few months, only about sixty were still alive.

Nor was this by any means all the waste of human life by disease during the earlier years of the Virginia colony, for literally hundreds perished in the process of becoming acclimated.[7]   Professor E. L. Bogart points out:[8]   "It has been estimated that in the first decade of the colony's existence 1,650 persons had sailed for Virginia, of whom 300 had returned to England and 350 remained in the colony; these figures indicate that about 1,000 persons perished in the interval.  In 1624, when the charter was revoked by the king and Virginia became a crown colony, the total number of emigrants was put at about 5,600 and the residents in Virginia at 1,200; the remainder had either died or fled back to England."

The colony did not develop rapidly under the control of the London Company.  One great mistake made by the company, perhaps, was the conviction that the slow development of the colony was attributable to the type of government operating there.  As a matter of fact, one governor after another was sent over to take charge of the colony, with varying degrees of success.  In just how far the governmental system may have been responsible for the colony's slow development must remain largely a matter of conjecture, but it is evident that political organization was less important than the economic readjustments which were necessary for the survival of English colonists in their new environment.

In 1622, after the Indian massacre, the colony faced ruin and the company, bankruptcy.  "The fear of your want of corn," wrote an official of the company to the colonial governor, "doth much perplex us, seeing so little possibility to

---

[7] "In 1614 the Spanish Ambassador in England wrote to Philip III that he had heard the London Company had asked for permission to withdraw the settlers from Virginia as the enterprise had turned out so expensive, but that this request had been denied, it being suggested that 'it was well to preserve that place, altho it be good for nothing more than to kill people and to afford an outlet to them from here; since in this Kingdom here they grow and multiply so as to be innumerable.' "— Alexander Brown, *Genesis of the United States*, Vol. II, p. 681.

[8] *Economic History of the American People* (1932), p. 58.  Reprinted by permission of Longmans, Green & Co., New York.

supply you; the public stock being utterly exhausted, and last year's Adventures made by Private men not returned— we have no hope of raising any valuable Magazine." [9] On account of commercial disappointment in the colony, the company had become divided into two factions, which finally engaged in a bitter quarrel that led to a government investigation of the "whole business" of the company. Hence, in 1624, when it had become evident that a receivership for the company was inevitable, King James annulled the charter and the company ceased to exist.

It should be remembered, however, that it was this company which had taken over the initial settlement under the original patent and had persevered, despite all discouragements from within and without, until the colony eventually became almost self-supporting. About seventeen years had been consumed in this effort; probably more than four thousand settlers had perished in the New Land, and as much as £200,000, or about $1,000,000, had been expended by the company. Yet, at last Virginia had become a permanent colony, and in tobacco growing there had been found a type of agriculture that insured the stability of the economic future of the colony.

## MARYLAND

In contrast to Virginia, Maryland was founded by an individual proprietor. The charter was granted by Charles I to George Calvert, the first Lord Baltimore, who died before the patent passed the Great Seal; and the charter was subsequently issued to his son, Cecilius Calvert, the second Lord Baltimore, in 1632. The land embraced in this grant was between the Potomac River and the 40th parallel of latitude, which was then the southern boundary of New England.

In asking the King for this grant, Calvert had two pur-

---

[9] *Manuscript Records of the Virginia Company*, Vol. III, Pt. 2, pp. 23a–25.

poses in view: first, to found in America a semifeudal state over which he would be ruler and from which he would secure revenue; and second (and perhaps of questionable sincerity), to provide a refuge for his persecuted fellow Roman Catholics.

In granting the charter, the King was probably aware of the desirability of having a buffer state between Virginia and the Dutch in New Netherlands; for, in 1631, the governor and the council of Virginia had complained that the "injurious Dutch doe come even to our doors."

It is said that Calvert drew up the charter with his own hand, merely leaving for the King a blank in which to place his signature. According to its provisions, Calvert and his heirs were made the *proprietaries* of the territory and were to have powers almost equal in extent to those of a feudal lord. The settlers were to be exempt from every form of regal taxation, but the proprietor—supposedly with the concurrence of the settlers—was to have authority to levy taxes and to collect tolls and duties. For all rights and privileges the proprietor was to pay to the King annually a quitrent of two Indian arrows and one fifth of the gold and silver mined in the province.

In November 1633, Calvert's son Cecilius sent out to the territory his brother Leonard, in command of two vessels loaded with supplies and implements; three Jesuit priests; and over two hundred laboring men, many of whom were Protestants. These settlers landed near the mouth of the Potomac and there founded a town which they called "St. Marys." The location was favorable because the site was surrounded with fields cleared by the Indians. The tribes in the neighborhood had been at war with the Susquehannas and were glad to sell the land and move across the Potomac. "We bought from the King (of the Indians)," wrote Father White, "thirty miles of that land, delivering in exchange axes, hatchets, rakes, and several yards of cloth."

Apparently all went well at first. The Calverts viewed the enterprise largely as a business venture and within two years invested some £40,000 in it. Land in varying amounts was granted to the settlers, and peaceful relations were established with the Indians. The colony was soon operating on a well-established basis. In 1639, Andrew White wrote to Cecilius Calvert [10] that their estate was "every day bettering itt selfe by encrease of Planters and plantations and large cropp this year of Corne and Tobacco." But, almost from the first, the colony experienced considerable trouble with William Claybourne, secretary of Virginia, who had established a trading post on Kent Island and who claimed the land now occupied by the Calvert colony. On a few occasions fighting occurred, and for a short time the colony actually came under the control of Claybourne; finally, moreover, Calvert had to resort to political manipulation and litigation to regain his control. Despite trouble of this kind, settlers flocked to the colony, both on account of its liberal land policy and on account of freedom from religious intolerance. Prosperity followed the cultivation of the fertile soil, and in time the Calvert family derived an enormous annual revenue from the colony.

## THE CAROLINAS

For nearly half a century after the founding of Jamestown, the broad belt of territory between Virginia and Spanish Florida lay unoccupied. However, as early as 1562, some Huguenots under the command of Jean Ribault, having left France because of religious persecution, had landed at Port Royal. When they landed, it was springtime, and the beauty of the scenery around the shores greatly delighted the weary voyagers. Everywhere there were stately cedars, magnolias, and wide-spreading oaks, and the air itself was "sweet with the fragrance of the rose

[10] *Calvert Papers*, Vol. I, p. 202.

and the jasmine." Ribault and his followers immediately laid the foundation of a fort, hoisted over it the flag of France, and with due ceremony took possession of the country for their King. Ribault left twenty-six men to complete and to garrison the fort, while he himself sailed home for additional settlers. But dissension arose among the guards, and, after murdering one commander of the fort and choosing another, they built a small vessel and, ill-equipped for the journey, set sail for home. In mid-ocean, after they had eaten one of their own men, an English ship picked up the survivors and carried them to England.

Two years later, another group of Huguenots had come to St. Johns River and built another fort. In 1565, Ribault had brought over additional settlers. But a Spanish fleet followed in close pursuit, and the Huguenots had hardly landed before the Spanish fell upon the settlers and killed every one. The French had failed to establish a colony in this region, and at the same time the Spanish had left the field to the north open for the English.

During the last quarter of the sixteenth century, futile attempts were made by Raleigh's ill-fated colonies to plant a settlement on Roanoke Island. Then, on account of the early failures and the swamp-girt coast, further efforts to colonize this middle region directly from Europe were abandoned for a long period of years.

In the meantime, even before Jamestown was two years old, Virginians began to explore the upper waters of several streams which flow into the Albemarle and Currituck Sounds. By 1625, the region as far south as Chowan was familiar to hunters and land-seekers. Four years later, Charles I granted the province of "Carolina" to his attorney-general, Sir Robert Heath. Although there are reasons for believing that Heath's assigns made an unsuccessful attempt later on to plant a colony within the grant, no settlement was made immediately; and the Virginia Assembly forthwith presumed to issue exploring and trading permits in "Carolina." In this manner the character of the country gradually became known to the Virginians.

Since the soil, climate, vegetation, and animals of the Albemarle region were the same as those of southeastern Virginia, it was natural that the planters of the established colony should gradually move southward in order to increase their activities and to get good meadowlands. Exactly when this expanding movement of the Virginia settlers began cannot be determined. But it is known that, in 1653, a Virginia clergyman, Roger Green by name, obtained a grant of ten thousand acres for the first one hundred persons who would settle on the Roanoke River south of Chowan, and one thousand acres for himself. It is believed by historians that he collected a small group of dissatisfied Virginians, presumably religious dissenters, and planted Albemarle, the first permanent settlement in what is now North Carolina. Whether Green founded Albemarle or whether settlers were already there, the fact remains that North Carolina received its first permanent settlers from Virginia.

During the next twenty years, sporadic attempts were made to establish other settlements in this region. For example, it is alleged that, in 1660, a number of New Englanders, desiring to raise cattle, settled at the mouth of the Cape Fear River; however, probably on account of the Indians, the colony soon disappeared. By 1663 the practice of purchasing land directly from the Indians of the region had become so common that the Virginia Assembly resolved to disregard the natives and required that patents should be obtained for such lands under the laws of Virginia. The earliest settlements were characterized mainly by isolation and lawlessness, and the important colonization of the Carolinas really began in the territory which is now South Carolina.

By means of two charters—one in 1663, the other in

1665 [11]—and regardless of Spanish claims, Charles II granted to eight of his so-called "Cousins and Counsellors" the province of "Carolina," which was defined as the territory lying between Virginia and Florida and stretching westward to the "South Sea."

In granting this charter, the King not only proposed to reward the *grantees* for their loyal support of the old monarchy, but hoped that "Carolina" would become a natural source of supply of those products which England was importing from southern Europe. Hence, the grantees were to have, use, and enjoy their "province" without restraint, except that the laws made by them from time to time were to be approved by the freemen in the colony, and the grantees were to pay annually to the King 20 marks and a quarter of the gold and silver found there.

Although the grantees, or *Lord Proprietors,* declared that their motives were "a laudable and pious zeal for the propagation of the Christian faith" and a desire to enlarge the King's dominions, nevertheless, they believed that their territory would yield them enormous profits, if properly colonized and governed. Hence, one of them, the Earl of Shaftesbury, employed the eminent political theorist of the day, John Locke, to draw up a plan for the economic and political organization of the province.

When completed, this plan embodied a synthesis of the theoretical scheme of Plato's Republic and the historical features of thirteenth-century feudalism. In the words of Professor Beard: [12] "This task the learned bookman discharged by drafting one of the most fantastic documents now to be found in the moldering archives of disillusionment." Nevertheless, these plans—termed "The Fundamental Constitutions of Carolina"—were adopted and signed by the proprietors in 1669, and thereupon declared

---

[11] The second charter was merely a modification of the first, in order to extend the width of the territory granted to include the Albemarle settlement on the north and two additional degrees on the south.

[12] *Rise of American Civilization,* p. 66.

to be unalterable. Four later editions of the "Constitutions" were prepared, and for the next thirty years the proprietors tried continually to induce the colonists, especially in the southern part of the province, to accept them.

The proprietors agreed to contribute £500 sterling each as an initial payment, and, thereafter, to contribute £200 sterling each annually for a period of five years. With this money they purchased three ships and loaded them with stores and some one hundred fifty colonists. In April 1670, this colony disembarked at the mouth of the Ashley River. There they began to lay out a town, which later was known as "Old Charles Town." Unfortunately, the site was little more than a marsh and therefore unhealthful. But food was available. The forests were filled with wild game; the river furnished plenty of fish and oysters; and for a short time corn and venison could be bought from the Indians. Coastwise trade with Virginia was soon established. Consequently the colony survived and, in 1671, had increased in population to about four hundred.

Soon settlers crossed the Ashley, and there, "on the first highland," established "New Charles Town," which eventually became Charleston. The older settlement was not abandoned immediately, but migration from there to the new town became increasingly rapid. "The Town which two years since had 3 or 4 houses," wrote Thomas Newe in 1682,[13] "hath now about a hundred houses in it, all which are wholly built of wood, tho here is excellent Brick made, but little of it." The proprietors were lavish in their aid. From 1680 to 1682, there was a considerable influx of new settlers, composed in the main of French Huguenots and English Dissenters, and by 1682, the colony had a total population of about twenty-five hundred.

During the first decade of proprietary control, the Albemarle settlement did not fare nearly so well. In 1667,

---

[13] Letter of Thomas Newe to his "most Honourd Father," in *American Historical Review*, Vol. XII, p. 323.

Governor Drummond, a clergyman and the first *appointee* of the proprietors, summoned an assembly which enacted several laws for the purpose of attracting settlers. One of these exempted new settlers from taxation for a year; another released them for five years from liability for debts contracted elsewhere. Consequently the character of the newcomers thus attracted was such that the Virginians named the colony "Rogues' Harbor." However, by 1677, the number of tithables, or working hands between the ages of sixteen and sixty, in the colony was only about fourteen hundred, and one third of these were Indians, negroes, and women. The proprietors blamed the colony itself for not making greater progress, and used this lack of development as the reason why they themselves disproportionately aided the colony on the Ashley River.

Nevertheless, many of the first settlers were not derelicts, but men seeking freedom either from ecclesiastical bigotry or from economic exploitation. Furthermore, subsequent settlers, whose character was on a par with that of other American colonists, were often considered lawless because they resented the intolerable dictatorship of some of the proprietors' appointed governors. As Dr. Edwin A. Alderman has said: "The key to North Carolina character in this inchoate period is the subordination of everything —material prosperity, personal ease, financial development —to the remorseless assertion of the sacredness of chartered rights . . ." against the arbitrary control of the proprietors. In other words, constant wrangling and sometimes revolt occurred because the government imposed upon the settlers was for the most part highly theoretical and inefficient. The hold of the proprietors, however, was very weak; Locke's plan was soon modified, and then it gave way to rapidly changing schemes of control.

Until after the first decade of the eighteenth century, the settlers of Albemarle and Charleston had from time to time struggled against these proprietary systems of control, both economic and political. Otherwise, things had gone relatively well. The Indians had for the most part remained peaceful, and subsistence had been obtained by direct appropriation, elementary production, and trade. Settlements had begun to push southward from Albemarle. This movement necessarily drove the Indians from their hunting grounds and incensed them against the whites. Likewise the rapidly growing colony at Charleston aroused the jealousy of the Spaniards in Florida, who feared further loss of their Indian fur trade as well as possible encroachment upon their own frontier.

Almost inevitably, therefore, but quite unexpectedly, the Tuscarora Indians, in 1711, suddenly attacked the settlements along the Pamlico and the Neuse, and within two hours slaughtered two hundred ten settlers. The few whites who escaped fled to Albemarle, leaving behind in the hot September sun their unburied dead and their settlements in ashes and desolation. Again, in 1712, trouble broke out with these Indians, and it was accompanied by an epidemic of yellow fever. However, by means of the concerted action of the Carolina colonies, a decisive blow was struck, and the remnant of the Tuscaroras fled to join the Iroquois in New York.

Three years later, at the insistence of the Spaniards, who furnished the guns, knives, and hatchets, the Yemassee Indians, who lived near Port Royal, attacked the settlers along the Pocataligo River and killed every person whom they found. Thence they rushed up the coast toward Charleston, murdering all whites and burning every house. Fortunately, Governor Charles Craven with two hundred fifty men blocked their advance and routed them. Nevertheless, the Indians twice more, and with far greater numbers, attempted to destroy Charleston. Probably more than four hundred settlers were killed in these struggles, before the Indians were finally defeated and routed to the Spaniards in Florida.

On account of these Indian ravages, the Carolina colonies were greatly retarded in their development, and many settlers, becoming discouraged, left the province. The proprietors had received very little return on their grants, and, on a moderate estimate, the quitrents in the Carolinas were in arrears to the amount of £9,500. For these reasons the proprietors, in 1729, sold their rights in the Carolina colonies to the King for £50,000. Thereafter, the two groups of settlements centering around Albemarle and Charleston became separately governed provinces, known as "North Carolina" and "South Carolina."

## GEORGIA

Georgia, the last of the Southern as well as the last of the Thirteen Colonies, was established for two purposes: as a philanthropic experiment, and as a stiategic outpost in English imperialistic expansion.

Originally the territory south of the Savannah River, which later comprised Georgia, was granted to the Lord Proprietors of "Carolina." Although during their control no colony was planted there, a continuous interest was manifested in the region. Colonial promoters persistently urged that settlements be established in this zone to safeguard the Carolina settlements against the Spaniards in Florida. In 1720, the Board of Trade in England, convinced by such arguments, planned to encourage the establishment of settlements in the region. But for more than a decade thereafter, their plan was frustrated both by the indifference of higher English authorities and by the policy of the Lord Proprietors of the Carolinas to check all further efforts at expansion southward.

In 1724, Purry, an ambitious colonial promoter, proposed to the Board of Trade that they settle six hundred Swiss in this unoccupied territory south of the Savannah River. A year later, he appeared before the Lord Proprietors of "Carolina" and argued that his projected colony "would not only strengthen that Province but be a Barrier to the rest of his Majesties Colonies upon the Continent of America." [14]  Nothing came of this proposal except promises of aid which were soon made impracticable by modifications.

About five years later, Robert Johnson, royal governor of South Carolina, appealed directly to the Board of Trade to encourage settlements in this zone for the avowed purpose of protection against the Spaniards. The next year (1730), the Board of Trade decided definitely to comply with the request, and forthwith to project colonization into this border region.

In 1729, the House of Commons had appointed a *gaols committee,* under the chairmanship of James Oglethorpe, to investigate the situation of the debtors who filled the prisons of England. As suspected, the findings indicated that conditions in many instances were intolerable and wholly unacceptable in a society such as that envisaged by the leaders of the growing humanitarian movement. Thus, concurrently, there appeared both the need for a strategic colony on the American frontier south of the Carolinas, and the problem of numerous debtors and paupers who had become a social burden in England but who could be shipped across the Atlantic to form this frontier outpost.

In 1732, James Oglethorpe and nineteen other trustees, as a corporate body, secured from King George II a charter for the territory extending from the Savannah southward to the Altamaha and from their heads westward to the "South Sea." These proprietors were given the land in perpetuity and the power to govern it for twenty-one years, with this exception: the Crown reserved the right to appoint officers who should collect the King's revenue in the province, and an annual accounting was to be made to the home government for all the receipts and expenditures of the province. To honor the King, the tract was styled "Georgia"; and, to express the overt purpose for establishing settlements there, an official seal was adopted,

---

[14] C. O. 5:292, p. 149. Quoted by Verner W. Crane in *Southern Frontier,* p. 286.

having on it silkworms and the motto *Non Sibi Sed Aliis*.

In order to meet the expenses of the colony, in 1732, Parliament granted £10,000, and, annually thereafter until the beginning of the war with Spain, amounts varying from £2,500 to £16,000. In addition, contributions were widely solicited. Governor Robert Johnson, of South Carolina, issued a proclamation in which he declared, among other things, that he was authorized "to take and receive all such voluntary contributions as any of his Majesty's good subjects of this province shall voluntarily contribute towards so good and charitable a work as the relieving of poor and insolvent debtors, and settling, establishing and assisting poor Protestants of what nation soever as shall be willing to settle in the said [Georgia] colony." The newspaper and periodical press, which was fairly well developed in England by 1730, was enlisted in behalf of the project to an extent never before realized in the case of other colonies.

In November 1732, Oglethorpe, as governor and general, set out from England with one hundred thirty persons, representing thirty-five families. Although these colonists had come from the pauper classes, the group was selected only after careful investigation, and was made up of carpenters, bricklayers, farmers, and mechanics. They reached Charleston in January 1733. With the assistance of Governor Johnson, they arrived in February at a selected place on a bluff overlooking the Savannah River, some ten miles from the sea. Here they founded the city of Savannah, the original plan of which in several respects resembled that of an old English village community. Each colonist was allotted fifty acres, consisting of a town lot, sixty by ninety feet; a garden lot of five acres adjoining the town; and, further out, a farm of forty-four acres and one hundred forty-one poles.

Slavery was prohibited because the founders of the colony believed that it would interfere with free white labor and that it might prove dangerous in case of a fron-

tier war with the Spaniards. Traffic in rum and spirituous
liquors was prohibited for industrial reasons. Nor could
any one person own more than five hundred acres of land.
In time, however, all these prohibitions were removed, and
Georgia came to have practically the same characteristics
as the other Southern colonies—namely: slavery, rum, and
plantations.

In 1734, there arrived a number of German Protestant
exiles from Salzburg, who established a settlement nearby
called "Ebenezer." Two years later, an armed colony
founded "Frederica," at the mouth of the Altamaha, on
the Spanish border. Several other settlements were
planted, and the number of colonists gradually increased
until, in 1752, Georgia had a population of 2,381 whites
and 1,066 negroes. Through the diplomacy of Oglethorpe,
peace was established with the nearby Creek Indians; and,
through his generalship, the Spanish, in 1742, were foiled
in their attempt to capture "Frederica." Thereafter the
Spaniards avoided Georgia. However, the colony did not
prosper to any great extent economically; the reason for
this was, perhaps, mainly due to the type of settlers, many
of whom were thriftless and indolent by nature.

Finally, in 1752, after twenty years of control, the
trustees surrendered their charter and Georgia became a
royal province. During their control they had expended
upon the colony about £154,000. Approximately £130,000
of this amount had been granted by Parliament, and
nearly all the remainder had been raised by subscription.

To plant the five Southern colonies had been a slow
and hazardous task. Between the founding of Jamestown
and that of Savannah, a period of one hundred twenty-
five years had elapsed and countless lives had been lost
on account of disease and Indian attacks. There had been
encountered hardships and privations which tested the
stamina and challenged the courage of the settlers to the
utmost. The risk of planting these colonies had been assumed in each case by colonial proprietors: in Virginia,

by a joint-stock company; in Maryland, by a family; in the Carolinas, by the Lord Proprietors; and in Georgia, by the trustees. England had trusted to the initiative of her citizens to establish these colonies for the sake of profits. Georgia alone was a partial exception.

Within a comparatively short time after they had become permanently established, all the colonies, with the exception of Maryland,[15] were taken over by the Crown and made into royal provinces. By 1760, the Southern colonies occupied a considerable fringe along the seaboard; in Virginia, people were beginning to settle the Shenandoah Valley and were exploring the Alleghenies.

### England's Colonial System

Although the English system of colonial control was more favorable to the Southern than to the Northern colonies, nevertheless, it both retarded and stimulated the economic development of the South.

According to a nationalistic theory of commerce known as *mercantilism,* which prevailed in England as well as throughout Europe from the sixteenth to the eighteenth centuries, colonies were considered primarily as a source for raw material which could not be produced at home and as a market for finished products produced by the home country. Great emphasis was placed upon the acquisition of money, not because business men of seventeenth-century England, as sometimes stated, considered money and wealth synonymous, but rather because they had grasped the quantity theory of money in its essentials and sought to avert the maldistribution of gold and silver among the nations. Such a condition required, they thought, a *favorable balance of trade,* which meant a surplus of commodity and service exports over imports, with the balance settled in precious metals. Colonies, since they existed solely for the benefit of the home country, were always to

---

[15] Even Maryland was managed directly from London for twenty-five years.

furnish a favorable balance of trade and also an abundance of staple products for the home country.

In order to apply the mercantilistic theory, Parliament in the course of time enacted a whole series of trade regulations. At first, England had no fixed system for governing the commercial development of her colonies, and only occasional orders in council of a mercantilistic cast were issued during the reigns of the first Stuarts. However, in the Puritan dictatorship of Oliver Cromwell, the Government undertook definitely to promote England's commerce by passing the first Navigation Acts, of 1650 and 1651. Following these, a series of acts—those of 1660, 1662, 1663, and 1673—were passed by the Parliament of the restored Stuarts; and, finally, in the reign of William and Mary, the provisions of these acts were summarized and somewhat clarified in the Navigation Act of 1696. During the first decades of the eighteenth century, there was a pause in further mercantilistic legislation that was of great importance to the Southern colonies. But, with the Peace of Paris in 1763, England annexed new territory in America for future development and markets, and then, with new determination, undertook to extend and to enforce her commercial regulations. The provisions and effects of the various commercial regulations as they concerned the Southern colonies, will be reserved for later discussion.

The passage of laws regulating colonial industry and trade made necessary the establishment of machinery for their enforcement. At the beginning of colonization, the regulation of the plantations and their trade lay in the hands of the King and his Privy Council. It was this Council which dealt in London with the Virginia Company before and after its dissolution. Parliament had not yet begun to legislate for the colonies. From 1630 to 1660, committees, or special commissions, were employed to inquire into colonial affairs. In 1660, two trade commissions were created: one for domestic trade, and the other for the foreign plantations. The *Council for Trade* consisted of sixty members and was instructed to consider how the manufacture, navigation, and trade of the United Kingdom might be improved. The *Council for Foreign Plantations* consisted of forty-eight members, and was set up in order "to make the colonies understand that their head and center is here [England]" and to enforce the Navigation Acts. The personnel of these Councils included ministers, privy councillors, merchants, and other persons familiar with trade. However, neither of these Councils functioned very effectively, probably because their membership was entirely too large and unwieldy. In 1670, the membership of the Council for Foreign Plantations was reduced to ten persons, with annual salaries ranging from £300 to £700. The next year, six noblemen were added to this Council.

In 1672, the Council for Trade and the Council for Foreign Plantations were combined to form the *Council for Trade and Foreign Plantations*. This was a purely advisory body to the Privy Council and was abolished in 1674. However, the next year, the work of the Council for Trade and Foreign Plantations was intrusted to a committee of twenty-one members of the Privy Council. This new committee was to be known as the *Lords of Trade* and was to be a permanent body, having its own clerks. In 1688, the whole Privy Council was made a standing committee for trade and plantations. In 1696, the Lords of Trade was superseded by a *Board of Commissioners for Trade and Plantations*. The latter was the *Board of Trade,* and until the Revolutionary War it handled all matters pertaining to the American colonies. It instructed the colonial officials, reviewed colonial legislation, received colonial petitions, and made recommendations to Parliament or to the Privy Council about colonial industry and trade. Although the Board of Trade had supervisory powers over the colonies, all of its resolutions were subject to review by the King and the Privy Council. Matters dealing with the finances of the colonies were usually referred by the Board of Trade to the Lords of the Treasury or to the

Commissioner of the Customs. The Bishop of London was *ex officio* a member of the Board of Trade, as he exercised jurisdiction over the affairs of the Anglican Church in the colonies.

In the early days of the colonies some person was sent occasionally by one or more colonies to England on a special mission. As time went on and the relationship between the colonies and the home country became more complex, these colonial *agents* became a regular part of the colonial administrative system. They were officially the business representatives of the colonies in the British Capital.

Another important feature of the colonial administrative system was the establishment, after 1660, of *Admiralty Courts* one of the chief duties of which was to try cases involving vessels seized for violating the Navigation Acts. At the close of the seventeenth century, seven of these Admiralty Courts had been established in the American colonies. In Maryland, Governor Nicholson received from the Lord High Admiral of England a commission of *vice admiral* and, vested with that authority, established Admiralty Courts in the colony for the trial of offenses against the Acts of Trade. Ships from the royal Navy were stationed in colonial waters to seize violators of navigation and trade laws. To collect customs duties, England sent collectors and, at the same time, comptrollers to check the work of the collectors.

Notwithstanding the comprehensive organization of her colonial administrative system, England seldom enforced her navigation and trade laws effectively. From 1631 to 1681, she made four attempts to extend her control over the colonies, but each time she was thwarted by political exigencies at home. Added to this difficulty was the growing practice of smuggling the "enumerated" articles from the colonies directly to the continental countries. Generally, however, the Southern colonies during their early history, since they were primarily plantations for the production of export staples, fitted well into the mercantilistic scheme of things; and until 1763, when England entered definitely upon a course of imperialism, it was seldom that they were irritated by English control.

### Bibliographical Note

The most scholarly work dealing with the economic aspects of English history as a background for American colonization is E. Lipson, ECONOMIC HISTORY OF ENGLAND, Volumes II and III (London, 1931), especially Volume II, *Age of Mercantilism*. W. J. Ashley, *Economic Organization of England* (London, 1914), also contains much valuable information. For more succinct treatments, see E. P. Cheyney, *European Background of American History* (New York, 1904); and *Economic History of Europe* (Boston, 1928), by Melvin M. Knight, Harry Elmer Barnes, and Felix Flugel.

On the founding of the Southern colonies, much has been written. However, most of the studies have been made from the political and institutional point of view rather than from the economic. The definitive works on the colonial period are H. L. Osgood's *American Colonies in the Seventeenth Century*, three volumes (New York, 1904–1907), and *American Colonies in the Eighteenth Century*, four volumes (New York, 1924); but Osgood purposely omits a discussion of economic development, though he frequently refers to economic factors. For Virginia, the most comprehensive study yet made is P. A. Bruce, *Economic History of Virginia in the Seventeenth Century*, two volumes (New York and London, 1895). To be mentioned also are: E. P. Cheyney, "Some English Conditions Surrounding the Settlement of Virginia," in the *American Historical Review*, Volume XII, pages 507–528; and Wesley Frank Craven, "The Dissolution of the London Company for Virginia," in the *American Historical Review*, Volume XXXVII, pages 14–24. References to economic factors may be found in Thomas Jefferson Wertenbaker, *Virginia Under the Stuarts, 1607–1688.* (Princeton, 1914); and in John Holladay Latané, *Early Relations between Maryland and Virginia* (New York, 1895). Of the earlier works on Virginia, Robert Beverley, *History of Virginia*, Reprint Edition (Richmond, 1855); and John D. Burk, *History of Virginia from its earliest settlement to the present day,* four volumes (Petersburg, 1804–1816), contain invaluable information. For Maryland, see N. D. Mereness, *Maryland as a Proprietary Province* (New York, 1901); Frederick Robertson Jones, *Colonization of the Middle States and Maryland* (New York, 1904); and Bernard Christian Steiner, *Beginnings of Maryland, 1631–1639* (Baltimore, 1903), *Maryland During the English Civil Wars* (Baltimore, 1906), and *Maryland under the Commonwealth, a Chronicle of the Years 1649–1659* (Baltimore, 1911). Up to the present time very little has been done in the economic history of colonial North Carolina. Most studies deal with the political aspects and make only casual reference to economic conditions. The most important of these works are: F. L. Hawks, *History of North Carolina* (Charleston, 1858); C. L. Raper, *North Carolina, A Study in English Colonial Government* (New York, 1894); Samuel Ashe, *History of North Carolina*, Volume I (Greensboro, N. C., 1908) and Volume II (Raleigh, N. C., 1925). For South Carolina, Edward McCrady has made two valuable studies: *History of South Carolina under Proprietary Government, 1670–1719* (New York and London, 1897), and *History of South Carolina under the Royal Government, 1719–1776* (New York and London, 1899). Also, see W. Roy Smith, *South Carolina as a Royal Province* (New York and London, 1903). The best study yet made of the economic aspects of colonial Georgia is Verner Winslow Crane's *Southern Frontier, 1670–1732* (Durham, N. C., 1928). Of a more general nature and emphasizing mainly the political aspects is C. C. Jones, Jr., *History of Georgia,* two volumes (Boston, 1883).

The best short work of a general nature but emphasizing particularly the economic aspects of colonization is M. W. Jernegan, *American Colonies, 1492–1750* (New York, 1929). O. P. Chitwood, *History of Colonial America* (New York, 1931), is a satisfactory textbook dealing in a general way with the subject of colonization, and offers considerable material on the Southern colonies. An invaluable aid to further reading in this field is the *Guide to the Study and Reading of American History,* Revised Edition (New York, 1912), by Edward Channing, A. B. Hart, and F. J. Turner.

On the subject of the English colonial system, the fundamental works are the various volumes by G. L. Beer. These include: *Origins of the British Colonial System, 1578–1600* (New York, 1908); *Old Colonial System* (New York, 1912); and *British Colonial Policy, 1754–1765* (New York, 1907). Dealing specifically with the English colonial administrative system is Charles M. Andrews, *British Committees, Commissions, and Councils of Trade and Plantations, 1622–1675* (New York, 1908). An excellent summary of the system is also found in Percy Scott Flippin's *Royal Government in Virginia, 1624–1775* (New York, 1919). The theory of mercantilism is brilliantly treated by Othmar Spann in *History of Economics*, Chapter II (New York, 1926). Presenting a different interpretation are: J. W. Harrocks, *Short History of Mercantilism* (London, 1925); and Gustav Schmoller, *Mercantile System and Its Historical Significance* (New York, 1896).

# CHAPTER III

# Agriculture in the Colonial South

## Experimental Period

THE agricultural history of the Southern colonies begins with an experimental period during which the chief purpose of the colonists was to achieve self-sufficiency. The first settlers at Jamestown thought that they could grow the same kinds of crops in Virginia soil as in their homeland; for, within two months after their arrival, on the area of about four acres which they had cleared in order to get timber for the fort, they sowed wheat and planted the seeds of fruits and vegetables brought from England. Although little came of this planting, they cleared more land and, the second year, sowed more wheat. They soon discovered, however, that, while the plant shot up to an amazing height in the extraordinarily fertile soil, the kernels unfortunately would not harden into grain.

Even though these crops failed, the colonists were still not thrown absolutely upon their own resources to discover plants and farming methods adapted to the new conditions; they could, and did, learn many of their first lessons directly from the Indians. It must be remembered that from the coastal Indians, who were not pure nomads, our ancestors learned how to grow two crops, corn and tobacco, which have played a prominent part in our agrarian economy.

In 1609, the Jamestown settlers learned how to cultivate corn (maize) and planted about forty acres with it. This grain brought in a good harvest; its cultivation was extended until, in 1614, the settlers planted about five hundred acres. The method usually followed was that of the Indians. First, the trees were deadened by girdling the bark of the trunk, and by building a fire near the roots. The next year, corn was planted in the clearing in holes at about 4- or 5-foot intervals, and, if the land was near a stream, a small fish was occasionally thrown into the hole beside the seed for fertilizer. As the corn grew, a hill of dirt was piled up around the roots. Between the hills squashes and pompions were often planted. This method of cultivation had already been used so extensively by the Indians that the colonists, on account of so many such clearings, frequently miscalculated the number of Indian inhabitants in the vicinity.

In 1612 at Jamestown, John Rolfe, the famous husband of Pocahontas, produced a small crop of tobacco which Ralph Hamor considered as "strong, sweet, and pleasant as any under the sun."[1] The method used in setting out and curing this crop was that learned from the Indians, which, though crude, was followed almost exactly by subsequent planters for about fifty years. First, the seeds were planted at intervals in finely pulverized soil. Then, after the plants had put out four or five leaves, the main stem was budded and the suckers kept pulled off in order to force the growth of the leaves. Finally, when the dew was on the leaves, the tobacco was harvested and heaped in a pile to dry.

Besides the cultivation of corn and tobacco, the early colonists learned from the Indians how to grow many vegetables and fruits that are indigenous to America—such as sweet potatoes, squashes, and several varieties of beans, and watermelons and strawberries. They also began to cultivate several European plants. Rye and Irish potatoes[2] were grown in 1630; flax, hemp, and hops, probably

---

[1] Quoted by T. J. Wertenbaker, *The First Americans, 1607-1690*, p. 22.

[2] Originally the Irish (or white) potato was probably carried, about 1550, from South America to Spain. It spread from there into other European countries.

about 1645; and buckwheat, in 1650. Even cotton was
planted at Jamestown during the first decades of its settlement. In 1609, a few horses, sheep, and swine were brought
over; in 1611, sixty cows were imported by Governor Dale;
and, in the summer of the same year, one hundred cows
and two hundred dogs were brought over by Sir Thomas
Gates.

Thus, by means of experimenting and readaptation, the
early colonists established the bases for Southern agriculture. During the whole colonial period, however, agricultural practices were extremely crude. Since the first
settlers had very few animals, the chief implements were
hand tools. These included the hoe, which consisted of
an ill-formed blade fastened to an unpeeled sapling that
was used for the handle; shovels; spades; sickles; scythes;
frows; and pickaxes. The plow was employed very little
and was a clumsy affair of wood; the iron plow was not
invented until 1797. In 1618, only one serviceable plow
was to be found in the colony; and, some thirty years later,
there were only one hundred fifty such implements. Grain
was sown broadcast by hand. When ripe, it was cut with
a hand sickle, and then threshed with a flail or by driving
horses over it. As a general rule, cattle were unhoused;
it was believed in the Southern colonies that housing and
milking cows during the winter might kill them. Fertiliz-
ing the land was temporarily unnecessary and was,
therefore, neglected.

During the early days at Jamestown, the most urgent
problem of the colonists was that of finding an export
product to exchange for the imports which were so badly
needed. There was no gold to be found, nor could ordinary grains—such as wheat, barley, rye, and oats—be used
for exports, because England, being an agricultural land,
had an abundance of these staples. The London Company,
realizing this fact, actually imported Italian experts to
teach the colonists how to grow silk, for which there was a
European demand; but the project failed. Then an effort

was made to raise grapes, in order, if possible, to establish a wine industry; but this also failed. For a time despair ruled at Jamestown, the colony appeared about to fail, and there was talk of the colonists' returning to England.

Fortunately for the colony a profitable export commodity was at last found in tobacco. Its use had been introduced by John Hawkins into England as early as 1565, and thereafter a demand for it had developed rapidly. In 1573, Harrison, in his *Description of England,* noted: [3] "In these days the taking in of the smoke of the Indian herb called 'Tobacco,' by an instrument formed like a little ladle, whereby it passeth from the mouth into the head and stomach, is greatly taken up and used in England against Rheums and some other diseases engendered in the lungs and inward parts and not without effect." In fact, the consumption of this plant spread so rapidly through England that, in 1604, King James I, becoming alarmed at the outflow of specie for its purchase, issued his "Counter Blast to Tobacco," in which he stated that some of the gentry "were bestowing three, some four hundred pounds a year upon this precious stink"; and, after a considerable *argumentum ad hominem,* he concluded by denouncing the use of tobacco as "a custom loathsome to the eye, hateful to the nose, harmful to the brain, dangerous to the lungs, and in the black stinking fume thereof nearest resembling the horrible Stygian smoke of the pit that is bottomless." [4] About eight years later, Pope Urban VIII published a decree against all church members who used snuff. But, despite King and Prelate, loyal subjects and churchmen formed into a national habit what was damned as a vice; and by 1612, when John Rolfe planted his first crop at Jamestown, the English people were already expending £200,000 a year for tobacco from the West Indies and Trinidad.

After Rolfe's first crop at Jamestown, small quantities

---

[3] R. B. Morgan, *Readings in English Social History,* p. 266.
[4] *Ibid.,* p. 352.

were sent from there to England at different times during the next four or five years. The first important shipment was not made, however, until 1619. This comprised 20,000 pounds and brought nearly $11,000, if estimated in present-day American money. With almost one accord, the colonists now turned to the production of tobacco, and thereafter the exports increased rapidly, often doubling and trebling the preceding year's production, until the supply far outran the demand for tobacco at profitable prices.

On the one hand, there was a rapidly developing demand for tobacco; on the other, there were available potential resources for producing the supply. Moreover, on account of the small bulk in proportion to value, tobacco was especially suitable for exporting. For these reasons it became the staple commodity of Virginia, Maryland, and, to a less extent, the Carolinas.

Similarly, rice, indigo, and cotton passed through a stage of experimental culture and finally, in the areas of the South adapted to their production, became the dominant crops, primarily because of foreign demand. The grain crops—wheat, corn, oats, barley, and rye—were relegated to the position of supplementary products in the regions producing the staple exports and, with westward expansion, were produced mainly in the back regions that were remote from river transportation to the Atlantic ports.

## Analysis of the Agricultural System

The Northern colonies, because of soil and climate, could not produce the staple export crops, but they had other resources upon which to build a successful economic future. The Southern colonies had to produce these crops, or fail.[5] Hence, the questions arise:· What kind of economic or-

[5] "The most important feature of economic life in a colony or newly settled community is its commercial connection with the rest of the world. Upon this more than upon any other circumstance depends its prosperity."—G. S. Callender, *Selections from the Economic History of the United States*, p. 6.

ganization was evolved for the production of these crops? In what proportion were the factors of production combined? And, what were the effects upon the social and the political life of the section under consideration?

## LANDHOLDINGS

On account of the discovery made by John Cabot in 1495, the King of England claimed for himself absolute sovereignty over the whole territory of aboriginal North America not already occupied by the subjects of other Christian monarchs. To him belonged all the land; and those of his subjects whom he had designated as grantees became *tenants-in-chief*, for which privilege they owed him fealty. In turn, they were privileged *ipso jure* to apportion the land among the settlers either in the form of *leaseholds* or *freeholds*. Thus, from the legal viewpoint, the whole colonial land system pyramided up to the King.

Originally, the Indians held the land by virtue of prior occupancy, and therefore it became necessary in some manner to dispossess them of the required areas. At first their rights to the land, though never recognized as permanent, had entitled them to enough compensation at least to keep them on good terms with the colonists. For example, the first Virginians, shortly after landing, purchased the island of Jamestown for a small amount of copper. Subsequently, the policy generally followed was that of extermination. There were presumably two reasons for this: The English through experience had found the Indians filthy, squalid, and treacherous; and, having no conception of a legal sale, the Indians had often insisted upon joint occupancy of the land with the whites. At any rate, the problem was more or less a temporary one, for there were only about 150,000 Indians east of the Mississippi River, and they had no effective tribal organization to stop the white man's aggressive seizure of the land.

As already noted in the preceding chapter, the King originally granted the land in Virginia to a company; that in Maryland, to an individual; and that in the Carolinas and Georgia, respectively, to a few individuals. But these royal grants exerted only a slight influence upon the development of the land system and, perhaps at most, merely influenced the ultimate establishment of the boundaries of these colonies. As a matter of fact, the land system had an internal growth conditioned, primarily, by the system of agricultural production which happened to be adapted to the given region and, secondly, by the legal system of inheritance used there.

**Land system in Virginia.** The first settlers of Virginia, who founded Jamestown, did not immediately receive land in severalty, nor in communal ownership. Instead, they were bound in "common servitude" to the London Company. But ownership was not long in evolving. According to the *Colonial Records,* in Virginia as early as 1613, Bermuda planters were given a *tenantship-at-will* on small tracts of the company's land at a yearly rent of three barrels of Indian corn and a month's service to the colony. In 1616, others, who likewise had been made tenants of the company, were granted the privilege for eleven months during the year of producing their maintenance on small rented farms, and were allowed to hire labor. After 1617, certain corporate rights to land were given to associations of planters. A few land grants, as well, were given to individuals. In 1619, under Sir George Yeardley, private ownership to land in severalty was established in Virginia.

Subsequently, there were three general methods by which an individual might acquire land: through purchase, as a reward for meritorious service, and in return for headrights.

In 1619, a demand was made of the representative assembly that every resident shareholder of the company be given land as a dividend. This request was granted, and everyone who owned stock was to receive for each share one hundred acres of land "upon the first division" and one hundred acres more when the grant was "seated."

Since the price of a share of stock was £12 10s., the price of an acre of land was roughly only about 60 cents. This fact, of course, influenced persons of means to purchase considerable numbers of these shares. About one third of the company's shareholders settled in Virginia, and perhaps another third of them sent over representatives. Later on, however, when Virginia became a royal colony, land in the northern neck could be bought at from 5 to 10 shillings a hundred acres. Finally, in 1705, a title to the public land at the rate of 5 shillings for every fifty acres was allowed, provided that a house be built and three acres planted within three years.

On account of meritorious service Captain Newport, as early as the time of Captain John Smith, received seventy-one shares of the company's stock. Sir Thomas Dale was allotted the equivalent of £700 in land at the usual rate of £12 10s. a hundred acres. In 1651, Charles I gave his favorite page, Edward Prodger, two thousand acres in Virginia. In fact, it frequently happened that ministers, physicians, public servants, and even ordinary laborers were rewarded, at least partially, by gifts of land.

Finally, land might be acquired by the title known as *headrights*. These rights were limited at first to shareholders; but, when the colony became a royal province, they were extended by law to all residents in Virginia. Under this scheme every property owner who met the cost of importing a person was entitled to fifty acres in the first division and fifty acres more in the second division. Thus, a planter could secure, not only additional land, but at the same time the labor necessary to cultivate it.

In early Virginia, the policy of the government had been to establish a system of small landholdings. At one time, because of fear of speculation, the government had even refused to sell land. Likewise, the system of headrights was intended to parcel out small units of land. Under the administration of the company, aside from the shareholders, no one could get a valid title to land without settling on it.

But this purpose did not long prevail. From 1626 to 1632, the average landholdings acquired under single patent did not exceed 160 acres, and the largest individual holding was 1,000 acres; while from 1634 to 1650, the average was about 446 acres, and the largest holding about 4,000 acres. During the next fifty years, the average was 674 acres; and between 1695 and 1700, the average was 688 acres, and there were seven holdings ranging from 5,000 to 10,000 acres, and one for 13,400 acres. After the turn of the century, the size of holdings seems to have increased so much that, in 1685, "although the population of Virginia did not exceed the number of inhabitants in the single parish of Stepney, London, nevertheless they had acquired ownership in plantations that spread over the same area as England itself." In 1705, the legislature attempted to check this concentration of landholdings by limiting the size of patents to 4,000 acres. Despite this fact, there were living in the colony about the middle of the eighteenth century men who had much larger estates. Robert Carter and William Byrd, owned, respectively, almost 60,000 and over 179,000 acres.

The individual acquisition of large areas of land, popularly known as *plantations,* was due primarily to the system of producing tobacco. Planters naturally attempted to get maximum profits from the sale of this product. They were, thus, required to reduce costs through combining the factors of production at a ratio which they considered most effective. According to James C. Ballagh: [6] "Tobacco was thought to demand a minimum of fifty acres of arable land per negro, and as an overseer was dear unless he had twenty negroes under him, a thousand acres of arable land was necessary for the profitable use of capital in tobacco planting. This area was further increased by

---

[6] THE SOUTH AND THE BUILDING OF THE NATION, Vol. VI, p. 153.

the need of timberland to furnish the casks for the tobacco and winter employment for the labor, and a cattle range was also needed for supplying provisions." Furthermore, it was found that tobacco culture quickly exhausted the arable land and necessitated the frequent use of new land, which was less expensive than the improvement of the old. Therefore, profitable production of tobacco led to extensive rather than intensive agriculture.

After Virginia became a royal province, the usual method of acquiring land was by means of the title of headright. Under this law every person who paid his passage to the colony received fifty acres, and he was given an additional fifty acres for every person imported by him. In other words, the size of a grant depended upon the number of headrights presented to the government. By this method, since transportation charges of an emigrant averaged about £6, the land received by the person paying the charges cost little more than a shilling an acre. Hence, by means of a moderate outlay, a planter could secure a large estate and, at the same time, laborers with which to till it.

This liberal device by which land might be acquired was made even more generous, subsequently, by fraudulent practices. Sometimes unscrupulous planters obtained headrights in consideration for money paid for members of their own family who were born in the colony and had never crossed the ocean, or for their own journeys to and from England. In 1651, one patentee crossed the ocean eight times and received 400 acres. One man is said to have taken a list of names from the tombstones at James-town and to have sworn that the persons thus named had come to America to stay and that they had no land. Through corrupt practices in the land office, clerks frequently made out headrights simply from lists of names and sold them for from one to five shillings apiece. Lawyers indulged so flagrantly in manipulating land titles, made uncertain by faulty surveys or by failure to "seat" the original grants, that for several years they were ex-

cluded from practicing in the colony.  But this doing away
with legal service merely added to the entanglements and
facilitated the fraudulent acquisition of land.  Speculators
also became active and acquired for later resale millions
of acres of the best lands of the backcountry.  Thus,
either by fraud, favoritism, or speculation, as well as by
honest practices, individuals in colonial Virginia acquired
landholdings ranging all the way from a few hundred to
several thousand acres.

These plantations—acquired primarily for the production of tobacco and secondarily for the social prestige of
the family—were maintained intact until after the Revolution by a system of inheritance based upon the laws of
entail and primogeniture.  By the law of entail, it was
provided that the owner of land could not sell or give
away his estate; and, by the law of primogeniture, "where
there are two or more males in equal degree the eldest
shall inherit; but the females altogether."  However, these
laws, long established in England, do not appear to have
been operative to any general extent in Virginia during
the seventeenth century, because of the very low-
capitalized land values and the scarcity of independent
employment for the younger sons.  In general the sons
shared equally, but sometimes the eldest son was permitted
to select his division of the estate.  According to Bruce,[7]
the first entail mentioned in Virginia records did not take
place until 1653.  However, thirty-five years later, it appears that a York County man bequeathed all his land and
tenements to his eldest son *in ventre*,[8] the living children
being daughters.  Thereafter the practice became general,
and during the eighteenth century practically all great
estates were willed according to the laws of entail and
primogeniture.  Thus there was created in colonial Vir-

[7] Philip A. Bruce, *Economic History of Virginia in the Seventeenth Century*, Vol. I, p. 487 *et seq.*

[8] *In ventre sa mère* is a legal phrase which loosely means "that may be
born hereafter."

ginia east of the Blue Ridge, a landed aristocracy. In Virginia west of the Blue Ridge, a different kind of economic order evolved. There, at the beginning of the Revolution, most of the settlements were new, though the land had actually been granted much earlier.

Even as far back as 1754, according to Governor Dinwiddie's report to the Board of Trade, the land up to the Allegheny Mountains had "been greatly taken up, and some remain'g to be settled." [9] Other records, however, indicate that progress in taking up this land was slower than Governor Dinwiddie's report might lead us to suppose. Actually, few settlements had been established there, on account of the Indians, until after the French and Indian War. But soon a great westward movement began, and the demand for new land became almost insatiable. From March 1772 to July 1774, 1,164 grants were made for approximately three hundred thousand acres scattered from Princess Anne to Augusta County; and from March 1774 to March 1775, the surveyor's record of Fincastle County shows that 354 grants were actually surveyed.

The economic order established in this region consisted of small independent proprietors whose average unit of land varied from three hundred to four hundred acres, because the method of farming adapted to the region, on account of soil and distance from the seaport, was that of diversification of crops and not of tobacco culture alone. Furthermore, instead of employing negro labor, as did the tobacco planters east of the Blue Ridge, these farmers had no slaves, or very few, for their method of farming made slave labor highly unprofitable. A comparison of the two sections, east and west of the Blue Ridge, does not imply, however, that all settlers in this colony were either great or small landholders. In both sections there were many poor and landless whites.

**Land systems in other Southern colonies.** The land systems in Maryland, the Carolinas, and Georgia came to

[9] *Dinwiddie Papers*, Vol. I, p. 362.

resemble that of Virginia in principle, but in all the colonies they differed somewhat in detail.

In Maryland, Lord Baltimore intended to establish two classes of landholdings: large estates resembling the old English manors, and small peasant farms. In 1633, 1636, 1642, and 1648, he issued conditions of acquiring land. The first issue contained offers made to the colonists before they left England. It provided that each free planter should pay for his outfit and transportation, which amounted to about £20. Every married man complying with this condition was to receive one hundred acres of land; and his wife, one hundred acres if she accompanied him to the colony. For each adult servant, he was to receive one hundred acres, and, for each child under sixteen years of age, fifty acres. In 1636, the proprietor offered each adventurer who would import five male settlers between the ages of sixteen and fifty, two thousand acres in perpetuity, subject to a quitrent of 20 shillings a year. In 1642, the amount of land granted to each individual settler of adult age was reduced from one hundred acres to fifty. Such grantees were required to pay a quitrent of 10 pounds of wheat and, as a general rule, received an inferior grade of land to that acquired by the holders of large estates. In 1648, the conditions for acquiring land were made especially elaborate. Grantees were required to erect manors; to reserve one sixth of each manor as a demesne; and to pay the proprietor rent, as under the original grant.

Here, as in Virginia, the profitable cultivation of tobacco soon affected the land system; and, in order to acquire the desired estates, similar methods were used. Headrights were manipulated; grants were obtained for meritorious services and consideration; surplus and lapsed and escheated lands were sometimes absorbed into existing plantations; and the laws of entail and primogeniture, though less extreme than in Virginia, were operative. Thus, by 1676, there were established sixty manors of

three thousand or more acres each. A certain Eltonhead
had received a grant of ten thousand acres; and Charles
Carroll, of Prince George County, had received twenty
thousand acres. However, in 1683, due mainly to fraudulent headrights, by proclamation of the proprietor, land
could be obtained thereafter only by the payment of purchase money, the sum being payable partly in tobacco and
partly in specie.

In the Carolinas under the proprietors, every freeman
was given: one hundred acres of land for himself, one hundred for his wife, one hundred for each child, one hundred
for each man servant, and fifty acres for each woman
servant; but the grantee was required to pay a quitrent,
usually of one-half penny an acre.

In North Carolina, the policy of the proprietors favored
moderate landholdings; it became customary to limit
single grants to six hundred or six hundred forty acres.
After the colony became a royal province, certain London
merchants were given large grants. McCulloch was granted
1,200,000 acres on the headwaters of the Pedee and the
Cape Fear, with the provision that no rents were to be
paid by him to the Crown for a number of years, and that
he subdivide this grant into baronies of 12,500 acres each.
In 1744, Lord Granville was given the entire northern half
of the province, from east to west. Of this he sold 100,000
acres to a group of Protestant refugees, called Moravians,
who established on it a communistic settlement and, in
1766, founded the old part of the city of Winston-Salem.
Plantations of one thousand to three thousand acres were
not uncommon. As a general rule, however, small landholdings predominated in North Carolina, because the
rivers and harbors were not such as to furnish navigation
for the export of agricultural products, and because the
colony was largely settled by poor immigrants from other
colonies.

In South Carolina, as in Virginia, a dual land system
developed. In the Tidewater section, large estates became

the rule.  In the middle and upper country, small landholdings predominated.

As already noted in the preceding chapter, the Earl of
Shaftesbury, one of the grantees of the Carolinas, decided
to establish an aristocracy with graded social classes and
went so far as to have John Locke draw up a theoretical
plan for such a system.  This plan was frustrated by the
exigencies of the new environment, but the land system
eventually developed to meet the requirements for the
profitable production of rice and indigo as exports.[10]

It is generally believed that rice was introduced into
the colony in 1694 by Governor Smith.  At any rate, it
was not long thereafter before the planters discovered that
it could be made to yield large profits if cultivated by
negro labor upon sufficient areas of the lowest and richest
lands.  For this reason its production rapidly increased.
Within thirty years after its introduction, 100,000 barrels
were exported from the colony; and in 1761, the value of
the quantity exported amounted to more than $1,500,000.
About 1745, indigo culture was successfully introduced into
the colony by Eliza Lucas.  This product also became a
profitable export and was produced in rapidly increasing
quantities in the lowlands of the Tidewater counties.  The
amount exported in the year 1747–1748 was 134,118
pounds; in 1754, 216,954 pounds; and in 1775, 1,150,662
pounds.

It was no doubt on account of the profits that could be
had from the production of these export crops, rice and
indigo, that the demand for land increased, not only for
new plantations, but also for additional units to be added
to existing plantations.  Consequently, irregular modes of

---

[10] In an effort to establish Locke's scheme, a dozen or more individuals
in the Carolinas were created *landgraves* and were issued patents calling
for forty-eight thousand acres of land each.  To persons of a lower rank,
called *caciques,* patents were issued calling for twenty-four thousand
acres each.  But, in most cases, these grants were never located or surveyed, and subsequently their legality, for that reason, was denied.

obtaining grants, as well as of extending them, came into existence. Patents, as a rule, were issued before the land was surveyed, and frequently as much as one fourth of an original grant was added to it after the payment of a small fee to the surveyors. In one case, for example, an attempt was made by this method to add eleven hundred acres to a tract of only fifty acres. Furthermore, during the colonial period the land office was sometimes closed for several years at a time, and in the interim not only was conveyance informal, but much ungranted land was actually claimed on the allegation that it was purchased from the Indians. By such methods there came into existence plantations whose annual value of products ranged from £10,000 to £20,000, and nowhere else in America was the plantation system developed in such an extreme form as in the Tidewater section of South Carolina.

This, however, was not the case in the middle and upper regions of the colony. There, the early grants made by Governor Robert Johnson were on the basis of fifty acres for each new settler, and on account of the distance to the seaport there was no general demand for large plantations for the production of export crops.

In Georgia, the plantation system did not begin to develop until the colony became a royal province. The trustees refused to grant estates in fee, and made grants only *in tail male*,[11] because the trustees thought that grants in fee might attract too many Spaniards and Frenchmen from Florida and Louisiana. The grants that were thus made *in tail male* were limited to fifty acres a settler. At Savannah such grants were even divided into three parts: one eighth of an acre for a house and garden in Savannah, four and seven-eighths acres at a distance from town, and forty-five acres "at a considerable Remove from thence." Slavery, which comprised most of the labor on the plantations, was prohibited in the early years of Georgia's existence.

---

[11] *In tail male* means to the male heir in the line of descent.

After Georgia became a royal province in 1752, new patents were substituted which, in the name of the King, reconveyed the lands in "free and common socage" to the grantees. Furthermore, fee simple grants of two hundred acres to each family head—with fifty acres more for each member of the household, white or black—were sold at the rate of £5 a hundred acres, provided that the grantees and their assigns paid an annual quitrent of 2 shillings a hundred acres, and annually cleared and cultivated at least five acres in every hundred of their grant. As a consequence, along with the usual amount of fraud, large tracts of thousands of acres were organized into plantations, and a land system similar to that in the other Southern colonies was finally established.

## Labor

Considered from the viewpoint of status, *labor* as an essential factor of production in the Southern colonies was composed of three classes: free contract labor, servitude, and slavery.

**Free contract labor.** The earliest colonial immigrants brought with them some *free contract laborers*—that is to say, laborers serving for wages. But because of the extraordinary effort required to establish a colony, most of the colonists were *contract laborers-on-the-shares,* more under military supervision than self-direction. Thus, in early Virginia, the *Adventurers of the Persons* (planters who came as colonists) were theoretically free laborers who had contracted with the Virginia Company for a number of years, provided they received their maintenance during the period and participated in the dividends of 'the company, if any. After five years, which was the period established by royal instructions for a system essentially communistic, the company established seven-year contracts, which either specifically excluded hired laborers from the colony, or reduced them to a status of "general and common servitude." A few years later some of these "ancient planters" were given small tracts of land, and in other cases slight modification was made in this "common servitude." With the exception of some personal servants and soldiers who received wages, there were never many free laborers in the Southern colonies, for abundant land could be acquired so cheaply by free laborers that most of them refused to work for wages which were not prohibitively high for planters to pay.

It is probable that free skilled labor received four or five times the amount that similar labor brought in England. In Virgina, before the influx of indentured servants. a day's work of an unskilled laborer brought, in addition to food, a pound of tobacco valued at one shilling, or, ordinarily, a wage equivalent to a week's wage for similar labor in England. In Georgia, while slavery was prohibited. wages for hired help were three times the English rate. Indeed, the situation in America, springing from an abundance of land and a scarcity of labor, was quite the reverse of that in Europe.

Since free labor was not available for the plantations, compulsory labor was deemed necessary. It was not difficult to inaugurate such a system, for in Europe there was a surplus of laborers who could be used for this very purpose.

**Servitude.** As Max Weber says: [12] "A plantation is an establishment with compulsory labor, producing garden products especially for a market." In the Southern colonies compulsory labor began, and for several years predominated, in the form of servitude as distinct from slavery. In the colonies *servitude,* as a form of labor organization, meant the temporary and partial loss of personal and political liberty to transported colonial laborers, in order to satisfy obligations incurred by them. Such laborers, termed *indentured servants* and *redemptioners,* were of two general classes: voluntary and involuntary.

---

[12] *General Economic History,* p. 79.

The *voluntary indentured servants* were those persons who, seeking a new start, came over of their own free will. In order to pay for their passage, which ranged from £6 to £10 sterling, they bound themselves into servitude for a term of years to sea captains, planters' agents, and even professional speculators, who, on arrival in America, reimbursed themselves by selling the time of such servants to the highest bidder. As distinguished from indentured servants, the *redemptioners* did not bind themselves beforehand, but were given transportation by the shipmaster, with the understanding that, on arrival, they would indenture themselves to someone who could pay for their passage. If the immigrants failed to do this, the shipmaster could sell them himself. Sometimes, *soul-drivers* would purchase fifty or more such servants from a shipmaster, and drive them about the country like sheep, to sell them at a profit.

*Involuntary indentured servants* were those who were brought over against their will, and consisted of criminals and kidnapped persons.

In England during the seventeenth and eighteenth centuries, there were at different times from one hundred sixty to over three hundred crimes punishable by death. However, in judicial practice, many of these capital offenses were no longer punished as such; and, when there arose an urgent demand for labor in the colonies, justices often commuted the death penalties to fourteen years of servitude in the colonies, or the penalty of whipping and branding, to seven years. Thousands of persons were deported in this manner from England. If adjudged by modern standards, by no means all of them were criminals. They would probably be classified into three groups: vicious, or real, criminals; political and religious offenders; and paupers. The real criminals were counterfeiters, robbers, and murderers. Some were carriers of disease, and practically every one of them was a menace to the colonists. As early as 1670, Virginia passed an act prohibiting the im-

portation of criminals. England confirmed the act and
made it apply to other colonies, but in 1717, Parliament
in effect repealed it by passing another act. Thereafter,
convicts were continually sent to the colonies.

In the *Virginia Gazette,* May 24, 1751, a writer declares:
"When we see our papers filled continually with accounts
of the most audacious Robberies, the most cruel Murders,
and infinite other Villanies perpetrated by Convicts transported from Europe, what melancholy and what terrible
Reflections must it occasion . . . These are some of the
Favours, Britain. Thou art called Mother Country; but
what good mother ever sent thieves and villains to accom-
pany her children; to corrupt with their infectious vices
and to murder the rest?"

Regardless of vigorous colonial protests, many undesir-
ables were sent to Virginia and especially to Maryland.
In fact, J. T. Scharf, a Maryland historian, declares that
twenty thousand felons were imported into that colony before the Revolutionary War.[13]

A large number of involuntary servants consisted of political and religious offenders who were often persons of
considerable intelligence and independence, but who had
come into conflict with the established order of church
and state. The Cavaliers, during the Puritan dictatorship
of Oliver Cromwell, were political offenders; and the
"gentle Quakers," at different times, were considered religious offenders who might be sold into servitude. Debtors
and the starving poor, though the latter may have committed only minor offenses, such as petty thievery and so
on, were, under the penal code of the period, classified with
highwaymen and murderers.

In addition to convicts who were sent to America, the
supply of indentured servants was further augmented by
kidnapped persons. Press gangs, spirits or crimps, and
other professionals regularly kidnapped both adults and
children, and sent them to America. Often members of

---

[13] *History of Maryland,* Vol. I, p. 371.

families, on account of the law of primogeniture, conspired with these agencies to rid themselves of the eldest son, who, under the law, would have become sole heir to the estate. Sometimes parents in abject poverty indentured their own children for a price and had them spirited away to America. Indeed the business of kidnapping grew so rapidly that, by 1627, probably 1,400 or 1,500 children had been sent across the Atlantic; forty years afterwards, according to official estimates, no less than 10,000 persons were thus spirited away to the colonies every year. In 1671, Parliament passed an act making kidnapping a crime punishable by death.

As to the number of indentured servants in the Southern colonies at any given time, only estimates can be made. Sir William Berkley estimated the number in Virginia in 1671 as 6,000. Another authority says that, by 1683, there were 12,000 in the colony, which probably was the greatest number there at any one time. It appears from the Virginia land patents that, between the years 1635 and 1705, there came to the colony annually between 1,500 and 2,000 indentured servants, which statistics would make a total for the seventy years of from 100,000 to 140,000.

But it must be remembered that, since the average servitude was about four years for each servant, at least one fourth of the number in the colony annually became free laborers who, if they chose, could acquire fifty acres of land. If allowance is made for deaths and escaped servants, it becomes evident that the proportion of servants to the total population at any one time was not more than 10 to 20 per cent. How many of these were convicts is largely a matter of conjecture, but it appears that, up to the time of the Revolution, about 50,000 had been sent from England into Virginia and Maryland.

According to a census of Maryland in 1752, there were 8,851 servants (of whom 1,981 were convicts) in a free population of 98,357. In 1771, two thirds of the school teachers in that colony were convicts. In Maryland, according to James T. Adams:[14] " . . . the proportion of indentured servants and convict laborers to the entire population seems to have remained fairly constant, at about nine per cent, but as the figures for servants include practically no small children, whereas these are included in the population figures, the proportion of servants to all adults in the colony would be much greater, perhaps twenty-five per cent."

In the Carolinas and Georgia, servitude never became very extensive. At the time that these colonies were being settled, slavery was replacing servitude in Virginia and Maryland. In North Carolina, the distance from good harbors tended to preclude the early development of an extensive plantation system. In South Carolina, the miasmatic rice swamps and indigo plantations soon killed off white laborers. By 1708, out of a total population of 9,580, there were only 120 surviving white servants. In Georgia, the trustees, though prohibiting slavery, encouraged servitude, on the assumption that it was best suited to the character of the settlers. According to their plan, Welsh, English, and German servants were to be indentured for periods of from four to fourteen years, and rights to their service were to be sold at prices ranging from £2 to 6 shillings. Presumably, the price was too high as compared with the returns, and servitude had hardly begun in Georgia before it was replaced by slavery. On one occasion, out of a shipload of sixty-one German servants sold at Savannah for £6 a head wholesale, only nineteen could be distributed, one each, to husbandmen.

Most of the servants transported to the Southern colonies were unskilled laborers, though several artisans and some in the professions bound themselves in servitude. In the *Virginia Gazette*, March 28, 1771, is an advertisement which describes a shipload of servants as follows: "Just arrived at Leedstown, the Ship *Justitia* with about one

---

[14] *Provincial Society, 1690–1763*, p. 98.

Hundred Healthy Servants.    Men, Women and Boys, among which are many Tradesmen—viz. Blacksmiths, Shoemakers, Tailors, House Carpenters and Joiners, a Cooper, a Bricklayer and Plaisterer, a Painter, a Watchmaker and Glazier, several Silversmiths, Weavers, a Jeweler, and many others.    The Sale will Commence on Tuesday, the 2d of April, at Leeds Town on Rappahannock River.    A Reasonable Credit will be allowed, giving Bond with Approved Security to Thomas Hodge."

Servitude as a system of labor had one serious drawback. It was temporary, and, at the expiration of the term of years for which a servant was indentured, the planter was compelled to seek a new servant.    This fact necessarily kept the supply of labor too small to develop the plantation system to its largest and most profitable extent, though it was by means of headrights for servants that it had been made possible in many instances, legitimately or by fraud, to acquire the land for the plantations.    Hence, slavery, as a permanent and cheap labor supply, solved this problem and superseded servitude.

Whether or not servitude eventually would have been crushed out of existence by the accumulating power of freed servants, who migrated to the back regions of the colonies, is a moot question.    It is highly improbable that such would have been the case for many generations; unfortunately, numerous indentured servants, especially the involuntary ones, became merely one of the sources of poor white trash in the South.

**Slavery.**    The first slaves to be introduced into the English colonies in America were brought in 1619, when a piratical Dutch vessel, manned chiefly by Englishmen, stopped at Jamestown and sold the colonists twenty negroes.    For several years thereafter, the importation of negroes was only casual.    Indeed, in 1648, there were only three hundred negroes in Virginia; and as late as 1671, there was only one negro slave to every three indentured white servants, or two thousand of the former to six thousand of the latter. Nor were many slaves brought into either Maryland or the Carolinas before the last quarter of the seventeenth century.

This slow development of slavery in the Southern colonies was due mainly to these reasons. In the first place, slaves in large numbers were not to be had, because the Spaniards, the Portuguese, and especially the Dutch monopolized trade and made it dangerous for the English even to approach the African trading stations. Secondly, because of the demand of the West Indies for this type of labor, prices paid for slaves were kept much higher than the cost of indentured servants, which at most included only a little more than their transportation from Europe.

Toward the close of the seventeenth century, there began a marked acceleration in the development of slavery in the Southern colonies; and by 1683, this form of labor organization had practically superseded servitude in the case of unskilled labor. Three factors were primarily responsible for this change. Great numbers of negroes were sent to the Atlantic coast for sale. At last, the English traders had been able to wring from the Dutch a share in the slave trade; and in 1662, the Royal African Company was chartered, which twenty-five years later was given the exclusive monopoly of trade between the African Gold Coast and the British colonies. Furthermore, in 1713, when the famous Asiento was signed by England and Spain, granting the former the exclusive right, for thirty years, of importing African slaves into Spanish possessions, a strong impetus was given the traffic, and the high seas soon swarmed with slavers. Even in New England, where slavery was hopelessly unremunerative and, therefore, looked upon with increasing hostility, numerous persons seeking high profits fitted out ships and engaged in the African slave trade, to bring thousands of negroes into the Southern colonies. Both in England and the colonies, white servant labor had decreased because of the increasing demand for it in those mechanical trades requiring skilled labor. Hence, cheap negro labor came to be the only adequate supply of unskilled labor.

As time went on, planters came to realize that a negro slave was a more profitable investment than an indentured white servant, because the negro being property could be treated as such, his children *de jure* became the property of the planter, and the subsistence of the negro cost less than that of the white servant.  As white labor in the Southern colonies became scarcer and dearer, negro slave labor became more plentiful and relatively cheaper.

While the statistics on slavery in the Southern colonies prior to 1790 (the First Federal Census) are not entirely trustworthy, they do indicate roughly the extent to which that "peculiar institution" had developed at different times. In 1705, 1,800 negroes were brought into Virginia; and in 1715, that colony had 23,000.  In 1708, Governor Seymour, of Maryland, writing to the Board of Trade, stated that 2,290 negroes were imported into that colony from midsummer 1698 to Christmas 1707.  In 1712, there were 8,330 negroes in Maryland.  In 1700, North Carolina had 1,100; and in 1708, South Carolina had 4,100.

Thus, during the early part of the eighteenth century, the total number of negro slaves in the Southern colonies was probably more than 36,000.  Indeed, it has been estimated that, in 1721, when the slave trade was at its height, negroes in Virginia comprised more than half of the total population; in Maryland, nearly half; in North Carolina, about one third; and in South Carolina, as much as four sevenths.  By 1723, negro slaves were being imported into Virginia at the rate of 1,500 or 1,600 a year.  In 1732, North Carolina had 6,000.  According to Du Bois, South Carolina, from 1733 to 1766, received about 3,000 slaves annually.  About 1738, the trustees, yielding to pressure, allowed the gradual introduction of slavery into Georgia.

Just how many negro slaves there were in the Southern colonies about the time of the Revolution is difficult to estimate.  According to Edward Channing,[15] who does not distinguish between slaves and free negroes, the number of blacks in 1760 was 299,000, distributed as follows:

POPULATION OF SOUTHERN COLONIES BEFORE
THE REVOLUTION

| Colony | Total | Whites | Blacks |
|---|---|---|---|
| Maryland | 164,000 | 108,000 | 56,000 |
| Virginia | 315,000 | 165,000 | 150,000 |
| North Carolina | 130,000 | 110,000 | 20,000 |
| South Carolina | 100,000 | 30,000 | 70,000 |
| Georgia | 9,000 | 6,000 | 3,000 |
|  | 718,000 | 419,000 | 299,000 |

Again, it has been estimated by Du Bois that, in 1776, the total number of slaves in the Southern colonies was 436,000, apportioned as follows: [16] Virginia, 165,000; Maryland, 80,000; North Carolina, 75,000; South Carolina, 110,000; and Georgia, 16,000.  It is a conservative estimate to say that, by the time of the Revolution, the number of negro slaves in the Southern colonies was about 40 per cent of the total population, though the proportion varied from 30 per cent of the total population in Georgia to about 70 per cent in South Carolina, and half of all the Southern slaves at that time were in Virginia alone.

The increase of slaves in the Southern colonies, particularly in Virginia and South Carolina, was so rapid that the danger of slave insurrections not only became imminent, but one such uprising actually did occur in South Carolina in 1739.  Moreover, some of the colonies became so overstocked with negroes that the value of these chattels began to decline.  The fear of insurrection and the declining value of slaves led some colonies to attempt to restrict the importation of negroes.  Thus, Virginia, from time to time during the eighteenth century, sought to hinder the im-

[15] *History of the United States* (1922), Vol. II, p. 491.  Reprinted by permission of the Macmillan Company, New York.

[16] *Industrial Resources,* Vol. III, p. 130.  Quoted from the *Liberator,* February 23, 1849.

portation of slaves by placing heavy duties on them. From 1732 until the Revolution, there were only about six months in which slaves could be brought into Virginia free of duty. In South Carolina, also, after the insurrection, the assembly sought to check the importation of negroes by imposing a kind of sales tax. An act provided that taxes ranging in amount from £10 to £100, according to the height of the slave and the purchase date, should be paid every time a negro slave was bought or sold. Within fifteen months from the passage of the act, £10 had to be paid for the purchase price of a negro over four feet ten inches in height, who had not been in the colony six months; and during the subsequent years, £100 had to be paid on the first purchase price of every such slave.

The attempts of the Southern colonies to curb the slave trade were usually nullified, however, by the veto of the royal governors or of the British Board of Trade, which at all times was under the dominance of a powerful pressure group of English merchants and shipowners. Thus, in 1754, the instructions to Governor Dobbs, of North Carolina, read: [17] "Whereas acts have been passed in some of our plantations in America for laying duties on the importation and exportation of negroes to the great discouragement of the merchants trading thither from the coast of Africa . . . it is our will and pleasure that you do not give your assent to or pass any law imposing duties upon negroes imported into our Province of North Carolina."

Peter Fontaine, of Virginia, wrote in 1757, as follows: [18] "But, our Assembly, foreseeing the ill consequences of importing such members [negroes] amongst us, hath often attempted to lay a duty upon them which would amount to a prohibition, such as ten or twenty pounds a head, but no Governor dare pass such a law, having instructions to the contrary from the Board of Trade at home. By this

---

[17] *North Carolina Colonial Records,* Vol. V, p. 1118.

[18] Reprinted by permission of the publishers, The Arthur H. Clark Company, from their *Documentary History of American Industrial Society,* by J. R. Commons. Vol. II, p. 29.

means they are forced upon us, whether we will or will not.  This plainly shows that the African Company hath the advantage of the colonies and may do as it pleases with the ministry."

Although the Southern colonies could not stop the importation of slaves, they were permitted by the English Government to develop codes defining the legal status of negro slaves.  In Virginia, such statutes usually were based upon the English common law; in South Carolina, where the treatment of negroes was more inhuman, they were based upon the laws of the sugar plantations in the West Indies.  The colonists considered all such laws necessary, not only to insure a maximum efficiency of the slave system, but even to protect the very lives of the planters against the slaves, many of whom at that time were savages direct from Africa.

Slavery, despite its inherent drawbacks, continued to flourish and spread, especially in the Coastal Plain region of the South, mainly because such a system of labor yielded profits to the planters.  One writer on the American tobacco trade concludes: [19]  "We can not agree with those 'abolitionists' and economists who maintained that the Southern planter was working against his best economic interests by employing slave instead of free white labor.  The relative value, as a source of income to the large plantation owner, was on the side of the Negro slave.  The following table represents, in brief, the profits derived from the exploitation of slave labor:

| *Annual Outlay* | | | *Annual Return* | |
|---|---|---|---|---|
| (1) Interest on capital invested in slaves (£50) | £2 | 10s. | (1) Two hogsheads tobacco | £16 |
| (2) Interest on farm capital required per slave | 2 | | (2) Corn, etc. | 4 |
| (3) Living expense of slave | 3 | | | |
| TOTAL COST | £7 | 10s. | | £20 |

Net profit: £12 10s. per year per slave.

[19] Meyer Jacobstein, *Tobacco Industry in the United States* (1907), p. 18.  Reprinted by permission of the Columbia University Press, New York.

The net cost per slave of seven pounds, ten shillings represented an investment of about one hundred pounds. The income of twenty pounds was, therefore, equivalent to twenty per cent profit on the total capital investment, less the sum necessary to replace the fund."

## CAPITAL

*Capital* defined as a producing surplus created by man was relatively scarce in the colonial South. Of the two classes of capital, *producers' goods* and *durable consumers' goods,* the latter was quantitatively more important.

The technology of the colonists was, of course, simple. Their agricultural implements were the kind used by European peasants in the twelfth century and, in some instances, by the Egyptian subjects of Rameses II. An inventory of almost any colonial plantation would have shown only the following items: axes, mattocks, spades, wooden plows, harrows, several sorts of hoes, scythes, rakes, forks, flails, a fanning mill, and some wooden carts.

At first, the bitter struggle for existence in the wilderness made it impossible for the settlers to accumulate much capital in the form of durable consumers' goods. In fact, during the whole colonial period the numerous small farmers had only humble dwellings and the simple furniture common in that time. With the opening of the eighteenth century, however, the planters, profiting from their agricultural exports, began to build beautiful mansions and surrounded them with flower gardens, broad lawns, and neatly trimmed hedges. Within such mansions were spacious rooms, graceful staircases, and large fireplaces. The furniture was usually imported from England or even occasionally brought in from France. There were tables, chairs, and settees of carved mahogany, the latter two sometimes upholstered in the finest Prussian leather. There were imported candlesticks, clocks, mirrors, chests, highboys, and beautiful oak and walnut bedsteads, as well as less expensive articles such as iron pots, pewter dishes, copper kettles, and stone bottles, crocks, and mugs. Moreover, there were all the necessary textile machines, such as spinning wheels, looms, and the like, which were housed in a small building nearby.

There is no way to measure in terms of money the total value of colonial capital. The system of direct exchange of commodities, along with a confused and unstable monetary system and the lack of records, precludes even an attempt at reliable estimate. Nevertheless, it is plainly evident that, in the plantation system of combining the factors of production, physical capital in the form of producers' goods was minimized and kept at the lowest possible ratio in proportion to land and labor.

## THE ENTREPRENEUR

The planter in the plantation system of production was the *entrepreneur*. He was the one who took the initiative to procure land, labor, and capital; assumed the risk of their combination; and received the profits or suffered the losses. That he was wasteful and lived in idleness and gayety, as some writers have alleged, is certainly contrary to the nature of his function and, as a rule, is not evidenced by historical fact. The planters' families, however, like the families of some present-day rich men, were often given to ostentatious consumption. Money was spent in acquiring an education, though in many instances this matter was left entirely in the hands of the younger members of the family, because frequently, as evidenced by colonial records, neither the father nor the mother could read or write. With few exceptions, the early planters in the South were merely *nouveaux riches*, without aristocratic lineage. By the accumulation of property and economic power, this group brought into existence the so-called "Southern aristocracy," much in the same manner as the European aristocracy had been developed generations earlier.

## THE PLANTATION SYSTEM

Thus far, the factors of production have been examined separately; when viewed together, the result is the *plantation system* as developed in the Southern colonies.

The central figure, of course, was the *entrepreneur,* the planter himself. Immediately under his direction was the *overseer,* who directed the slave labor. Next, especially on the larger plantations, there were *drivers,* trusty slaves who acted as assistants to the overseer. Finally, at the bottom of this pyramidal organization were the *slaves* themselves, who, as time went on, were divided into different classes: field hands, blacksmiths, carpenters, house servants, plantation cooks, nurses, and so on.

To get efficient work from the slaves, three methods were commonly employed: by specific assignment of tasks to a given person; by the gang system, where a driver set the pace and the rest were expected to follow; and by punishment.

The large plantation was a community within itself, astir almost continuously with some form of activity. Bruce, in his *Economic History of Virginia in the Seventeenth Century,* says: [20] "Each plantation stood apart to itself. It had its separate population; it had its own distinct round of occupations." Yet a common problem of plantation organization was that of getting efficient work done by slave labor. At "sunup" the negroes were driven into the fields, and worked until dark. Their noonday meal usually consisted of water and hoecake; each negro took with him to the field some water and a small amount of meal, and when, at the proper hour, a fire was built, the negro, having moistened his meal with water, placed it on his hoe and held it over the fire until it was baked. Other negroes were put to work as carpenters, tanners, coopers, weavers, distillers, or at whatever tasks such a community might require to meet its needs. Even during

---

[20] Vol. II, p. 568.

the night, in some instances, work went on, and at times guards were appointed to keep watch over the slaves.

It must not be imagined, however, that all the land, or even a great part, of any given plantation was under cultivation, and that the country presented a picture of one prosperous colonial estate after another. On the contrary, travelers observed that the plantations were very scattered, that great strips of woodland intervened between the plantations, that within the plantations much land had never been cleared, and that great tracts of worn-out land lay idle and barren. Nevertheless, the early planters were generally fairly prosperous.

Perhaps the best way to secure an accurate picture of the earlier plantation system is to quote from a letter written, in 1686, by William Fitzhugh to Dr. Ralph Smith: [21] "At first the Plantation where I now live contains a thousand acres, at least 700 acres of it being rich thicket, the remainder good hearty plantable land, without any waste either by marshes or great swamps the commodiousness, conveniency and pleasantness yourself well know, upon it there is three quarters well furnished with all necessary houses: grounds and fencing, together with a choice crew of negroes at each plantation, most of them this country born, the remainder as likely as most in Virginia, there being twenty-nine in all, with stocks of cattle and hogs at each quarter, upon the same land, is my own Dwelling house furnished with all accommodations for a comfortable and gentile living, as a very good dwelling house with rooms in it, four of the best of them hung and nine of them plentifully furnished with all things necessary and convenient and all houses for use furnished with brick chimneys, four good Cellars, a Dairy, Dovecot, Stable, Barn, Henhouse, Kitchen and all other conveniencys and all in a manner new, a large Orchard, of about 2,500 Aple trees most grafted, well fenced with a Locust fence, which

[21] "Letters of William Fitzhugh," in *Virginia Magazine of History and Biography,* Vol. I, pp. 395–396.

is as durable as most brick walls, a Garden, a hundred foot square, well pailed in, a Yeard wherein is most of the foresaid necessary houses, pallizado'd in with locust Punchens, which is as good as if it were walled in and more lasting than any of our bricks, together with a good Stock of Cattle, hogs, horses, mares, sheep etc., necessary servants belonging to it, for the supply and support thereof. About a mile and half distance a good water Grist miln, whose tole I find sufficient to find my own family with wheat and Indian corn for our necessitys and occasions up the River in this country three tracts of land more, one of them contains 21,996 acres, another 500 acres and one other 1,000 acres, all good convenient and commodious Seats and W$^{ch}$ in a few years will yield a considerable annual Income. A stock of Tob$^o$ with the crops and good debts lying out of about 250,000$^{lb}$ besides sufficient of almost all sorts of goods, to supply the familys and the Quarter's occasion for two if not three years. Thus I have given you some particulars, which I thus deduce the yearly crops of corn and Tob$^o$ together with the surplusage of meat more than will serve the family's use, will amount annually to 60,000$^{lb}$ Tob$^o$ W$^{ch}$ at 10 shillings p.C$^{os}$ 300 pounds p. annum and the negroes increase being all young and a considerable parcel of breeders will keep that stock good for ever. The stock of Tob$^o$ managed with an inland trade will yearly yield 60,000 lb Tob$^o$ without hazard or risque, which will be both clear without charge of house keeping or disbursements for servants clothing."

In time the plantation system became exploitative and wasteful. Land was cultivated without fertilization until it was completely exhausted; then a new area was cleared and the former tract abandoned. It has been estimated that this method required as much as seventy acres of fresh land annually to run even a small plantation. On the rice and indigo plantations white servants could not be used, and the health of black slaves was soon impaired. In fact, on rice and indigo plantations belonging to absentee owners, slaves were frequently killed off through mistreatment because it seemed cheaper to replace the older ones with new negroes than adequately to care for the older ones with food and shorter working hours. "If a work could be imagined peculiarly unwholesome, and even fatal to health," wrote a European upon visiting a rice plantation in South Carolina, "it must be that of standing like the Negross [negroes] ancle and even mid-leg deep in water, which floats on ouzy mud; and exposed all the while to a burning sun, which makes the very air they breathe hotter than the human blood; and these poor wretches are then in a furnace of stinking, putrid effluvia; a more horrible employment can hardly be imagined, not far short of digging in Potosi."

The law of diminishing returns, however, both in the sense of a physical productivity combination and a profit yielding combination, was operative to the extent that it soon caused modifications in the plantation system— namely, in the expansive utilization of land and in the shift in labor from white servants to cheap negro slaves.

Nevertheless, it must be noted that the fundamental results of the plantation system were of three kinds: economic, social, and political. In the first place, the system gave rise to a one-sided economic order. Thus, the large-scale agriculture which developed, though precariously dependent upon a passive commerce and foreign markets, diverted labor and capital disproportionately from everything else and left the South, later on, without adequate manufactures. Furthermore, the plantation system tended to concentrate wealth in the hands of a relatively small class, with the result that class distinctions evolved. Thus, there were the so-called *aristocrats*, the *small farmers*, the *poor white trash*, and the *negro slaves*. The distinction among the whites was sometimes carried into churches and lecture rooms, where seats were allotted according to economic status. There evolved in politics the theory of decentralization of government, known decades later as

*State rights.* In practice, the planters of the Tidewater aristocracy dominated the whole political organization, a fact which caused Thomas Jefferson to declare, in 1780, that "in Virginia 19,000 men below the Falls give law to more than 30,000 living in other parts of the state."[22]  In fact, the great planters—many of whom were conservative on account of their wealth—were the managers of the colonies; while the smaller farmers were, for the most part, the aggressive faction in nearly every struggle for democracy.

## Governmental Regulation of Agriculture

Governmental regulations affecting agriculture in the Southern colonies may be considered under three general classes: regulations by the colonial governments to insure a supply of certain agricultural products; regulations by the English Government covering export and import trade; and legislative efforts on the part of the colonists to regulate prices.

### REGULATIONS CONCERNING AGRICULTURAL PRODUCTS

Although there was never a definite legislative policy in the Southern colonies to insure a supply of essential products, there were sporadic laws for this purpose. As early as 1619, the Virginia legislators took up the subject of hemp and flax legislation, as a war measure. They ordered that the county courts should distribute a quart of flaxseed and a quart of hempseed to each *tithable;*[23] and that at the end of every year each tithable should deliver to the tithing master one pound of dressed hemp and one of flax, or two of either, and swear that it was his own

---

[22] Thomas Jefferson, *Notes on Virginia* (edited by Ford), p. 157.

[23] The Anglican Church was the established church of the colony, and it was supported by compulsory levies, called *tithes.* The persons who paid these levies were called *tithables* and included all male persons above sixteen—later eighteen—years of age, and all negro, mulatto, and Indian women above sixteen. By 1769, free negro, mulatto, and Indian women were excluded from the lists.

growth. This law remained in effect for several years. In 1624, when the colony was threatened with a bread famine, the government decreed that a public granary should be established in every parish, and that each adult male should deposit a bushel of grain therein after the harvest. In 1630, and several times thereafter, it was enacted that, for every worker on a plantation, two acres of land should be planted in corn, and that anyone who was found delinquent in this matter should forfeit all of his tobacco. In 1642, it was further ordered that constables should inspect the cornfields and enforce the law governing the planting of corn. On another occasion, the government required each landholder to plant ten mulberry trees for every one hundred acres; and in 1657, legislation was enacted to encourage the growing of hops. In the same year, acts were passed prohibiting the export of horses and sheep from the colony.

In Maryland, the first settlers soon began to plant tobacco to the exclusion of corn, preferring to buy their grain from the Indians or to import it from the other colonies. Hence, the government, seeing grave danger in an insufficient supply of grain, decreed that everyone who planted tobacco should also grow two acres of corn. This law was renewed several times until 1654. Fifty years later, again in an effort to encourage the production of grain, Maryland passed an act prohibiting the importation, from Pennsylvania or the lower countries, of any breadstuffs, beer, malt, or horses. In later years this act was periodically revived.

In South Carolina as early as 1723, the colonial legislature granted a bounty on indigo culture. Later this was repealed because it was too heavy a burden upon the public. In 1748, Parliament granted a bounty of 6 pence a pound on all indigo exported directly to England.

It appears, thus, that both the colonial authorities and Parliament tried at different times to induce the colonists to substitute other crops for tobacco, but the yield from such crops was relatively inadequate and, therefore, all such laws proved ineffective.

## REGULATIONS BY THE ENGLISH GOVERNMENT

In Chapter II it was pointed out that mercantilism during the colonial period was in theory commercial nationalism.[24] Briefly stated, its implication was that there should be at least a counterpoise between the export and the import trade with foreign countries, to prevent an unfavorable balance of trade and the consequent outflow of gold. There was to be a strong navy, to insure national security. Colonies were to be the source of raw materials for the mother country and, in turn, a market for her exports. Nor were other nations to be permitted to trade with such colonies, lest the mother country be weakened by the carrying off of her colonial resources. Restrictions on trade during the colonial period followed as a matter of course.

From the very outset restrictions were enacted to control the tobacco trade. In 1619, in order to encourage the Virginia planters, the cultivation of tobacco was forbidden in England. In 1621, when it became evident that tobacco could be grown on a profitable scale in Virginia, Parliament immediately enacted a law which practically prohibited the importation of foreign tobacco into England by levying discriminating duties in favor of colonial tobacco and against all foreign tobacco. In the same year, the Privy Council forbade the export of any product of Virginia to any foreign country until such product had been landed in England and had paid the English duties.[25] Although this order was repeated several times, it was nevertheless evaded, and a considerable part of the tobacco trade fell into the hands of the Dutch. About thirty years

[24] See Chapter II, section on "England's Colonial System," page 54 of this text.

[25] King James I, through agents known as *farmers of revenue*, experimented with a monopoly on tobacco, but this practice proved unsatisfactory to the colonists. See *Chalmer's Annals*, p. 46.

later, Parliament, in an effort to cripple the Dutch trade and to satisfy English merchants clamoring for preferential treatment in colonial trade, began the enactment of a whole series of restrictive regulations known as the *Navigation Acts*.

Thus, according to the Navigation Act of 1650, foreign vessels were forbidden "To come to or Trade in, or Traffique with" any of the English colonies in America, unless licensed by the English Government. On the other hand, the colonies were forbidden to have "any manner of commerce or Traffique with any people whatsoever." That is to say, the Southern planters, regardless of high profits in other markets, were compelled to trade solely with England. The next year, there was passed another act, which excluded all foreign ships from carrying on commerce between England and any of her colonies and which required all foreigners to employ British ships to carry exports to England or her colonies. Furthermore, by an act passed in 1660, seven "enumerated" products of the colonies (sugar, tobacco, raw cotton, ginger, indigo, fustic, and other dye woods) could be landed only at British ports. European goods could not be imported after 1663 into the colonies, except in British, or British colonial, ships sailing from British ports.

In subsequent years the list of "enumerated" articles was extended more and more; and, after 1766, in order to prevent the colonists from buying manufactured goods on the Continent, non-enumerated articles had to be shipped to England, Ireland, or some country south of Cape Finisterre. From time to time supplementary acts were passed to strengthen the administration of these various regulations. For example, in 1673, such an act provided that every outbound vessel from the colonies loading with enumerated articles must be bonded or pay specific export duties.

If all these acts had been strictly obeyed, the Southern planters would have been limited to a very narrow market, and left essentially to the mercy of profiteering British merchants. But England had no administrative machinery adequate for the strict enforcement of these acts, and, occasionally, smuggling made them almost totally ineffective.[26]

## LEGISLATIVE EFFORTS TO REGULATE PRICES

As time went on, it became the chief problem of the tobacco planters to obtain profitable prices for their crops. Their legitimate market was, according to British restrictions, almost exclusively in the hands of British merchants. However, continual wars in Europe sometimes cut off from the British merchants the foreign markets where they were accustomed to dispose of their tobacco, bought from the Southern planters; and, at the same time, this deprivation caused other nations to grow tobacco for themselves.

Moreover, London merchants who acted as planters' agents often took advantage of their clients. For instance, a planter might send, at his own risk, a shipment of tobacco to a merchant, trusting the latter would sell it at a price that would cover, in addition to a profit for himself, freight, duties, and commission. In return, the merchant was authorized to purchase European goods for the planter and to charge them against the proceeds from the tobacco sale. This practice usually left the planter indebted to the merchant, who would then require the planter to ship him the next crop also. Since the merchant was both creditor and buyer, he usually tried to fix the price of tobacco so as to keep the planter continuously in debt.

Finally, the production of tobacco in the colonies increased at an unprecedented rate and, according to Alexander Spotswood, was "far disproportioned to the con-

---

[26] On November 23, 1763, Governor Thomas Boone, of South Carolina, wrote to the British Secretary of State that he had had eleven years' acquaintance with nearly every "province of America" and that he was convinced it was necessary now to take steps to prevent illegal trade.— *Bulletin to Halifax,* Am. and W. I., p. 223.

sumption that could be made of it in all the markets which the war had left open, and by natural consequence lowered the price to a great degree." [27]    Although there are no strictly accurate statistics on the production and prices of tobacco in the American colonies, the following estimate [28] is perhaps as reliable as any.   Tobacco prices fell from time to time, and, if one is to believe the many complaints in colonial letters and records extant in that period, the planters sometimes suffered heavy losses.

TOBACCO STATISTICS FOR THE AMERICAN COLONIES

| Year | Production of Leaf Tobacco, Pounds | Price per Pound in Cents Instead of English Pence |
|------|-----------------------------------|---------------------------------------------------|
| 1618.............. | 20,000 | 54.75 |
| 1620.............. | 55,000 | 54.75 |
| 1639.............. | 1,500,000 | 6.08 |
| 1688.............. | 29,147,000 | 3.08 |
| 1765.............. | 75,482,000 | (1763) 2d. |
| 1774.............. | 101,828,617 | ? |
| 1790.............. | 130,000,000 | 3.40 |

In order to obtain better prices, various attempts were made by means of legislative enactments to fix the price, to improve the quality, and to diminish the quantity of tobacco grown.   During the period from 1620 to 1640, not only did the Virginia Assembly fix the price of tobacco in terms of English money, but it also fixed other commodity prices in terms of tobacco.

In 1629, the assembly passed a law prohibiting the colonists from raising more than three thousand plants for each tithable worker, unless the family consisted wholly of women and children.   In 1630, the number of plants permitted was reduced to two thousand for each member of a family.   Next, the assembly attempted to diminish the amount grown by limiting the period of planting.   The act of 1661 declared [29] that there should "no tobacco be

---

[27] Letter of Alexander Spotswood to the British Council of Trade, Virginia, 1710. See VIRGINIA HISTORICAL SOCIETY COLLECTIONS, Vol. I, pp. 72–74.

[28] See U. S. Department of Agriculture, *Yearbook* (1908), pp. 681–689.

[29] W. W. Hening, *Statutes of Virginia,* Vol. II, p. 119.

planted after the tenth day of July and that whosoever shall either directly or indirectly plant or replant or cause to be planted or replanted any tobacco after the said tenth day of July shall forfeit ten thousand pounds of tobacco to the use of the publique." In 1679, Virginia prohibited the importation of tobacco, from "Carolina or other localities," into her territory—there to be "laid on shore, sold or shipped." [30] Further attempts were later made by the Virginia Assembly to limit the maximum number of pounds that each planter could produce for each cultivator employed, and governmental inspectors were even ordered to destroy the poor grades of leaf in order to diminish the supply.

Finding that none of these laws accomplished their intent, the Virginians blamed the failure upon the Maryland Assembly, which refused to coöperate in a general plan to limit the production of tobacco. The theory behind all such legislation assumed that the demand for tobacco was practically inelastic and that prices for it could be raised merely by controlling the supply. If Maryland had joined with Virginia in such an attempt, the result would have been as futile as it was for Virginia alone. What the planters needed during the decades of falling tobacco prices, was a wide, unrestricted market instead of the monopoly market which was partially effected by British restrictions.

### Bibliographical Note

The definitive work on Southern agriculture prior to the Civil War is Lewis C. Gray, *History of Agriculture in Southern United States to 1860* (Washington, 1933). Invaluable notes on the history of agriculture in the Southern colonies can be found in several general works dealing with the history of American agriculture. The most informative of these are: Lyman Carrier, *Beginnings of Agriculture in America* (New York, 1923); and, in the *Cyclopedia of American Agriculture* (New York, 1907–1909), Volume IV, two articles: one by G. K.

---

[30] *Ibid.*, Vol. II, p. 445.

Holmes, "Aboriginal Agriculture—The American Indian," and the other by T. N. Carver, "Historical Sketch of American Agriculture." Virginian agriculture is exhaustively treated by Philip Alexander Bruce in his *Economic History of Virginia in the Seventeenth Century; An Inquiry into the Material Condition of the People; Based upon Original and Contemporaneous Records*, two volumes (New York, 1896). Several essays have been written dealing specifically with Indian agriculture. In the *American Mercury*, January 1929, Cornelia H. Dam has written an interesting article on "Tobacco among the Indians"; in *American Anthropology*, January-March 1907, George Bird Ginnel has a valuable explanation of "Tenure of Land Among the Indians"; and, in the *William and Mary Quarterly*, October 1910, Hu. Maxwell has an instructive article on "The Use and Abuse of Forests by Virginia Indians."

The land system in the Southern colonies has received considerable attention from students of American colonial history. In the JOHNS HOPKINS UNIVERSITY STUDIES IN HISTORICAL AND POLITICAL SCIENCE, there is a monograph dealing specifically with the land system of colonial Maryland: Clarence Pembroke Gould, *Land System in Maryland, 1720-1765* (Baltimore, 1913). To be noted, also, is an article in the *Maryland Historical Magazine*, June 1908, entitled "First Land Grants in Maryland; A Note of All the Warrants for the Granting of Land in Maryland." Bruce, *op. cit.*, describes the methods of granting land in Virginia; and Thomas J. Wertenbaker, *Planters of Colonial Virginia* (Princeton, 1922), discusses in complete detail the size of landholdings. Incidental information concerning the colonial rice plantations may be found in D. D. Wallace, *Life of Henry Laurens* (New York, 1915).

The labor system of the Southern colonies has received extended treatment. The most important works on this subject are: E. I. McCormac, *White Servitude in Maryland, 1634-1820* (Baltimore, 1904); J. C. Ballagh, *White Servitude in the Colony of Virginia* (Baltimore, 1895); J. S. Bassett, *Slavery and Servitude in the Colony of North Carolina* (Baltimore, 1896); J. R. Brackett, *Negro in Maryland* (Baltimore, 1889); E. McCrady, "Slavery in the Province of South Carolina, 1670-1770," printed in the *Annual Report of the American Historical Association* (1895), pages 631-673; James A. Padgett, "The Status of Slaves in Colonial North Carolina," in the *Journal of Negro History*, Volume 14, pages 300–327; Elizabeth Donnan, "The Slave Trade Into South Carolina Before the Revolution," in the *American Historical Review*, Volume XXXIII, pages 804–828. Exceptional notes on the labor system in the Southern colonies may be found (especially Chapters I and III) in M. W. Jernegan's *Laboring and Dependent Classes in Colonial America, 1607–1783* (Chicago, 1931). Of interest, also, is J. D. Butler's article "British Convicts Shipped to American Colonies," published in the *American Historical Review*, Volume II, pages 12–34. The results of many earlier studies have been brought together by U. B. Phillips in *American Negro Slavery* (New York, 1921), and by far the best history of Southern agriculture is the germane portion of this work. Another excellent study, which in some respects breaks new ground in Southern history, is A. O. Craven, *Soil Exhaustion as a Factor in the Agricultural History of Virginia and Maryland, 1606–1860* (Urbana, Ill., 1926). The best treatment of early agriculture in North Carolina is W. Niel Franklin, "Agriculture in Colonial North Carolina," in the *North Carolina Historical Review*, Volume 3, pages 539–574.

For a brief discussion of the tobacco industry in the Southern colonies, see Meyer Jacobstein, *Tobacco Industry in the United States* (New York, 1907). Outside of primary sources there is very little information to be found which deals satisfactorily with the problem of colonial tobacco prices. To be mentioned, however, is Lewis Cecil Gray's, "The Market Surplus Problems of Colonial Tobacco," published in two issues of the *William and Mary Quarterly:* October 1927, pages 231–245, and January 1928, pages 1–16. For an enlightening discussion of the English commercial system, see St. George L. Sioussat's article "Virginia and the English Commercial System, 1730–1733," in the *Annual Report of the American Historical Association* (1905), Volume I, pages 71–97.

# CHAPTER IV

# Industry in the Colonial South

MANUFACTURING in the Southern colonies was of secondary importance to agriculture and, for the most part, was carried on simply to supply local and plantation needs. At first, the Virginia Company attempted to establish manufactures in the Jamestown colony. Skilled laborers from England, Italy, Germany, and the Baltic countries were brought in for the purpose of erecting sawmills and ironworks and for manufacturing glass, tar, and potash. Soon, however, certain factors became operative that retarded the development of these industries and diverted attention chiefly to agriculture.

## Factors Affecting Manufacturing

During the colonial period, factors unfavorable to the development of manufacturing in the South greatly outweighed those which might have served as a stimulus to this well-rounded economic development.

As a basis for manufacturing there was in the Southern colonies an ample supply of raw materials, such as timber, minerals, and certain agricultural products. From pine forests could be had ship timber, pitch, tar, rosin, and turpentine; and from oak forests, staves for barrels and boards for various purposes. In some localities there were iron and coal awaiting utilization; and grains, flax, hemp, hides, and wool could be procured from farms and plantations. Furthermore, it was difficult and expensive to procure necessaries from abroad. At that time the colonies were isolated from Europe on account of sailing facilities; the vessels were slow and required from four weeks to four months, or sometimes even more, to cross the Atlantic. Necessarily supplies of goods were irregular; and often, when they did arrive, they did not fit the consumer demand of the colonists. Transportation costs were high, sometimes ranging over £3 per ton. Even as late as 1793, according to Tenche Coxe, the cost of all transportation charges from Europe to America amounted to more than 20 per cent of the English price of cotton goods. The difficulty and the expense of procuring foreign goods acted as a sort of protective tariff for colonial manufacturers.

From time to time the colonial governments, in order to encourage manufactures, enacted laws giving assistance in the form of bounties, premiums, and subsidies. In 1662, Virginia granted a bounty of 5 pounds of tobacco for every yard of woolen cloth made in the colony. Twenty years later, this was increased to 6 pounds of tobacco and made to include both woolens and mixed fabrics. Maryland, in 1682, enacted a similar law granting a bounty of 10 pounds of tobacco for a yard of linen. In 1770, South Carolina gave a bounty of 30 per cent upon the value of linen and linen thread made in the colony. Virginia, in 1661, and South Carolina, in 1711 and in 1753, granted bounties for potash produced in the colony; and in 1745, Virginia granted bounties for the production of saltpetre. In 1693, Virginia authorized the justices of the peace in every county to give annually three premiums of 800, 600, and 400 pounds of tobacco for the best pieces of linen of specified length and breadth produced. A Maryland statute of 1740 was similar, except as to the amount of the premium. In 1712, South Carolina offered a reward of £50 each to the first two persons establishing potash works in the state. Similarly North Carolina provided for rewards to producers of potash. Subsidies were given in some of the Southern colonies for the manufacture of salt and ships' supplies.

Although it appears that compulsory manufactures were perhaps confined to Virginia, that colony at an early date enacted a statute requiring mechanics, by prohibiting them from engaging in agriculture, to follow their own trade. In 1661, the colony passed an act requiring each county to establish one or more public tanneries; in 1666, another act required each county to establish within two years a public loom with a weaver.

During the colonial period, leather was in great demand for clothing: both for boots and shoes, and for breeches and waistcoats for men and petticoats for women. Leather was used also for bedding, for harnesses, and for saddles. Hence, to assure an adequate supply, each of the Southern colonies took steps to encourage tanning by discouraging, or sometimes even prohibiting, the export of hides. As early as 1662, the governor and the council of Maryland passed an ordinance prohibiting the exportation of untanned hides. A similar ordinance was enacted in 1681. Prior to 1690, Virginia passed several laws prohibiting the export of hides, under penalties so heavy that they amounted to prohibitive export duties. In 1764, North Carolina imposed export duties on hides; in 1772, South Carolina imposed export duties on both hides and leather; and Georgia, in 1773, imposed an export duty on hides.

Although land grants to encourage manufactures were not so common in the Southern as in the Northern colonies, they did occur. In 1769, for example, Virginia furnished 100 acres of land and slaves to a Frenchman to introduce wine making in the colony; and at one time, South Carolina leased a plantation for the purpose of introducing silk culture. In 1719, the Maryland Assembly offered 100 acres of land to any citizen who would set up iron furnaces and forges in the colony.

By granting monopoly privileges to the owners of salt works, both Virginia and South Carolina tried to insure a supply of salt. These colonies at various times also granted patents to individuals for new machines, for new processes, and, at least in one instance, for a medical compound.

The factors unfavorable to the development of industry

were numerous.   Skilled labor was scarce and relatively expensive.   Frequently the supposedly skilled, indentured immigrants knew very little about their trades; in order to establish a manufacture, it sometimes became necessary to import skilled laborers from the Continent.   Spotswood's iron furnace in Virginia was operated by Germans, and the incipient silk industry in Georgia was carried on by the same nationals.   Furthermore, because of the scarcity of skilled laborers and the ease with which they could obtain land, masters had to pay high wages.   When the colonial period closed, spinners were paid from 10 to 30 cents per day; weavers, about 40 cents; blacksmiths, nearly 70 cents; shoemakers, 73 cents; and shipbuilders, about 90 cents. These wages, though low according to present standards, were relatively high as real wages, because of the low commodity prices at that time.

Moreover, a serious lack of fixed and working capital existed in the colonies.   During the colonial period there was required for establishing a manufacture relatively less fixed capital than would be necessary at present, for at that time buildings could be constructed of wood, which was generally near at hand; machines were of the simplest kind; and power, in most instances, could be harnessed from a stream by means of a cumbersome water wheel. Nevertheless, a large capital was needed in the case of ironworks: furnaces were usually constructed of imported bricks, great tracts of land had to be purchased in order to get wood for charcoal, and slaves had to be brought in to carry on the heavy work.   But, whatever the requirements for fixed capital, the supply was limited.   At first, it was furnished by the British; later on, by a few planters; sometimes, by mechanics and tradesmen themselves out of their previous earnings; and, occasionally, by Northern colonists who had accumulated a surplus and were seeking profitable investments.   To obtain adequate working capital was still more difficult, because, once a plant was established and the product put on the market, slow transportation, long credits, and the necessity of selling other goods taken in exchange for the product compelled the manufacturer to wait much longer than is necessary at present for returns. In other words, the flow of working capital was very slow, and therefore a greater amount was required to keep the plant continually operating.

An extensive market was lacking in the colonies. Although the trans-Atlantic market stimulated in the Southern colonies the production of such staples as tobacco, rice, and indigo—and sometimes lumber and ship supplies— nevertheless, the distribution of a sparse population over wide areas greatly checked the growth of manufacturing. In 1688, the populations of Virginia and Maryland together were only about 75,000; and that of the Carolinas, including the present area of Georgia, was not more than 10,000. The total population of the Southern colonies was only about 85,000. In 1699, Jamestown was described to the Board of Trade as having "not above twenty houses" and as the only place in Virginia that could be called a town. During the eighteenth century the population increased more rapidly; and in 1760, there were probably 718,000 persons in the Southern colonies, of whom about 40 per cent were negroes. Transportation by means of boats and horses and wagons was such that a wide market for distant communities could not be established, especially for the heavier products. Consequently goods besides those imported, which were mainly for the large plantations and the communities near the coast, were produced by household industry and local manufacture.

England, in accordance with the mercantile theory, enacted laws to prevent the creation of colonial industry in competition with her home industry. For this purpose Parliament enacted the Woolen Act of 1699. This law provided, under heavy penalties, that no wool, woolen cloth, or yarn produced in the colonies could be shipped to any other plantation or to any other place whatsoever. In 1706, London merchants petitioned the Board of Trade to compel colonial planters to clothe their servants and slaves in British woolens, but no law was enacted at that time.  In 1731, the British merchants again petitioned the Lords of Trade to suppress all manufacture of woolens, hats, and shoes in the colonies.  Only the Hat Act of 1732 resulted from this petition, and it provided that American-made hats could not be shipped from one colony to another, or to England or Europe; that no master could have more than two apprentices; and that no person could manufacture felt hats unless he himself had been an apprentice for seven years.  Furthermore, negroes could not be employed in such manufactures.  Finally, in 1750, Parliament passed the Iron Act.  This prohibited in the colonies the erection of new slitting or rolling mills, plating forges, and steel furnaces.  The penalty to be imposed for the violation of this act was a fine of £200.  The colonists were still permitted to make kettles, salt pans, and cannon; and, to encourage iron smelting, they were allowed to ship bar iron free of duty into Great Britain.

Although these acts appear drastic, they actually had little effect upon manufacturing in the Southern colonies, because the colonial manufacturers of cloth and hats could not have competed even in a *laissez-faire* market with the low-cost producers of England, and the Iron Act of 1750 came too late to greatly affect the development of that industry before the Revolution.

## Industrial Systems

In the Southern colonies there existed simultaneously: household industry, a quasi-domestic system, and manufactures in the more modern sense.

*Household industry,* as the term implies, went on in the household, and the finished products were consumed by the household group.  The raw materials used were almost wholly grown, or otherwise produced, by the family itself.

Although it is impossible to know the quantity of goods made at home, abundant evidence shows that the practice prevailed in practically every colonial home. A contemporary writer, in Maryland in 1679, has left a description of plantation life, in which he says: "The servants and negroes, after they have worn themselves down the whole day . . . have yet to grind and pound the grain . . . for their masters and all their families, as well as themselves and all the negroes." Another early writer tells of a pioneer planter in the Tidewater region who "sows yearly store of hemp and flax and causes it to be spun; he keeps weavers and hath a tan house, causes leather to be dressed, hath eight shoemakers employed in the trade, hath forty negro servants, bringing them up to trades in his house."

By visiting Mount Vernon, one can today see how a colonial plantation was equipped for household industry. There Washington had a smithy, charcoal burners, brick kilns, a flour mill, and establishments for weavers, shoemakers, masons, coopers, and carpenters. He even had a vessel in which to carry produce to market. Numerous commodities were produced in practically every colonial household; they fall roughly into the following classifications: foods and drinks; textiles, clothing, and shoes; household furniture and utensils; agricultural implements; and candles, soap, and miscellaneous necessities.

There was also prevalent in the Southern colonies a *quasi-domestic system;* this was somewhat similar to the European domestic system. Under the former system, merchants furnished raw materials to independent artisans who carried on the actual process of manufacture in their own dwellings. In turn, the merchants took the finished products to sell them in the markets. Throughout the colonies, however, any person might furnish the raw materials and take the finished products for use rather than for sale. In other words, instead of a situation in which all of the processes were being carried on at home, specialization began to develop, and independent artisans in the settlements were often called upon to complete the manufacture of certain commodities.  For example, cording and fulling came to be done outside of the home, but spinning and weaving continued to be done in the home.  Usually sawmills and grist mills were operated by independent proprietors for the toll they received from the raw materials furnished them by the colonists.  In fact, this system was sometimes regulated by legislation—mainly to protect the consumers.  Thus, in Maryland, a law provided that not more than one sixth of the grain could be taken for toll; in Virginia, a law required millers to grind for their customers in regular turn.

*Manufactures* existed in the Southern colonies, but there were no factories, for the factory began with the application of steam to industry—that is to say, at the end of the eighteenth century.  A *manufactory* may be defined as an industrial organization—consisting of an entrepreneur; wage-earners or apprentices; and a furnace or a mill driven by animal, wind, or water power—operating as a unit to manufacture goods to be sold in a market at a profit.  With this connotation in mind, it is correct to say that there were in the Southern colonies some manufactures of iron, textiles, lumber, and a few miscellaneous products.  In the descriptions of specific industries, some notice will be taken of technology and processes; but, whether the products were produced in a home, in a toll mill, or in a manufactory, the same processes were generally used for the production of the given commodity.

## Development of Specific Industries

For convenience, the specific industries developed in the colonial South may be classified under the following general heads: forest industries; textile industries; industries based on agricultural resources; mining industries; and miscellaneous industries.

### FORESTS

In the Southern colonies the forests formed the basis for lumbering as an industry, for shipbuilding, for the making of naval stores, and for the production of potash.

Three centuries ago, the eastern seaboard, except for a few Indian clearings, was covered with a continuous belt of forests. As the white population increased, much of this timber had to be destroyed to make room for an expanding agriculture. At the same time, much was used both for domestic purposes and for exports. Indeed, timber, in the absence of other available materials, was absolutely indispensable to the colonists for building houses and barns, for manufacturing their own furniture and implements, and for constructing their fortifications. Moreover, during the colonial period, such forest products as sawed timber, masts, shingles, clapboards, staves, headings, hoops, potash, pearlashes, and naval stores were of considerable commercial value as exports.

In order to obtain forest products, the work at first was done by hand with axes, saws, and wedges. But, because of the scarcity of labor and the increasing demand for timber, it became necessary to have sawmills. There were no circular saws. Instead, a mill consisted of little more than an ordinary crosscut saw fastened at both ends to some sort of apparatus so that the saw could be moved, by water power, up and down as the log was slowly pushed forward against it. Although artisans were sent to Virginia as early as 1620 to erect a sawmill, evidently none was completed before 1652. In Georgia, however, sawmills were among the first enterprises, and during the eighteenth century they became common throughout the Southern colonies.

Although shipbuilding was confined largely to New England, ships were built nearly every year in the Southern colonies. A survey of shipping in the colonies, in 1769, shows the number and tonnage of vessels built in the Southern colonies as follows:

COLONIAL SHIPPING, 1769

| Colony | Three-Masted Ships or Square-Rigged Vessels | Two-Masted and One-Masted Ships or Schooners and Sloops | Tonnage |
|---|---|---|---|
| Maryland............. | 9 | 11 | 1,344 |
| Virginia............... | 6 | 21 | 1,269 |
| North Carolina........ | 3 | 9 | 607 |
| South Carolina......... | 4 | 8 | 789 |
| Georgia.............. | 0 | 2 | 50 |

In the same year, however, Massachusetts alone built nearly twice as many vessels, if measured by tonnage; or, that state had a tonnage of 8,013, as compared with the South's total of 4,059.

On the other hand, the production of naval stores was one of the leading industries in the Southern colonies and ranked second only to tobacco in exports from Maryland and Virginia. By 1700, pitch, tar, and naval stores in general had become the chief exports of both North and South Carolina. In 1720, Boone and Barnwell wrote that they had made about 6,000 barrels of .pitch and tar in North Carolina and that sloops from New England had carried it to Great Britain. In 1734, Gabriel Johnston wrote to the Board of Trade that there were more pitch and tar made in the two Carolinas than in all the other American provinces and "rather more in North than in South Carolina." Just before the Revolutionary War, the annual exports of turpentine, pitch, and tar had reached nearly 200,000 barrels, which if valued according to present-day standards, yielded about $225,000.

Still another forest product of considerable importance as an export was potash. This product was mainly incidental to the clearing of land, and was made from the ashes of hardwoods, such as oak, birch, and hickory. When the trees were cut down and burned, the ashes were collected and put in an ash-hopper, usually a V-shaped container made of boards. Then, by leaching them, lye was obtained. This, in turn, was boiled in iron pots until the water evaporated, leaving a brownish residue called potash. If the residue was placed in a hot oven and the carbon burned out, the product was pearlash, which was considered more valuable than potash. Both potash and pearlash were used for bleaching and soap making, and were in great demand in England.

## TEXTILES

In the Southern colonies, wool was the material most commonly used for cloth making, but there was also some production of linen and cotton goods, and even a little silk.

The London Company sent sheep with the first colonists to Jamestown; and forty years later there were in Virginia about 3,000 head, which yielded an annual clip of about 6,000 pounds, or approximately one pound of wool for every eight colonists. No doubt, dogs, wolves, and sometimes British restrictions greatly hindered sheep-raising; but the colonists slowly increased their flocks until, by the end of the seventeenth century, it was common for a planter to have from 50 to 100 head. Sheep-raising was especially significant in the upland regions, where wool became one of the chief products. Washington tried in every way to encourage sheep-raising, and he himself kept a flock of from 700 to 800 head.

At first all the processes of making woolen fabrics were carried on in the home. The sheep were sheared by hand. The wool was then cleaned: the grease and burrs, which together comprised about half the weight of the clip, were removed. In turn, the cleaned wool was carded, combed, and worked into rolls. Then, it was converted into yarn by processes of drawing out and twisting. For this purpose spinning wheels, now valuable as antiques, were used. The yarn was dyed either with indigo or the juices of certain plants, or with the bark of such trees as butternut, chestnut, dogwood, oak, hickory, and sumach. Afterwards, it was either knit or woven. If woven, crude wooden looms were used. Finally, the cloth itself had to be put through a process called "fulling," in order to shrink the cloth and give it the desired compactness. The cloth was run through soapy warm water and pounded with heavy wooden mallets. In this fashion it was possible to produce a cloth that did not show the weave; the material was known as "broadcloth." Fulling was the heaviest work connected with cloth making and soon became a specialized process carried on outside the home. In 1692, a fulling mill was erected in Virginia; and before the close of the colonial period, the colony had fulling mills in various localities. In North Carolina, a fulling mill was erected before 1790 for dressing fine and coarse woolens.

Although for several years the making of woolen fabrics in the Southern colonies was not very extensive, nevertheless, when crop prices fell and British imported clothing became scarcer, the colonists turned more and more to this industry. Thus, by 1660, because of the low price of tobacco, the colonists began to supply their own needs for clothing, and official encouragement was given them in the form of bounties and public looms. Thereafter, the making of woolen fabrics not only became common but also tended to increase rapidly as the foreign market for colonial exports became more restricted. Woolen manufactures remained local, however, chiefly because the quality of the commercially produced homespuns—such as linsey-woolsey and jeans—was not satisfactory and because the market for inferior cloth was small.

Flax and hemp ranked next to wool in the manufacture of colonial textiles. England did not look with disfavor upon the production of these materials as she did in the case of wool; she hoped to supplement from the colonies her own inadequate supply of these materials for sailcloth and cordage. However, most of the flax and hemp was used for domestic purposes, though some of both was produced annually by practically every planter and farmer.

Usually the clothing for negroes was made on each plantation by negro women. The cloth was a coarse mixture of wool or cotton with flax or hemp, the warp being necessarily of hemp or flax thread while the woof was of wool or cotton, according to the locality. It was not until the population had begun to press back into the interior that flax culture reached large proportions. Especially was this true in western Virginia and western North Carolina. Because of the remoteness of the frontier settlements, the spinning and weaving of these materials continued almost until the Civil War. For many persons in the colonies, hempen cloth and linen of different degrees of fineness constituted the principal articles of clothing. Undergarments, bed linens, and table covers of nearly all classes were made from flax. Linen served most purposes for which cotton is now used. Flax and hemp, like wool, were processed mainly in the home. The breaking and heckling were usually done by men or stout wenches, while the corking, spinning, weaving, bleaching and dyeing (if the material was linen) were processes carried on by the housewife and her daughters. Some women developed great deftness in producing ornamented linen, some specimens of which have come down to posterity as treasured heirlooms.

Cotton was not indigenous to America. Reference is made to cotton in a Hindu hymn written fifteen centuries before Christ. It was probably introduced into America from the West Indies. At any rate, in 1609, its cultivation began at Jamestown; and by 1621, it was listed among the marketable products of the colony. Cotton was cultivated in the Carolinas certainly before 1664, and in Georgia, in 1735. In Virginia in 1705, according to one report, "the quality of Goods and especially Clothing imported of late not being sufficient for supplying the Country Many of the Inhabitants . . . have this last year planted a considerable quantity of cotton." Yet, cotton culture as a whole made slow progress in the Southern colonies and was confined mainly to garden plots. The reasons were: cotton was a far more difficult fiber than flax to process and could be spun at that time only by being mixed with flax; and during most of the colonial period, technological improvements for the manufacture of cotton cloth were still in the experimental state. The cultivation of cotton in the South did not begin on an extensive scale until after the rise of the factory system, which, in the United States, dates from 1790, when Samuel Slater set up an Arkwright-type textile mill at Pawtucket, Rhode Island.

At the approach of the Revolution, when England was exporting from the West Indies and elsewhere considerable quantities of cotton into the Northern colonies, attention was focusing upon the possibility of increasing cotton production in the South. In 1774–1775, Alexander Hamilton wrote as follows about the future production and manufacture of cotton in this country: "With respect to cotton, you do not pretend to deny that a sufficient quantity may be produced. Several of the Southern Colonies are so favorable to it that, with due cultivation, in a couple of years they would afford enough to clothe the whole continent. As to the expense of bringing it by land, the best way will be to manufacture it where it grows, and afterwards transport it to the other colonies."

The demand for silk in England and the impossibility of growing silkworms there caused English rulers to insist upon sericulture in the Southern colonies. James I, in 1619, ordered the Virginians to abandon the cultivation of tobacco and to raise silk. Three years later, he sent over John Bonell to give instructions in silk culture; and the colonial government, for a few years, paid a bounty of 50 pounds of tobacco per pound of raw silk. But neither King nor rewards could effectively divert the energies of the Virginians from tobacco culture to the raising of a less profitable product. Georgia, however, made more persistent efforts to establish sericulture. In 1750, that colony exported 118 pounds of raw silk; in 1765, 138 pounds; in 1770, 290 pounds; and between 1758 and 1766, probably 20,000 pounds of cocoons were delivered to Savannah, though scarcely more than 1,000 pounds were exported to England. A small quantity of silk was manufactured in the South; and some persons of distinction, like Mrs. Pinckney of South Carolina, boasted of silk garments made in the colonies. Yet sericulture in America, in spite of encouragement by the rich and those who aped the rich, was sporadic and soon languished.

## INDUSTRIES BASED ON AGRICULTURAL RESOURCES

Corn and grist mills driven by water power were common in the Southern colonies. These mills were small and seldom had a capacity of even one hundred bushels of grain per day. The grinding was done by means of two millstones, one placed above the other. The grain was run between them, poured from a hopper through a hole in the upper stone. A few mills of this type still exist in certain mountain regions of the South.

Many agricultural products had to be prepared for market by the use of capital and labor. The required processes in most cases were relatively simple. Thus, tobacco was prepared by drying, sorting, and packing the leaves. Rice was cleaned, polished, and packed. Meat was cured and salted, or pickled, before packing for export.[1] Indigo processes were more complicated and specialized; they included fermentation, evaporation, and drying, before the coloring matter could be reduced to marketable cakes.

The manufacture of leather was carried on both as a household industry and in separate tanneries. As already noted, Virginia, in 1661, required each county to provide for at least one tanner, one currier, and one shoemaker.

---

[1] For example, in 1763, the list of exports from Virginia and Maryland included £15,000 worth of pickled pork, beef, ham, and bacon.—*American Husbandry*, Vol. I, pp. 256–257.

However, because of the increasing demand for leather, further legislation was unnecessary. Tanneries as a specialized type of business became common in the older communities, though the household production of leather continued in the frontier settlements.

In colonial times the processes of leather making were relatively simple. A tannery was usually merely a shed equipped with a series of vats. The hides were moved from one vat to another for the purpose of dehairing, defleshing, and tanning. In the tanning vat, the hides were laid between layers of tanbark and covered with water, which leached the tannin from the bark onto the hides. Almost a year was required to complete this process, as well as some skill on the part of the tanner, who had to rely upon his senses of smell and touch, also, to aid him in accurately timing the process. Next, the leather was treated—usually by a currier—with oils and various substances to soften, preserve, and color it. This process was done solely with hand implements. The leather articles most commonly produced in those days were harnesses, saddles, boots and shoes, gloves, vests, breeches, petticoats, and many smaller items such as hinges and straps. Shoemaking, like dentistry in later periods, was largely a peripatetic occupation.

Brewing was mainly a household industry and was carried on in nearly every home in the Southern colonies. Indian corn, barley, wheat, and even rice were malted for fermentation. Little of the beer, ale, and wine produced could be exported, and most of it was consumed almost immediately. The Southern colonists were, however, no thirstier than the Northern colonists, who not only exported large quantities of rum, but also drank plenty of hard liquor, beer, and homemade cider.

## MINING

The first attempt to manufacture iron on the American Continent was made in Virginia in 1619. In that year, skilled workmen were sent over to set up three ironworks in the colony. A forge was built at Falling Creek. Two years later, a "gentleman," John Berkley, came over to take charge of the enterprise. Altogether, the Virginia Company expended no less than $20,000 or $25,000 in setting up a going concern.[2] In 1622, both the works and the workmen were destroyed by Indians. After this tragedy, iron manufacturing was not resumed in Virginia for about one hundred years; and it was not until 1716 that the industry was founded on a permanent basis in the colony.

Two years before that time, forty Germans—men, women, and children—coming via London from the Sieg Valley in Germany, had arrived at the colony destitute. The men were skilled ironworkers and had come to Virginia on account of a severe depression in the iron industry in Germany. Without protest, Governor Spotswood had paid the £50 charged for their passage and had immediately stationed them on the northwestern frontier just beyond the falls of the Rappahannock. There he had built for them a blockhouse, fortified it with two cannon, and named it, in their honor, "Germanna." He had intended that this outpost, which was thirty miles beyond any English settlement, should be a guard against the Indians, and more especially that it should afford an opportunity to open up silver mines, as soon as he could secure the royal sanction. Discovering that there was iron ore instead of silver in this region, he quietly took out a patent in 1716 in the name of William Robinson, who was then clerk of the council, for 3,229 acres of land, which included the iron beds at Germanna. Then, at his own expense, he set the German immigrants to making iron.

Soon Spotswood, Augustine Washington (the father of the President), and others started operating furnaces on a larger scale than any before in America. Most important

---

[2] In 1621 in the House of Commons, Sir Edwin Sandys said that the Virginia Company had erected four ironworks in the colony at a cost of £4,000.—*Commons Journal*, Vol. I, p. 622.

of these establishments was the Principio Company, which operated four furnaces and two forges on the Chesapeake and the Potomac.  With this company were associated the Washingtons, on whose Virginia land some of the works were located.  Both British capital and colonial capital were invested in these enterprises, and it has been estimated that one of the larger Virginia plants cost £12,000, which included the furnace, 100 slaves, and 1,500 acres of forest land.

Iron ore was worked during the early part of the eighteenth century in the Valley of Virginia west of the Blue Ridge.  According to Lesley's "Iron Manufactures Guide," in 1725, Pine Forge was erected three and a half miles north of New Market, in Shenandoah County; in 1757, another forge was built on Mossy Creek, fifteen miles north of Staunton; and in 1760, a furnace was built in the same vicinity.  In Maryland, besides the operations of the Principio Company at the head of the Chesapeake Bay, other works were built at various times during the colonial period.  As early as 1742, a rolling mill was erected on the Big Elk River five miles north of Elkton.  Although a small quantity of pig iron—about one ton—was exported from North Carolina to England as early as 1729, there are no authentic accounts of the location or the dates of the earliest ironworks in that colony.  In South Carolina, it appears that the first ironworks were not erected until 1773, and that they were destroyed by the Tories during the Revolution.  In Georgia, no development in iron manufacturing occurred during the colonial period.

Prior to the Revolution practically all the iron produced in the South was from bog ore.  The industry in general was composed of two classes: establishments conducting only primary processes such as smelting and steel making; and reproductive manufactories such as rolling mills, slitting mills, and foundries.  Colonial furnaces were similar in principle to modern furnaces, except that charcoal was used exclusively for fuel and the air draught was created by hand- or water-driven bellows. To make steel, pig iron was hammered into bars; and these were packed in boxes between charcoal and then placed in a retort where they were slowly carbonized by being kept for several weeks at a high degree of heat. Hollow ware, like pots and kettles, was moulded. Similar to the distribution of Spotswood's furnaces, these products were marketed by peddling from house to house. Other articles, such as plowshares and hoes, were made by plantation or community blacksmiths.

As indicated above, England tried to encourage the colonial production of raw materials to be exported for British industry and, at the same time, to prevent the colonial manufacture of products that would compete with the exports of British producers. Therefore, the main purpose of the first Southern furnaces was to produce pig iron for export to England. These exports began about 1718 with a consignment of less than 4 tons. In 1730, the amount of pig and bar iron exported was about 2,000 tons; in 1763, the amount exported from Virginia and Maryland was valued at £35,000.

The reason for the development, though comparatively small, of the iron industry in the Southern colonies before the Revolution was the lack of charcoal in England during the seventeenth century, which caused the British iron industry to decline. Accordingly the demand for colonial pig iron increased. Furthermore, the high cost of importing heavy iron articles gave the colonial ironmakers a protection which was approximately the equivalent of a 25 per cent ad valorem duty.

In 1612, for the first time in America, bricks were made in Virginia; and one of the earliest exports from that colony was a cargo of bricks to the Bermudas. However, the Southern colonies did not begin to develop brickmaking extensively until near the close of the colonial period, when there began to appear, especially in the towns, spacious brick houses. The first settlers of Georgia made some pottery, which they sent to South Carolina; and just before the Revolution, potteries were established in North Carolina at Salem, and in South Carolina at Camden. In spite of the fact that there was plenty of kaolin in the colonies, no porcelain works were developed, partly because there was a lack of the necessary skill and partly because it was still a period of pewter plates. Sporadic attempts were made to establish glassworks. In 1609, a glassworks was erected in South Carolina. Glass beads and trinkets were given to the Indians in exchange for foods and furs. This plant was destroyed the next year by the Indians, and for many years thereafter, no important attempt at glassmaking was undertaken in the Southern colonies.

### Miscellaneous Industries

A few household industries not heretofore described and other industries of minor importance must be mentioned to complete the chronicle of Southern industrial progress before the Revolution. Candle making was carried on in nearly every colonial home. Candles were made either by dipping and redipping a wick of yarn or flax into melted tallow until the desired size was obtained, or, as in later days, by moulding the tallow in metal candle moulds.

Another household industry was the preparation of maple syrup or sugar, especially common in Virginia and Maryland and in the frontier settlements where there happened to be maple trees. The process consisted in first tapping the trees, when the sap began to rise, by boring holes through the bark and inserting spiles made of hollow alder wood to lead the sap into buckets. The sap was then boiled in large iron kettles until a syrup was formed, or still further boiled until there was left only a sugar residue, which was finally cut into small cakes. This industry, like "molassy-making" and "apple butter stirrings," was part of the romance of colonial times, and afforded an opportunity for social gatherings at a time when the joys of friendly intercourse were few indeed.

In the Southern colonies, little attention was paid to

fishing. According to John Smith's *Advertisements for Unexperienced Planters,* published in 1631: "Now although there be fish in the rivers, yet the rivers are so broad and we so unskillful to catch them, we little trouble them, nor they us." However, Burnaby, in 1760, wrote of the Potomac: "These waters are stored with incredible quantities of fish, such as sheepshead, rockfish, drums, white pearch, herrings, oysters, crabs, and several other sorts. Sturgeon and shad are in such prodigious numbers that one day, within the space of two miles only, some gentlemen in canoes caught about six hundred of the former with hooks which they let down to the bottom and drew up at a venture when they perceived them to rub against a fish; and of the latter above five thousand have been caught at a single haul of the seine." Nevertheless, fishing as an industry in the South did not attain much importance until the decades just preceding the Civil War.

Another industry, which was, in fact, only in its incipient stage and can scarcely therefore be recognized as an industry, was that of coal mining. As early as 1701, William Byrd referred in a letter to coal deposits that had been found at "ye Manakan Town"—an Indian town near Richmond. "We went up to ye Cole," he wrote, "w'ch is not above a mile and a half from their settlement on the great upper Creeke, w'ch, riseing very high in great Raines hath washed away the Banke that the Coal lyes bare, otherwise its very deep in the Earth, the land being very high, and near the surface is plenty of Slate." The first coal mine opened in the South was at Richmond in 1750, and for years this was the only important source of coal in America. No doubt the following were the reasons for this slow development of what is now a major American industry: wood was abundant, and there was no demand for coal except from a few blacksmiths.

The total amount of goods manufactured in the Southern colonies at any given time cannot be determined, because the colonial records are mainly descriptive and seldom statistical. Nevertheless, it is evident that agriculture was the predominant occupation throughout the colonial period and that manufacturing, though finally of considerable variety, was local and widely scattered.

Perhaps Robert Beverley, in 1705, slightly exaggerated the situation, yet there was truth in his remarks when he said: [3] "They have their clothing of all sorts from England; as linen, woolens and silk, hats, and leather. Yet flax and hemp grow nowhere in the world better than there. Their sheep yield good increase and bear fleeces, but they shear them only to cool them. The mulberry tree whose leaf is the proper food of the silkworm, grows there like a weed and silkworms have been observed to thrive extremely and without hazard. The very furs that their hats are made of perhaps go first from thence; and most of their hides lie and rot, or are made use of only for covering dry-goods in a leaky house. Indeed, some few hides with much ado are tanned and made into servants' shoes, but at so careless a rate that the planters don't care to buy them if they can get others; and sometimes perhaps a better manager than ordinary will vouchsafe to make a pair of breeches of a deerskin. Nay, they are such abominably ill husbands that though their country be overrun with wood, yet have they all their wooden wares from England; their cabinets, chairs, tables, stools, chests, boxes, cart-wheels, and all other things even so much as their bowls and birchen brooms to the eternal reproach of their laziness."

As late as 1769, there was still an unfavorable trade balance against the Southern colonies, although, whenever Southern trade statistics are analyzed, due allowance must be made for the importation of slaves. (See table, p. 126.) Indeed, the Southern colonies, because of their system of agricultural production of export staples and their lack of

---

[3] Robert Beverley, *History of Virginia* (London, 1705), p. 58.

TRADE OF GREAT BRITAIN WITH THE COLONIES, 1769[4]

| Colony | British Imports from Colonies | | | British Exports to Colonies | | |
|---|---|---|---|---|---|---|
| | £. | s. | d. | £. | s. | d. |
| Virginia and Maryland........ | 714,943 | 15 | 8 | 759,961 | 5 | 0 |
| Carolinas................... | 327,084 | 8 | 6 | 405,014 | 13 | 1 |
| Georgia................... | 58,340 | 19 | 4 | 82,270 | 2 | 3 |
| TOTAL............... | 1,100,369 | 3 | 6 | 1,247,246 | 0 | 4 |

adequate domestic manufactures, were dependent upon foreign markets throughout the colonial period.

## Bibliographical Note

Of the various studies on the economic development of the South, practically none deals exclusively with the establishment and consequent development of industry in the Southern colonies. However, invaluable notes can be gathered from V. S. Clark, *History of Manufactures in the United States, 1607–1860* (Washington, 1916); J. L. Bishop, *History of American Manufactures from 1608 to 1860–1866*, three volumes (Philadelphia and London, 1868); and R. M. Tryon, *Household Manufactures in the United States, 1640–1860* (Chicago, 1917).

There is need for a monograph on the lumber industry in the Southern colonies. J. E. Defebaugh, *History of the Lumber Industry of America*, four volumes (Chicago, 1906–1907), is the only general work of any value on the subject.

There has been very little written on the history of naval stores and shipbuilding in the Southern colonies. Henry Hall, *Report on the Ship-building Industry of the United States*, TENTH CENSUS (1880), Volume VIII (Washington, 1884), is quite inadequate but is the only available material on the early period.

On the textile industry in the Southern colonies, valuable information may be discovered in A. H. Cole, *American Wool Manufacture*, two volumes (Cambridge, Mass., 1926).

An adequate and scholarly treatment of the iron industry in colonial Virginia is presented in Kathleen Bruce's *Virginia Iron Manufacture in the Slave Era* (New York, 1931). The best

---

[4] Figures compiled from Hazard, *United States and Commercial Register*, Vol. I, pp. 4–5.

history of the Principio Company will be found in the *Pennsylvania Magazine of History,* Volume XI, pages 63, 190, 288. J. B. Pearse, *Concise History of the Iron Manufacture of the American Colonies up to the Revolution* (Philadelphia, 1876), contains some valuable information.

P. A. Bruce, *op. cit.*, gives an interesting account of industry in general in colonial Virginia.

# CHAPTER V

# Population in the Colonial South

IN THE Southern colonies a social complex existed among the different immigrants. Besides the English, there were Germans, French, Scotch-Irish, Irish, Jews, Negroes, and a few other nationalities most of whom had come to these shores either for economic or for religious reasons, or because they had suffered from tyranny or had been forcibly imported. How far the peculiar characteristics of each of these groups influenced economic development and ideals cannot be determined quantitatively; but there is little doubt that such characteristics do have qualitative effects and that different types of peoples prefer different occupations and articles of consumption. It is well, therefore, to consider briefly the several nationalities that settled in the colonial South.

## Total Population

Although there are no authentic statistics of total population in the Southern colonies, a few estimates have been made which, perhaps, are fairly reliable. According to Bancroft, the population of the Southern colonies in 1688–1689 was as follows: [1] Maryland, 20,000; Virginia, 58,000; and the Carolinas, 5,000; or, a total for the section of 83,000. In 1760, according to Channing's estimate, the population was: Maryland, 164,000; Virginia, 315,000; North Carolina, 130,000; South Carolina, 100,000; and Georgia, 9,000; or, a total for the section of 718,000, of which 419,000 were whites. Finally, in 1776, according to

---

[1] George Bancroft, *History of the United States* (15th Edition), Vol. II, p. 450.

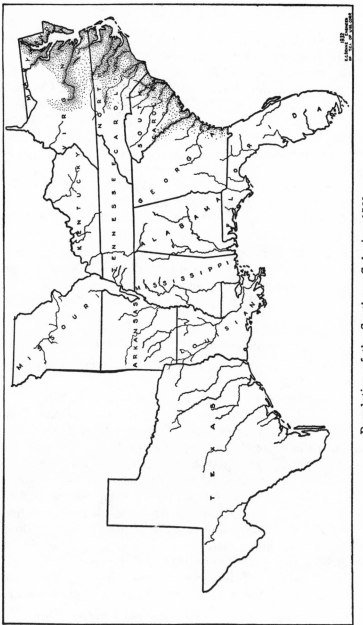

Population of the Southern Colonies, 1760

estimates made by the Continental Congress as a basis on which to apportion the expenses of the Revolution, the white population was as follows: [2] Maryland, 174,000; Virginia (including Kentucky), 300,000; North Carolina (including Tennessee), 181,000; South Carolina, 93,000; and Georgia, 27,000; or, a total for the section of 775,000. Bancroft doubts the accuracy of this estimate. Hanna, after careful research including an actual count of names in colonial land books and parish records, estimated the population for 1775 as follows: [3] Maryland, 134,000; Virginia (including Kentucky), 325,000; North Carolina (including Tennessee), 206,000; South Carolina, 90,000; and Georgia, 34,000; or, a total for the section of 789,000. At any rate, it appears from every available source that prior to the Revolution the total white population of the Southern colonies never reached one million and, at most, did not even equal the present population of the city of Baltimore.

## Distribution of Nationalities

Of the total white population, by far the greater proportion were English.

The settlements in Virginia east of the Blue Ridge were almost exclusively English, but those west of the Blue Ridge included other groups. Why the English predominated in the older settlements of the colony is not difficult to understand. The plantation system, which in several respects was a replica of the English manorial system, required for its existence a supply of cheap labor. Before the availability of negro slaves, the English poor supplied this demand. The planters were obliged to draw their laborers from those classes who were willing, or could be compelled, to submit to servitude. Since more or less coercive recruiting of laborers was possible at that time mainly in England, most of the Virginia white servants

---

[2] Edward Channing, *History of the United States*, Vol. II, p. 491.
[3] Charles A. Hanna, *Scotch-Irish*, Vol. I, Chap. VI.

were English. According to tradition, many English Cavaliers fled to Virginia on account of the quarrel between the Royalists and the Puritans; a searching inquiry into the facts, made by Wertenbaker, shows, however, that this was not the case and that only a few Cavaliers actually came to Virginia.[4]

Maryland, like Virginia, was settled principally by the English. From the beginning, Lord Baltimore adopted a policy of religious toleration, and the colony soon began to draw men of different creeds. Within a few years, the Protestants became so numerous that they were about to dominate and assimilate the Catholics by sheer force of numbers. This result was prevented by the Toleration Act of 1649, which granted religious freedom to all those who professed to believe in Christ. Then, in 1691, when the colony became a royal province, the Church of England was established, the public exercise of Catholic worship was proscribed, and Catholic immigrants were prohibited from entering the colony. Such a policy tended to check immigration from continental Europe. Moreover, Maryland, like Virginia, required cheap laborers and, before slavery developed in this country, obtained them with least difficulty from England.

In the Carolinas, the first three permanent settlements were established by English-speaking people; subsequently, both North and South Carolina received many immigrants of English origin. North Carolina, especially, became a refuge for honorable poor from Virginia as well as for criminal indentured servants. Unfortunately, from this latter class came some of the poor white trash whose ranks after the Civil War were augmented by numbers of "carpetbaggers" and who today have, for the most part, been pushed onto the marginal land areas of the South. However, as time went on, more orderly and thrifty settlers

---

[4] "The widespread belief that during the years from 1645 to 1660 Virginia was the refuge of large numbers of English Cavaliers is entirely without foundation in fact."—T. J. Wertenbaker, *First Americans* (Vol. II of HISTORY OF AMERICAN LIFE), p. 306.

came in, not only of English descent, but of other stocks as well—many of whom, as in Virginia, located in the back-country.  In South Carolina, there was also a constant influx of English immigrants, but this colony was by far more cosmopolitan than any other Southern colony and was the only one that developed an urban society.

Georgia, though the youngest of the Southern colonies, was peopled direct from England.  As already noted, James Oglethorpe established the first settlement there with a group chosen from thirty-five English families.  Who these persons were and what was their legal and economic status matter little, for it was the subsequent immigration of both English and other nationalities that really formed the basis for Georgia's development.  Nor must too much emphasis be placed upon this colony in the pre-Revolution-ary scheme of things, for in those days it was scarcely more than a backwoods outpost.  Thus, the English out-numbered every other group in the Southern colonies.  In the earliest settlements, the greater part of the aristocratic planters, small landholders, and indentured servants were largely English.  In the backcountry, they were mingled with other groups, such as Germans and Scotch-Irish. Despite the presence of a number of nationalities, however, the South was basically English in language, institutions, and laws.

The Scotch-Irish were the next most important group in the Southern colonies.  In 1611, James I, in an effort to subdue the rebellious Irish, confiscated the land belong-ing to the natives in six of the northern counties of Ulster and regranted it to English speculators.  The land was then leased to settlers from the Scottish lowlands.  Despite political and religious vicissitudes, the settlers prospered and their descendants came to be known as Scotch-Irish. "A paradoxical fact regarding the Scotch-Irish is that they are very little Scotch and much less Irish.  That is to say, they do not belong mainly to the so-called Celtic race, but they are the most composite of all the people of the British

Isles.  They are called Scots because they lived in Scotia;
and they are called Irish because they moved to Ireland.
Geography and not ethnology has given them their name.
They are a mixed race through whose veins runs the Celtic
blood of the primitive Scot and Pict, the primitive Britain,
the primitive Irish, but with a larger admixture of the later
Norwegian, Dane, Saxon and Angle." [5]

About the end of the seventeenth century, the British
Government began to enact laws to protect English trade
from Irish competition.  Prohibitive duties were laid upon
Irish exports; in 1704, the Test Act was passed, declaring
the Scotch-Irish outlaws, though at the same time compelling them to pay tithes for the support of the Church
of Ireland.  Finally, between 1714 and 1718, the absentee
landlords doubled and, in some cases, trebled rents.  On
account of such economic exploitation and religious intolerance, the Scotch-Irish hated England.  From 1719 to
about 1782, they poured into America.  At first some came
to New England, but they could not adjust themselves to
the Puritan mode of life and therefore moved on.  Most
of them, however, came to Pennsylvania, and from there
many emigrated southward.  In Virginia, they settled in
the Shenandoah Valley and beyond, in the territory that
is now a part of Tennessee and Kentucky.  In North Carolina, they pushed back into the Piedmont and "had come
before the Revolutionary War to be the strongest element
in the population of the colony." [6]  Likewise, several
thousand located in the backcountry of South Carolina
and in Georgia.  In other words, practically the whole frontier was occupied predominantly by Scotch-Irish.  According to fairly reliable estimates, in 1775, they were
probably distributed somewhat as follows: [7]

---

[5] Henry Jones Ford, *Scotch-Irish in America* (1915), p. 521.  Reprinted
by permission of the Princeton University Press, Princeton, N. J.

[6] John Fiske, *Old Virginia and Her Neighbors* (De Luxe Edition), Vol.
2, p. 373.

[7] Charles A. Hanna, *Scotch-Irish* (1902), Vol. I, Chap. VI.  Reprinted by
permission of G. P. Putnam's Sons, New York.

DISTRIBUTION OF SCOTCH-IRISH, 1775

| State | Number of Scotch-Irish |
|---|---|
| Maryland | 30,000 |
| Virginia | 75,000 |
| North Carolina | 65,000 |
| South Carolina | 45,000 |
| Georgia | 10,000 |
| TOTAL | 225,000 |

The Scotch-Irish were peculiarly well fitted for pioneer life. In the words of F. J. Turner, they were "the cutting edge of the frontier." [8]   They were aggressive, bold, and steadfast, especially in the defense of Presbyterianism.   In business, they were shrewd and practical to such an extent that it was reported of them: "They kept the Sabbath and everything else that they could lay their hands on."   In politics, they were individualists, and would fight to the death for human freedom.   During the Revolutionary War, they were among America's staunchest champions for independence from England.   Moreover, eminent men like Jackson, Calhoun, and Wilson traced their ancestry to this sturdy stock.

The first list of planters in Virginia contained some German names.   Both Augustine Herrmann, who established the tobacco export trade there, and Johannes Lederer, who was the first explorer of the Allegheny Mountains, were Germans.   The first iron furnace in the colony was erected by German miners brought from Westphalia.   Most of the early Germans in Virginia, however, came as indentured servants and, upon the expiration of their indenture, acquired land in the outlying regions of the colony.   Usually they were the second wave of frontier settlers, buying out the Scotch-Irish or following after them; but later on the Germans, especially from Pennsylvania and Maryland, settled side by side with the Scotch-Irish in the Shenandoah Valley and farther westward, along the frontier.

In Maryland, most of the Germans came from Pennsyl-

[8] F. J. Turner, *Frontier in American History*, p. 103 et seq.

vania. There, as in Pennsylvania, they were usually mis-
named the "Dutch." In North Carolina, Germans began
coming in during the early part of the eighteenth century.
Thus, in 1710, 650 Germans from the Palatinate and 1,500
Swiss founded "New Berne." About a decade later, the
Moravians settled Rowan County. However, there were
never so many Germans in North Carolina as in South
Carolina. In 1732, the Germans and the Swiss founded
"Purryville" in South Carolina and, a few years later,
poured into Charleston by the hundreds.

In Georgia, in 1731, German Mennonites and Herrn-
huters settled on St. Simon's Island, near Savannah; and
in 1734, about 1,200 German Protestants who had been
driven from Salzburg came into the colony and founded
"Ebenezer" about thirty miles above Savannah. Thus, as
in the case of the Scotch-Irish, most of the Germans were
pushed into the backcountry beyond the older settlements,
which had been established mainly by the English. Faust,
historian of the German element, estimates the number of
Germans in these colonies at the beginning of the Revolutionary War as follows: [9]

### DISTRIBUTION OF GERMANS, 1775

| State | Number of Germans |
|---|---|
| Maryland and Delaware | 20,500 |
| Virginia and West Virginia | 25,000 |
| North Carolina | 8,000 |
| South Carolina | 15,000 |
| Georgia | 5,000 |
| TOTAL | 73,500 |

During the colonial period, most of the German immigrants were peasants, though a few were artisans. Nearly
all of them came over as indentured servants. Eventually
they became excellent farmers in the South. However,
their influence upon the political and social organization of
the Southern colonies was less in proportion to their num-

---

[9] Statistics compiled from Albert Bernhardt Faust, *German Element in
the United States,* Vol. I, p. 285.

bers than that of any other group. This may have been due partly to their early poverty; yet it was, perhaps, due more especially to their language. Because they could not read English, they were frequently considered illiterate; Benjamin Franklin even went so far as to say that they were "generally the most stupid of their nation." During the Revolution, many of them rallied to the cause of American freedom, though some, as in Georgia, were prominent Tories. In subsequent years, there were contributed to the American Nation from this stock several distinguished scholars, scientists, and leaders.

In 1685, when Louis XIV revoked the Edict of Nantes (granted by Henry of Navarre in 1598 to give protection to the Huguenots), thousands of Huguenots fled from France. They were good, thrifty citizens of that nation, and for this reason they were welcome almost everywhere. As Bancroft says: [10] "Every wise government was eager to offer refuge to the upright men who would carry to other countries the arts, the skill in manufacture, and the wealth of France. Emigrant Huguenots put a new aspect on the north of Germany, when they constituted towns and sections of cities, introducing manufactures before unknown. A suburb of London was filled with French mechanics; the Prince of Orange gained entire regiments of soldiers, as brave as those whom Cromwell led to victory; a colony of them reached even the Cape of Good Hope. In our American Colonies they were welcome everywhere."

To these refugees the warm climate of Virginia and South Carolina was especially attractive, and the British Government actively encouraged their immigration to the Southern colonies. In 1700, about 700 or 800 came to Virginia. Upon their arrival, they received special attention from the colonial government, for it was hoped that they would establish a profitable wine industry in the colony. At a place called "Manakinton," they were granted

[10] George Bancroft, *History of the United States* (15th Edition), Vol. II, p. 179.

a tract of 10,000 acres of land from the extinct Manakin Tribe of Indians. Here they established a settlement. In the spring of 1701, a visitor reported that he had seen "about seventy of their huts; being most of them very mean, there being upwards of fourty of y'm betwixt ye two Creeks, w'ch is about four miles on ye River, and have cleared all ye old Manacan ffields for near three miles together." [11] But this settlement did not prosper. In October of 1701, Governor Mason wrote: [12] "Ye ffrench Refugees is most of them, gone to Maryland, and have left an ill distemper behind them." In 1707, another group of them, becoming dissatisfied with this settlement, removed to the Trent River, in North Carolina.

The chief group of Huguenots in the Southern colonies were in South Carolina. They settled principally at Charleston, though there were six separate settlements in the colony. How many Huguenots came to the South is not known and cannot be accurately ascertained. Jones estimates that at least 15,000 came to America, and that they came in small groups to several of the colonies.[13] Wilson fixes the number of French Protestants in South Carolina alone as 6,000.[14]

At any rate, the influence of the Huguenots in the South has been far greater than their numbers indicate. As pointed out by Hirsch: [15] "Their inventions and discoveries and those of their descendants came into general use in the South. Skilled in nearly all the industries in France and of sturdy industrious habits they could not do otherwise than influence the economic activities of their environment.

---

[11] Virginia Historical Society, "The State of the French Refugees," in *Documents Chiefly Unpublished Relating to the Huguenots' Emigration to Virginia,* p. 42.

[12] *Ibid.,* p. 44.

[13] Howard Mumford Jones, *America and French Culture,* p. 102.

[14] Robert Wilson, *Transactions of the Huguenot Society of South Carolina for 1897,* No. 4 ("The Huguenot Influence in Colonial South Carolina"), pp. 26–38.

[15] Arthur Henry Hirsch, *Huguenots of Colonial South Carolina* (1928), p. 264. By permission of the Duke University Press, Durham, N. C.

. . . In Guerrard's 'Pendulum Engine' for pounding rice, in the natural monopoly on the manufacture of salt, in the introduction of indigo, and in the marked improvements in the growth of rice, silk and wine, as well as in cultural endeavours the French Protestants played an important part."

Of the miscellaneous nationalities the Jews probably constituted the most important group. They were confined principally to South Carolina and Georgia. Virginia contained very few Jews until toward the close of the eighteenth century. "A Muster of the Inhabitants of Virginia," in 1633, contains the names of Elias Legardo, Joseph Moise, and Rebecca Isaacke. Twenty-five years later, Moses Nehemiah is mentioned in the legal records of the colony as a litigant trying to compel a creditor to receive payment in coin instead of tobacco. In Maryland, the famous Toleration Act (1649) provided that no person professing belief in Jesus Christ should in any wise be molested on account of his religion, but any person blaspheming or denying "Jesus Christ to be the Son of God" should be punished by death and his goods and lands forfeited. Until the penalty clause was omitted in 1654, this law had the effect of practically excluding Jews from the colony. From that year until the latter part of the eighteenth century, there was only a slow percolation of Jews into Maryland, and those who remained there quietly exercised, rather than openly professed, their faith. During the colonial period, there were only a few Jews in North Carolina. This paucity in numbers was due to the fact that the colony was less important commercially than the other colonies, and it was also due to illiberal governmental provisions. In South Carolina, the Jews never suffered from the civil and religious persecutions usually applied to them in other colonies; hence, by 1750, they had come to form a significant element in the population of this colony. Most of them came from London and, as is characteristic of their race, engaged chiefly in merchandising. However,

Moses Lindo, who arrived from London in 1756, became interested in the indigo manufacture and made it one of the principal industries in the colony. A number of Jews, also, came to Georgia. The second vessel that reached the colony brought forty. These came to Savannah without the sanction of the trustees of the colony; consequently, a committee was appointed to prepare for publication in England a statement of the matter and to announce that the trustees did not purpose "to make a Jew colony in Georgia." General Oglethorpe took little heed of this report, and by 1733, one third of the entire population of Savannah were Jews. After Oglethorpe returned to England, however, an intolerant spirit arose in the colony and some of the Jews removed to Charleston.

There were, likewise, only a few Irish in the Southern colonies. Nearly all of these came over, not in groups, but individually as indentured servants, though, it is said, during the early part of the eighteenth century one group of about 500 Irish Protestants were induced by the proprietors to settle along the southern border of South Carolina. Generally, because of their language, ignorance, and Catholic religion, the Irish were not wanted in any of the Southern colonies. In 1699 and again a few years later, Maryland passed an act to prevent too great a number of Irish Papists from being imported into the province; in 1716, South Carolina even excluded them, charging them to be "scandalous characters."

Finally, of course, there were Indians and Negroes; the former were to be exterminated; and the latter, to be segregated as slaves.

Thus, at the time of the Revolution, the population of the Southern colonies—excluding the minor elements, the Negroes and the Indians—was a physically homogeneous group composed exclusively of white stocks from Britain, France, and Germany. These, indeed, were the stocks from which, through amalgamation, sprang the people of the true "Old South," and upon which later additions must be regarded as "extraneous grafts."

### Bibliographical Note

Scattered through Volume II of Edward Channing's *History of the United States* (New York, 1905) may be found several references to the population of the Southern colonies. A pioneer work dealing exclusively with the number of inhabitants in the colonies is Franklin B. Dexter, *Estimates of Population in the American Colonies* (Worcester, Mass., 1887). Interesting notes on the colonial population, and particularly the English settlers, may be collected from J. T. Adams, *Provincial Society, 1690–1763* (New York, 1927); and Thomas Jefferson Wertenbaker, *First Americans, 1607–1690* (New York, 1927). The latter are Volumes III and II, respectively, in the series HISTORY OF AMERICAN LIFE.

There are several valuable works dealing historically with the various nationalities in the United States. A scholarly treatment of the Scotch-Irish in the Southern colonies will be found in C. A. Hanna, *Scotch-Irish*, two volumes (New York, 1902); and in H. J. Ford, *Scotch-Irish in America* (Princeton, 1915). The most brilliant work dealing with the influence of the Scotch-Irish and other frontiersmen on American history is F. J. Turner, *Frontier in American History* (New York, 1920). Alfred P. James, however, has undertaken to minimize the importance of the Scotch-Irish in western Pennsylvania, Kentucky, and West Virginia. For his discussion, see "The First English-Speaking Trans-Appalachian Frontier," *Mississippi Valley Historical Review*, Volume 17, pages 55–71. The most scholarly treatment of the German element is Albert Bernhardt Faust, *German Element in the United States with Special Reference to Its Political, Moral and Social, and Educational Influence*, two volumes in one (Boston, 1927). C. D. Bernheim, *German Settlements in North and South Carolina* (New York, 1872), contains some valuable data, but his discussion must be used circumspectly.

Charles W. Baird, *Huguenot Emigration to America*, two volumes (New York, 1885), is an interesting general treatment of the Huguenot element, though much of the work has no value from an economic viewpoint. Arthur H. Hirsch is the accepted authority on Huguenots in South Carolina. His writings on this subject are: *Huguenots of Colonial South Carolina* (Durham, N. C., 1928), which is a searching inquiry into their early settlements in the colony, their economic and social life, and their influence; and "French Influence on American Agriculture in the Colonial Period with Special Reference to Southern Provinces," *Agricultural History*, January 1930, pages 1–9. Louis Fosdick, *French Blood in America* (New York, 1911), is an excellent source of information. Also to be mentioned is J. G. Rosengarten, *French Colonists and Exiles in the United States* (New York, 1907).

Numerous books have been written about the Jews in America, but the most reliable sources of information on this subject, so far as early history in the South is concerned, are: *Publications of the American Jewish Historical Society*, especially Volumes 1, 2, 6, 12, and 20; Lee Levinger, *History of the Jews in the United States* (New York, 1930); and Anita Libman Lebeson, *Jewish Pioneers in America, 1492–1848* (New York, 1931).

For the Irish in the Southern colonies, see: Thomas D'Arcy McGee, *History of the Irish Settlers in North America* (Boston, 1850); and A. J. Theband, *Irish Race in the Past and Present* (New York, 1893).

# CHAPTER VI

# Finance in the Colonial South

A CCORDING to Aristotle: "Government was created to make life possible and exists to make life good." But it is equally axiomatic, at least in modern times, that the existence of any government presupposes the existence of some system of public finance. The institution of private property, production, and the exchange of products in a civilized community requires an adequate supply of money, or counters of purchasing power.

## Money and Credit

In the Southern colonies neither the early settlers nor subsequent immigrants brought with them, severally or collectively, enough money to carry on the essential colonial trade. From the first there was a scarcity of money and credit for carrying on both domestic and foreign trade. Basically it was a scarcity of capital and not a scarcity of money from which the early settlers suffered; for if they had had adequate capital to establish manufactures to supply the domestic market with goods and, at the same time, could have continued the export of agricultural staples, the balance of trade would have been favorable and money would have flowed in. However, it must be remembered that the British mercantile policy, in so far as possible, aided in keeping the balance of trade against the colonies. Therefore, since money—certainly specie— was drained out and large debts accumulated against the colonists, they were practically compelled to resort to various mediums of exchange. This situation created the problem of establishing a standard or, at least, a money

142

of account—that is to say, a money in which people could reckon and negotiate.  Thus, the colonists were face to face with the most fundamental problems of money and credit.

## METALLIC MONEY

The early settlers brought with them some English coins and the British money of account—namely, the concept of pounds, shillings, and pence, in which prices and debts were expressed.  As time went on, sporadic attempts were made to coin for domestic use small amounts of the lesser denominations.  In 1645, the General Assembly of Virginia ordered 10,000 pounds of copper to be bought and coined into 2-pence, 6-pence, and 9-pence pieces, but there is no evidence that these proposed coins were actually put into circulation.  In 1722, William Wood, presumably a needy courtier, obtained permission in England to coin money for the American colonies.  These coins were farthings, halfpennies, and pennies, and are known to numismatists as *Rosa Americana*.  In 1772, the Virginia Assembly invested £1,000 sterling in copper and had that amount struck off in England into coins known as *Virginia halfpennies*.  These were probably circulated in 1775 and 1776, for specimens are sometimes found in the state, though Thomas Jefferson once declared, "Coppers have never been in use in Virginia."  In Maryland as early as 1660, Lord Baltimore issued silver coins in denominations of 12 pence, 6 pence, and 4 pence.

Despite these sources and the possible trickle of coin from England in the course of trade, the chief source of metallic money in the colonies was not in English coinage.  The most common coins in the Southern colonies were Spanish and Portuguese; they came in mainly through trade with the West Indies.  Of such coins the most familiar was the Spanish dollar, or *piece-of-eight*.  This was a silver coin of eight *reals,* or *ryals,* and, if accurately valued, was equivalent to 4s. 6d.  But these coins were seldom of the same weight and fineness, mainly because, after leaving the Spanish mint, they were often either impaired by *clipping* or reduced in weight by *sweating*—that is to say, small particles of the metal were removed by shaking a number of them together violently in a bag. On account of this inequality in size and weight, and in accordance with Gresham's law, the heavier coins tended to disappear from circulation. Moreover, the colonies attempted to put different values upon these coins as legal tender equivalents of English money. In Virginia, for the purpose of attracting more coin, the value of a Spanish dollar was 6 shillings; in Maryland, 7½ shillings; in North Carolina, 8 shillings; in South Carolina, 32½ shillings; and in Georgia, 5 shillings. Indeed, the confusion was so great that, in 1704, England tried to simplify matters by declaring that the maximum equivalent of a Spanish piece-of-eight should be 6 shillings. This action, of course, proved as futile as the colonial efforts to regulate by statutory law the price of silver. Nevertheless, these coins were eagerly sought; and Virginia, in 1645, declared the Spanish dollar, inclusive of the subsidiary coins of halves, quarters, and eighths, to be the monetary standard of the colony.

Besides Spanish silver coins in the Southern colonies, there were also in circulation French silver *crowns* and *livres* and some foreign gold—such as, the *guinea;* the *pistole;* and the Portuguese *moidore, johannes,* and *joe.* It may be noted that, in 1765, Maryland's delegates to the Stamp Act Congress acknowledged in foreign coins the receipt of their expenses: [1]

|  | £. | s. | d. |
|---|---|---|---|
| 409 Spanish pistoles at 27s. | 532 | 3 | 0 |
| 5 Half johannes at 57s. 6d. | 14 | 7 | 6 |
| 4 French pistoles at 26s. 6d. | 5 | 6 | 0 |
| 1 Moidore | 2 | 3 | 6 |
| 1 Half moidore | 1 | 1 | 9 |
|  | 575 | 1 | 9 |

[1] Edward Channing, *History of the United States* (1922), Vol. II, p. 498. Reprinted by permission of the Macmillan Company, New York.

Most of these coins were introduced when products were smuggled into foreign ports without reciprocal trade. However, this influx of coin was not extensive enough to offset the unfavorable balance of trade with England, and in spite of the welter of heterogeneous coins that came in, the colonists never had an adequate supply of metallic money as a medium of exchange.

## COMMODITY MONEY

In the absence of a sufficient supply of metallic money, the colonists had to resort for a medium of exchange to such substitutes as commodities and paper. When commodities were used, it was necessary to select those that were generally acceptable and least perishable—for example, tobacco and rice, though other products were sometimes used.

In Virginia, tobacco was used as a medium of exchange as early as 1619; and in that year, the assembly passed a law making the price "three shillings the beste and the second sort at 18d. the pound." In 1642, tobacco was virtually made legal tender by a law prohibiting the enforcement of contracts made payable in money. However, as time went on, it became impracticable to transfer the tobacco itself from hand to hand; hence there evolved a system of warehouse certificates which could be used instead of actually handling the tobacco. In 1727, the assembly legalized the issuing of such certificates, or *tobacco notes*. Government warehouses were established and inspectors appointed to receive the tobacco, to grade and inspect it, and, thereupon, to issue notes to the owner. In 1734, a further innovation was made in the form of *crop notes*. These were issued in a similar manner, but called for particular casks of tobacco that had been branded with a mark to correspond with the same mark on some particular notes.

By 1750, tobacco certificates were the predominant medium of exchange in the colony. Debts, contracts, legacies, and other financial transactions were expressed, not in the English money of account, but in pounds of tobacco. These certificates soon caused losses either for the payer or the payee, whenever the price of tobacco rose or fell within the duration of the financial contracts. If it rose, the payer lost, because he still had to give the payee just as many pounds as he was obliged to when the contract was made. Conversely, when the price fell, the payee lost to the extent of the difference between the estimated price at the time the contract was made and the realized price at the time of payment. Tobacco prices often fluctuated widely, with the result that this medium of exchange effected hardships, especially for salaried persons and taxpayers.

In order to remedy the trouble, futile efforts were made, through legislative control of production, to stabilize the price of tobacco. In 1755, the Virginia Assembly passed the so-called *Two-Penny Act,* which allowed a person to pay his taxes either in tobacco or in coin, at the rate of 2 pence for each pound of tobacco. No doubt this measure would have tended to relieve the taxpayers, but in 1758, the British Government disallowed the act. The tobacco certificates as a medium of exchange had caused so much confusion in the colony that occasionally violence had been prevented only with considerable difficulty. Nevertheless, even after the Two-Penny Act was nullified, the ministers brought up a test case known as the "Parson's Cause," in which Patrick Henry denied the right of the British Government to veto a Virginia law—a fact which is of interest here as an indication of the crystallization of sentiment against the British mercantile policy.

In Maryland, likewise, tobacco was used for money, and there was similar confusion in the payment of taxes in tobacco or in coin. Yet there seems to have been less trouble in Maryland than in Virginia, for, at the beginning of the eighteenth century, the Maryland Assembly agreed that the sheriffs should receive all public dues either in coin or in tobacco, at the election of the payer, because, as an early committee report indicated, the poor inhabitants could not procure enough coin to pay the levy.

In South Carolina, rice was the chief commodity used as money. In 1719, the assembly made rice "delivered in good barrels upon the Bay at Charleston" receivable for taxes. The next year, a tax of 1,200,000 pounds of rice was levied, and, as in the case of tobacco certificates in Virginia, *rice orders*, or *certificates*, were issued against the supply at the rate of 30 shillings for each one hundred pounds. These certificates were circulated from hand to hand; were legal tender for all purposes; and were protected against counterfeiting, since such act was declared a felony without benefit of clergy.

Besides tobacco (which was used as money chiefly in Virginia and Maryland and, to a lesser extent, in North Carolina) and rice (which was used as money chiefly in South Carolina), other commodities, such as corn or wheat, and lumber, were sometimes used for the same purpose. In 1682, Virginia decreed that flax, hemp, washed wool, tar, and lumber should be legal tender. In 1715, the assembly in North Carolina made a still more extensive list of commodities legal tender. As reported by Governor Johnson to the Board of Trade, this list included not only the specified commodities but also the legal value of each: [2]

COMMODITIES USED AS LEGAL TENDER, 1715

|  | £. | s. | d. |
|---|---|---|---|
| Indian Corn per Bushel.............. |  | 1 | 8 |
| Tallow per Pound.................. |  | 0 | 5 |
| Beaver and Otter Skins per Pound..... |  | 2 | 6 |
| Butter per Pound................... |  | 0 | 6 |
| Raw buck and Doe Skins per Pound.... |  | 0 | 9 |
| Feathers per Pound................. |  | 1 | 4 |
| Pitch per Barrel full gauged........... | 1 | 0 | 0 |
| Pork per Barrel..................... | 2 | 5 | 0 |
| Tobacco per 100 cwt................ |  | 10 | 0 |

[2] Letters of Governor Johnson to the Board of Trade (1749), in *Colonial Records of North Carolina* (edited by W. L. Saunders), No. LV, pp. 920–921.

| | | |
|---|---|---|
| Wheat per Bushel..................... | 3 | 6 |
| Leather Tann'd uncurried per Pound... | 0 | 8 |
| Wild Cat Skins per piece.............. | 1 | 0 |
| Cheese per Pound.................... | 0 | 4 |
| Drest Buck & Doe Skins per Pound.... | 2 | 6 |
| Tar per Barrel full gauged............. | 10 | 0 |
| Whale oil per Barrel................. 1 | 10 | 0 |
| Beef per Barrel..................... 1 | 10 | 0 |

Again, Gresham's law—that cheap money tends to drive out dear money—seems to have been in operation while these commodities were used as mediums of exchange. According to Governor Johnson's report, this method of financing had a particularly "damaging" effect on the revenues, because "so many commodities of the worst sort were only paid."

## Paper Money

The next step, usually taken by the Southern colonists to supplement their inadequate supply of specie, was an emergency measure to meet the expenses of war or defense. In South Carolina, for example, the assembly, to defray the expenses of the expedition against St. Augustine in 1703, issued the first paper money circulated in that colony. This issue consisted of £6,000 of notes bearing 12 per cent interest, which were to be canceled by the receipts from duties, and £2,000 in taxes to be levied during each of the years 1703 and 1704. These notes, however, were not retired as proposed, and the funds set aside for the purpose were diverted into other channels. Again, in 1707, £11,000 of additional bills were issued; in 1708, £5,000 more; and in 1710, £3,000 more. In 1710, of the total of £25,000 of bills outstanding, only £9,000 were retired. In 1711, for the purpose of assisting North Carolina in the war with the Tuscarora Indians, there were issued £4,000 of *Tuscarora bills*. In 1712, in compliance with the so-called *Bank Act*, £52,000 more were issued, of which £32,000 were placed at interest. In 1715, an additional £35,000 were voted; and by 1731, the amount of notes outstanding equalled £106,500. There was no fund for their repayment and cancellation. Inevitably these issues depreciated with each new issue. By 1716, the value of the South Carolina paper money was only one fourth that of standard British money, and by 1749, only one seventh.

In 1755, when Virginia could neither borrow nor raise by taxation the funds necessary to help finance the French and Indian War, the assembly issued £20,000 in *treasury notes* to be redeemed "next June." [3] Like the notes in South Carolina, these were to bear interest, but at the rate of 5 per cent instead of 12. The notes were also made legal tender for all debts except quitrents. During the next two decades, Virginia issued £614,746 of notes, all of which were to be repaid from future tax receipts. Unlike South Carolina's paper money, these notes had been conservatively issued in relation to income available for repayment. Hence, in 1769, it was reported that there were available from taxes £11,000 more than would be required for the redemption of the notes then outstanding.

The other Southern colonies tried issuing small amounts of paper money. Maryland, in 1733, had issued bills of credit to the amount of £90,000. For redeeming them, a duty of 15 pence was levied on every hogshead of tobacco exported. In subsequent years, the colony issued a total amount of £46,000; but in 1764, Maryland had redeemed all of her paper money. In 1729, North Carolina authorized the issue of £40,000 in bills of credit, £10,000 of which were used in redeeming old bills and the rest were distributed among the precincts for circulation. No other Southern colony suffered from an overissue of paper money as did South Carolina.

Nevertheless, Parliament, realizing the possible danger from an inflated currency, especially to creditors, enacted a law in 1763 "to prevent paper bills of credit, hereafter, to be issued in any of his Majesty's Colonies or plantations

---

[3] George T. Starnes, *Sixty Years of Branch Banking in Virginia,* p. 9.

in America, from being declared to be a legal tender in payment of money, and to prevent the legal tender of such bills as are now subsisting from being prolonged beyond the periods for calling in and sinking the same." [4] As a matter of fact, however, paper money was to play its last and most important role in the Southern colonies during the Revolution.

## BILLS OF EXCHANGE

Trade with England was carried on mainly by means of bills of exchange, which almost obviated the necessity of money as a medium of exchange and helped England to keep the balance of trade in her favor.

This method of carrying on trade, as it operated between Virginia and England, has been concisely described by Dr. George T. Starnes: [5] "The English merchants, as a rule, had factors in the colony to whom they shipped manufactured commodities, and from whom they received cargoes of tobacco. In such transactions between the Virginia planters and the English merchants, the bill of exchange played an important role. The English traders, who bought large quantities of Virginia tobacco, instead of paying in merchandise or money sterling, usually gave the planter a bill of exchange on some English merchant with whom they had a balance to their credit. The planter then sent the bill of exchange to his correspondent in England for collection and credit. The planter could, then, at any time have his correspondent ship him such manufactured commodities as he desired; or he could draw a bill of exchange on his representative for the purpose of settling an account with some other English merchant."

Similarly in the other Southern colonies, trade with England was commonly carried on by means of bills of exchange

---

[4] U. B. Phillips, *Plantation and Frontier* (Vol. II of DOCUMENTARY HISTORY OF AMERICAN INDUSTRIAL SOCIETY), p. 24.

[5] *Sixty Years of Branch Banking in Virginia*, p. 3. Reprinted by permission of the author.

drawn by traders or by shipcaptains on British merchants. The chief difficulty in the use of such bills was that in the circuitous travels of the bills and the long intervals before they were presented for redemption, the balance to the credit of the drawer was often overdrawn and the bills were protested. In order to remedy this defect, both Virginia and Maryland imposed heavy penalties on the drawer of a bill that was returned protested. During the last quarter of the seventeenth century, Maryland imposed for such an offense a penalty of 20 per cent of the bill, besides all legal costs. In spite of all difficulties, however, most large payments were made by bills of exchange. Such bills were of the simpler class, being drawn directly on the purchaser of the exported products, and not on a bank or banker. Otherwise, much confusion might have been eliminated.

## Public Finance

In the Southern colonies, public finance was relatively a simple matter, for there were few public demands and, consequently, no great need for taxes. A survey of the finances of the colonies casts some light, however, upon the tax systems later evolved in the Southern States.

### Virginia Taxation System

In Virginia there were two different forms of taxation. The British Government, in accordance with its Navigation Acts, established a revenue system which was entirely under its control, the officers being appointed by the Crown. Besides the royal system the colonists had their own method of raising revenue for their local needs.

Since this was the practice in nearly all the Southern colonies, the Virginia system may be taken as a typical example; it will be explained somewhat in detail as to the kinds of taxes actually adopted and the methods of their administration. The taxes may be summarized as follows:

A. General taxes for the colony.
    1. Direct taxes:
       (a) Poll taxes.
       (b) Land taxes.
    2. Quitrents.
    3. Customs duties:
       (a) Export taxes—
          *1.* On tobacco.
          *2.* On hides.
       (b) Import taxes—
          *1.* On liquor.
          *2.* On slaves.
          *3.* For tonnage dues.
B. Local taxes.
    1. County levies:
       (a) Poll taxes.
    2. Parish levies:
       (a) Tithes.

The relative importance of each of these taxes in the fiscal system varied from time to time, but usually the poll taxes were the principal source of revenue for the colonial assembly, while the quitrents and customs duties were the principal source for the British Government. The land tax was tried occasionally, though it was never carried beyond an incipient stage. The poll tax, on the other hand, was exploited on practically every occasion requiring an extraordinary expenditure. This difference in emphasis upon the land tax and the poll tax was perhaps due to the fundamental character of the two taxes. In theory a *land tax* is based upon "possession as a measure of ability to contribute"; while a *poll tax* in a slave society, where capital and labor combine in one person, is a tax both upon possessions and upon productive ability.

Everyone who held land in the colony was required to

pay annually to the King a *quitrent* of 2 shillings per one hundred acres.  From 1624 to 1684, the British Government paid little attention to the collection of these *feudal dues* and allowed them to come under local control.  Until the eighteenth century, they were paid in tobacco, but thereafter, in either tobacco or current money.  After 1684, under the supervision of the British Government, the quitrents became an important source of revenue.  Although a large portion of the receipts from this source had previously been left in the colony, after 1745, nearly all the receipts were sent to Great Britain.  Evasion of quitrents was common.  Estates of fifty and sixty thousand acres often yielded less in quitrents than plantations of one third their size.  An early writer declared, moreover, that, if the British Government should demand the payment of the arrears of quitrents, many Virginians would be forced to resign their patents to huge tracts of land.

In addition to the general taxes, there were also two local levies: the county poll tax and the parish tithe.  The *county poll tax* constituted the sole source of revenue for the counties.  Whenever a county court required a certain amount of revenue for a given expenditure, it was necessary, first, to fix the rate of the poll, and, then, to make the assessment upon the basis of the list of tithables furnished by the assembly.  If the yield happened to be more than was immediately necessary, the surplus had to be turned over to the sheriff for the use of the assembly.  On the other hand, the *parish tithe* was a levy imposed upon everyone for the support of the established church.  The part required for the minister's salary was fixed in rate and assessed by the assembly; the part needed for the general expenses was fixed by the parish.  The whole tithe had to be collected and spent locally by the vestry.  The following statistics enumerate the levies of Christ Church Parish, Virginia: [6]

---

[6] Compiled from Christ Church Parish, Virginia, *Vestry Book* (1663–1767).

LEVIES IN CHRIST CHURCH PARISH, VIRGINIA

| Year | Number of Tithables | At Pounds of Tobacco per Poll | Total Number of Pounds |
|---|---|---|---|
| 1732 | 1,208 | 39 | 47,112 |
| 1742 | 1,330 | 27½ | 37,193 |
| 1752 | 1,336 | 28½ | 38,076 |
| 1762 | 1,442 | 21 | 30,282 |
| 1767 | 1,454 | 30 | 43,620 |

Seemingly all these local and general taxes would have made a system under which the total tax burden was necessarily heavy, but this was not the case. The rates of most of the taxes were relatively low. For example, in the decade immediately preceding the Revolution, when the population of Virginia was probably around 300,000, the poll tax yielded only from £1,000 to £5,000; the customs duties, from £6,000 to £9,000; and the quit.ents, from £4,000 to £5,000 per year. Likewise, the rates of the parish levy, as indicated by early vestry books, averaged only about 30 or 40 pounds of tobacco per tithable. Many of these taxes, moreover, and especially the quitrents, were widely evaded. To check this evasion, every revenue law enacted by the assembly carried with it a penalty for violation, and often threats were made to publish the names of the sheriffs who were in arrears for taxes.

To handle the several revenues, the administrative organization in the eighteenth century, when the system was well established, included about twenty royal and about one hundred and fifty provincial officials, who may be classified as follows:

A. Officers in charge of customs duties:
   1. Royal collectors.
   2. Naval officers.
   3. Comptrollers of the customs.
   4. Surveyor-generals of the customs.
   5. Searchers.
   6. Collectors of the duty on liquors.
   7. Collectors of the duty on slaves.

    8. Collectors of the duty on skins and furs.
    9. Collectors of the duty on servants.
B. Central officers for entire revenue system:
    1. Auditor.
    2. Receiver-general.
    3. Treasurer.
C. Local revenue officers:
    1. Sheriffs.

Those of the royal officers who were connected with the customs duties formed, not only in Virginia, but in nearly all the colonies, a kind of system of search and espionage, both to collect customs and to prevent fraud among themselves. In fact, they were England's especially delegated agents to enforce her policy of colonial control. After 1691, the treasurer functioned no longer as a royal official but as an appointee of the assembly. Out of the treasurer's office evolved the separate office of auditor, which was first authorized by an act of the Virginia Assembly in 1664. In 1705, on account of the growing suspicion of fraud, a receiver-general's office was established, by royal appointment, to share the auditor's duties. Finally, in every county a sheriff was maintained whose chief function was to collect taxes. Usually, however, he was one of the planters appointed to this office by the governor and the council. As a tax official, he was "his Majesty's immediate officer in the county to collect all quit-rents, escheats and deodands." [7] After 1660, he was also the sole collector of all local taxes. Prior to that time, the church wardens themselves collected the parish tithes. Thereafter, for convenience, the sheriff usually collected the church tithes at the same time that he collected the county and public poll taxes.

---

[7] Cyrus H. Karraker, *Seventeenth-Century Sheriff*, p. 138. "From very early times it had been the custom in England for the sheriff to seize for the King, where the deodand belonged to the King, anything which had by accident caused the death of a person. The thing seized was then sold and given to charity, that is, to God."—*Ibid.*, p. 138.

The two systems, the one royal and the other colonial, were apparently administered together.  Not only did the sheriffs act as agents for both systems, but the central officers, the treasurer and the auditor, though appointed by the assembly, also functioned at the same time as agents of the British Government.

### Systems in Other Southern Colonies

The fiscal systems of the other Southern colonies resembled that of Virginia in a general way as to kinds of taxes and type of administrative machinery used; yet, that of each colony differed in emphasis placed upon certain taxes and in administrative details.

**Maryland.**  During the one hundred and forty-two years of proprietary government, revenues were derived largely from poll taxes, which were levied by "even and equal assessment" upon every poll, irrespective of ability or wealth, and which were usually paid in tobacco.  However, increasing public wants from time to time caused the rate to be raised and the scope extended to include more taxables.  In 1641, a "subsedye" was enacted which provided that every free person, male or female, should be taxed at the rate of 15 pounds of tobacco for every person over twelve years of age residing in his family, and, further, that every servant belonging to a non-resident should be thus taxed.  The next year, the expenses of the members of the General Assembly were levied upon the respective hundreds which they represented.  In 1650, every freeman was required to pay a poll tax of 4 pounds of tobacco and cask for the "muster master Gen'rall's ffee."  In 1662, a per capita tax of 25 pounds of tobacco was levied for the support of the lieutenant general; and in 1694, a tax of 40 pounds of tobacco was assessed upon each freeman for the support of the Anglican clergy.

Besides the poll tax, an export tax was imposed for the benefit of the Lord Proprietor, and subsequently, at short intervals, licenses, tobacco and tonnage duties, anchorage

taxes, and special fees were levied. Quitrents were imposed
by the most efficient system in the colonies. In 1642, the
rate was 2 shillings for every one hundred acres of land,
and in 1660, the rate was increased to 4 shillings. By 1774,
the Lord Proprietor was receiving annually over £8,000
from this source. Various forms of tangible property, such
as slaves, cattle, excess landholdings, and silver plate, also
came to be taxable—to be levied upon for a kind of supplementary poll tax—and in 1756, a crude sort of land tax was
imposed.[8]

The administration of these taxes differed from that of
the Virginia system in that the taxes were paid to the Lord
Proprietor, through his agents; during the eighteenth century, however, a few taxes were levied for the King of
England, despite the fact that he had expressly renounced
in the Maryland charter the right to tax this province.

**North Carolina.** The colonial government at first derived its revenue from quitrents and the sale of lands. As
time went on, both customs duties and poll taxes were
imposed, as in the other Southern colonies, though only
twice before the Revolution was a land tax levied. Of
these sources of revenue the most important was the poll
tax. In fact, whenever an extraordinary expenditure was
required or a redemption fund was to be provided for bills
of credit, the poll tax was immediately resorted to. According to Coralie Parker:[9] "The rate per poll ranged anywhere
from 3s. in 1740 to 16s. 4d. per taxable in 1760." After
1740, the tax was usually levied upon all white males over
eighteen years of age and upon all slaves over sixteen years
of age. This extensive use of the poll tax was not acci-

[8] In 1695, a small export duty on furs was substituted for a license tax
that had been imposed on fur traders since 1650. But neither of these
sources of revenue was important. Presumably, only skins of small animals were exported from Maryland, and the duty on these ranged from
4d. on beavers to ¾d. on raccoons. From 1695 to 1698, inclusive, the
duty on furs from the colony was only £154 4s. 9¾d. See: *Archives of
Maryland*, Vol. XIX, p. 276; and *Colonial Office Papers*, Vol. 5, p. 749.

[9] Coralie Parker, *History of Taxation in North Carolina During the
Colonial Period, 1663–1776*, p. 120.

dental; for it was generally held that such a tax on labor would fall on the chief source of wealth, since abundant land without labor was of little value. Customs duties were of only slight importance, because most of the North Carolina coast was inaccessible; nor was any emphasis placed upon a land tax, principally on account of the quitrents.

As in the other colonies, the administrative machinery in North Carolina included the local officers and a group of persons responsible to the proprietors or, as they were later on, to the Crown. The administration of the poll tax was relatively simple. The sheriff merely made a list of the taxables in his jurisdiction and sent it to the secretary of the colony, who then supervised the collection of the levy according to the list. Conversely, the quitrents were less easily collected. On several occasions the colonists objected to the rates, and among the early backwoodsmen the whole question of quitrents was constantly being agitated. At first, a receiver-general came annually to Edenton and Bathtown to collect the quitrents, but the taxables generally failed to meet him. Later, collectors were sent into each of the several districts. Despite all efforts, the system of quitrents was never an unqualified success under the proprietors and, when North Carolina became a royal province, was practically neglected as a source of revenue.[10] During the years 1745 to 1748, the receipts from quitrents rose as high as £400, but in other years, fell as low as £146. As a result, in 1752, the salary of Governor Gabriel Johnson, which was £1,000 a year and was to be paid out of the quitrents, was in arrears to the amount of more than £13,000.[11]

**South Carolina.** Revenues were derived from both direct and indirect taxation, fees, fines, licenses, and quitrents. During the first twelve years of the colony's life,

---

[10] Beverley W. Bond, *Quit-Rent System in the American Colonies,* p. 115 *et seq.*

[11] *North Carolina Colonial Records,* Vol. 19, p. 77.

no taxes at all were imposed; in 1682, however, steps were taken to levy a "tax of £400 for defraying the public charges of the province." Thereafter, as the need for revenue increased, various levies were made, until South Carolina came to have a fiscal system almost as comprehensive as that of colonial Virginia.

Although the records do not indicate how the first levy was raised, it appears that customs duties were the earliest form of taxation in the colony. In 1691, the colonial government passed an act imposing a small export duty on deer, beaver, otter, fox, bear, and raccoon skins, which at that time were the chief exports. As early as 1695, an import duty was laid upon liquors, tobacco, and provisions; but, in so far as the preserved records show, the earliest general customs duty law was that of 1703. This law provided an extensive tariff schedule. Specific duties were imposed on ale, beer, brandy, cider, wine, biscuit bread, flour, molasses, sugar, salt fish, cocoanuts, logwood, and several other articles. An ad valorem duty was imposed on all articles not enumerated, except salt. A duty of 10 shillings a head was imposed on negro slaves imported directly from Africa, and 20 shillings on those brought from the other colonies. However, the duty on slaves was for a sumptuary rather than a fiscal purpose, because the colony was having entirely too large an influx of negroes. In 1717, the ad valorem duties under this act were raised to 10 per cent, and the specific also were raised on most articles.

Ordinarily these duties amounted to about £4,500 annually, or about £1,000 in excess of public expenditures. These expenditures were as follows: [12]

PUBLIC EXPENDITURES IN SOUTH CAROLINA, 1720

| | |
|---|---|
| For stipends to 10 ministers of the Church of England... | £1,000 |
| For finishing and preparing fortifications.............. | 1,000 |
| For officers and soldiers doing duty in forts........... | 600 |
| To the governor...................................... | 250 |
| For military stores................................... | 300 |
| For accidental charges............................... | 400 |

[12] Compiled from *Carroll's Col.*, Vol. II, p. 259.

After the first quarter of the eighteenth century, Governor Glen reported that in the colony there were no taxes upon either real or personal property, and that the public revenues were all raised by the customs duties just described. Of these sources of revenue the most important was the export duty on furs and deerskins. In the Southern colonies Charleston was the center of the fur trade. By 1730, more than 80,000 deerskins were annually exported from that port; and a decade later, when Augusta had become the western entrepot for the fur trade with the Indians, over £20,000 worth of furs were sent annually from there to Charleston. The following table shows the exports of deerskins from Charleston and the duties collected on them from 1731 to 1736: [13]

DEERSKIN TRADE AT CHARLESTON, 1731-1736

| Date | Deerskins (Number) | Duties (Currency) | | |
|---|---|---|---|---|
| | | £. | s. | d. |
| March 25, 1731 to March 25, 1732........ | 86,771 | 2,169 | 5 | 9 |
| March 25, 1732 to March 25, 1733........ | 74,483 | 1,862 | 1 | 9 |
| March 25, 1733 to March 25, 1734........ | 96,523 | 2,413 | 1 | 6 |
| March 25, 1734 to March 25, 1735........ | 84,958 | 2,123 | 19 | 0 |
| March 25, 1735 to March 25, 1736........ | 81,017 | 2,025 | 8 | 9 |

Customs duties soon became inadequate to provide funds for the retirement of the continually increasing issues of bills of credit. Hence, in 1739, a tax of 10 shillings per head was levied on all negroes and other slaves within the colony, and a tax of 10 shillings for every one hundred acres of all land except that appropriated for churches and public use. Again, in 1758, another act was passed which not only increased the rates on slaves and land but also imposed a poll tax on all free negroes, and introduced a crude form of income tax levied on the profits of county storekeepers and the incomes of physicians and surgeons. Even annuities and money loaned out at interest were

---

[13] Compiled from Verner W. Crane, *Southern Frontier, 1670-1732*, Appendix A.

taxed.  Finally, in 1760, this levy was extended to all trades and professions, except that of the clergy, and, in addition, a tax was imposed upon the value of lots, wharves, and buildings in towns, villages, and boroughs.  Before long, these direct taxes were relatively more important than all the others.  In 1746, which was an average year, the yield from this source as compared with the other sources is clearly indicated below: [14]

SOUTH CAROLINA REVENUE RECEIPTS, 1746

| | |
|---|---:|
| Direct taxes | £52,827 |
| Duties | 23,848 |
| Liquor licenses | 2,661 |
| Fines and forfeitures | 287 |
| Quitrents | 7,000 |
| TOTAL | £86,623 |

As in Virginia, these levies were administered by a system of local and royal officers, functioning separately or as an organized group.

**Georgia.**  While under the control of the trustees, Georgia was saved from bankruptcy mainly by General Oglethorpe, who drew upon his private fortune to meet the general expenses of the colony.  After the charter was surrendered to the Crown, public officers of the colony had to be paid from public revenues.  Various taxes were imposed, such as quitrents; an impost duty on rum; and a tax on houses, lands, negroes, and money at interest.  Of these the quitrents were the most important.  The rate was fixed at 4 shillings for every one hundred acres of land.  In 1773, when the annual expenses were between £3,000 and £4,000, the quitrents were the source of the greater part of the colony's income.  The fiscal system of colonial Georgia was in no significant respect different from that of the other Southern colonies, except that the revenue receipts were mainly from quitrents.

---

[14] Compiled from *Statutes* III; *Com. House Journal Ms.* XXV, XXII; and *Public Records Ms.* XX.

The chief sources of revenue in the Southern colonies were poll taxes and indirect taxes, especially export duties. Property taxes were not extensively used, because as a rule the lawmakers themselves had large landholdings and numerous slaves. Quitrents, though in common use, were a mere carry-over from British fiscal history and, with few exceptions, were of no great importance. The fiscal systems of the Southern colonies consisted mainly of tax measures that were evolved empirically to meet the most essential public needs.

### Bibliographical Note

No complete financial history of the Southern colonies exists. For brief treatments of money and credit, see: Henry Phillips, Jr., *Historical Sketches of the Paper Currency of the American Colonies Prior to the Adoption of the Federal Constitution,* First Series (Roxbury, Mass., 1865); "The Spanish Dollar and the Colonial Shilling," *American Historical Review,* July 1898. On the medium of exchange in Virginia, see P. A. Bruce, *Economic History of Virginia in the Seventeenth Century,* two volumes (New York, 1907), especially Volume II, Chapter XIX. For a satisfactory treatment of bills of exchange in colonial Virginia, see George T. Starnes, *Sixty Years of Branch Banking in Virginia* (New York, 1931), Chapter I. In the JOHNS HOPKINS UNIVERSITY STUDIES IN HISTORICAL AND POLITICAL SCIENCE there are two volumes which deal with the subject of money and credit in Maryland: C. P. Gould, *Money and Transportation in Maryland, 1720–1765* (Baltimore, 1915); and Kathryn L. Behren's *Paper Currency in Maryland, 1727–1789* (Baltimore, 1923). For an excellent discussion of the currency situation in Maryland, see "Trade and Industry in Colonial Maryland," *Journal of Economic and Business History,* May 1932, Volume IV, pages 512–538.

William Z. Ripley, *Financial History of Virginia, 1609–1776* (New York, 1893), is the pioneer study of Virginia's early fiscal system, but this study, on account of the recent availability of much additional documentary material, needs revision. Of some value, also, is Percy Scott Flippin, *Financial Administration of the Colony of Virginia* (Baltimore, 1915). Lewis Mayer,

*Ground Rents in Maryland* (Baltimore, 1883), contains a brief discussion of colonial taxes. Some notes on taxes and customs duties can be found in M. S. Moriss, *Colonial Trade of Maryland, 1689–1715* (Baltimore, 1914). The only satisfactory treatment of the fiscal system in colonial North Carolina is Coralie Parker, *History of Taxation in North Carolina During the Colonial Period, 1663–1776* (New York, 1928). Chapter VI of W. Roy Smith's *South Carolina as a Royal Province 1719–1776* (New York, 1903) is a brilliant summary of the financial history of that colony. Practically nothing has been written on the early fiscal system of Georgia; brief reference is made to the early period in E. M. Banks, *Economics of Land Tenure in Georgia* (New York, 1905). Beverley W. Bond, Jr., *Quit-Rent System in the American Colonies* (New Haven, Conn., 1919), is the only authoritative treatment of that subject. To be mentioned also in this connection is *Studies in State Taxation* (Baltimore, 1900), edited by J. H. Hollander. This is a volume in the JOHNS HOPKINS UNIVERSITY STUDIES IN HISTORICAL AND POLITICAL SCIENCE; Parts I, II, and V, respectively, contain short sketches of the colonial fiscal systems of Maryland, North Carolina, and Georgia.

# CHAPTER VII

# The Revolutionary War

THE American Revolution was not an accidental breach between England and her adolescent colonies. In a large measure it was the culmination of economic causes that began far back in colonial history.

From the beginning the colonies evolved slowly toward self-government. Removed from England by three thousand miles of tossing sea, the early settlers felt somewhat secure from the royal will. Their environment tended to make them self-reliant, and countless regulations of English society became burdensome and useless in the forests of the New World. Along the westward-moving frontier, settlements were established that were practically out of touch with the older communities. Hence, as new generations grew up—of those inhabitants who had never seen England—it was inevitable that they, accustomed to the freedom of the forest, should exhibit a frame of mind different from that of their kinsmen across the sea. It was a new spirit born of a new world.

Until 1763, England in reality had followed a policy of "salutary neglect" in governing her American colonies. From time to time she had enacted laws governing colonial trade and industry. In fact, within the interval from the adoption, under Cromwell, of the Navigation Acts in 1651 to the Stamp Act of 1765, England enacted a series of trade regulations sufficient to satisfy the most ardent mercantilist. In 1672, an act had been passed requiring certain enumerated articles to be sent to England, and all imports to America to be shipped via England. Thus British merchants were to be assured of the right to handle the colonial trade, and England was to be made an entrepot for the benefit of the British. In 1699, a statute had been enacted prohibiting the export of wool or wool cloth from the colonies. In 1719, a statute prohibited in the colonies the production of iron in practically every form. In 1732, an act forbade the export of hats from the colonies. In 1750, a statute prohibited the erection of iron furnaces in the colonies. These acts, in general, however, either were not enforced or were evaded. Until after 1765, England had no administrative machinery for their effective enforcement.[1]

During more than fifty years after the settlement of Jamestown, there was no permanent British governing body to supervise the colonies. Throughout the seventeenth century, a continual struggle existed between the Crown and Parliament; each tended to counteract the efforts of the other in governing the colonies. For nearly two decades after 1667, Dutch wars, Popish plots, and fear of the French prevented England almost completely from enforcing her colonial policy. Although, in 1696, the Board of Trade was instituted for the purpose of supervising the colonies, this body had no executive power and devoted itself entirely to making recommendations and to hearing complaints. Above the Board of Trade and aside from the Privy Council, which served as a kind of court of appeals, was the Secretary of State for the Southern Department. From 1724 to 1748, the occupant of this office was the Duke of Newcastle, whose chief characteristics as an administrator were timidity and procrastination. England sent governors to her royal colonies and appointed councillors who were expected to uphold her laws, but in several instances the colonial assemblies succeeded in shearing these royal officers of their authority.

The acts governing colonial industry and trade were also made less effective by smuggling, which, according to some

[1] See "England's Colonial System," in Chapter II, page 54 of this text.

authorities, was carried on systematically by many of the colonists. The colonial governments sometimes condoned the violation of the restrictive laws. Virginia, in 1660, went so far as to issue an invitation for all countries to trade with her. At a later date a member of the British Board of Trade urged that a law be enacted to the effect that persons committing the same offense twice should be tried in England, because the juries in the colonies would not find guilty any countryman of theirs.

England herself, through the enactment of measures advantageous to the colonies, did much to ameliorate the effect of her restrictive laws. By a preferential system of customs duties, she gave the colonies much lower rates on some domestic commodities—such as, tobacco, indigo, and potash—than on foreign commodities. By means of bounties and other financial inducements, she also encouraged the colonists to engage in the production of certain commodities, as for example, naval stores. Added to these advantages was the protection from rival nations that was afforded the colonies by the British Army and Navy.

After the Treaty of Paris in 1763, which closed the French and Indian War and eliminated France as a colonial rival, England undertook the reorganization of her whole colonial empire.

## The Trans-Allegheny

One of the first problems presented was the control of the Trans-Allegheny territory. Under the old regime, the Indians, exploited by fur traders and land-grabbers and influenced by the French, had turned in savage attacks upon the colonists. Hence, to secure future peaceful relations with the Indian tribes, it was proposed that the home government should establish one central system of Indian administration and should regulate the fur trade. It was proposed, also, that the power of granting western lands be taken out of the hands of colonial governors, in order to prevent squabbles over conflicting land titles and espe-

cially over the vague territorial limits set out in some of
the early colonial charters. To carry out these proposals,
the Proclamation of 1763 "reserved to the Indians," at
least "for the present," all the territory between the crest
of the Allegheny Mountains on the east and the Mississippi
on the west, and from "the new province of Florida on the
south" to 50 degrees north latitude. Colonial governors
were ordered to grant no warrants of survey and to pass
no patents for any lands in that region; those inhabitants
who had inadvertently settled there were required to move;
and every person who desired to carry on trade with the
Indians was required to give bond for observing such rules
as the British Government might at any time establish
"for the benefit of the said trade."

To many of the colonists the Proclamation of 1763 came
like a thunder clap. Because they did not understand its
real purposes, it was to them nothing less than an arbitrary
barrier to their natural expansion westward.

For more than a decade before this proclamation, Virginia had made vigorous efforts to promote western settlements. All settlers "on the waters of the Mississippi" and
in Augusta County, which stretched to the "utmost limits
of Virginia," had been exempted for fifteen years from
paying all public, county, and parish levies. Between 1743
and 1760, Virginia had granted more than 3,000,000 acres
of land in that region. Among the grantees were many
men prominent in Virginia or in adjoining colonies. There
were also great land companies. The Loyal Land Company had received 800,000 acres; the Greenbrier Company,
100,000; and the Ohio Company, 500,000 acres. George
Washington had 20,000 acres near the mouth of the Great
Kanawha. All of these landholders voiced in no uncertain
terms their opposition to the British measure. Washington, Walker, Lewis, Nelson, and other Virginians even
decided to treat the proclamation as a "scrap of paper."

In February 1774, further instructions to royal governors
ordered that land in the unoccupied portions of the prov-

inces should be surveyed, and lots of not less than one hundred and not more than one thousand acres should be sold at auction, at a minimum price of 6 pence per acre, with an annual quitrent of one-half pence sterling per acre. These instructions were met with bitter protests. In the spring of 1774, Thomas Jefferson, being unable to attend the Virginia Assembly, wrote to that body: he considered as "fictitious" the doctrine that all lands originally belonged to the King. Even the governors of Virginia, North Carolina, South Carolina, and Georgia reported adversely upon these instructions. Finally, in 1774, when it appeared that the rich lands of the Kentucky and Ohio regions might be granted to a British company sponsored by George Grenville, the British Prime Minister, the anger of colonial land speculators knew no bounds, and many men who had been loyal to the British Government became supporters of revolutionary doctrines.

### British Revenue Legislation

Another problem confronting England was that of raising revenue to meet the requirements for imperial defense. For more than fifty years the expenditures for protecting the colonies had continually increased. From 1708 to 1711, England had increased her debt by nearly £2,000,000, solely for naval protection for her colonies. In later years it had become necessary to maintain, along the frontiers of New York and North Carolina, outposts against the Indians and to spend large sums annually in an effort to keep the Indians pacified. According to Lord Sheffield, on account of the American colonies, Great Britain by 1739 had expended £31,000,000, and by 1755, £71,500,000. The Seven Years' War had cost England over £82,000,000 and had increased her debt to over £130,000,000, the largest war debt in English history up to that time. Moreover, the British Government was convinced that it would require a standing army of 10,000 men to protect her vast American territory. To maintain such an army, according to an official estimate of that time, would cost annually about £300,000. At the same time the British Navy would require annually about £1,500,000. To meet these requirements, the British Government turned to her American colonies, because the British landowners, even before the Seven Years' War, were already paying a tax which they thought excessive—6½ shillings per pound, or approximately 30 per cent of their income, not including tithes and poor rates; and because the colonists, prior to 1763, had not been called upon to pay anything like their share of the expenditures for defense.

The first act for the purpose of shifting part of the burden of defense to the colonies was the Sugar Act of 1764, which superseded the Molasses Act of 1733. This new act lowered the import duty on molasses and raised the duty on refined sugar; it also forbade the importation of rum and placed a discriminatory tax on Portuguese and Spanish coffees, wines, and various other articles and on French and Oriental textiles, unless imported via England. It further provided strict regulations governing the bonding and registration of shipmasters, and heavy penalties for the violation of the law.

In 1764, Parliament forbade the issue of bills of credit in the colonies, and thereby prevented the paper money abuses to which many colonists were subjected. Nevertheless, this act aroused resentment among both Northern debtors and hard-pressed planters of the South.

It had been the intention of the British Government, when the Sugar Act was passed, to require the colonies to pay to the Exchequer about £150,000 annually. The revenue from the Sugar Act, however, fell far short of that amount, and it became necessary to levy an additional tax. George Grenville proposed a direct tax in the form of "certain stamp duties," and asked the colonial governors to suggest any form of taxation that would be more acceptable. Failing to elicit any satisfactory reply, he presented the matter to Parliament; in February 1765, "a listless and half-empty House of Commons," and "a still more listless and empty House of Lords" passed the Stamp Act. This act provided that the colonists should place stamps, varying from a halfpenny to £10, on legal papers, such as licenses, deeds, mortgages, and writs; on commercial documents, such as contracts, inventories, and advertisements; and on pamphlets, newspapers, almanacs, playing cards, and dice. It provided, in addition, that fines varying from £5 to £50 should be imposed on those neglecting to use the proper stamp; that those who sold almanacs and newspapers not duly stamped should forfeit 40 shillings; and that persons counterfeiting the stamps should be punished by death. This act, with its far-reaching taxes and harsh enforcement provisions, met with violent opposition in the colonies. Even English merchants and manufacturers, because of the alarming drop in the American demand for their goods—due to a colonial boycott—petitioned for its repeal. Consequently the British Government repealed the act in March 1766.

The next year, the British Government again tried to tighten the mercantilistic regulations and to raise revenue in America. Charles Townsend, Chancellor of the Exchequer, induced Parliament to pass three measures which are known as the *Townsend Acts*. The first of these provided for the strict enforcement of the British trade regulations by Commissioners appointed by the King and paid out of the British Treasury; the second imposed duties on glass, lead, painters' colors, paper, and tea imported into the colonies; and the third suspended the New York Assembly. These acts proved to be even more unpopular than the notorious Stamp Act, and out of the widespread opposition there developed within a few months an elaborate system of commercial boycott, which caused great losses to British merchants. As in the case of the Stamp Act, British merchants and manufacturers petitioned for the repeal of the Townsend Acts. Yielding to this request, Parliament, in 1770, repealed all of the Townsend duties, except the tax of 3 pence per pound on tea.

For three years after the partial repeal of the Townsend Acts, there were practically no political disturbances in the colonies. Then, in 1773, the British Government, in order to rescue the East India Company from threatened bankruptcy, passed the Tea Act, which was designed to grant to that company a virtual monopoly of the sale of tea in the American colonies. The news of the passage of this act spread consternation among colonial business men. Not only would it mean the loss of a lucrative business, but they feared also that similar monopolies would be granted to British merchants for the sale of other colonial imports. Moderate counsels no longer availed to keep order.

In Boston, men disguised as Indians boarded some vessels of the East India Company, and emptied £18,000 worth of tea into the harbor. At Annapolis, a tea ship, the *Peggy Stewart*, was burned. In New York, "The Association of the Sons of Liberty" declared a boycott against all persons attempting to bring tea into port. In Philadelphia, eight thousand colonists ordered Captain Ayers to return a cargo of tea to England, and he obeyed. In Charleston, tea was unloaded from a vessel of the East India Company by planters, and placed in warehouses belonging to the colony; three years later, the tea was sold at auction for the benefit of the American colonies.

In England, Parliament proceeded to pass punitive measures known as the *Intolerable Acts*. The port of Boston was closed to foreign commerce; the Massachusetts charter of 1691 was revoked and town meetings without the sanction of the governor were prohibited; persons accused of murder in resisting the enforcement of British laws were to be sent to England for trial; British troops were to be quartered in the towns of Massachusetts; and the boundaries of Quebec were to be extended to the Ohio River.[2] With these acts, England definitely entered upon a policy of coercing her colonies; but the immediate effect of the Intolerable Acts was to cause other colonies to rally to the support of Massachusetts. Finally, in 1775, when Parliament, by means of the Prohibitory Act, put a commercial ban on all of her American colonies, the *impasse* was complete—the only way out was war.

The colonies might not have drifted so rapidly toward the Revolution had England undertaken to impose new revenue measures on them during a period of prosperity. During the decade preceding the Revolution, there occurred a severe economic depression in England, due, perhaps, mainly to the necessary readjustments incidental to the industrial and the agrarian revolutions. This depression affected exports from American colonies to the extent that prices declined on almost all products, and especially on Southern staples. At the same time the cost of producing tobacco was beginning to increase; for the wasteful method of continuously growing that crop upon the same land without rotation or fertilizers had exhausted the fertility of the best land, and poorer, or marginal, land had to be brought into cultivation, at a proportionately smaller yield per unit of capital and labor. In the face of this depression in the South, any increase in taxes or new restrictions on trade affected the colonists more severely than might have been the case in more prosperous times when the world market could have taken the exports at profitable prices.

## Southern Radicalism

It must not be supposed, however, that every colonist was an enthusiastic patriot for American independence. Certainly at the beginning, the Revolution was a minority war, and even after three years, many colonists favored

---

[2] The Quebec Act was really not one of the Intolerable Acts, although it was passed at the same time.

union with the British Government upon "Constitutional principles," rather than independence. The Southern colonies, from the viewpoint of British loyalism, were divided into three classes: backcountry and frontier settlers, many of whom despised Britain; large planters and other colonists in the Tidewater region, who, for specific reasons, determined to escape from British control; and loyalists, who refused to support the American cause.

Many of the backcountry and frontier settlers were radicals. In comparison with the great landholders, they owned relatively little property, yet they bore practically an equal burden of taxation. In Virginia, on account of the system of the apportionment of only two burgesses to each county regardless of size or population, the planters in the Tidewater section, which was comprised of the smallest counties, enjoyed a decided political advantage over the small farmers in the backcountry. In North Carolina, the population of the backcountry had suffered not only from heavy taxes, quitrents, and illegal fees, but also from corrupt sheriffs, court officials, and tax collectors. During 1766 and 1768, meetings to remedy the situation were held in what is now the north central part of the state. At the first meeting, the members formed an association and pledged themselves to correct these practices. In 1768, four thousand of these *Regulators,* as they called themselves, assembled in a meeting to demand adjustment of their taxes. Practically no relief was obtained from the British Government, and in 1771, the movement culminated in the Regulators' Rebellion, which was crushed in the Battle of the Alamance by the militia under Governor William Tryon. In South Carolina, similar protests reached a crisis in 1769, but there was no bloodshed. In these circumstances, when the opportunity came, many of the backcountry and frontier settlers in the Southern colonies supported the Revolution, in the hope that they could destroy the economic and political control not only of Britain but also of the conservative colonial planters.

However, in Georgia, the frontier settlers were pro-British in their sympathies, because they depended largely upon the home government for protection against the Creek Indians.

There were several large planters and other more or less prominent colonists who had specific reasons for supporting the Revolution. In the first place, the ire of some colonial planters and speculators, who had acquired or were eager to acquire land beyond the Alleghenies, was aroused by the British Proclamation of 1763, which, temporarily at least, forbade colonial governors from making grants of land in that region. Again, several of the Tidewater planters were heavily, or even hopelessly, in debt to British merchants. In 1736, Colonel Byrd, of Virginia, was "selling off land and negroes to stay the stomach" of his hungry British creditors. According to Thomas Jefferson, Virginia planters owed no less than £2,000,000, and "these debts had become hereditary from father to son, for many generations, so that the planters were a species of property annexed to certain mercantile houses in London." Jefferson himself owed Jones & Farrell, of London, and Kippen & Company, of Glasgow, about £10,000. As additional evidence of the colonists' debts, the British merchants, in 1791, submitted a statement to the English Government, showing the debts due them from Americans in 1775. This statement indicated that the total, inclusive of both principal and accrued interest, amounted to £4,930,656, of which £4,137,944 was due from the Southern colonies. Virginians alone owed £2,305,408. To relieve these debtors, Thomas Jefferson and Patrick Henry in an extralegal meeting of the Virginia Assembly proposed that all payments on British debts be stopped. During the Revolution, five hundred Virginians seized the opportunity to pay their debts to British merchants in depreciated currency. Colonial expenditures were generally met from colonial taxes; the balance left amounted to several thousand pounds, but it could not be used by the colonial governments since it had to be paid into the British Treasury. Colonial assemblies, as the depression deepened and taxes became still more burdensome, naturally opposed such an unsound fiscal policy.

In the loyalist group were some rich merchants; some professional men, such as lawyers and college authorities; nearly all of the royal officers; many of the Anglican clergymen; several *nouveaux riches,* who tried to ape the British aristocracy; and those persons who were economically dependent upon well-to-do loyalists. In Virginia, loyalism predominated in two sections: at Norfolk, in the southeast; and at Fort Pitt, in the northwest. Many residents of Norfolk were Scottish merchants who, as agents and factors for British houses, had nothing in common with colonial radicals. At Fort Pitt, a frontier trading post, loyalism was kept alive by Dr. John Connolly, whom Governor Dunmore had placed in charge of the fort. In South Carolina, loyalists comprised almost half of the population and were especially numerous in Charleston. In each of the other Southern colonies, however, they were a minority group.

As in every modern war, propaganda was used to arouse feeling: orators harangued meetings of the colonists and urged action in the defense of human liberty; stories were told of atrocities committed by Hessians, the German mercenary troops of the British Army; and fancy painted dark pictures of oppressed and martyred citizens, if the cause should fail. Hence, toward the close of the Revolution, there came to be a far greater solidarity of opinion against Britain than there was in 1776.

## Financial Effects of the Revolutionary War

When the colonies united to carry on war against Britain, the first problem was to provide the necessary resources. The Continental Congress, which was an emergency body, had no revenue, and the colonies were unwilling to be taxed by the Congress. Even if the entire supply of specie in the colonies could have been made available for the war, the amount would not have been more than $6,000,000 to $30,000,000. The Continental Congress had to resort to other sources in order to secure the necessary revenue, and used as methods the issuing of bills of credit, the making of requisitions upon the states, and borrowing.

Within a week after the Battle of Bunker Hill, Congress authorized the issue of $2,000,000 in bills of credit (or paper money). Thereafter, increasing amounts were issued in rapid succession until, by the end of the year 1779, there had been authorized no less than forty issues, totaling $241,552,780. These were as follows: [3]

ISSUES OF PAPER MONEY AUTHORIZED BY CONGRESS, 1775–1779

| Year | Number of Resolutions Authorizing Issues | Amounts |
|------|:---:|---:|
| 1775 | 3 | $   6,000,000 |
| 1776 | 4 | 19,000,000 |
| 1777 | 5 | 13,000,000 |
| 1778 | 14 | 63,500,300 |
| 1779 | 14 | 140,052,480 |
| TOTAL | 40 | $241,552,780 |

The bills of credit were distributed among the separate colonies approximately in proportion to population, including negroes. Moreover, it was understood that each colony was to provide for the sinking of its portion of the bills by levying a sufficient amount of taxes, which could be paid by the individual taxpayers to the state either with these bills or with specie. In turn, the states, having received the bills for taxes, were to pass them on in payment of taxes to be laid upon the states by Congress. Because Congress had no power of taxation, this arrangement practically placed the obligation of redemption upon the several states, until such time as a responsible national government

---

[3] Compiled from Davis Rich Dewey, *Financial History of the United States,* p. 36.

could be organized. Then, since the states failed to support their credit and since the paper money was issued far in excess of the current need for a medium of exchange, depreciation increased from year to year, and the prices of all commodities and services rose correspondingly. At one time Washington declared that "a wagon load of money will scarcely purchase a wagon load of provisions." Price conventions were called to fix prices of goods in terms of paper money, but the value of this currency continued to fall. In 1780, Congress provided for the redemption of the outstanding Continental currency at the rate of 40 to 1 in "new tenor" bills, which were to be issued by the states and indorsed by the United States. These new bills depreciated to such an extent that the "old tenor" bills in the South were worth only about 1,000 to 1 in specie. In a short time most of the Continental currency had disappeared from circulation. Finally, in 1790, the United States Treasury redeemed $6,000,000 of the remaining amount outstanding at the rate of one cent on the dollar. The balance of the Continental currency was probably lost or destroyed.

The next method of raising money was by requisitions. From November 1777 to October 1779, Congress made four requisitions upon the states for a total of $95,000,000 in paper money, but received only $54,667,000. From August 1780 to March 1781, Congress made three requisitions for a total of $10,642,988 in specie, but received only $1,592,-222. In short, according to Professor C. J. Bullock, the net revenue obtained from all requisitions in specie and translated into specie value amounted to only $5,795,000.[4]

In 1779, Congress resorted even to requisitioning commodities: the states were asked to furnish such supplies as beef, pork, corn, flour, and hay. Virginia, for example, was requested to contribute 20,000 bushels of corn. In 1780, Congress made a general call for supplies, each state being

---

[4] C. J. Bullock, *Finances of the United States, 1775–1789*, p. 123 *et seq.*

left free to furnish what it could. In return for such supplies the Army quartermasters were ordered to issue certificates. It has been estimated that the states received
for requisitioned commodities certificates which, if reduced
to a specie value, would have been equivalent to $16,-
708,000.

Although there were never made out full and correct
statements of what each state paid and failed to pay Congress, yet, from the Treasury report of May 4, 1790, it
appears that during the years 1779 to 1781, inclusive, the
payments of three Southern States, in valid drafts upon
their treasuries, were received by Congress as follows:
Maryland, $116,000; Virginia, $278,000; and North Carolina, $73,000. From the beginning of the Revolution to
1790, according to Alexander Hamilton, Congress received
from and paid to Southern States the following amounts,
"reduced to specie value:" [5]

### PAYMENTS BETWEEN CONGRESS AND SOUTHERN STATES, 1775–1790

| State | Paid to State | Received from State |
|---|---|---|
| Maryland | $  609,617 | $  945,537 |
| Virginia | 482,881 | 1,963,811 |
| North Carolina | 988,031 | 219,835 |
| South Carolina | 1,014,808 | 499,325 |
| Georgia | 679,412 | 122,744 |

The South, especially toward the end of the war, contributed heavily in provisions, the value of which is not included in Hamilton's estimates.

During the Revolution, Congress secured some funds by
means of loans, both domestic and foreign. In each state,
loan offices were set up to dispose of *indented certificates,*
which, being in denominations from $300 to $1,000 and
bearing interest ranging from 4 to 6 per cent, were some-

---

[5] Data compiled from U. S. Treasury, *Report* (May 4, 1790). Hamilton admitted that his report did not show the "actual specie value,"
because he could not ascertain it in every instance.

what similar to coupon bonds. Between $60,000,000 and $70,000,000 worth of these certificates were sold; if evaluated in specie, they would have amounted to about $7,500,000. Besides such certificates, there were miscellaneous issues, by quartermasters and other Army officers, which have to be included in the total expenses of the war. Alexander Hamilton reported that these obligations, outstanding in 1790, amounted to $16,708,000. Furthermore, in 1782 and 1783, $1,272,842 in short-time loans was secured from the Bank of North America. Foreign loans obtained during the Revolution were as follows: [6]

FOREIGN LOANS, 1777–1783

| Year | France | Spain | Holland |
|------|--------|-------|---------|
| 1777 | $ 181,500 | | |
| 1778 | 544,500 | | |
| 1779 | 181,500 | | |
| 1780 | 726,000 | | |
| 1781 | 1,737,763 | $128,804 | |
| 1782 | 1,892,237 | 45,213 | $720,000 |
| 1783 | 1,089,000 | | 584,000 |
| TOTAL | $6,352,500 | $174,017 | $1,304,000 |

In addition to all these funds—consisting mainly of paper money—raised by the Continental Congress, practically every one of the states issued paper money on its own account, although some states already had outstanding obligations. The amount of paper money thus issued by the states between 1775 and 1783 was $209,524,776, or an amount which, according to Professor Laurence Laughlin, "nearly doubled the outstanding bills of credit burdening the same community." [7]

The paper money issues in Southern States were as follows: [8]

---

[6] Davis Rich Dewey, *Financial History of the United States* (1895), p. 46. Reprinted by permission of Longmans, Green & Co., New York.

[7] J. Laurence Laughlin, *Money, Credit and Prices,* Vol. II, p. 152.

[8] Compiled from J. W. Shuckers' *Brief Account of the Finances and Paper Money of the Revolutionary War,* p. 127.

PAPER MONEY ISSUES IN SOUTHERN STATES, 1775–1783

| Year | Maryland | Virginia | North Carolina | South Carolina |
|------|----------|----------|----------------|----------------|
| 1775 | $535,000 | $ 875,000 | | |
| 1776 | 415,000 | 1,500,000 | | |
| 1777 | | 2,700,000 | | |
| 1778 | | 2,700,000 | $ 2,125,000 | |
| 1779 | | | 2,500,000 | $1,250,000 |
| 1780 | | 30,666,000 | 3,600,000 | |
| 1781 | | 87,500,000 | 26,250,000 | |
| 1783 | | | 100,000 | |
| TOTALS | $950,000 | $125,941,000 | $34,575,000 | $1,250,000 |

GRAND TOTAL: $162,716,000

Of the paper currency issued by the several states during the Revolution, these Southern States issued over 92 per cent—Virginia alone, over 60 per cent.

To carry on the war, both Congress and the several states in a blundering way issued bills of credit, which did not rest, for redemption, upon a sound basis of taxation. The result was that paper money depreciated in value; this change tended to drive out specie and, in turn, still further depreciated paper money until, by the end of the war, the country was on the verge of bankruptcy.

All of these points must be considered in the general background for the fiscal problems of the Southern colonies during this period. Until after the Revolution the Confederation was simply a temporary makeshift to unify the colonies against England.

## VIRGINIA

As the royal government in Virginia disintegrated during the years 1774 to 1776, the colonial treasury rapidly became exhausted. The supply of £15,000 or £20,000 in gold and silver reserves moved to Europe to settle trade balances, and the entire amount of £54,391 of paper currency then outstanding became irredeemable. To meet this situation, the Revolutionary government, while it was still in the incipient stage, had to rely upon voluntary subscriptions, raised either by county committees or by the delegates to the general conventions. Patriotic feeling was sufficiently widespread that, in July 1775, the Virginia Convention, though without legal right, actually levied taxes and appointed fiscal officers and committees. The tax system developed during the colonial period was continued but modified to meet the new requirements. Loyal citizens replaced the officers of the Crown, and a few minor changes were made in the legal qualifications for officeholders. As in colonial days, the treasurer, the auditor, and the sheriffs continued to be the most important officers.

As the war progressed, the tax scheme was broadened to tap every available source of revenue. Thus, Virginia had simultaneously: specific taxes, poll taxes, licenses, customs duties, and miscellaneous taxes of several kinds, for during this period not only land and vehicles were specifically taxed but also cattle, horses, and slaves. In 1781, a levy of 6 shillings per head was imposed upon "neat cattle"; in 1782, there were levies of 3 pence for "cattle of all ages," and 2 shillings for every horse, mare, and colt. Five years later, the tax on cattle was repealed. Slaves were taxed specifically, because it was generally held, in accordance with a curious statute of 1705, that they were a "kind of real estate." Thus, in 1779, the assembly levied against every owner for each of his slaves a tax of £5, which was reduced later to 10 shillings per slave. It appears, however, that throughout the period considerable importance was attached to the slave tax, because it fell almost wholly upon the large planters.

When the Revolution began, the poll tax was still important; by 1779, the rate had been raised to £3. Later this tax became less and less important, and the emphasis shifted to a land tax. In 1777, for the first time in the history of Virginia, an ad valorem tax was laid, though only temporarily, upon property.

License taxes were not used extensively by the new government. Besides marriage licenses and licenses upon attorneys, physicians, apothecaries, and surgeons, a tax of 10 shillings was imposed upon each £100 of a merchant's stock in trade. The assembly continued to rely upon customs duties, though the war seriously disrupted the foreign trade of Virginia, and several additional miscellaneous taxes had to be levied to meet urgent needs as the war progressed.

### ADDITIONAL TAXES LEVIED BY VIRGINIA ASSEMBLY DURING THE REVOLUTION

| Year | Tax | Basis | Rate |
|---|---|---|---|
| 1777 | Income | Amount of all salaries and of "neat income" of all officers. | 10 shillings of every £100 |
| 1780 | Income | Annual profits of "all publick officers" not fixed by certain salaries. | 1 shilling of each £1 |
| 1777 | Liquor | All spiritus liquors distilled within the commonwealth. | 6 pence per gallon |
| 1780 | Liquor | Brandy. | 10 shillings per gallon |
| 1777 | Legal Process | Original subpoena writ. | 5 shillings each |
| 1788 | Legal Process | Final judgments in district courts, deeds, wills. | 6 shillings each |
| 1779 | Money | Monies which any person possesses. | 30 shillings of every £100 |
| 1780 | Money | Monies which any person possesses. | 15 shillings of every £100 |
| 1780 | Mortgages | Mortgages. | 20 shillings on each mortgage |
| 1781 | Tobacco | Collected, for inspection fee, by inspectors from owners of tobacco. | 5 shillings per hogshead |
| 1780 | Windows | Glass windows. | 1 shilling each |
| 1782 | Billard Tables | Every billard table. | £15 each |

It is interesting to note the disposition made of religious taxation and other religious legislative measures. During the colonial period such taxation, mainly for the purpose of paying clergymen's salaries, had been accepted as a legitimate function of government. Hence, it was natural, upon the formation of the new commonwealth, to propose that the assembly continue the levy on taxpayers. The unfavorable reaction to this proposal was immediate and became cumulative. From 1738, when Governor Gooch granted the privilege of worship to some Presbyterian ministers in the Shenandoah Valley, to the close of the Revolution, the Scotch-Irish Presbyterians in the back counties grew so rapidly in influence that they may be said to have gained toleration; they were indefatigable in their efforts to defeat such legislation. The Baptists, also, opposed the established church and the powers of the vestry. The struggle for religious liberty went on simultaneously with the fight for civil liberty. Public opinion, as expressed by petitions from nearly fifty counties, clearly disapproved such legislation, and gave official sanction to Jefferson's famous indictment in a letter to François Jean: [9] "This body [clergy] though shattered, is still formidable, still forms a *corps,* and is still actuated by the *esprit de corps.* The nature of that spirit has been severely felt by mankind and has filled the history of ten or twelve centuries with too many atrocities not to merit a proscription." This form of taxation was eventually discarded because it was incompatible with the American concept of freedom.

Theoretically, the administration of the tax system under the new commonwealth appears quite simple. The sheriffs, as the immediate tax officials of the state, were expected to apply the tax levies, to collect the revenues arising therefrom, and to forward the amount, less their commission, to the central officers of the state.[10] Practically, the arrangement did not work effectively for various reasons. After the taxes had actually been collected by the sheriffs, it was difficult to get the money into the state treasury. During these early days great risk was involved in conveying large sums of money long distances, where vast stretches of wooded country had to be traversed in order to reach Richmond. As a matter of record, robberies fre-

---

[9] Thomas Jefferson, *Correspondence* (edited by Ford), p. 14: Letter to François Jean, Marquis de Castellux, September 2, 1785.

[10] Sheriffs frequently received for their labor a commission which amounted to 50 per cent of the revenues collected.

quently occurred. Moreover, sheriffs and collectors sometimes deliberately avoided settlement with the state
treasury, as is evidenced by official notices printed in the
*Virginia Gazette* at that time, and fraud was also perpetrated on various occasions both by taxpayers and sheriffs.

The most flagrant practice was that which involved
collecting taxes and afterwards turning in the taxpayer's
name as delinquent.[11] Furthermore, there was a widespread
use of counterfeit money in payment of taxes.[12]

The worst difficulties encountered, however, arose from
the inflation of the currency—a situation which grew directly out of the policy adopted for financing the war.
The policy from the first placed main reliance for finances
upon the issue of paper money, with taxes pledged to redeem it.  As the need for funds increased, the issues
increased and more taxes were pledged; but by means of
this vicious spiral, the currency eventually became worthless.

In 1779, there was outstanding in the state of Virginia
£2,636,682 of paper money; in May 1780, this amount was
nearly doubled by an issue of £2,000,000.  Certain duties
and the window tax were pledged to redeem it.  Should
these taxes prove deficient, the old capitol buildings at
Williamsburg were to be sold.  In October of the same
year, the auditor, acting upon authority from the assembly,
issued £10,000,000; and in 1781, due to the distressing
needs arising from the British invasion, an additional
£36,125,000 was printed.  The effect was inevitable.  The
rate of exchange of paper money into specie rose by leaps
and bounds: in January, it was 75; in April, it was 100 to
1; by August, 700; and by December, 1000 to 1.  In July
1781, all this paper currency ceased to be legal tender and
the state would no longer accept it for taxes.  From October 1780 to October 1781, the total receipts of the state,

---

[11] *Calendar of Virginia State Papers*, Vol. VII, p. 127:  Letter of Wm. C.
Williams to the governor, 1784.
[12] *Ibid.*, p. 59.  See also *House Journal* (December 17, 1781), p. 43.

including the paper money emitted, were £60,823,216, but at the end of the year, the treasury had an actual deficit of £3,277,000.

Financial disaster seemed imminent. Prices rose to ridiculous heights. Horses were valued at from £3,000 to £4,000 each; cows, at £500; pigs, at £100; and negroes, at £10,000. Army officials complained that all public faith was gone and that provisions could not be bought for the Army at any price in paper money. In such circumstances taxes were of little avail.

"We find ourselves," declared Jefferson, "cheated in every essay by the depreciation intervening between the declaration of the tax and its actual receipt."

"There was no coin in the country," points out another authority,[13] "the circulating medium had only a nominal value, and nothing could be more arbitrary than the prices affixed in the interior to tobacco, hemp, flour, deerskins, and other commodities receivable in kind in the payment of taxes. An astute and unscrupulous sheriff or deputy sheriff, aided by an unprincipled pettyfogger and availing himself of the authority of law, could render the rich uncomfortable and reduce men of moderate means to beggary. Hence the enormous fortunes made by the sheriffs, some of which have descended to our times; and hence the terrible malediction upon sheriffs which was entered by Patrick Henry in the present Convention."

Realizing the worthlessness of these paper issues, the assembly set about to remedy the situation. The first step was to provide that all paper money, except the issues authorized in 1780 and turned in for taxes, should be burned. By October 1781, this money ceased to be legal tender, and tobacco was, as in earlier times, the medium of exchange. Consequently a plan was adopted whereby all paper money hitherto issued was to be funded. To avoid the difficulties that would naturally arise from such

---

[13] *Papers of Alexander White*, in VIRGINIA HISTORICAL SOCIETY COLLECTIONS, Vol. X, p. 73.

a procedure, the assembly reduced all taxes and made them payable in flour, hemp, deerskins, and specie.

After the war had ended in 1783, the assembly, by requiring the payment of all taxes in specie, again attempted to place the state upon a sound financial basis. Such payment was impossible on account of the condition of the country. Nor was there, before 1790, anything like a systematic collection of taxes in the state.

## OTHER SOUTHERN STATES

**Maryland.** During the Revolution, Maryland issued only $950,000 in paper money, which was by far the smallest amount emitted by any Southern State. But this amount plus the part of the national issues allocated to the state made it necessary to readjust the fiscal system and, as in Virginia, to tap all available sources of revenue. In the interval between the fall of the proprietary government and the creation of the state government, revenue was raised by contributions from citizens, who were asked to come to the aid of the new government. Those who refused were advertised as *Tories* and suffered the consequences of public opprobium. After the state government was organized in 1777, a relatively comprehensive tax system was inaugurated, the new levies including license taxes, an income tax, and a heavy property tax. Although the income tax had only an unsatisfactory trial—being levied in 1777 and again in 1779, and disappearing thereafter—the general property tax, authorized in 1777, was successfully administered. In fact, this property tax was levied for specific purposes at intervals during the next generation, and finally became the cornerstone of the state's subsequent fiscal system. As in Virginia, loyal citizens replaced royal officials in the administrative machinery, which was somewhat modified to meet the exigencies of the new regime.

**North Carolina.** The principal expenses of North Carolina during the Revolution were met by the issue of paper money. As in the other states, the acts authorizing such issues required that certain taxes be levied for the redemption of paper currency. Most of the taxes used for this purpose were excise duties and poll taxes. Both the scope and the rate of these taxes were increased when the needs for revenue became more imperative. In 1783, the General Assembly taxed cattle at 20 shillings per head; slaves, anywhere from £20 to £40 each, according to age; and carriages, phaetons, stagecoaches, and other "carriages of pleasure," at the rate of 5 shillings (in specie) per wheel. Besides the state taxes there were also parish taxes. These were for specific local purposes, and were laid upon property over £100 in value. A poll tax was levied upon those persons who had less than £100 in property. Practically the same difficulties that were encountered in Virginia arose in the administration of this system: defalcations, the use of counterfeit money, inflated prices, and evasion were the chief problems that made the task of raising revenue exceedingly difficult.

**South Carolina.** During the transition period from colony to commonwealth, the extralegal body in South Carolina, known as the *Provincial Congress,* made use of bills of credit to meet the expenses of the Revolution. Each of these bills was indorsed by three responsible citizens. Subsequently, as in other Southern States, new series of bills were issued at frequent intervals to meet the increasing revenue requirements. Of these issues the most important were the following. In November 1775, the government authorized the printing of £120,000; in February 1776, three thousand bills of £50 each; in March 1776, £350,000; and in October 1776, £130,000, plus the authority to borrow a sum not exceeding £500,000. In December 1776, two issues were authorized: one of £308,000, valued in Spanish milled dollars; the other of £307,384. Again, in February 1777, authority was granted to issue £500,000 in dollar bills, and to borrow another £500,000. In March

1778, an issue of £100,000 was authorized; and in 1779, the government authorized $1,000,000 to be printed and a loan of $4,000,000 to be made.

The first issues retained their value fairly well until April 1777, when they began to depreciate. Thereafter the public finances of the state were caught in the vicious spiral of depreciation, new issues of paper money, and inevitable increased depreciation. In May 1780, when Charleston was captured by the British, paper money ceased to circulate. Three separate levies had earlier been laid on lands and negroes, to secure the necessary revenue for military expenditures. In 1777, one third of a dollar was levied on each negro, as well as on each unit of one hundred acres of land. The next year, this tax was doubled; in 1779, it was raised to one dollar in specie, or about $20 in paper money value at that time. Finally, when it became evident that this kind of fiscal system was fallacious —that nothing was to be gained from attempts to stabilize the value of paper money by additional issues, or from payments of new revenues by the use of such money—the General Assembly, in 1782, passed "An act, for repealing the laws which make Paper Currency or Bills of Credit, a legal tender in payment of debts in this state." [14]

**Georgia.** During the Revolution few changes were made in the fiscal system of Georgia. Import duties and other taxes were laid on practically the same classes of property as had been levied under the Crown. In 1783, at the insistence of the Privy Council, the house passed a bill imposing a tax of a quarter of a dollar on each unit of land of one hundred acres; a quarter of a dollar on each negro, whether slave or mulatto; a quarter of a dollar on each town lot; one dollar on each free negro; and two dollars on each male inhabitant twenty-one years old or over, who was not cultivating so much as five acres of land or who was not engaged in a mechanical trade or profession.

---

[14] *Statutes at Large of South Carolina*, Vol. IV, pp. 508–509.

Thus, it appears that the Revolutionary War did not change the tax forms comprising the fiscal system of each of the Southern colonies nearly so much as it extended the scope and the rate of the existing taxes. It did, however, change the administrative system to the extent, not only of replacing Crown officers with *patriots,* but also of eliminating the whole system of petty British officials, whose chief function had been to prevent evasion.

As is characteristic of war times, fear, economic self-interest, and propaganda caused feeling to run high. In 1777, the Continental Congress recommended to the states that the real and personal estates of loyalists be seized and sold, and the receipts invested in the certificates of the Continental Loan Office. To comply with this request, Virginia, during October of the same year, passed a general sequestration law, which provided that debts due British subjects from Virginia citizens should be paid into the loan office of the state, and that the real and personal property in Virginia belonging to British subjects should be seized. In November 1777, North Carolina confiscated the property of both loyalists and British merchants. The next spring, Georgia passed a similar act.

From the fiscal viewpoint, all such *escheated* property did not add a great deal to state revenue. In Virginia, for example, prior to 1790, only about 34,066 acres of land were confiscated. Furthermore, the total loss of all the Tories in the Thirteen Colonies, by colonial estimate, was only about $40,000,000; even by British estimate, the amount did not exceed $15,000,000.

## DEBT ASSUMPTION MEASURES

After 1781, when the Articles of Confederation went into effect, these Southern States made a gallant effort to restore their financial stability. In Virginia, James Madison urged the adoption of a "pay-as-you-go" policy; and in South Carolina, Governor Guerard called for retrenchment and a state bank, "that so, we may accomplish the full and honorable discharge of our debts." [15]

The state treasuries, however, were allowed to suffer from the accumulation of large arrears in taxes. In Maryland, the total amount of tax arrears for 1784–1785 was £97,000. In Virginia, the assembly sometimes postponed the date on which taxes fell due, and arrears reached such a volume that, in 1787, the treasury received more than £33,000 in back taxes, or nearly one fourth the year's receipts from taxes. In North Carolina in 1788, the treasurer collected £54,131 as arrearages from previous years, or half again as much as the year's receipts in current taxes. No uniform monetary system had as yet been established for the Thirteen Colonies, and during the two years 1785–1786, the issue of paper money by states was once more agitated. North Carolina, South Carolina, and Georgia authorized new issues, which soon depreciated and added to the fiscal confusion.

The establishment of the new Federal Government in 1789 laid the foundation for a sounder fiscal system in these Southern States.

Upon entering the Union, the states brought with them a burden of indebtedness. Chiefly through the initiative of Alexander Hamilton, the Federal Government assumed the debts incurred by the states to meet the expenses of the Revolution. For a while such a proposal was opposed by these Southern States, as their debts, in proportion to population, were less than those of the North. Finally, through a compromise locating the Federal Capitol on the banks of the Potomac, enough Southern votes were secured to pass the assumption scheme through Congress. According to this plan of assumption, the Federal Government floated a loan to take up such debts, and subscriptions to the loan were received in certificates previously issued by the states for war purposes. The specific amount for which

---

[15] *South Carolina Gazette,* February 19, 1784.

each state could subscribe was fixed by law. For these Southern States, the permitted and assumed amounts were as follows: [16]

FEDERAL ASSUMPTION PLAN ADOPTED AFTER THE REVOLUTION

| State | Amount Permitted by Law | Amount Actually Assumed |
|---|---|---|
| Maryland | $ 800,000 | $ 517,491 |
| Virginia | 3,500,000 | 2,934,416 |
| North Carolina | 2,400,000 | 1,793,804 |
| South Carolina | 4,000,000 | 3,999,651 |
| Georgia | 300,000 | 246,030 |
| TOTAL | $11,000,000 | $9,491.392 |

The amount of Southern debt assumed by the Federal Government was 51.2 per cent of the total amount assumed for the Thirteen Colonies. Thus the South, despite its original fear, actually had more than its proportional part of the total debt assumed, and secured, in addition, a favorable settlement of the question of the location of the Capitol.

In the case of South Carolina, however, it was found that, beyond the amount originally assumed by the Federal Government, a balance of $1,447,173 was still due to that state for expenditures made for war purposes. Hence, additional certificates of funded stock for that amount were given to the state, and these certificates eventually were paid by the United States.

The Federal Government also undertook the establishment of a uniform monetary system. A mint was set up; bimetallism was adopted, and gold and silver were made legal tender for all debts; and the several states were prohibited from issuing bills of credit.

While this was a step in the right direction, a new source of confusion soon arose, and temporarily hindered the states from adjusting their fiscal problems. Instead of each state

---

[16] Compiled from Davis Rich Dewey's *Financial History of the United States*, p. 93.

issuing paper money, private banks throughout the country issued notes. So great was the flood of bank-note issues that again, as in earlier days, practically all coin was driven from general circulation. Nevertheless, an evolution had set in toward a sound monetary system, and this trend acted as a check on fiscal extravagance in the South.

It should be noted that the Federal Constitution prohibited any state from taxing exports and imports. Hence, after 1789, it became necessary for the various commonwealths to abandon customs duties, which in Virginia and South Carolina had been one of the chief sources of revenue. To replace this loss, the Southern States turned to a property tax as a necessary substitution. Another reason for the new form of taxation was the small landholder class, who, having gained legislative power under the new state constitutions, tried to shift the burden of taxation to the large plantation owners.

### Effect of the Revolutionary War on Agriculture

During the Revolution, agriculture in the South was retarded by the scarcity of laborers, by the decline in the foreign market demand for staple crops, and by the issuing of bills of credit.

Although military activity in the South prior to 1780 was of slight consequence, men were mobilized in varying numbers from most of the communities. With the progress of the war, mobilization increased, until the total number of soldiers enlisted from this section ranged all the way from over 13,000 in Georgia to over 51,000 in Virginia. Enlistment figures during the war are given on page 193. It is, therefore, reasonable to assume that this withdrawal of men—mainly from agriculture—in a measure was responsible for the somewhat smaller yield in crops.

The disruption of foreign commerce with England had a more clearly defined effect on Southern agriculture. As noted elsewhere, England was the chief buyer of Southern products, especially tobacco. Prior to the Revolution, the

SOUTHERN TROOPS IN THE REVOLUTIONARY WAR
(ENLISTMENT BY YEARS)

| State | 1775 | 1776 | 1777 | 1778 | 1779 | 1780 | 1781 | 1782 | 1783 |
|-------|------|------|------|------|------|------|------|------|------|
| Maryland . | ........ | 3,329 | 7,565 | 3,307 | 2,849 | 2,065 | 2,107 | 1,280 | 974 |
| Virginia... | 3,180 | 6,180 | 11,013 | 7,836 | 7,573 | 6,986 | 6,116 | 2,204 | 629 |
| North .... Carolina . | 2,000 | 4,134 | 1,281 | 1,287 | 4,920 | 6,132 | 3,545 | 1,152 | 697 |
| South .... Carolina . | 4,000 | 6,069 | 2,000 | 3,650 | 4,500 | 9,132 | 3,000 | 3,152 | 139 |
| Georgia... | 1,000 | 2,300 | 2,173 | 3,873 | 837 | 1,272 | 750 | 1,325 | 145 |
| TOTAL | 10,180 | 22,012 | 24,032 | 19,953 | 20,679 | 25,587 | 15,518 | 9,113 | 2,584 |

annual tobacco exports from Southern colonies amounted
to one hundred million pounds, most of which were sold
to British merchants. During the war, the average annual
exports of tobacco declined to about fifteen million pounds.
Moreover, the Revolution injured the indigo planters, both
by curtailing their market and by depriving them of the
British bounty. Even the cultivation of rice in the Carolinas was temporarily affected by a decline in market demand and by the seizure of slaves by the British troops.
Not long after the Revolution began, the legislatures of
Maryland, Virginia, and South Carolina urged that cotton
be cultivated, presumably for the needs of the Continental
Army, and it is safe to assume that the production of wool
slightly increased; but agriculture in general declined.

As money depreciated and confidence in the monetary
systems declined, there was so much uncertainty about
prices that the profit motive was greatly affected. Farmers
had to be appealed to on patriotic grounds to produce
enough surplus beyond their own needs in order that the
Army might obtain food and clothing.

## Effect of the Revolution on Manufactures and Trade

Just before the Revolution, appeals were made to the
Southern colonies to join in the non-importation agreements concerning British goods. At that time, because the
Southern colonists had no general interest in manufacturing their own goods, such appeals probably had slight

effect; but when the Revolution began and there was a sudden stoppage of imported British goods, an urgent demand arose in the colonies, both for war supplies and for ordinary manufactured goods. Consequently the South was compelled to turn to manufacturing, though it did so on a far smaller scale, with the exception of household industries, than did the North.

To supply the military demand for iron, a line of furnaces and forges was extended from New Hampshire to South Carolina. In Virginia, the assembly subsidized such undertakings, and in North Carolina, the assembly appropriated £5,000 to purchase or lease existing ironworks in Guilford County. In South Carolina, after the only iron furnace in the state was destroyed by the Tories early in the war, several unsuccessful efforts were made to reëstablish the industry. In Maryland, from eighteen to twenty bloomeries were operated at capacity, while the Principio works, in that state, were used to manufacture cannonballs. At Chiswell, Virginia, lead deposits were worked. Both the salt and saltpetre industries were speeded up throughout the South.

In Baltimore in 1776, a linen and woolen factory was opened, subsidized by the state. In Virginia at the beginning of the war, it was estimated that Augusta County alone was producing enough Osnaburgs to supply the entire population of the state. In South Carolina, however, manufacturing fared badly; there, the Tories burned loom houses and killed sheep, "even when these could not be used for food."

Aside from such efforts to supply military needs, the disorganized economic conditions in the South compelled the people, for the most part, to supply their wants by such home industries as could be maintained in those perilous times. During this period the planters frequently, not only employed their poorer white neighbors at spinning and weaving, but even trained their slaves in household industries. By 1789, home industries in the South were more active than similar industries in the North, and they did not decline in production until after the War of 1812.

The Revolutionary War, like all wars, exacted its toll of life and economic well-being. In Virginia, trade was stagnant, the courts were closed, and civil government was practically suspended. In Maryland, though the hostile troops had devastated no communities, many lives had been lost, tobacco culture was made unprofitable, and debt had accumulated. In North Carolina, political and economic disorder abounded. For seven years South Carolina had been the battleground of contending forces, and during these years she was raided and ravished, from the mountains to the seacoast, by the British Army. Industry was destroyed; homes and factories were burned; livestock and farming implements were either destroyed or stolen; and the people were virtually bankrupt. In Georgia, vast areas lay in waste. The stock of slaves was depleted by the loss of 4,000, carried away by Tory refugees. The indigo industry was ruined by the loss of the British bounty.

Colonial finances had to be readjusted, agriculture and industry rejuvenated, and trade resumed with Great Britain. The foreign trade of America, as it had been before the war, was now destined to remain predominantly British, "because British traders understood American business conditions much better than French, Dutch, and Spanish traders did. The people of Great Britain knew what goods were wanted in America. The common language of the two peoples and their common blood contributed to the development of their commerce with each other." [17] The old Navigation Acts, which had reserved the British markets in several cases for colonial exports, were gone; and the United States was discriminated against as were other nations. While imports from Great Britain temporarily increased, exports to Great Britain declined to a point where the United States did not have enough

---

[17] Johnson, Van Meter, Huebener, and Hanchett, *History of Domestic and Foreign Commerce of the United States*, p. 126.

specie to settle her unfavorable trade balance. These circumstances led to a severe crisis, which affected nearly every type of economic activity. In 1786, however, there began in business and trade an upswing that soon led to economic recovery.

## Beneficial Changes in the South

Despite the cost in life and property the Revolutionary War brought about certain changes which ultimately benefited the South.

Of primary importance was the effect of the war upon the system of landholdings; the Revolution contributed largely to a legal reform which tended toward a more equitable system of landholding. The large estates of Tories—such as those of Lord Fairfax in Virginia and Sir James Wright in Georgia—were broken up into small parcels and sold to farmers. The old legal devices of primogeniture and entail, which had kept large estates undivided from generation to generation, were cast into the discard. In Maryland, this result had come about just before the Revolution. In Virginia, soon after the signing of the Declaration of Independence, a law was enacted which "released from entail at least half, and possibly three quarters of the entire 'seated' area of Virginia." [18] By 1790, all of the states had abolished primogeniture and had placed both sons and daughters on an equality in the matter of landed inheritance. Quitrents and church tithes were abolished—the former, because there was no further obligation to the King; and the latter, because Americans demanded freedom for religious worship according to the dictates of conscience.

Another beneficial change was the release from British control of all the vacant land west of the Allegheny Mountains, which, by the royal Proclamation of 1763, had been legally closed to settlement. Prior to the Revolution, only

---

[18] Harry J. Carman, *Social and Economic History of the United States,* Vol. I, p. 317.

a few frontiersmen had ventured beyond these mountains. John Sevier had established Watauga, in east Tennessee; Daniel Boone had migrated into Kentucky, and in 1779, James Robertson had founded a settlement called "Nashboro" (now Nashville), in middle Tennessee. When this vast western area was freed from British restrictions, a great westward migration began, which ultimately reached the Pacific coast.

There was, too, a growth of liberalism, which expressed itself in reactions against slavery—particularly in Virginia —against the Anglican Church, and against economic and political inequality. At the close of the Revolution, despite economic distress, the South faced a great opportunity.

## Bibliographical Note

Since about 1900, historians have, by a more scientific method than that of their predecessors, reappraised and rewritten the history of the American Revolution. The colonies have been considered as an integral part of the British Empire, and more attention has been given to the economic causes of the war. Foremost among the studies written from this viewpoint is C. M. Andrews, *Colonial Background of the Revolution* (New Haven, Conn., 1924). Charles and Mary Beard, *Rise of American Civilization*, two volumes (New York, 1927), contains a brilliant discussion of the underlying factors leading to the Revolution; and H. E. Egerton, *Causes and Character of the American Revolution* (Oxford, England, 1923), is a fairly impartial study by an Englishman. C. H. Van Tyne, *Causes of the War of Independence* (New York, 1922), is an interesting recapitulation of political causes, but makes little mention of economic causes. A particularly illuminating chapter on the American Revolution is to be found in A. M. Schlesinger's *New Viewpoints In American History* (New York, 1928). Among the studies dealing with specific casual factors are to be mentioned: C. W. Alvord, *Mississippi Valley in British Politics*, two volumes (Cleveland, 1917); Archibald Henderson, "A Pre-Revolutionary Revolt in the Old Southwest," in the *Mississippi Valley Historical Review*, Volume 17, pages 191–212; and W. P. Breed, *Presbyterians and the Revolution* (New York, 1876). For a discussion of the Revolution in Virginia, see: H. J. Eckenrode, *Revolution in Virginia* (Boston, 1916); C. R. Lingley, *Transition in Virginia from Colony to Commonwealth* (New York, 1910); and Isaac S. Harrell, "Some Neglected Phases of the Revolution in Virginia," in the *William and Mary Quarterly*, July 1925, pages 159–170. Some valuable material is given in David Ramsay, *History of the Revolution in South Carolina*, two volumes (Charleston, 1809).

The activities of the loyalist element of the population have been treated by C. H. Van Tyne, *Loyalists in the American Revolution* (New York, 1902); and by I. S. Harrell, *Loyalism in Virginia* (Durham, N. C., 1926). The part taken by the colonial merchants in the Revolution is developed by A. M. Schlesinger, *Colonial Merchants and the American Revolution* (New York, 1918), Volume LXXVIII in the COLUMBIA UNIVERSITY STUDIES.

One of the most complete works upon American financial history is A. S. Bolle's *Financial History of the United States,* three volumes (New York, 1879–1885). The first volume covers the years 1774–1789. Some valuable notes may be had from W. G. Sumner, *Finances and Financiers of the American Revolution,* two volumes (New York, 1891). A brief but careful treatment may be found in Davis Rich Dewey, *Financial History of the United States, 1775–1789* (Madison, Wis., 1895), in the UNIVERSITY OF WISCONSIN BULLETIN; J. W. Shuckers, *Brief Account of the Finances and Paper Money of the Revolutionary War* (Philadelphia, 1874); and Ralph V. Harlow, "Aspects of Revolutionary Finance, 1775–1783," in the *American Historical Review*, October 1929, pages 46–68.

Valuable notes on the finances of the Southern States for this period may be had from: T. Pitkin, *History of the United States*, two volumes (New Haven, Conn., 1828); and Allan Nevins, *American States During and After the Revolution, 1775–1789* (New York, 1924). Among the special studies on the subject may be mentioned: H. S. Hanna, *Financial History of Maryland, 1789–1848* (Baltimore, 1907); *Studies in State Taxation,* edited by J. H. Hollander (Baltimore, 1900), Series XVIII in the JOHNS HOPKINS UNIVERSITY STUDIES IN HISTORICAL AND POLITICAL SCIENCE; W. F. Dodd, "Effects of the Adoption of the Constitution on the Finances of Virginia," in the *Virginia Historical Magazine*, Volume 10. The reaction of the settlers in the backcounties to political control by Tidewater landholders is clearly shown in John Spencer Bassett's "The Regulators of North Carolina (1756–1771)," in the *Annual Report of the American Historical Association* (1894), pages 141–212. Some illuminating facts on the administration of taxes in the last days of the colonial period may be found in Chapter IX of C. H. Karraker, *Seventeenth-Century Sheriff* (Chapel Hill, N. C., 1930).

Otto C. Lightner in his *History of Business Depressions* (New York, 1922) has a somewhat exaggerated description of the depression following the Revolution.

Charles A. Beard, *Economic Interpretation of the Revolution* (New York, 1913), is the accepted treatise on the subject.

J. F. Jameson, *American Revolution Considered as a Social Movement* (Princeton, 1926), is a summary of some of the changes wrought by that war.

# CHAPTER VIII

# Land and Population of the Ante-Bellum South, 1783–1860

**B**ETWEEN 1776 and 1836, the area of the South was more than doubled, reaching approximately its present territorial limits. Between 1790 and 1860, the total population of the section increased from 1,966,372 to 12,-315,374, or about 531 per cent.

It is the purpose of this chapter, to elaborate on this territorial expansion: particularly, to describe the method of acquiring landholdings in the new area; to note the increase, density, and ethnic composition of the population in the ante-bellum South; and so far as possible, to indicate the extent of the westward migration of population from the older Southern communities.

## Territorial Expansion and Landholding

The definitive treaty of peace between England and the United States, concluded at Paris on September 3, 1783, recognized the boundaries of the United States as extending from the Atlantic Ocean and the St. Croix River, on the east, to the Mississippi River, on the west; and from the 45th parallel, the St. Lawrence River, the Great Lakes, and the Lake of the Woods, on the north, to the northern boundary line of Spanish Florida, on the south. The Florida line eventually ran from the Mississippi River, along the 31st parallel, to the Chattahoochee; down to the mouth of the Flint; and thence, in a straight line, to the source of the St. Marys and, along that river, to the sea. Such, roughly stated, were the territorial limits of the new nation.

## Trans-Allegheny

To whom did the Trans-Allegheny lands belong? to the Federal Government, or to the original states that had claims based upon royal charters? The ink was scarcely dry upon the Declaration of Independence before there arose in the Second Continental Congress a dispute about this question which threatened to disrupt the Government. The "landless states" persistently urged that such territory should become the public domain of the Central Government. This question was not finally settled until twenty-five years later.

In 1776, Virginia had enacted a resolution making Kentucky a county of Virginia; and two years later, she had declared the region northwest of the Ohio River to be a part of Virginia, and named the vast territory the "County of Illinois." Both Virginia and North Carolina claimed the territory which eventually became the state of Tennessee. Land offices were opened by both states to sell tracts in the same Trans-Allegheny territory. North Carolina was not in any haste to cede this territory to the Federal Government, though she was frequently prodded by Congress to do so.

In 1783, Governor Alexander Martin wrote to the North Carolina delegation in Congress: [1] "Perhaps Congress may be dissatisfied with the mode of our land office being opened, as we have made no concession of any part of our western lands." The reason for this attitude, according to one writer, was that "a melon was to be cut, but the meat was intended for North Carolinians alone, and the rind for others, including the National Government." [2] In other words, the best land was to be sold to "home-folks," and afterwards the remainder would be ceded to the Federal Government. Furthermore, North Carolina was careful to stipulate in her act of cession that all such grants must be

---

[1] *North Carolina State Records*, Vol. XVI, p. 919.
[2] S. C. Williams, *Beginnings of West Tennessee*, p. 41.

satisfied.  Thus it turned out North Carolina had already granted so much land in Tennessee that it was not worth while for the Federal Government to open a land office in that territory when it was finally ceded to the United States in 1790.

Virginia, North Carolina, South Carolina, and Georgia each claimed western lands extending to the Mississippi; Maryland, along with Delaware, New Jersey, New Hampshire, and Rhode Island, had no claims on western land. The latter group, particularly Maryland, were afraid of losing power in the Federal Government should the other Southern States eventually become so extensive.  Therefore they sought to have the western lands ceded to the Federal Government, and, since the Articles of Confederation required unanimous ratification before they could go into effect, Maryland was able to force cession by refusing to ratify the Articles until Virginia agreed to give up her western lands.

In 1781, Virginia ceded her northwestern claims, with the exception of 6,000 square miles between the Scioto and the Little Miami Rivers—a territory reserved to redeem her military certificates.  In 1792, Kentucky, which Virginia had claimed as a county, became a state.  In 1782, South Carolina gave up her western land claims; North Carolina followed in 1790, and Georgia, in 1802.

Before the Trans-Allegheny lands were ceded by the several Southern States to the Federal Government and before there was anything like a uniform method of grants, much of this territory had been sold by the states to settlers and speculators, and numerous squatters, without having any title to their lands, had settled in various localities.

### Louisiana Territory

Between 1789 and 1860, the United States acquired by purchase or by annexation additional territory amounting to 2,181,186 square miles.  The primary cost of these acquisitions was about $55,000,000.  Up to 1849, an estimate

of the total expenditures was as follows: to France for
Louisiana (1803), $15,000,000, with $8,529,353 interest;
to Spain for Florida (1819), $5,000,000, with $1,489,763 interest; to Georgia, $1,250,000, with $1,832,000 interest; for
Yazoo claims, $4,282,757; to Mexico, $15,000,000; for the
cost of the Mexican War, following the annexation of Texas
in 1845, $217,175,577; to Texas, for the cost of the removal
of the Indians to lands beyond the Mississippi, and the
Gadsden Purchase, about $30,000,000. The total in 1849
approximated $300,000,000. Of these acquisitions the most
important—such as the Louisiana Territory of 1,182,752
square miles, Florida, and Texas—either were made when
a Southerner was President or were prompted by Southern
influence. Yet only 496,455 square miles of this new territory went to the South as a slaveholding section.

The political aspects of this division of territory have
been discussed at length by other writers. The present text
deals only with the system of landholding that existed in
the regions added to the South. From the standpoint of
economic development, it must be recognized that the lower
Mississippi Valley was basically French, and that Florida
and Texas were basically Spanish.

Although the present state of Louisiana comprises only
a fraction of the original French territory of that name,
French institutions, particularly the legal system of landholding, have had permanent effects on the entire area. In
colonial times the land tenure was almost *franc-alleu,* or
what roughly corresponds to the English system of fee
simple. The unit of land was the *arpent,* an area of slightly
more than an acre. Grants were made under the French
law *Coutume de Paris* in what was known as *seigneurie*—
that is to say, land was granted by a superior lord on the
condition that the grantee render him military assistance
in time of war; the practice was somewhat similar to the
feudal system of Europe.

Some of the most extensive grants in Louisiana were
made by the notorious "John Law's Company of the West."

These tracts, as granted, usually faced a body of water and extended in depth two or three times the frontage. Some comprised as much as, and a few even more than, a square league—7,056 arpents. Later grants were oblong in shape and were so laid out as to leave a vacant strip between every two lots. This strip subsequently was divided between the plantations. The plan prevented legal confusion about conflicting titles.

When the Spanish came into this territory during the last decades of the eighteenth century, practically no changes were made.[3] French remained the official language; immigration was retarded; and few important land grants were authorized. In 1801, by the Treaty of San Ildefonso, Spain retroceded the territory to France. In 1804, following the Louisiana Purchase, the Federal Government passed an act annulling all Spanish land grants made in the territory subsequent to the Treaty of San Ildefonso.

The state of Arkansas was originally a part of the Louisiana Purchase. In 1718, John Law obtained in this region a grant of land twelve miles square, and planted a colony of Germans about seven miles above Arkansas Post. He built storehouses, pavilions for officers, and cabins for workmen. Within the next three years, about seven hundred persons, including many married men and their families, came to the settlement. When they learned of Law's financial failure, they left the settlement and located near New Orleans. The history of this grant practically covers the attempts to establish important French landholdings in the Arkansas region.

When the Spanish came into the Louisiana Territory, one of their governors, Baron de Corondelet, made many land grants. Not only did such grants, according to Spanish law, have to be made by a commandant, but the land had to be surveyed and each transaction approved by the

---

[3] France ceded Louisiana to Spain in 1763.

Spanish governor at New Orleans. After the Louisiana Purchase the United States courts respected all perfect titles to such grants; however, much litigation resulted on account of the indefiniteness of several large grants. The most noted was the Winter's grant, of about one and a half million acres. This grant was contested until 1848, when it was finally declared void. Unfortunately, the uncertainty of title to this large tract greatly retarded the development of the country about Arkansas Post.

Missouri was also part of the Louisiana Purchase and prior to American control was governed by much the same laws as other French territory in the Mississippi Valley. The first permanent settlement was established at St. Genevieve, probably between 1730 and 1752. In 1764, the site of St. Louis was selected by Pierre Laclede Ligueste, who sent Auguste Chouteau to found a village there for the headquarters of Maxent, Laclede & Cie., fur dealers at New Orleans. Similar to the Gulf coast models, the town was laid out in oblong lots, but with the additional feature of out-lots of forty to eighty arpents and of fields of varying areas adjacent to the town. No land was surveyed beyond this limit, and claims to such land rested on possession.

Land grants in the territory within the state of Alabama were greatly complicated because of the respective claims of Spain, France, England, and Georgia. To understand the situation, it is necessary to sketch briefly the early history of the region.

In 1540, or eighty years before the Pilgrims arrived at Plymouth, Hernando de Soto, with six hundred and twenty men, landed at Tampa Bay, crossed Georgia and entered Alabama. This group, in its search for gold, visited Coosa, Tallasee, and other Indian towns, and then passed by Piachee to Maubila (the original name of Mobile), and proceeded thence up the Tombigbee Valley into Mississippi. Since discovery was the basis of possession, this territory first belonged to Spain. Nevertheless, one hundred and sixty years later, Sieur de Bienville transferred his French colony from Biloxi to Dog River, on Mobile Bay, and erected Fort St. Louis de la Mobile. In 1711, he moved to the present site of Mobile. A few years later English fur traders from Georgia built a fort at Ocufuskee. In 1763, when France ceded the Trans-Allegheny country to Great Britain, the part of Alabama south of Selma and Montgomery was included in the "District of West Florida," and the unoccupied country to the north belonged to the "County of Illinois." Montgomery lay in Florida, and Wetumpka, in Illinois. In 1779, Galvez, the Spanish governor of Louisiana, with two thousand soldiers, captured Mobile, which, in population, was practically a French town. The Spaniards then held the country until 1798 as a part of Florida. Georgia also claimed, under her royal charter of 1665, great parts of Alabama and Mississippi, but in 1798 and 1802, she ceded them to the United States for $1,250,000.

Under the French regime, Mobile was the capital of Louisiana. Hence, land, as in other French settlements, was granted according to the *Coutume de Paris*. The town lots were twelve and one half by twenty-five *toises* (a *toise* being six feet) in dimensions. Besides lots, there were several larger grants. For example, Madame de Lusser, in lieu of a pension for her husband, who was killed in the Chickasaw War, received a tract of land "south of the fort and running a mile westward." Bienville, the so-called "Father of Alabama," on a highland facing the bay had a *"maison avec jardin,"* which perhaps included several arpents.

After England had acquired the region by the Treaty of Paris in 1763 and, in turn, had acquired from the Indians the area about the Bay and the Tombigbee River, she attempted to establish a land system calculated to attract settlers. By an ordinance of November 1, 1765, she authorized the Privy Council to grant one hundred acres of land to each head of a family and an additional fifty acres to each person, whether white or black, connected with the family. She contemplated a land system in Alabama similar to that which she had tried in her other Southern colonies. Besides these grants, British officers and soldiers of the late war with France were to be given, instead of pensions, land in the following amounts: field officers, 5,000 acres; captains, 3,000 acres; subalterns, 2,000 acres; non-commissioned officers, 200 acres; and privates, 60 acres. The grantee was to locate his own claim—a practice which led to much overlapping and subsequent disputes.

Many of these grants were never occupied. Therefore, when the Spaniards came into control of this region during the last decades of the eighteenth century, they disregarded many of these English grants and issued land rights *de novo*. The Spanish also made many concessions contingent upon the obtaining of proper papers from the officer who had succeeded the one in command at the time of the original concession. Even the United States subsequently recognized some of these informal grants. After the Treaty of San Ildefonso, one half of Mobile was bought by an American physician from the Spanish interpreter who was in charge of treaty negotiations. Land speculation was common all over "West Florida" for three or four years after this treaty.

The situation was still further complicated because the United States, while claiming that the district extending to the Perdido was a part of the Louisiana Purchase, delayed in occupying it, and therefore left it in the *de facto* possession of Spain. On the other hand, Spain assumed that the territory east of Pearl River belonged to her, and continued granting lands according to Spanish law. Before the War of 1812, Americans began to occupy this territory, and eventually it was admitted into the Union as part of the states of Alabama and Mississippi. Only one course was left in dealing with the land grants made in the region—

namely, to declare void every grant made by the Spaniards after the Treaty of San Ildefonso in 1801.

As already suggested, the territory within the present state of Mississippi was a part of old Louisiana. The first settlements were established by the French at Natchez, on the seacoast near Biloxi, and up the Yazoo. The land grants at these places were in accord with the *Coutume de Paris,* already described in connection with other French settlements in the lower Mississippi Valley.

In 1763, according to the Treaty of Paris, Mississippi was included in the territory ceded by France to England, and it belonged to the so-called "County of Illinois." While the land was under British control, the same system of grants was followed as in Alabama during the same period. In 1779, Galvez captured Natchez. Three years later, a few New England and Carolina immigrants and Royalists captured Natchez, only to have it recaptured by the Spaniards. When "West Florida" was confirmed to Spain by a treaty in 1783, the United States occupied the eastern side of the Mississippi Valley up to the disputed Florida boundary. A disagreement, due to a secret clause in the Treaty of 1783, arose between the two nations as to whether the boundary lay at 31 degrees latitude or at the Yazoo River. At last, in 1795, Spain yielded, and Congress formed the disputed area, from the Mississippi to the Chatta-hoochee, into the "Mississippi Territory." Thus, by 1800, the area of the present state of Mississippi lay in the following jurisdictions: from the Gulf to 31 degrees, in Spanish Florida; from 31 degrees to the parallel of the Yazoo, in "Mississippi Territory"; and from the Yazoo northward nearly to Tennessee, in Georgia. This latter section was acquired by Congress, in 1802, from Georgia in the notorious "Yazoo Claims Settlement." Had there been extensive settlements in Mississippi at that time, there would have been much confusion of titles; but, since population was sparse and settlements were tiny villages, little difficulty arose over land titles.

### FLORIDA

In contrast to the Mississippi Valley territory, Florida was originally Spanish. St. Augustine, established in 1565, remained for nearly a century and a half a distinctly Spanish settlement. In 1586, Sir Francis Drake destroyed this settlement, but it was soon rebuilt by the Spaniards. In 1696, a Spanish colony of about three hundred persons established Pensacola. In 1719, this town was captured by the Frenchman Bienville, and then was deserted until 1722, when it was rebuilt on Santa Rosa Island. In 1765, Pensacola was built on its present site, on the mainland. Eighteen years later, the town was captured by Galvez in his coast-wide seizure for Spain. However, St. Augustine and Pensacola were forts rather than true colonies, established to carry on production and therefore requiring land, and the *adelantados* (titled Spaniards) were interested primarily in explorations for gold and in the exploitation of the Indians.

In 1763, after the Treaty of Paris, only a few Spaniards remained in Florida, and the English, during this short occupancy, granted land there according to the English tenure used in Alabama and Mississippi. In fact, land ownership in Florida really began with the British. When the Spanish for the second time came into possession of Florida, in 1783, the English grants were mostly confiscated and the lands were regranted, sometimes in areas of several hundred arpents. Finally, after the United States purchased this territory by a treaty ratified in 1822. the various titles were dealt with in the same way as those in Louisiana, Alabama, and Mississippi.

### TEXAS

Originally Texas was a part of Mexico, and unlike Florida, which was under the control of far-away Spain. this vast region was directly under Spanish control centering in Mexico City. There were, however, only a few

Spanish settlements in Texas, the most important being San Antonio. On the other hand, there was so much *entrada y conquista* (penetration and conquest) that it can be truly said most of this vast territory under Spanish possession was without law and order.

In so far as there was a land system, it was based upon the Mexican division of the land into *labores* (an area unit of one hundred and seventy-seven acres). Lands were usually obtained from the government through an *empresario*—a grantee, or contractor, who received a large tract on condition that he would settle on it, at his own expense and within six years, a specified number of families, apportioning to each a legally authorized amount of land. In return for this service, the *empresario* was usually allowed as a premium for every hundred families he settled, five *sitios* (a *sitio* being a square league, or twenty-five million *varas*) of grazing land and five labores of arable land.

Probably the most important Spanish grant made in Texas was the one to Moses Austin in 1820, which, on account of his death, the next year passed to his son Stephen F. Austin. After spending a year (1822) in the Mexican Capital, Austin received a formal grant to establish the settlement for which informal permission had been given to his father.

This grant was in accord with a general law which provided "that to each of three hundred families one labor [177 acres of land] should be given for farming and twenty-four additional labores for stock-raising. The total amount was a *sitio*, or square league. More might be given those who had many children or might deserve special consideration."[4] Furthermore, the colonists were permitted to choose their land from any section they desired. Consequently, this type of American settlement soon became scattered over the "extensive region bounded by San Jacinto

---

[4] Cardinal Goodwin, *Trans-Mississippi West (1803-1853), A History of Its Acquisition and Settlement*, p. 167.

and Lavaca Rivers on the east and west, by the Gulf on the south, and by the San Antonio-Nacogdoches Trail on the north." [5]

Three additional grants were made to Austin himself, and others were made in rapid succession to several Americans. Colonies were established along the Nueces and the Trio, and in the region around Gonzales, but many of the grants were nullified because the grantees failed to carry out their contracts.

Eventually American settlers outnumbered the Spaniards and, as a result of a perhaps inevitable clash, made Texas into an independent republic. About a decade later (1845), the republic was admitted as a state into the Union—an act which was partly responsible for the war with Mexico. Unlike other states, Texas retained her public lands when she entered the Union and subsequently sold most of them in her own way. She changed her land system to resemble the system used by the United States Land Office.

In summing up the story of westward expansion, it should be repeated that land grants were made by the original Southern States to the Trans-Allegheny territory prior to the cession of their chartered claims to this territory, and that little ungranted land was actually turned over by some of the states to the Federal Government. Moreover, in the Southwest prior to American possession, individual grants were made to considerable areas: by the French and Spanish, in the lower Mississippi Valley; by the Spanish, in Florida and Texas; and by the British, along the Gulf Coast. Many of these grants beyond the Alleghenies were in relatively large units; thus, a nucleus for the system of large landholdings existed in these regions before the advent of cotton as a staple crop. It therefore cannot be accurately said that cotton culture was solely responsible for the existence of large landholdings in the new territory of the South.

---

[5] *Ibid.*, p. 168.

## FEDERAL LAND SYSTEM AFTER THE REVOLUTION

Following the acquisition of this vast territory, the Federal Government established a land system over the groundwork of all prior grants, recognized most of these as valid, and proceeded to dispose of the remaining ungranted lands, with the exception of the public lands of Texas.

At first, the policy of the Government was to sell the land for the benefit of the Federal Treasury, and thereby to extinguish the national debt. Between 1783 and 1800, public land was sold in tracts of only 640 or more acres. From 1801 to 1820, Congress reduced the minimum acreage that could be sold to an individual to 80 acres, and the lowest price to $1.25 per acre. From 1821 to 1840, the minimum acreage that could be sold to an individual was further reduced to 40 acres, and the lowest price fixed at $1.25 per acre.[6] Such land policies, however, especially the earliest one, were unfavorable to settlement; for, as Thomas Jefferson had said in 1776:[7] "The people who will migrate to the westward . . . will be a people little able to pay taxes. . . . By selling the lands to them, you will disgust them, and cause an avulsion of them from the common union. They will settle the land in spite of everybody.

---

[6] The early development of the Federal Government's land policy may be summarized as follows:

| Act | Minimum Purchase (Acres) | Minimum Auction Price Per Acre | Condition of Sale |
|---|---|---|---|
| 1796........... | 640 | $2.00 | ½ Cash (cash deposit and remainder in 30 days). ½ Credit for 1 year. |
| 1800........... | 320 | $2.00 | ¼ Cash. ¼ Credit for 40 days. ¼ Credit for 2 years. ¼ Credit for 4 years. |
| 1804........... | 160 | $2.00 | Terms practically same as in Act of 1800. |
| 1820........... | 80 | $1.25 | Cash. |
| 1832........... | 40 | $1.25 | Cash. |

[7] *Works of Jefferson* (edited by Ford), Vol. II, pp. 239–240: Letter to Edmund Pendelton.

. . . I am at the same time clear that they [the lands] should be appropriated in small quantities."

Finally, the Government abandoned the purely financial policy of disposing of public lands and adopted a social policy which was calculated to attract settlers. Thus, in 1841, Congress passed a preëmption act, withdrawing certain lands from sale to the general public and reserving them for sale to actual settlers, who were permitted to purchase small areas upon which they had already settled, or squatted, at a fixed minimum price of $1.25 per acre.

A rectangular system of surveying was adopted from the first, and a survey had to be made prior to the sale of all public lands. The form of land tenure was *"allocial"*—that is to say, land was to be held in fee simple by the purchaser and could be freely transferred, and estates of persons dying intestate had to be divided equally among all the heirs. This system was especially important, for it meant a deathblow to all relics of feudalism which had been inherited from Europe.

In connection with the disposition of public lands, it may be noted that the receipts from sales in the South from 1833 to 1840 were as follows:

RECEIPTS FROM LAND SALES, 1833–1840

| State | Amount |
|---|---|
| Alabama | $ 7,251,460 |
| Arkansas | 3,110,377 |
| Florida | 516,408 |
| Louisiana | 3,240,369 |
| Mississippi | 10,068,973 |
| Missouri | 6,880,880 |
| TOTAL | $31,068,467 |

This amount constituted almost 45 per cent of the total receipts from land sales by the Federal Government during the period. It also indicates roughly the rapidity of westward migration from 1833 to 1840.

### Increase, Density, and Ethnic Composition of Population

There were several causes which brought settlers into the new regions of the South and which pushed the frontier westward.

At the close of the Revolutionary War, the Southern States were heavily in debt; depreciated paper currency had driven out specie, and individual insolvency was common. Production of tobacco for export had declined to such an extent that slavery, which had been profitable in Virginia and Maryland, could scarcely be supported. As a result many persons turned westward for new lands and freedom from debt. New settlements followed from the natural increase in families, generation after generation pushing their farms farther and farther up the frontier valleys and across the prairies.

Sometimes there were more specific reasons for westward migration. For example, in 1828, when gold was discovered in northern Georgia, hundreds of people rushed into that region. Some settled there on small farms, while others moved farther on to better lands. Moreover, land speculators, as well as Revolutionary veterans—by realizing on the scrip which they had received for military service—took up new lands.

In the years between 1825 and 1832, South Carolina underwent far-reaching economic changes. The indigo plantations had already ceased to be profitable; the rice planters had lost their old prosperity; and, due to continuous cultivation without crop rotation or the use of fertilizers, the soil of many cotton plantations was nearly exhausted. Consequently, when the price of cotton fell after 1825, it became necessary for the inhabitants to seek the advantages of large estates of unexhausted soil, in order to make a profit from cotton cultivation. In 1832, Haynes, of South Carolina, in his speech in the senate, declared, though doubtless with some exaggeration, that the condition of South Carolina was "not merely one of unexampled depression, but of great and all-pervading distress" with "the mournful evidence of premature decay, . . . merchants bankrupt or driven away—their capital sunk or transferred to other pursuits—our shipyards broken up—our ships all sold. . . . If," he continued, "we fly from the city to the country, what do we there behold? Fields abandoned; the hospitable mansions of our fathers deserted; agriculture drooping; our slaves, like their masters, working harder, and faring worse; the planter striving with unavailing efforts to avert the ruin which is before him." [8]

In short, the planters of South Carolina felt the growing competition of the cotton crops from the virgin soil of the Southwest and, at the same time, saw in the protective tariff, enacted by Congress for the development of Northern manufactures, another source of distress. To escape from their already impoverished condition, some South Carolinians moved westward.

From 1830 to 1850, a further decline of cotton and tobacco prices and a general financial depression furnished a new impetus for still greater migration. Many persons deliberately chose the Southwest, while others, hoping to find some new opportunity though uncertain where, drifted aimlessly from the region of their misfortunes. "The Southerner packed up his household goods," says Pooley, "faced the west, and travelled by the most convenient road." Further illustration of this characteristic attitude is given in the answer made by a North Carolina man, who, traveling westward with all his earthly possessions, was asked where he was going. "No where in pertick'lar," he answered; "me and my wife thought we'd hunt a place to settle. We've no money, nor no plunder—nothin' but just ourselves and this nag—we thought we'd try our luck in a new country." [9]

Yet one of the most striking facts about this migration

[8] *Register of Debates*, Vol. VIII, Pt. I, pp. 80–81.
[9] William Vipond Pooley, *Settlement of Illinois from 1830 to 1850*, p. 353.

is that most of it was in parallel lines westward, though some persons moved into the Northwest, while a few went into the North. To a certain extent, the movement of the center of population in the United States was a gauge of the changes in the South. Tending westward along the 39th parallel, the point moved about forty-one miles, with a slight southern angle, between 1790 and 1800, as settlers occupied the Northwest Territory and the land acquired from the Carolinas and Georgia. The Louisiana Purchase produced an additional westward and southward trend between 1800 and 1820. The acquisition of Florida brought the center of population in 1830 to its farthest southern point. From 1830 to 1840, the center moved northward; but by the end of the next decade, on account of Texas, it was 38 degrees 19 minutes west. Finally, from 1850 to 1860, it again shifted northward and moved eighty-one miles westward.

From the statistics of population, there appear to have been at least three waves of westward migration into the new territory of the ante-bellum South. First, settlers moved westward into Kentucky and Tennessee during the Revolutionary War and after the Peace of 1783 had removed British restrictions from this territory. By 1790, the First Census gave Kentucky a population of 73,677, and Tennessee, 35,691. The next migration followed certain technological improvements in the textile industry, particularly the invention of the cotton gin in 1793, which made possible the profitable cultivation of the short-staple variety of cotton. Hitherto, the labor of picking the seeds by hand from this variety of plant—which is the only one suited to cultivation in the uplands—had prevented its extensive culture. Thereafter, the cotton area was rapidly extended inland, away from the Tidewater region. As Judge Johnson, of the United States Supreme Court, pointed out:[10] "The whole interior of the Southern States was

---

[10] See E. C. Brooks, *Story of Cotton*, p. 99.

languishing, and its inhabitants were emigrating for want of some object to engage their attention and employ their industry, when the invention of this machine at once opened views to them which set the whole country in active motion." Finally, technological innovations lowered the cost of manufacturing cotton goods to such an extent that market demand increased rapidly. This change was reflected also among the planters; as a result of it, more and more persons engaged in cotton culture, and thus pushed the frontier of production farther and farther westward. The business crises of 1825 and 1837 sent increasing numbers of persons into the Southwest, just as, until recent years, practically every depression has been an impelling force toward westward migration. Financial failure and unemployment in the older regions of the country drove many to seek new lands beyond the established communities.

The distribution of population over the ante-bellum South was irregular. In some regions, there were rather compact settlements; in others, homes were sparse, and long distances intervened between communities. In 1860, the density of population per square mile ranged from 56.26 in Maryland to only 2.39 in Florida and 2.27 in Texas. Up to 1820, the one hundred and twenty-seven miles of westward movement of the center of population was made chiefly by native Americans, but in the next forty years, the change of two hundred and thirty miles was due mainly to the foreign element that came to America during this period.

The tide of immigration to the United States increased between 1820 and 1834 from 8,385 persons per year to 65,305. In 1838, it fell to 38,914, but in 1854, it reached 427,833. Thereafter it gradually decreased, until it fell to 153,640 in 1860. In 1830, the census showed 10,326 aliens in the South, whereas there were 97,506 in the North. In 1850, the South had a little more than 14 per cent of the total foreign-born population, and in 1860, about 13

TOTAL POPULATION: WHITES AND NEGROES[11]

| State | 1790 | 1800 | 1810 | 1820 | 1830 | 1840 | 1850 | 1860 |
|---|---|---|---|---|---|---|---|---|
| Maryland | 319,728 | 341,548 | 381,546 | 407,350 | 447,040 | 470,019 | 583,034 | 687,049 |
| Virginia | 747,610 | 880,200 | 974,600 | 1,211,405 | 1,239,797 | 1,421,661 | 1,421,661 | 1,596,318 |
| North Carolina | 393,751 | 478,103 | 555,500 | 638,829 | 737,987 | 753,419 | 869,039 | 992,622 |
| South Carolina | 249,073 | 345,591 | 415,115 | 502,741 | 581,185 | 594,398 | 668,407 | 703,708 |
| Georgia | 82,548 | 162,686 | 252,433 | 340,989 | 516,823 | 691,392 | 906,185 | 1,057,286 |
| Kentucky | 73,677 | 220,955 | 406,511 | 564,317 | 687,917 | 779,828 | 982,405 | 1,155,684 |
| Tennessee | 35,691 | 105,602 | 261,727 | 422,823 | 681,904 | 829,210 | 1,002,717 | 1,109,801 |
| Mississippi | | 8,850 | 40,352 | 75,448 | 136,621 | 375,651 | 606,526 | 791,305 |
| Missouri | | | 19,783 | 66,586 | 140,455 | 383,702 | 682,044 | 1,182,012 |
| Louisiana | | | 76,556 | 153,407 | 215,739 | 352,411 | 517,762 | 708,002 |
| Arkansas | | | 1,062 | 14,273 | 30,388 | 97,574 | 209,897 | 435,450 |
| Alabama | | | | 127,901 | 309,527 | 590,756 | 771,623 | 964,201 |
| Florida | | | | | 34,730 | 54,477 | 87,445 | 140,424 |
| Texas | | | | | | | 212,592 | 604,215 |
| TOTAL | 1,902,078 | 2,543,535 | 3,385,185 | 4,526,069 | 5,760,113 | 7,394,498 | 9,531,337 | 12,108,077 |

[11] Compiled from *Abstracts* of the UNITED STATES CENSUS.

PERCENTAGE OF INCREASE OF POPULATION[12]

| State | 1790 to 1800 | 1800 to 1810 | 1810 to 1820 | 1820 to 1830 | 1830 to 1840 | 1840 to 1850 | 1850 to 1860 | No. of Inhabitants Per Square Mile | |
|---|---|---|---|---|---|---|---|---|---|
| | | | | | | | | 1850 | 1860 |
| Maryland | 6.8 | 11.4 | 7.0 | 9.7 | 5.1 | 24.0 | 17.8 | 62.31 | 56.26 |
| Virginia | 17.7 | 10.7 | 9.2 | 13.7 | 2.3 | 14.6 | 12.2 | 23.17 | 23.74 |
| North Carolina | — | — | — | — | — | — | — | 19.30 | 18.99 |
| South Carolina | — | — | — | — | — | — | — | 27.28 | 23.01 |
| Georgia | 97.0 | 55.1 | 351.0 | 51.5 | 33.7 | 31.0 | 16.6 | 15.68 | 17.77 |
| Kentucky | 199.8 | 83.9 | 38.7 | 21.9 | 13.3 | 25.9 | 17.6 | 26.07 | 28.60 |
| Tennessee | 195.8 | 147.8 | 61.5 | 61.2 | 21.6 | 20.9 | 10.6 | 21.98 | 26.39 |
| Mississippi | | 355.9 | 86.9 | 81.0 | 74.9 | 61.4 | 30.4 | 12.86 | 16.90 |
| Missouri | | | 219.2 | 111.0 | 73.1 | 77.7 | 73.3 | 10.12 | 17.02 |
| Louisiana | | | 99.7 | 41.0 | 63.3 | 46.9 | 36.7 | 11.02 | 14.53 |
| Arkansas | | | | 113.1 | 21.0 | 15.1 | 107.4 | 4.01 | 8.06 |
| Alabama | | | | 142.0 | 90.8 | 30.6 | 24.9 | 15.21 | 18.45 |
| Florida | | | | | 56.8 | 60.5 | 60.5 | 1.47 | 2.39 |
| Texas | | | | | | | 182.2 | .89 | 2.27 |

[12] Compiled from *Abstracts* of the UNITED STATES CENSUS.

per cent. Of these immigrants the bulk came from Europe and included principally some English, Irish, Germans, and Scandinavians. The following table indicates, by percentages, the distribution of these four classes of immigrants in the ante-bellum South.

DISTRIBUTION OF IMMIGRANTS IN ANTE-BELLUM SOUTH

| Nationality | 1850 | 1860 |
|---|---|---|
| English | 9.17 | 8.90 |
| Irish | 10.60 | 11.24 |
| Germans | 21.56 | 16.85 |
| Scandinavians | 8.67 | 4.27 |

What were the influences which led the greater number of immigrants to settle in the North?

In the first place, the North was in a latitude to which most of the foreigners had been accustomed. Besides, there were many rumors current that the climate of the South was unhealthful.[13] Travel from Europe, however, naturally followed the principal direct routes to America, and transportation to the new lands of the South was more difficult and often hazardous. For example, it required from a week to ten days—at the risk of life itself—to make a trip up the Mississippi River from New Orleans to St. Louis. Nevertheless, the chief reason why many immigrants avoided the South was the lack of opportunity to make a living there, especially since most immigrants did not have the capital to become planters, and unskilled white laborers could not, and would not, compete with slave labor.

There were strong foreign groups in Baltimore, New Orleans, St. Louis, and Louisville. In 1812, according to one estimate, a third of the population of Baltimore was German. Toward the close of the ante-bellum period, there were several thousand Germans in Louisville, and over half of the foreign-born population in St. Louis was German.

---

[13] In 1823, Isaac Holmes gave the following advice to prospective immigrants: "The Southern States, as a permanent residence, even if slavery were not admitted, are not without their evils; the heat and insalubrity of the climate being sufficient to deter any European from fixing there."— Isaac Holmes, *An Account of the U. S. of America*, p. 142.

New Orleans had in proportion to slaves perhaps more free white laborers than any other Southern city. According to Olmsted, many Irishmen and Germans lived there, and "the majority of the cartmen, hackney-coach men, porters, railroad hands, public waiters, and common laborers, as well as of skilled mechanics, appear to be white men." [14]

Besides the direct European immigration into the new Southern territory, the population of this section was derived to a certain extent from the migration of farmers and planters from the Thirteen Original States—especially the first Southern States—and from the later migration of the professional and mercantile classes.

Before a more detailed account is given of the internal migration from the older Southern communities to the new territory of the South, the following points should be noted about the resident population.

In 1860, in addition to a total white population of 8,099,-760, there were 4,215,614 negroes in the South. Of these only 261,918 were free negroes. It appears that, while the white element in the population during the preceding three decades had increased 118.5 per cent, during the same time the slave element of the population had increased 97.1 per cent. [15]

WHITE AND NEGRO POPULATION IN THE SOUTH, 1830–1860

| Year | Whites | Negroes Free | Negroes Slaves | Per Cent of Negroes to Total Population |
|------|--------|--------------|----------------|------------------------------------------|
| 1830 | 3,660,758 | 166,550 | 2,005,475 | 37.2 |
| 1840 | 4,632,640 | 215,565 | 2,486,226 | 36.8 |
| 1850 | 6,222,418 | 238,187 | 3,204,051 | 35.6 |
| 1860 | 8,099,760 | 261,918 | 3,953,696 | 34.2 |

By no means did every white family in the South have slaves. In 1860, there were only 384,753 slave owners in the entire section. Nor were the slaves equally distributed among these owners. In that year, 7,929 owners

---

[14] Frederick Law Olmsted, *Journey in the Seaboard Slave States in the Years 1853–1854, with Remarks on Their Economy,* Vol. 2, p. 239.

[15] Compiled from *Abstracts* of the UNITED STATES CENSUS.

DISTRIBUTION OF SLAVES BY OWNERS, 1850[16]

| State | 1 Slave | Under 15 | Under 10 | Under 20 | Under 50 | Under 100 | Under 200 | Above 200 | Aggregate |
|---|---|---|---|---|---|---|---|---|---|
| Alabama | 5,204 | 7,737 | 6,572 | 5,067 | 3,524 | 957 | 216 | 18 | 29,295 |
| Arkansas | 1,383 | 1,951 | 1,365 | 788 | 382 | 109 | 19 | 2 | 5,999 |
| Florida | 699 | 991 | 759 | 588 | 349 | 104 | 29 | 1 | 3,520 |
| Georgia | 6,554 | 11,716 | 7,701 | 6,490 | 5,056 | 764 | 147 | 28 | 38,456 |
| Kentucky | 9,244 | 13,284 | 9,579 | 5,022 | 1,198 | 53 | 5 | ...... | 38,385 |
| Louisiana | 4,797 | 6,072 | 4,327 | 2,652 | 1,774 | 728 | 274 | 46 | 20,670 |
| Maryland | 4,825 | 5,331 | 3,327 | 1,822 | 655 | 72 | 7 | 1 | 16,040 |
| Mississippi | 3,640 | 6,228 | 5,143 | 4,015 | 2,964 | 910 | 189 | 27 | 23,116 |
| Missouri | 5,762 | 6,878 | 4,370 | 1,810 | 345 | 19 | ...... | 1 | 19,185 |
| North Carolina | 1,204 | 9,668 | 8,129 | 5,898 | 2,828 | 485 | 76 | 15 | 28,303 |
| South Carolina | 3,492 | 6,164 | 6,311 | 4,955 | 3,200 | 990 | 382 | 102 | 25,596 |
| Tennessee | 7,616 | 10,582 | 8,314 | 4,852 | 2,202 | 276 | 19 | 3 | 33,864 |
| Texas | 1,935 | 2,640 | 1,585 | 1,121 | 374 | 82 | 9 | 1 | 7,747 |
| Virginia | 11,385 | 15,550 | 13,030 | 9,456 | 4,880 | 646 | 107 | 9 | 55,063 |
| TOTAL | 67,740 | 104,792 | 80,512 | 54,536 | 29,731 | 6,195 | 1,479 | 254 | 345,239 |

[16] Compiled from *Report* of the UNITED STATES CENSUS.

had more than fifty slaves each; 174,503 owned less than five; and 165,093 owned between five and fifty. In ten Southern States, 56 planters owned between three hundred and five hundred slaves each. In Georgia, Louisiana, Mississippi, and South Carolina, 9 planters owned between five hundred and one thousand slaves.

A further analysis of the distribution of slaves shows that in 1850 about 400,000 may be classed as "Urban," while the remainder, or about 2,800,000, ' may be classed as "Rural." Of the latter number, about 60,000 were used in the cultivation of hemp; 125,000, in rice; 150,000, in sugar cane; 350,000, in tobacco; and 1,815,000, in cotton culture.[17] The remainder were employed in miscellaneous occupations. Thus, it appears that slavery had become predominantly a feature of cotton culture.

### Westward Movement of Population

There were two distinct sources of population migration into the new regions of the South: the internal migration from east to west, and the influx of people from Europe. As already noted, the number of foreign immigrants was much less than the number coming into the North; the foreign element did not constitute a large part of the total population of the Southern States under consideration. This fact appears clearly from the table on page 224.[18]

The *Old South* was by far the most important source of migration to the frontier. According to Pooley: [19] "Before 1850, Virginia had lost by emigration 26 per cent of her native-born free inhabitants. South Carolina had lost 36 per cent, and North Carolina 31 per cent. Further examination of statistics will, however, show that the movement was probably almost entirely within the limits of the planting states themselves. From 1831 to 1840,

---

[17] *Compendium* of the UNITED STATES CENSUS (1850), p. 178.

[18] Compiled from UNITED STATES CENSUS (1864), Volume on *Population*.

[19] W. V. Pooley, *Settlement of Illinois from 1830 to 1850* (1908), p. 334. Reprinted by permission of the University of Wisconsin Press, Madison.

LOCATION OF FOREIGN RESIDENTS, 1860

| Southern States | Per Cent Foreign | Other States | Per Cent Foreign |
|---|---|---|---|
| Alabama | 1.28 | California | 44.98 |
| Arkansas | 0.86 | Connecticut | 17.54 |
| Florida | 2.36 | Illinois | 18.97 |
| Georgia | 1.10 | Indiana | 8.75 |
| Kentucky | 5.17 | Iowa | 15.71 |
| Louisiana | 11.44 | Kansas | 11.84 |
| Maryland | 11.24 | Maine | 5.96 |
| Mississippi | 1.08 | Massachusetts | 21.13 |
| Missouri | 13.59 | Michigan | 19.91 |
| North Carolina | 0.33 | Minnesota | 33.78 |
| South Carolina | 1.42 | New Hampshire | 6.42 |
| Tennessee | 1.91 | New Jersey | 18.27 |
| Texas | 7.19 | New York | 25.73 |
| Virginia | 2.19 | Ohio | 14.03 |
| | | Pennsylvania | 14.81 |
| | | Wisconsin | 35.69 |

Georgia gained nearly 34 per cent in population; Alabama 91 per cent; and Arkansas 275 per cent. . . . In the next decade, while the percentages of increase were lower, the actual gain in population in these states was little less than in the preceding decade; and if Texas, which appears for the first time in the Census reports, be included, the increase was nearly 200,000 in excess of that of the preceding decade."

In turn, states, like Georgia and Alabama, which had been receiving new settlers, about 1850 began to lose large numbers by emigration westward into Mississippi, Louisiana, and Texas. According to a statement in the *Alabama Beacon,* published at Greensboro, during 1851 there had passed through Cardo, Louisiana, 343 families, with 2,359 whites and 1,556 negroes, 481 wagons and vehicles, 1,365 horses and mules, and 375 oxen. Of these emigrants the number from Alabama was 1,471; from Mississippi, 821; from Tennessee, 541; from Arkansas, 493; and from Georgia, 197.[20]

Most of the persons who migrated from the Old South prior to 1860, sought regions where conditions of soil, cli-

---

[20] *Alabama Beacon,* January 4, 1851.

mate, and topography were familiar, and especially where the cultivation of cotton was possible and more profitable than in the older areas.  As A. B. Hulbert points out: [21] "Long interstate series of good soils, peculiar prejudices brought from afar as to soils and agriculture, and finally reports of adventures in the interior of our land, exerted very positive influences on migration.  As illustrations of the first mentioned influence, the Pontotoc Ridge in Mississippi and the Chennenugga Ridge in Alabama may be cited as lines of social movement dictated by lengthy stretches of good lands.  That rich province of calcareous prairie soil in Louisiana, which breaks across the Texas line to its fullest dimensions, was a vital factor in the story of the interstate phases of the expansion of slavery."  There is little doubt that the migration of persons of Southern birth almost directly westward was due to climate, soil, and topography.  The following table indicates the distribution of persons migrating westward in 1850: [22]

### PERSONS OF SOUTHERN BIRTH IN SOUTHERN STATES WEST OF THE MISSISSIPPI RIVER, 1850

| STATE OF BIRTH | STATE OF RESIDENCE | | | |
| --- | --- | --- | --- | --- |
| | *Mississippi* | *Arkansas* | *Louisiana* | *Texas* |
| United States | 528,800 | 160,300 | 205,900 | 137,100 |
| Maryland | 4,300 | 300 | 1,400 | 500 |
| Virginia | 40,800 | 4,700 | 3,200 | 3,600 |
| North Carolina | 17,000 | 8,800 | 2,900 | 5,200 |
| South Carolina | 2,900 | 4,600 | 4,600 | 4,500 |
| Kentucky | 69,700 | 7,400 | 3,000 | 5,500 |
| Tennessee | 45,000 | 33,800 | 3,400 | 17,700 |
| Georgia | 1,300 | 6,400 | 5,900 | 7,600 |
| Florida | 100 | ......... | 400 | 400 |
| Alabama | 2,100 | 11,250 | 7,300 | 12,000 |
| Mississippi | 600 | 4,500 | 10,900 | 6,500 |
| Missouri | 277,600 | 5,300 | 900 | 5,100 |
| Arkansas | 2,100 | 63,200 | 800 | 4,700 |
| Louisiana | 700 | 1,100 | 145,500 | 4,500 |
| Texas | 200 | 300 | 900 | 49,200 |

[21] Archer Butler Hulbert, *Soil* (1930), p. 76.  Reprinted by permission of the Yale University Press, New Haven, Conn.

[22] Compiled from TWELFTH CENSUS, *Supplementary Analysis and Derivative Tables.*

It may be noted from the foregoing statistical survey that
the white population of the South in 1860 was far more
homogeneous than that of the North. There was no great
influx of new customs, habits, and doctrines that tended to
have a disturbing effect upon the economic life of the section. Slavery was taken for granted because it was a
function of an agrarianism adapted to the peculiar Southern
climate, soil, and market demand. On the other hand, the
great influx of foreign laborers into the North resulted in
a population which looked askance at Southern slavery,
because its unequal competitive nature was inimical to free
white immigrant labor. As the editor of the *Morehouse*
(Louisiana) *Advocate* pointed out: [23] "The great mass of
foreigners who come to our shores are laborers, and consequently come in competition with slave labor. It is to
their interest to abolish Slavery; and we know full well
the disposition of man to promote all things which advance
his own interests."

### Bibliographical Note

Valuable notes on territorial expansion and land policies may
be found in B. H. Hibbard, *History of the Public Land Policies*
(New York, 1924), which is a factual chronicle full of interesting
details; and P. J. Treat, *National Land System, 1785–1820* (New
York, 1910). The importance of land cessions is brought out
by H. B. Adams, *Maryland's Influence on Land Cessions to the
United States* (Baltimore, 1885), in the JOHNS HOPKINS UNI-
VERSITY STUDIES IN HISTORICAL AND POLITICAL SCIENCE. To be
noted also are: Francis P. Burns, "The Spanish Land Laws of
Louisiana," in the *Louisiana Historical Quarterly*, October 1928,
pages 557–581; S. G. McLendon, *History of the Public Domain
of Georgia* (Atlanta, Ga., 1924); William Rouse Jillson, *Ken-
tucky Land Grants* (Louisville, Ky., 1925); and Reuben Mc-
Kitrick, *Public Land System of Texas, 1823–1910* (Madison,
Wis., 1918).

There is a vast amount of literature on the subject of immi-

---

[23] Quoted by F. L. Olmsted, *Journey in the Seaboard Slave States*, Vol.
2, p. 238.

gration. For references to the South, the following are perhaps the best: UNITED STATES CENSUS (1835), *Report: Statistical View of the Population, 1790–1830;* W. J. Bromwell, *History of Immigration into the United States, 1819–1855* (New York, 1856); J. R. Commons, *Races and Immigrants in America* (New York, 1908); and William C. Hunt, "Immigration to the Southern States, 1783–1865", pages 595–606 of Volume V of THE SOUTH IN THE BUILDING OF THE NATION (Richmond, 1909). There is also a brief discussion of population in Edward Ingle's *Southern Sidelights* (Baltimore, 1896). For more specific studies of population movements in the South, see: T. P. Abernethy, *From Frontier to Plantation in Tennessee* (Chapel Hill, N. C., 1932), especially Chapter IV, and *Formation Period in Alabama, 1815–1828* (Montgomery, Ala., 1922), Chapter 6; R. S. Cotterill, *History of Pioneer Kentucky* (Cincinnati, 1917); and William O. Lynch, "The Influence of Population Movements on Missouri Before 1861," in the *Missouri Historical Review,* July 1922, pages 500–516.

A great deal has been written on the early settlement and land system of Texas, but the following are the most satisfactory works: Eugene C. Barker (Editor), *Austin Papers,* two volumes (Washington, 1924); Archibald Henderson, *Conquest of the Old Southwest* (New York, 1920); Cardinal Goodwin, *Trans-Mississippi West* (New York, 1922); Mattie Austin Hatcher, "The Louisiana Background of the Colonization of Texas, 1763–1803," in the *Southwest Historical Quarterly,* January 1921, pages 169–194; F. W. Blackmor, *Spanish Institutions in the Southwest* (Baltimore, 1888); M. Tiling, *History of the German Element in Texas from 1820 to 1850* (Austin, Texas, 1913).

D. H. Bacot, Jr., in an article entitled "South Carolina and the Whitney Cotton Gin," in the *South Carolina Historical and Genealogical Magazine,* July 1918, pages 151–152, describes the purchase of the patent of the cotton gin by South Carolina. An informative study of the opposition in South Carolina to the Tariff Acts of 1820, 1824, and 1827 is that of John L. Conger: "South Carolina and the Early Tariffs," in the *Mississippi Valley Historical Review,* March 1919, pages 415–433.

A succinct editorial on the land policy of the Federal Government as it affected the South is "Passage of the Homestead

Bill," in the *Richmond Whig and Public Advertiser*, March 19, 1860.

For a brief general summary of the territorial expansion and the population problems of this period, see E. L. Bogart, *Economic History of the American People* (New York, 1930).

# CHAPTER IX

# Agriculture in the Ante-Bellum South, 1783–1860

THE population of the ante-bellum South was pre-dominantly rural. In 1860, only three Southern cities had a population above 100,000, and Baltimore, the largest city in the section, had a population of only 212,418. Altogether, there were twenty-seven cities which had a population above 4,000. These cities were of two types: seaports or river ports, and state capitals. The many county seats and rural hamlets could scarcely be classed as urban, since they were mainly aggregates of farmers or plantation owners engaged in overseeing their nearby lands. The percentage of people living in Southern cities of over 4,000 inhabitants was only 7.8 of the total population of the section.

The ante-bellum South was predominantly agricultural, not merely because the Southern colonies had become accustomed to producing export crops for British markets, but primarily on account of the natural environment. There were few minerals, and there was little water power for manufacturing in the Coastal Plains and the Mississippi embayment. These resources lay farther back, in the Piedmont and the Highland regions. Men naturally devoted themselves to agriculture in those physiographic regions of the South where land was available and where mineral and power resources were scarce.

## Cotton

Although it had been demonstrated during the Revolutionary War that cotton could be raised in each of the

Southern States, few persons believed that it would become a profitable crop for market. Two factors combined to make it a staple crop and to spread its cultivation throughout the South wherever soil and climate proved suitable.

On the one hand, a new crop was needed in the South. The cultivation of tobacco was declining because of the exhaustion of the soil, which resulted from the one-crop system, and because of the partial loss of the British market, which during the war had turned to other sources of supply. Indigo was no longer profitable since the British bounty had been lost, and rice could be raised only in limited areas.

On the other hand, there was a new and continually growing demand for cotton. In England, inventions in spinning and weaving led to the establishment of the factory system. By means of these devices, cotton as well as wool could be profitably manufactured into cloth. In New England, where agriculture, on account of soil and climate, was practically limited to subsistence farming, especially during and after the War of 1812, which furnished artificial protection to that industry, men began to establish a cotton manufacture patterned after that in Britain. Furthermore, the old sources of cotton supply, the Levant and the West Indies, were incapable of further expansion. The South turned to cotton culture for the same reason that a business man goes into manufacturing—namely, by utilizing available resources, to supply a market demand at a profit.

However, cotton culture, notwithstanding Eli Whitney's gin, invented in 1793, did not make immediate progress in the South, as is sometimes alleged. In 1800, the total crop was only about 35,000 bales, and the production of this amount was confined mainly to South Carolina and Georgia. As late as 1820, these two states produced over one half of the total American crop. Outside of these states, cotton culture had spread into central North Carolina and southeastern Virginia as far as soil and climatic conditions permitted. Cotton culture entered upon

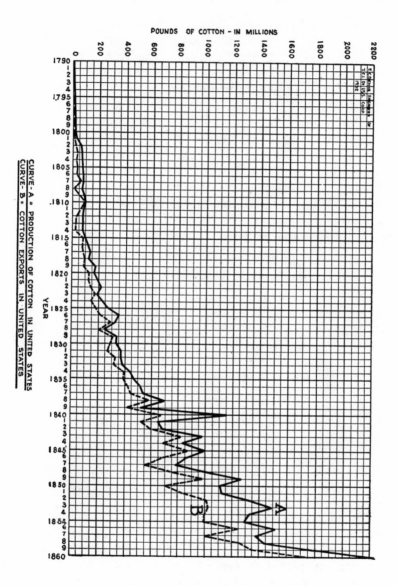

POUNDS OF COTTON - IN MILLIONS

YEAR

CURVE-A = PRODUCTION OF COTTON IN UNITED STATES
CURVE-B = COTTON EXPORTS IN UNITED STATES

231

its most rapid era of expansion, however, between 1820 and 1840, when the Southwestern lands were thrown open to settlement. The history of this expansion of cotton culture into the Gulf region and the lower Mississippi Valley falls into two rather distinct chronological periods, the first, from 1833 to 1837, when the settlement of the Southwest was being promoted by land speculators and newly established state banks; and the second, the period following the annexation of Texas in 1845. The largest increase in cotton production during the decade from 1850 to 1860 came from Texas. As the following table indicates,[1] until 1835, the Atlantic Coast States were the chief producers of cotton, and after that date, the Gulf States usually produced about two thirds of the total crop.

COTTON PRODUCTION, 1800–1860

| Year | Atlantic States (Bales) | Gulf States (Bales) | Total |
|---|---|---|---|
| 1800 | ---------- | ---------- | 35,000 |
| 1824 | 333,253 | 175,905 | 509,158 |
| 1830 | 522,062 | 348,353 | 870,415 |
| 1835 | 493,405 | 760,923 | 1,254,328 |
| 1840 | 642,287 | 1,535,654 | 2,177,532 |
| 1845 | 769,948 | 1,635,015 | 2,394,503 |
| 1850 | 751,271 | 1,345,435 | 2,796,706 |
| 1851 | 742,846 | 1,612,411 | 2,355,257 |
| 1852 | 839,625 | 2,175,404 | 3,015,029 |
| 1853 | 871,712 | 2,391,170 | 3,262,882 |
| 1854 | 788,649 | 2,151,378 | 2,930,027 |
| 1855 | 942,766 | 1,904,573 | 2,847,339 |
| 1856 | 910,192 | 2,617,653 | 3,527,841 |
| 1857 | 775,116 | 2,164,403 | 2,939,519 |
| 1858 | 746,562 | 2,367,900 | 3,114,962 |
| 1859 | 1,111,954 | 2,739,427 | 3,851,481 |
| 1860 | 1,480,000 | 2,920,000 | 4,300,000 |

Cotton was produced in the ante-bellum South under an extensive exploitation of land and labor, primarily, and with a minimum use of capital. The crop, like tobacco in the colonial period, was cultivated on a given tract of land until the fertility of that soil was practically exhausted,

---

[1] Compiled from U. S. Department of Agriculture, *Yearbooks*.

and then a new area was planted.  This system of "mining the soil" caused the need for new land and was one of the compelling factors for migration into the Southwest. "Olmsted," says Professor Broadus Mitchell, "chronicled passing in Mississippi during one day 'four or five large plantations, the hillside gullied like icebergs, stables and Negro quarters all abandoned and given up to decay.  The fertility of the soil might be preserved by throwing slopes into permanent terraces.'  But with Negroes at $1,000 a head and fresh land in Texas at $1.00 an acre nothing of this sort could be thought of." [2]

While there were exceptions in this practice of the exhaustive method of agriculture, and while practically no migratory shifting occurred in certain regions, like the fertile Black Belt of Alabama and Texas, there were, nevertheless, enormous tracts of exhausted and abandoned cotton lands in every Southern State.  The following table shows the amounts of improved and unimproved lands in 1860, and the difference in this respect between the South and the rest of the United States: [3]

LAND IN FREE AND SLAVE STATES, 1860

| Type of Land | Free States | Border States and Territories: Md., Ky., Ill., Mo. | Slave States |
|---|---|---|---|
| Improved Land (Acres)........ | 88,730,678 | 17,547,885 | 56,832,157 |
| Unimproved Land (Acres)..... | 72,983,311 | 27,474,315 | 143,644,192 |
| TOTAL QUANTITY (ACRES). | 161,713,989 | 45,022,200 | 200,476,349 |

Individual cotton planters owned plantations ranging from twenty or thirty thousand acres to even less than a hundred acres.  In several instances, as already pointed out in Chapter VIII of this text, large tracts of land had been granted to individuals even before cotton culture was

[2] Broadus Mitchell, *Frederick Law Olmsted, A Critic of the Old South* (1924), pp. 145–146.  Reprinted by permission of the Johns Hopkins Press, Baltimore.

[3] E. C. Seaman, *Essays on the Progress of Nations* (Second Series, 1868), Vol. II, p. 572.

established on a commercial basis. It must be emphasized that, while there was a tendency to utilize land in large units in the production of cotton, great plantations were not universal. Indeed, besides plantations there were many farms, some of which were as large as the smaller plantations. The difference between a farm and a plantation was one primarily of organization of labor and not of amount of land acreage. A *farm* may be briefly defined as a tract of land cultivated by free labor, while a *plantation* is a tract cultivated by slave labor.

In 1850, the number of cotton plantations in the South was 74,031. These were distributed as follows: Alabama, 16,100; Mississippi, 15,110; Georgia, 14,578; South Carolina, 11,522; Louisiana, 4,205; Tennessee, 4,043; North Carolina, 2,827; Texas, 2,262; Arkansas, 2,175; Florida, 990; Virginia, 198; and Kentucky, only 21.

Farmers—particularly in the Piedmont region—who owned no slaves sometimes devoted themselves to cotton growing, especially after the invention of the cotton gin; for this device made it possible for one man to clean three hundred and fifty pounds of cotton a day, whereas by hand it required one day to clean one pound. In other words, the labor factor, due to this device, could be minimized in proportion to the land factor so as to make it possible to produce cotton almost as profitably on a small area as on a large one, providing, of course, that the land was sufficiently fertile to produce a crop yearly without exhaustion and the subsequent need for new land.

Why were there large cotton plantations in the antebellum South if a large unit of land was not essential for an economical combination of the factors involved in cotton production?

For the sake of analysis, three reasons can be stated separately, although ordinarily no one reason alone is sufficient to explain the existence of almost any given large plantation.

Several large tracts of land had been granted to individuals in the lower South and the Southwest before cotton culture was introduced into these regions, and, as noted elsewhere, there was already a beginning of the system of large landholdings. Cotton culture meant merely the utilization of such estates for a specific purpose. Since cotton culture was carried on in a manner similar to the one-crop system of tobacco culture in colonial Virginia, it was necessary, so far as possible, to have large landholdings in order that the planter might shift his cotton fields from the area that became exhausted to a nearby new tract.

In the ante-bellum South, as in the colonial South, the ownership of a large plantation was the accepted criterion of social prestige. As a result, persons anxious to be classified among the "aristocracy" acquired as much land and as many slaves as possible. This motive seems to have been especially strong among those persons who, before migration, lacked the opportunity of realizing their social ambitions, for there have always been "the rich and those who ape the rich."

In 1857, a Scotchman traveling in the South gave this epigrammatical description: [4] "Niggers and cotton—cotton and niggers; these are the law and the prophets to the men of the South." Nor was this condition surprising, for cotton was the South's best *money crop,* and negro slaves were especially adapted to its cultivation. Little skill was required to plant, cultivate, and pick cotton. Employment in its production was almost continuous for about three quarters of the year. Not only negro men but also women and children could be used in the fields. At the same time, less was required for the maintenance of slaves in the warm climate than in the cooler climate of the border states and the lands farther north. Not least important was the fact that negroes in a cotton field could be supervised in groups, thus preventing "soldiering," which was characteristic of the discipline necessary when slaves were put on separate

---

[4] Stirling, *Letters from the Slave States,* p. 179.

jobs. Furthermore, it was seriously believed by some planters that white laborers could not survive in the semitropical sun of the cotton fields.

As a rule, new slaves were supplied to cotton planters by smuggling either from abroad or from the so-called "slave-breeding" states, because the foreign slave trade, though all the states had already passed laws to check it, was by an act of Congress prohibited in the United States after January 1, 1808. Unlike the colonial planters, the cotton planters had to rely for most of their slaves upon a relatively limited market.

It was generally believed that one negro was required for every three acres of cotton. The planters therefore were confronted with the problem of obtaining the "required number" of negro slaves at a price which, after maintenance and interest on the investment had been deducted, would yield a profit in the cultivation of relatively cheap land. To understand the prices which planters were willing to pay for slaves, it is necessary to consider both the supply and demand sides of the slave market.

As the plantation system expanded, the demand for slaves increased. In the older communities the planters purchased land from the farmers, who, in turn, moved farther west or into the backwoods. This process was repeated until the plantations were sometimes expanded to cover thousands of acres. For example, in Mississippi, Joseph and Jefferson Davis acquired an enormous plantation by buying up dozens of small farms from persons who, either on account of the encroachment of the plantation system or because of a depression, wished to move farther west. In Madison County, Alabama, practically all the surplus income of planters was invested in lands bought from small farmers who, having partially exhausted the soil, moved westward to new land.

As a rule, planters acquired these farms during a period of depression, and, when prosperity returned, they bought more slaves to cultivate their additional acres. There was an even greater demand for slaves on the plantations farther west. From 1820 to 1860, the increase of negro slaves corresponds somewhat roughly to the expansion of the Southwest and the increased production of cotton.

Many slaves were supplied by smugglers, though slave importation was explicitly prohibited by Federal law. According to one estimate, at least 270,000 slaves were smuggled into the United States from 1808 to 1860, inclusive. These were distributed as follows: between 1808 and 1820, 60,000; 1820 to 1830, 50,000; 1830 to 1840, 40,000; 1840 to 1850, 50,000; and from 1850 to 1860, 70,000.

By far the greater supply, however, came from the "slave-breeding" states. As slavery became a burden in the states of the upper South, on account of a decline in prices for their staple agricultural product, the increased demand for slaves in the lower South furnished a market for the slaves from the former states. When agricultural profits declined in the upper South, it became profitable to supply slave labor for the lower South. Evidence is not lacking on this point. In 1832 in the Virginia House of Delegates, Thomas Marshall declared: [5] "As the result of extensive inquiry, embracing the last fifteen years, that a very great proportion of the larger plantations, with from fifty to one hundred slaves, actually bring their proprietors in debt at the end of a short term of years, notwithstanding what would once in Virginia have been deemed very sheer economy, that much the larger part of the considerable landholders are content, if they barely meet their plantation expenses without a loss of capital; and that those who make any profit, it will in none but rare instances, average more than one and a half per cent, on the capital invested. The case is not materially varied with the smaller proprietors."

During the same session of the Virginia Assembly,

[5] Speech of Thomas Marshall in the Virginia House of Delegates, reprinted in the *Richmond Enquirer*, February 2, 1832.

Thomas Jefferson Randolph said:[6] "The exportation (of slaves to the other Southern States) has averaged 8,500 for the last twenty years. . . . It is a practice, and an increasing practice in parts of Virginia, to rear slaves for the market. How can an honorable mind, a patriot, and a lover of his country, bear to see this ancient dominion, rendered illustrious by the noble devotion and patriotism of her sons in the cause of liberty, converted into one grand menagerie where men are to be reared for market like oxen for the shambles."

The sale of slaves became the source of the largest profit of nearly all the slaveholders in the upper South. Thus, according to Frederic Bancroft, who has made an exhaustive study of this subject:[7] "Maryland and Virginia were almost exclusively slave exporting states. Texas was wholly an importing state; Florida and Arkansas were at first only a little less so. The Carolinas, Kentucky, and Missouri early began exporting and increased it, while continuing importations in variously lessening degrees. Until after the Mexican War, Georgia did not export many, and Alabama, Mississippi, and Louisiana imported almost exclusively, except when a few thousand were taken to Texas and interstate markets, like those of Mobile, Natchez, and New Orleans, [and] resold to neighboring states—but subsequently more and more slaves were removed from all those states to Arkansas and Texas in the hope of obtaining still cheaper land and more profitable opportunities to raise cotton."

Accounts of slave-breeding deliberately carried on to supply the slave market of the lower South, have no doubt been greatly exaggerated by unfriendly critics. For example, the Reverend Philo Tower, in 1856, spoke as follows:[8] "Not only in Virginia, but also in Maryland,

---

[6] Pamphlet copy of speech in the Virginia House of Delegates, January 21, 1832, pp. 12 and 15.

[7] Frederic Bancroft, *Slave-Trading in the Old South* (1931), p. 383. Reprinted by permission of the author.

[8] Philo Tower, *Slavery Unmasked*, p. 53.

North Carolina, Kentucky, Tennessee, and Missouri, as much attention is paid to the breeding and growth of negroes as to that of horses and mules. . . . It is a common thing for planters to command their girls and women (married or not) to have children; and I am told a great many negro girls are sold off, simply and mainly because they did not have children."

There is abundant and reliable evidence, however, to show that slave-breeding, though not generally in such an exaggerated form, was carried on in the South. According to John C. Reed, a native of Georgia, a graduate of Princeton University in 1854, and afterwards a practicing lawyer in his native state:[9] "Many of these older sections [of the South] turned, from being agricultural communities, into nurseries, rearing slaves for the younger states where virgin soil was abundant."

Besides the deliberate breeding of slaves, there was the natural increase on every plantation; this source within itself supplied great numbers for the market, since the planters in the older slave states could not support many additional negroes. This fact was recognized by the editor of the *National Era,* a rather moderate antislavery paper, in 1847, when he wrote:[10] "The sale of slaves to the South is carried on to a great extent. The slave holders do not, so far as I can learn, raise them for that special purpose. But here is a man with a score of slaves, located on an exhausted plantation. It must furnish support for all; but while they increase, its capacity for supply decreases. The result is he must emancipate or sell. But he has fallen into debt, and he sells to relieve himself of debt and also from the excess of mouths."

As a matter of fact, the interstate sale of negroes ran into the thousands. As estimated by Frederic Bancroft, after the most careful examination of original sources, the average annual interstate sale of slaves in the decade 1850–

[9] *The Brothers' War,* p. 432.
[10] *National Era,* June 10, 1847.

1860 was 55,151.[11] Despite this number, and the fact that slaves were seldom sold until they were over ten years of age, the supply was never sufficient. The demand for, and the supply of, slaves in the market can be followed in the advertisements of Southern newspapers. The following examples are typical.

In the *Village Herald,* of Princess Anne, Maryland, on January 7, 1831, an advertisement stated: "Cash for negroes for the New Orleans market and will give more than any purchaser that is now or hereafter may come into the market. Richard C. Woolfolk."

In the *Virginia Herald,* of Fredericksburg, Virginia, on January 2, 1836, the following appeared: "Cash for negroes:—We will give cash for 200 negroes between the ages of 15 and 25 years old of both sexes. Those having that kind of property for sale will find it to their interest to give us a call. Finnal and Freeman."

In the *Savannah Republican,* of December 18, 1858: "For sale. Likely country raised girl, 17 years old, capable servant; likely intelligent yellow girl child, five years, country raised; one man and his wife and 2 girl children, 8 and 4 years old, fieldhands; middle aged woman, good plain cook, washer and house servant; 2 likely girls, 8 and 11 years old; 2 boys, capable to saddle and harness, making intelligent good workmen; 2 men, 24 and 26 years old; several old men and women; 1 woman and 2 girl children, woman good cook; several other families. A. Bryan, Market Square."

And, as a final example, in the *Natchez Free Trader,* on February 26, 1836, this notice appeared: "For sale or hire—43 acclimated family negroes, of whom 38 are cotton pickers, and have been accustomed to the cultivation of cotton in a swamp plantation. For terms and further particulars apply to Alfred Cochran."

As would be expected from a consideration of the fore-

---

[11] *Slave-Trading in the Old South,* p. 405.

going facts relative to the demand for and the supply of slaves, the price paid for them by planters varied widely from time to time. The most reliable compilation of these prices has been made by Professor Ulrich B. Phillips. According to his conclusions, the average prices of prime field hands were as follows: [12]

PRICE OF YOUNG SLAVE MEN, ABLE-BODIED BUT UNSKILLED

| Market | 1800 | 1808 | 1813 | 1818 | 1828 | 1837 | 1843 | 1848 | 1853 | 1856 | 1860 |
|---|---|---|---|---|---|---|---|---|---|---|---|
| Washington, Richmond, Norfolk | $350 | $500 | $400 | $700 | $___ | $900 | $___ | $___ | $1,250 | $1,300 | $___ |
| Charleston, S. C. | 500 | 550 | 450 | 850 | 450 | 1,200 | 500 | 700 | 900 | ---- | 1,200 |
| Louisville, Ky. | 400 | ---- | 550 | 800 | 500 | 1,200 | _.• | --- | ----- | 1,000 | 1,400 |
| Middle Georgia | 450 | 650 | 450 | 1,000 | 700 | 1,300 | 600 | 900 | 1,250 | ---- | 1,800 |
| Montgomery, Ala. | --- | ---- | ---- | 800 | 600 | 1,200 | 650 | 800 | ----- | ---- | 1,600 |
| New Orleans, La. | 500 | 600 | --- | 1,000 | 700 | 1,300 | 600 | 900 | 1,250 | 1,500 | 1,800 |

The fluctuation in slave prices during this period should be considered against a background of general price levels. The world price level—and this must be taken as a basis, since cotton was largely an export crop—from 1815 to the discovery of gold in California in 1849, declined about 61 per cent; but from the latter date to 1865. it rose about 188 per cent. Therefore the high money prices paid for slaves after 1853 were due, not only to the extension of slave labor into the Southwest, but also to the general rise of prices. At the same time, however, cotton prices were imperceptibly declining, mainly on account of an extraordinary increase of production which temporarily outran the demands of the textile industry. Another element in the rapid rise of slave prices was the tendency for slave trading to become speculative, and the practice of buying slaves with the primary aim of reselling them later at an appreciated price.

In proportion to land and labor, cotton planters as a

[12] Compiled from U. B. Phillips, *American Negro Slavery*. Chap. XIX. Also see Lewis C. Gray, *History of Agriculture in Southern United States to 1860*, Vol. 2, pp. 663–667.

rule had only a minimum of capital, which consisted principally of plows, hoes, and wagons. As in the colonial period, most of the agricultural implements were made on the plantations or by local blacksmith shops. After 1825, however, the wooden plow gave way to the cast-iron plow. On several plantations and in almost every community, a Whitney gin and cotton presser were installed; and a few planters purchased a simple machine, invented by George G. Henry, of Mobile, Alabama, for the purpose of ginning, carding, and spinning cotton. In cultivating cotton, little or no machinery was used, and the use of fertilizers was almost unknown prior to 1860.

Much has been written about the life of the cotton planter himself. Page, in *Ole Virginia*, makes him a lesser saint. Harriet Beecher Stowe, in *Uncle Tom's Cabin*, shows him as uninterested in the welfare of his slaves. A host of less versatile reformers and self-appointed saviours of the South have used up much ink and paper in setting forth in glittering generalities the cruelty, immorality, and incompetency of the planter class. Fortunately, American scholars have succeeded in debunking most of these misconceptions. None has done more to discover and expose the truth about the ante-bellum South than Professor Ulrich B. Phillips, especially in his most recent book, *Life and Labor in the Old South*.

Obviously cotton planters, like other men, belonged to the species *homo sapiens* and, as such, differed widely from one another in ability and, sometimes, in beliefs and ambitions. No doubt there were planters who treated their slaves cruelly; but it stands to reason that this was the exception rather than the rule, since the monetary value of a slave, if nothing else, tended to safeguard him against any abuse that would impair his value. Furthermore, it must be remembered that slaves imported from Africa were savages who had no conception of civilized conduct and no experience in Anglo-Saxon behavior to serve as a premise for moral suasion in a system of social control. It has required generations of disciplined evolution to bring American negroes as a race to their present status. On the other hand, some planters treated their slaves very kindly, especially the "ole nigger mammies" who cared for the white children. In evidence of this, the South's testimony has been correctly and eloquently summarized by the distinguished editor and orator, Henry W. Grady.

By and large, however, the cotton planters, not unlike their contemporaries who owned factories in New England, looked upon labor solely from the viewpoint of making profit. What they desired was the maximum application of human energy in production at a minimum expense. This could be more easily exacted from slave labor than from free labor, especially in a country where there was an abundance of cheap land.

In ability, the planters differed widely from one another. Some had a formal education, most of them did not, and a few were even illiterate. Politically, they were individualists, resenting the authority of a bureaucratic and highly centralized government. In a sense, their social theory was analogous to that of the Roman *dominus* (lord and master). Most of the planters believed in organized churches and were members of some denomination. In 1860, there were 20,858 church buildings in the South, whereas the rest of the Nation, with a population almost three times as great, had only 33,151 churches. Furthermore, there is little evidence that planters as a class were excessive drinkers of spirituous liquors or that they gambled regularly, though there were individual planters who did both; and the fact that they did, became an interesting item of news.

As a rule, planters had little or no conception of efficiency in organization as a means of reducing the cost of production and consequently increasing the margin of profit from the sale of their crops. Moreover, they could not, like modern captains of industry, quickly dismiss their labor when profits failed to appear, and thereby create an "army of the unemployed." Slaves were more or less immobile.

They had cost large sums of money, and therefore could not be dismissed without loss. Of course, in the upper South, when there were no profits from crops, the slaves could be sold in the lower South or Southwest as long as these were profit-making regions. But toward 1860, with the fall of cotton prices, the problem of declining profits and positive losses became general on all the Southern plantations.

The chief ambition of most planters was to accumulate a great estate, consisting of land and slaves, in order to insure and to perpetuate the social prestige of their families. The regard that most planters had for their families is one of the most striking features of the social history of the South. No doubt this was due in part to the more or less isolated life of the family on the large plantation, for the members of such a family were necessarily brought together in a solidarity of companionship. The home, as both a producing and consuming unit, was also a social unit. The planter, perhaps unlike the modern city man of large affairs, had time to get acquainted with the members of his own family and to develop an affection for them, which he believed could best be symbolized by some tangible economic achievement.

Although the planter was the central figure on the plantation, there was still another person who performed an indispensable function in the organization. This person, "unnoticed in society, with no friends to record his services," was the overseer. As Professor John S. Bassett has said: [13] "The planter might plan and incite, and the slave might dig, plow, and gather into barns; it was the overseer who brought the mind of the one and the muscle of the other into coöperation." Generally he was drawn from the social class known as *yeoman farmers*, though sometimes he was brought up from the ranks of the poor landless

---

[13] John Spencer Bassett, *Southern Plantation Overseer as Revealed in His Letters*, p. 2.

whites. Not only was his education meager, but more often than not he was illiterate.

Toward slaves he usually took a contemptuous attitude, perhaps because he was reacting against his own social status. Yet he had to be a man of common sense and practical judgment, because upon him largely depended the success of the plantation, and even the prevention of the disintegration and breakdown of the institution of slavery. His importance in the plantation system is evidenced by the mere enumeration of his duties. He had to care for the slaves and the livestock. At all times he had to be present with the slaves when they were working, though he himself was permitted to do no work in their presence. Nor could he ever be absent from the plantation without the permission of the planter. He had to distribute food and clothing to the slaves, and to inspect the food cooked for them in the "big pot." At night he was expected to find out whether all the slaves were in their quarters, and to prevent any of them from running away. He also had to see that all sick slaves were cared for according to the general practices of the plantation. Negro cooks, nurses, and specialized laborers had to be appointed and supervised by him. All punishments were either inflicted by him, or ordered and supervised by him, though the slaves, as a rule, had the right of appeal to the planter. Indeed, the overseer was to the negroes the most hated symbol of slavery, for it was he who set the specific tasks and meted out punishment for non-performance of orders as well as for all infractions of rules and regulations. The overseer had to see that the slaves, if possible, produced enough grain, vegetables, and meat, especially bacon, to meet the plantation needs. Finally, he had to raise as much cotton—or other money crops, if his was not a cotton plantation—as possible without overworking the slaves.

For all these services, and many more too numerous to mention, he received annually a salary varying from $250 to $600, though on a few of the largest plantations he re-

THE PLANTER'S ANNUAL INVENTORY OF IMPLEMENTS AND
TOOLS, ON PLEASANT HILL PLANTATION,
DURING THE YEAR 1850

*Tone, Overseer*

| Implements and Tools | Number and Value at the Commencement of the Year | | Purchased During the Year | | Made on Plantation During Yr. | | Number and Value at Close Yr. | |
|---|---|---|---|---|---|---|---|---|
| | No. | Value | No. | Value | No. | Value | No. | Value |
| Waggons........ | 3 | $245.00 | 1 | $90.00 | | | 4 | $340.00 |
| Ox-carts......... | | | | | | | | |
| Horse-carts...... | 1 | 20.00 | 1 | 42.00 | | | 2 | 60.00 |
| Ox-chains....... | 1 | 3.00 | | | | | 1 | 3.00 |
| Ox-yokes........ | 1 | 2.00 | | | | | 1 | 2.00 |
| Plows........... | 32 | 144.00 | 7 | 56.20 | 1 | $10.50 | | |
| Cultivators...... | 6 | 20.00 | | | | | 6 | 20.00 |
| Sweeps......... | | | | | | | | |
| Scrapers........ | | | | | | | | |
| Shovel-plows.... | 6 | 30.00 | | | | | 6 | 30.00 |
| Planters......... | 3 | 10.00 | | | 3 | 15.00 | 4 | 20.00 |
| Harrows........ | 4 | 20.00 | | | 5 | 11.00 | | |
| Wheel-barrows... | 1 | 5.00 | | | 3 | 7.50 | 3 | 10.00 |
| Scoops......... | | | | | | | | |
| Setts Plow-harness........ | 10 | 40.00 | 3 | 3.50 | | | 10 | 40.00 |
| Setts Waggon-harness......... | 3 | 95.00 | | | | | 3 | 95.00 |
| Dung forks...... | | | | | | | | |
| Axes........... | | | 2 | 2.50 | | | 16 | 16.00 |
| Wedges........ | | | | | | | 8 | 4.00 |
| Hoes.......... | 16 | 4.80 | | | | | 20 | 5.00 |
| Spades......... | 2 | 2.00 | | | | | 2 | 1.50 |
| Shovels........ | 2 | 1.50 | | | | | 1 | 0.75 |
| Saws.......... | 4 | 18.00 | 1 | 3.00 | | | 5 | 21.00 |
| Adzes.......... | 2 | 3.00 | | | | | 2 | 3.00 |
| | | $663.30 | | $197.20 | | $44.00 | | $671.25 |

ceived as much as $1,000. Thus it appears that, while the
planter was *de facto* the entrepreneur, the overseer was his
paid manager in the plantation organization.

When the foregoing elements—land, slave labor, planter,
and overseer—are considered together, the result should be
a general conception of the plantation as an organized unit
for cotton culture. Perhaps the most complete extant

# THE PLANTER'S ANNUAL RECORD OF THE STOCK UPON PLEASANT HILL PLANTATION DURING THE YEAR 1850

*Tone, Overseer*

| | Number and Value at Commencement of Yr. | | Purchased During Yr. | | Sold During Yr. | | Number and Value at Close of Yr. | |
|---|---|---|---|---|---|---|---|---|
| | No. | Value | No. | Value | No. | Value | No. | Value |
| *Stock* | | | | | | | | |
| *Horses* | | | | | | | | |
| Work | | | | | | | | |
| Horses...... | 5 | $285.00 | 1 | $142.00 | | | 5 | $410.00 |
| Brood | | | | | | | | |
| Mares...... | 1 | 100.00 | 1 | 85.00 | | | 2 | 200.00 |
| Colts....... | 1 | 25.00 | | | | | 2 | 60.00 |
| *Jack* | | | | | | | | |
| *Mules* | | | | | | | | |
| Work | | | | | | | | |
| mules....... | 8 | 680.00 | | | | | 8 | 850.00 |
| Colts....... | | | | | | | | |
| *Cattle* | | | | | | | | |
| Bulls....... | 1 | 30.00 | | | | | | |
| Cows....... | 13 | 177.00 | | | 1 | $18.00 | 16 | 245.00 |
| Calves...... | 4 | 12.00 | | | 1 | 5.00 | 2 | 10.00 |
| Yearlings.... | 2 | 8.00 | | | | | 3 | 15.00 |
| 2 & 3 yr. | | | | | | | | |
| olds........ | 9 | 45.00 | | | | | 5 | 50.00 |
| Work oxen.. | | | | | | | | |
| Aged | | | | | | | | |
| Oxen....... | | | | | | | | |
| *Sheep* | | | | | | | | |
| Rams....... | 1 | 35.00 | | | | | 1 | 30.00 |
| Ewes....... | 44 | 89.50 | | | | | 42 | 84.00 |
| Wethers..... | 9 | 13.50 | | | | | 7 | 14.00 |
| Lambs...... | 11 | 11.00 | | | 4 | 18.00 | | |
| Goats....... | | | | | | | | |
| *Hogs* | | | | | | | | |
| Boars....... | 1 | 25.00 | | | | | | |
| Brood sows.. | 8 | 32.00 | | | 1 | 5.00 | 3 | 30.00 |
| Pigs........ | 37 | 37.00 | | | 2 | 10.00 | | |
| Shoats...... | 16 | 24.00 | | | | | 49 | 147.00 |
| Stock | | | | | | | | |
| Hogs....... | 79 | 300.00 | | | | | 53 | 159.00 |
| *Poultry* | | | | | | | | |
| Turkeys..... | 11 | 8.50 | | | | | 13 | 11.00 |
| Geese....... | | | | | | | | |
| Ducks...... | 5 | 1.25 | | | | | 16 | 480.00 |
| Fowls....... | 25 | 3.75 | | | 12 | 3.00 | 27 | 6.75 |
| | | $1,924.50 | | $227.00 | | $59.00 | | $2,801.75 |

THE PLANTER'S ANNUAL RECORD OF HIS NEGROES UPON
PLEASANT HILL PLANTATION, DURING THE YEAR 1850

MALES

| Name | Age | Value at Commencement of the Year | Value at End of the Year |
|---|---|---|---|
| John | 70 | $    50.00 | $    75.00 |
| Tone | 49 | 1,000.00 | 1,200.00 |
| Sandy | 38 | 600.00 | 800.00 |
| Edmund | 45 | 1,000.00 | 1,300.00 |
| Tiny | 40 | 700.00 | 950.00 |
| Solomon | 38 | 700.00 | 950.00 |
| Peter | | 700.00 | 950.00 |
| Isaac | 30 | 700.00 | 950.00 |
| Anthony | 25 | 800.00 | 950.00 |
| Scott | 25 | 800.00 | 950.00 |
| George | 20 | 750.00 | 1,000.00 |
| Jim | 27 | 800.00 | 950.00 |
| Detson | 20 | 700.00 | 900.00 |
| Bill | 18 | 700.00 | 900.00 |
| William | 24 | 1,000.00 | 1,100.00 |
| Charles | 10 | 500.00 | 650.00 |
| Henry | 9 | 375.00 | 400.00 |
| Henderson | 8 | 300.00 | 350.00 |
| Johnson | 6 | 250.00 | 275.00 |
| Stephen | 4 | 200.00 | 225.00 |
| Tom | 5 | 250.00 | 275.00 |
| Monroe | 4 | 200.00 | 225.00 |
| Daniel | 2 | 150.00 | 175.00 |
| Sim | 2 | 150.00 | 175.00 |
| Aaron | 3 | 175.00 | 200.00 |
| Jerry | 1 | 75.00 | 100.00 |
| | | $13,625.00 | $16,975.00 |

records of an ante-bellum plantation are the yearly account
books which E. T. Capell kept of his Pleasant Hill plantation from 1850 to 1860.[14] This plantation consisted of
1,485 acres and was located about seven miles east of
Centreville, Mississippi. The following tables show in detail the organization of the plantation and the "profits
realized" from it for the year 1850.

The chief problem of the planters was that which arose
from increasing the production of cotton while the market

[14] The complete set of these account books, except for one year, has
recently been acquired by the Louisiana State University.

THE PLANTER'S ANNUAL RECORD OF HIS NEGROES UPON
PLEASANT HILL PLANTATION, DURING THE YEAR 1850

FEMALES

| Name | Age | Value at Commencement of the Year | Value at End of the Year |
|------|-----|-----------------------------------|--------------------------|
| Hannah | 60 | $100.00 | $125.00 |
| Mary | 34 | 800.00 | 900.00 |
| Fanny | 23 | 800.00 | 900.00 |
| Rachel (Senior) | 32 | 675.00 | 750.00 |
| Martha | 27 | 675.00 | 750.00 |
| Celia | 25 | 675.00 | 750.00 |
| Rachel (Junior) | 24 | 675.00 | 750.00 |
| Diana | 31 | 600.00 | 700.00 |
| Chany | 32 | 600.00 | 675.00 |
| Lucy | 28 | 600.00 | 750.00 |
| Let | 28 | 550.00 | 650.00 |
| Azaline | 13 | 600.00 | 700.00 |
| Amanda | 13 | 400.00 | 600.00 |
| Sarah | 9 | 350.00 | 450.00 |
| Harriet | 8 | 300.00 | 400.00 |
| Bet | 7 | 350.00 | 400.00 |
| Hannah | 7 | 350.00 | 450.00 |
| Maryan | 7 | 275.00 | 300.00 |
| Ellen | 6 | 200.00 | 250.00 |
| Louisa | 5 | 175.00 | 200.00 |
| Susan | 4 | 200.00 | 250.00 |
| Melissa | 3 | 100.00 | 125.00 |
| Matilda | 5 | 200.00 | 225.00 |
| Jinny | 3 | 150.00 | 150.00 |
| Caroline | 3 | 150.00 | 150.00 |
| Frances | 2 | 100.00 | 125.00 |
| Laura | 1 | 100.00 | 125.00 |
| Amarintha | 1 | 75.00 | 100.00 |
| Saraan | 6 mo. | 75.00 | 100.00 |
| Rose | 6 mo. | 75.00 | 100.00 |
| Ann | | | 100.00 |
| Delia | | | 100.00 |
| | | $10,975.00 | $13,100.00 |

price of cotton fell and the cost of production remained
almost constant or even increased. The South's markets
for cotton were New York and Liverpool. Prior to 1820,
the annual crop was relatively small. From 1791 to 1795,
the average annual production was only about 5,200,000
pounds, and of this, 33.43 per cent was exported. During
the next five years, the average annual production rose to

DAILY RECORD OF COTTON PICKED ON PLEASANT HILL
PLANTATION DURING THE WEEK COMMENCING ON
30TH DAY OF SEPTEMBER, 1850

*Tone, Overseer*

| Name | No. | Mon-day | Tues-day | Wednes-day | Thurs-day | Fri-day | Satur-day | Week's Pick |
|---|---|---|---|---|---|---|---|---|
| Sanday | 1 | M. Basket | M. Basket | M. Basket | Cutting rice | Cutting rice | Sundry | |
| Scott | 2 | 95 | 107 | 118 | 108 | 107 | 120 | 655 |
| Solomon | 3 | 85 | 100 | 105 | 107 | 100 | 125 | 622 |
| Bill | 4 | 74 | 80 | 90 | 106 | 106 | 130 | 586 |
| Jerry | 5 | 110 | 150 | 160 | 150 | 154 | 170 | 894 |
| Isaac | 6 | 117 | 124 | 130 | 130 | 120 | 153 | 774 |
| Jim | 7 | 117 | 138 | 160 | 144 | 153 | 157 | 869 |
| Dotson | 8 | 70 | 80 | 108 | 106 | 118 | 127 | 609 |
| Peter | 9 | 100 | 108 | 105 | 100 | Gone to mill | 120 | 533 |
| Edmund | 10 | At shop | At shop | At shop | At shop | Cutting rice | Shelling corn | |
| Anthony | 11 | 95 | 104 | 114 | 112 | 117 | 120 | 662 |
| Chany | 12 | 100 | 108 | 118 | 110 | 105 | 130 | 677 |
| Diana | 13 | 102 | 115 | 118 | 116 | 120 | 121 | 692 |
| Martha | 14 | 89 | 104 | 112 | 105 | 50 | Sick | 460 |
| Celia | 15 | 84 | 90 | 90 | 103 | 100 | 103 | 570 |
| Rach | 16 | 100 | 120 | 120 | 116 | 116 | 117 | 689 |
| Lett | 17 | 64 | 80 | 84 | 60 | 64 | 86 | 438 |
| Rachel | 18 | 100 | 107 | 118 | 114 | 120 | 120 | 679 |
| Lucy | 19 | 86 | 104 | 112 | 107 | 110 | 110 | 629 |
| Azaline | 20 | 55 | 60 | 70 | 60 | 64 | 60 | 369 |
| Amanda | 21 | 50 | 55 | 55 | 60 | 63 | 60 | 343 |
| Charles | 22 | 45 | 50 | 60 | 50 | 50 | 50 | 305 |
| Henry | 23 | 39 | 38 | 38 | 37 | 36 | 30 | 218 |
| Sarah | 24 | 40 | 40 | 38 | 40 | 40 | 40 | 238 |
| | | 1,817 | 2,062 | 2,223 | 2,141 | 2,013 | 2,249 | 12,505 |

about 18,200,000 pounds, and 49.31 per cent was exported.
From 1810 to 1815, the average annual production increased
to about 80,000,000 pounds, and more than half was exported. The War of 1812 caused a great difference between
cotton prices in New York and in Liverpool, and incidentally was the source of several fortunes made at that
period in the North because it enabled those who had
money to buy up Southern cotton at a reduced price and
hold it until the return of peace. From 1824 to 1831, the

## THE PLANTER'S RECORD OF THE SALES OF COTTON, THE CROP ON PLEASANT HILL PLANTATION DURING THE YEAR 1850

| By Whom Sold & When | | No. of Bales | Average Weight | | | | Sold at Per Pound | Charges | | Net Amount of Account Sales | Net Per Lb. |
|---|---|---|---|---|---|---|---|---|---|---|---|
| | | | At Press | Per Sales | Loss | Gain | | Total on The Lot | Average Per Bale | | |
| J. B. Gribble | Septr 23 | 6 | 408 2/3 | 402 1/2 | 6 1/3 | | 13 3/8 | $19.52 | $3.25 1/3 | $303.48 | 12 56/100 |
| Do. Do. | Septr 30 | 6 | 435 | 433 1/3 | 1 2/3 | | 13 1/8 | 20.08 | 3.34 2/3 | 321.17 | 12 3/10 |
| Do. Do. | Octr 7 | 6 | 430 2/3 | 429 1/3 | 1 1/3 | | 13 3/4 | 20.47 | 3.41 1/6 | 333.86 | 12 7/8 |
| By | | | | | | | | | | | |
| E. T. Capell | Octr 24 | 7 | 433 5/7 | 429 5/7 | 4 | | 13 | 00.00 | 0.00 | 391.04 | 13 |
| E. T. Capell | Octr 31 | 7 | 429 2/7 | 425 2/7 | 3 4/7 | | 13 1/4 | 00.00 | 0.00 | 394.85 | 13 1/4 |
| E. T. Capell | Novr 7 | 7 | 443 3/7 | 440 2/7 | 3 1/7 | | 13 1/4 | 00.00 | 0.00 | 408.36 | 13 1/4 |
| | 1851 | | | | | | | | | $2,152.76 | |
| McKee Bulkley & Co. | May 19 | 7 | 426 4/7 | 440 2/7 | | 14 | 9 1/4 & 8 1/4 | 20.46 | 2.92 | 255.82 | 8 3/8 |
| Do. Do. | May 24 | 6 | 444 | 438 | 6 | 00 | 9 & 8 1/4 | 17.86 | 2.97 | 211.95 | 8 |
| Do. Do. | June 5 | 7 | 429 | 425 1/2 | 3 1/2 | | 9 & 8 | 19.91 | 2.84 | 235.88 | 7 7/8 |
| Buckley & Holt | April 12 | 6 | 434 1/6 | 443 | | 9 | 10 3/8 | 17.69 | 2.95 | 257.97 | 9 3/4 |

## THE PLANTER'S RECORD OF THE AMOUNT AND VALUE OF CROPS, &c., MADE UPON PLEASANT HILL PLANTATION, DURING THE YEAR 1850

| Produce of Plantation | On Hand, January 1 | | No. of Acres in Cultivation | Crops Made | Crops Sold | | On Hand, Close of Year | |
|---|---|---|---|---|---|---|---|---|
| | Quantity | Cash Value | | | Quantity | Net Return | Quantity | Cash Value |
| Cotton............ 400 lb. bales | 10 | $ 515.00 | 155 | 65 | 39 | $2,152.76 | 26 | $1,300.00 |
| Cotton-seed......... bu. | 1,400 | 350.00 | | 2,600 bu. | | | 2,600 bu. | 100.00 |
| Sugar .............. | | | | | | | | |
| Molasses .......... | | | | | | | | |
| Rice ............. bu. | 20 | 15.00 | 1 | 12 bu. | | | 20 bu. | 15.00 |
| Corn............. do. | 2,300 | 1,725.00 | 89 | 2,650 bu. | 60 | 25.00 | 2,400 | 2,400.00 |
| Egyptian Oats..... do. | 7 | 4.20 | | | | | | |
| Spring........... do. | 18 | 10.80 | 12 | 28 | | | 30 | 22.50 |
| Peas............. do. | 12 bu. | 12.00 | 20 | 5 bu. | | | 5 | 5.00 |
| Wheat........... do. | | | | | | | | |
| Rye............. do. | | | | | | | | |
| Millet........... do. | | | | | | | | |
| Sweet Potatoes..... do. | 300 | 150.00 | 9½ | 405 | 7 | 6.55 | 390 | 234.00 |
| Irish............ do. | | | ⅛ | 20 bu. | | | | |
| Turnips......... do. | | | | | | | | |
| Artichokes....... do. | | | | | | | | |

| Item | | Qty | Value | | | | Rate | Qty | Value |
|---|---|---|---|---|---|---|---|---|---|
| Hay | tons | 4,000 | 30.00 | 4,000 | 3 | | | 3,000 | 25.00 |
| Fodder | do. | 3,000 | 90.00 | 16,000 | | | | 10,000 | 100.00 |
| Shucks | do. | | | 5,000 | | | | 3,000 | 90.00 |
| Pea-fodder | do. | | | | | | | | |
| Millet-hay | do. | | | | | | | | |
| Pork | pounds | 7,500 | 375.00 | | | | | 3,150 | 157.00 |
| Bacon | do. | | | | | | | | |
| Beef | do. | | | | | 30 | 3.00 | | |
| Lard | do. | 600 | 60.00 | 160 | | | | 300 | 30.00 |
| Wool | do. | 137 | 20.00 | | | | | 160 | 24.00 |
| Feathers | do. | | | | | | | 1 | 2.50 |
| Hides | do. | | | | | | | | |
| Leather, Sides | | | | | | | | | |
| Do., Skins | | | | | | | | | |
| Shoes, pairs made | | | | | | | | | |
| Socks, do. knit | | | | | | | | | |
| Linsey, yards | | | | | | | | | |
| Jeans, do. | | | | | | | | | |
| Cotton Cloth, do. | | 93 | 9.30 | | | | | 490 | 49.00 |
| Do. Sacking, do. | | | | | | | | | |
| | | | $3,357.60 | | | | $2,187.31 | | |
| | | | $3,366.90 | | | | | | $4,554.00 |

253

THE PLANTER'S ANNUAL

SHOWING THE RESULT OF THE SEASON'S OPERATIONS—THE LOSS OR PROFIT

*Dr.*

To

| | | | |
|---|---|---|---|
| 1,485 Acres of Land, with the improvements, forming Plantation, at $5.00 per acre..................... | | | $ 7,425.00 |
| Interest on the same at six per cent................. | | | 445.50 |
| Negroes, as per Inventory at...................... | Page | I | 20,600.00 |
| Interest on the same at six per cent................. | | | 1,236.00 |
| Stock, as per Inventory at........................ | " | J | 1,940.50 |
| Interest on same, at six per cent................... | | | 116.43 |
| Stock purchased during the year, as per............. | " | J | 227.00 |
| Implements and utensils, as per.................... | " | K | 663.30 |
| Interest on same, at six per cent................... | | | 39.79 |
| Do. purchased during the year, as per.............. | " | K | 197.20 |
| Produce on hand at commencement of the year, as per. | " | L | 3,366.90 |
| Plantation expenses, as per statement at............ | " | N | 893.63 |
| | | | $37,151.25 |

production of cotton was practically doubled. At the same time, the price of cotton fell from 20 cents in 1825 to 10 cents in 1831. By the end of the next decade, production had again doubled in quantity, though the price declined to 8.92 cents per pound.

According to the price table on page 256, the lowest cotton prices occurred during the decades between 1840 and 1860; these prices, as already indicated, were almost simultaneous with the rise in the general price level. The fall in cotton prices may be accounted for only in part by the condition of the food crops in England. When food is dear in a country dependent upon foreign supplies for bread, a short harvest would tend to cause such a rise in grain prices as to absorb the earnings of the masses of the people for its purchase and to diminish the buying of clothing. To a certain extent this did happen in England around 1845.

It must be noted, in addition, from the same table that cotton prices began to decline rather rapidly about 1820, when the average annual production of cotton rose from about 80,000,000 pounds to over 140,000,000 pounds. In

BALANCE SHEET
UPON THE CROP OF PLEASANT HILL PLANTATION AT CLOSE OF 1850

*Cr.*

| | | | |
|---|---|---|---:|
| By | | | |
| Acres of Land, forming Plantation with improvements, at $5.00 per acre...................... | | | $ 7,425.00 |
| Negroes, as per inventory, at close of the year as per..Page | I | | 30,025.00 |
| Stock sold and used during the year, as per.......... | " | J | 54.00 |
| Do.   on hand at the close of the year, as per........ | " | J | 2,811.75 |
| Implements and utensils  do.   do.  as per........... | " | K | 671.25 |
| Produce of Plantation sold, as per.................. | " | L | 2,187.31 |
| Do.   of do.  on hand at close of the year, as per.. | " | L | 4,554.00 |
| | | | $47,728.31 |
| | | | 37,151.25 |
| Balance in favor of farm...................... | | | $10,577.06 |

other words, there is evidently some correlation between
the supply of cotton and the price paid for it. It is just
as evident that Southern planters generally failed to realize
this fact. Production was increased more and more, though
prices fell and the cost of production either remained
constant or increased.

In 1831, a speaker before the New York Institute, declared: [15] "I have been lately favored with a minute statement of the average product of five or six cotton plantations in two of the southwestern states, ascertained by
putting together the income of a good and a bad year.
The result of this statement is, that the capital invested
in these plantations yields from fifteen to twenty per cent
clear; and the net profit accruing to the proprietor, for
the labor of each efficient hand is two hundred and thirty-
seven dollars and fifty cents per annum; being a clear gain
of four dollars and fifty cents per week. It further appears
that on one of these plantations (and the same, though not
stated, is believed to hold of the other in due proportion)

---

[15] Quoted by Grenville Mellen's *Book of the United States* (1839),
p. 348.

worth altogether, for land, labor, and stock, ninety-two thousand dollars, the entire amount of articles paying duty annually consumed, is two thousand three hundred dollars. The average crop of this plantation, taking a good and a bad year, is fourteen thousand five hundred dollars."

AVERAGE ANNUAL PRICES FOR FIVE-YEAR PERIODS, 1791–1860, FOR MIDDLING UPLAND COTTON IN NEW YORK AND LIVERPOOL[16]

| Year | Per Cent of Crops Exported | Average New York Prices: Cents | Average Liverpool Prices: Pence |
|---|---|---|---|
| 1791–1795 | 33.43 | 31.7 | No data |
| 1796–1800 | 49.41 | 36.3 | No data |
| 1801–1805 | 56.38 | 25.0 | 15.4 |
| 1806–1810 | 65.38 | 18.9 | 18.4 |
| 1811–1815 | 52.83 | 14.8 | 20.5 |
| 1816–1820 | 67.38 | 26.2 | 16.7 |
| 1821–1825 | 72.93 | 16.2 | 9.2 |
| 1826–1830 | 82.84 | 10.9 | 6.5 |
| 1831–1835 | 82.57 | 11.9 | 8.0 |
| 1836–1840 | 83.15 | 13.0 | 6.7 |
| 1841–1845 | 84.03 | 7.7 | 4.7 |
| 1846–1850 | 74.46 | 8.7 | 5.2 |
| 1851–1855 | 76.51 | 9.6 | 5.4 |
| 1856–1860 | 79.51 | 11.5 | 6.7 |

No doubt planters made large profits while the market price of cotton remained relatively high as compared to the cost of production. But when cotton prices declined, the planters, unable to reduce their cost of production, realized less and less.

In 1853, an apparently well-informed writer described the situation as follows: [17] "Take a plantation well-improved and properly organized, with good buildings, gins, mills, teams, etc., on which there are one hundred slaves, old and young negroes. Let this be cultivated, free of rent or hire, for one year, or a series of years, and left in as

---

[16] Compiled from M. B. Hammond, *Cotton Industry* (1897), Appendix I; and *Cotton in Commerce* (1895)—both publications prepared in the Bureau of Statistics of the United States Treasury.

[17] J. D. B. De Bow, *Industrial Resources . . . of the Southern and Western States* (1853), Vol. I, p. 151 *et seq.*

good order as it was received; it is a fair calculation that such places, upon rich bottom land, will produce annually seven bales, weighing one hundred pounds, to each hand; but not near so much on 'uplands.' On such a plantation, with one hundred slaves, there would generally be found about sixty classified, average field hands—the whole property being worth about $100,000.

| | |
|---|---|
| Thus, fifty hands will produce 350 bales, of 400 pounds; this, sold at five cents per pound, will be $20.00 per bale—350 bales.......... | $7,000.00 |
| From which deduct, for sending to market and selling $2.50 per bale—350 bales........ | $875.00 |
| To feed 100 servants, to furnish hospitals, overseer's table, etc..................... | 750.00 |
| Deduct bagging and rope per bale—350 bales | 525.00 |
| To clothe 100 slaves, shoe them, furnish bedding, sacks for gathering cotton, etc......... | 750.00 |
| Wages to competent overseer.............. | 700.00 |
| Such planting requires 35 or 40 mules, will need an annual addition of about 4 or 5 to sustain the team......................... | 400.00 |
| Annual outlay to keep up farming tools of all descriptions, in wood and iron.............. | 250.00 |
| Taxes on the whole estate.................. | 350.00 |
| Medicine, doctor's bills, etc................. | 250.00 |
| Annual repairs of gins, mills, press, and purchasing new stands, etc.................... | 250.00 |
| Annual outlay for materials to keep in repair all the buildings needed. For nails, lime, plank, and such materials as cannot be had on the place............................ | 200.00 |
| Total expenses above named.......... | $5,300.00 |
| Leaves............................. | $1,700.00 |

"It is to be borne in mind that there are hundreds of small matters not enumerated here, which must be annually purchased, and added to the list of expenses; also, that nothing has been allowed for the support of the planter and his family, which should all be charged to the place, as his supervision is indispensable. Nor has anything been set down to meet those contingencies and incidental losses and costs, to which all such estates are liable, as the loss of servants from epidemics, the loss of whole teams from disease, the frequent accidents to gins and houses from fire, losses from overflows, breaking of levees etc.; and costs of making entirely new all the buildings, gins, etc., on the premises, occurring every fifteen or twenty years. If the reasonable charges are made for all these things, it will be readily seen the balance of $1,750 will fail to meet them. Thus it appears that it will cost 5 cents to produce cotton, and if the land is given, clear of rent, and the labor without hire, a judicious economy only could save the manager of such an estate from debt, if he be required to surrender the property to the owner, at the end of the year, in good condition.

"Nearly half the time in the last ten years, cotton has been sold for the planter on the lowlands, for about five cents per pound, a procedure which the most superficial observer must see has been ruinous; for it would appear, those immense estates not only pay no interest on the large investments, at those rates, but scarcely would the revenues support the charge of cultivating and sustaining them. It would require an extraordinary coincidence of favorable circumstances, to leave the smallest margin of profit to the planters. Their profits begin only when cotton advances above five cents, or the crop reaches beyond the ordinary average of seven bales to the hand; the latter no one ought to presume on, for he will as often fall below as rise above the average."

Obviously it is incorrect to conclude that no plantation made a profit during the years of falling cotton prices. There were a few planters who, when cotton prices were the lowest, derived from their crops an economic rent, which varied according to the fertility of their land. Many planters, however, derived no surplus above the cost of slave labor and capital, though the latter was so small a factor in proportion to the others that only a minimum of income need be imputed to it. Nevertheless, these *marginal* planters did not withdraw from production even when cotton prices fell so low as to cause a deficit—that is to say, the planters became *submarginal*. If an individual planter became insolvent, moreover, about all that happened was a transfer of legal rights to the ownership of the plantation. Cotton was king; and no planter, without increasing his risk, could readily turn to the production of other crops, because a plantation organized with slave labor was not only best adapted for cotton culture but was practically immobile. Negro slaves were not fitted for work that could not be closely supervised.

There could be no rational control of cotton production, for three reasons. The planter, as a rule, had only a meager knowledge of his market. Over three fourths of his crop had to be exported, and by far the largest factory demand for Southern cotton was in the region of Manchester, England. The planter had to commit his crop into the hands of a commission merchant and then to await the returns. The prices paid by commission merchants at Wilmington, Charleston, Savannah, Mobile, New Orleans, and other export towns, rose and fell only as quickly as the slow mails from England could carry the information. It was not possible to obtain much knowledge of probable demand, and sometimes cotton accumulated in such quantities that the British manufacturers bought it at their own bid. The cost of production on any given plantation could scarcely be reduced, because it was already at a minimum. The slaves, who comprised the chief item of operating expenditure, received only those supplies which were necessary to maintain subsistence. There could be no effective coöperation between planters for the control of total cotton production, mainly because planters, like present-day farmers, were individualists; through isolation of occupation and habitual self-reliance in making a living, individualism had become their mode of life.

## Other Staple Crops

As in the colonial period, tobacco, rice, and indigo were still cultivated as staple crops; besides these, there was sugar cane. All such products were produced on plantations with slave labor, but in comparison with cotton, they may be designated as the South's minor staples.

**Tobacco.** From 1790 to 1840, the production of tobacco was almost stationary. The Embargo and the War of 1812 were particularly disastrous to the tobacco planters. According to the *Special Report on Statistics of the Manufacturers of Tobacco*,[18] in 1806, exports of tobacco from this country amounted to 83,186 hogsheads, but in 1808, they fell to 9,576 hogsheads. In 1810, there were 84,134 hogsheads, but in 1814, they fell to only 3,125 hogsheads. In the older Southern States, due to the continuous cultivation of tobacco on land with no fertilizer, the soil was becoming impoverished to the extent that the yield was greatly reduced. The discovery of new methods of curing tobacco and the introduction of a "lemon-colored" leaf in North Carolina, with its subsequent spread into Kentucky, Tennessee, and Missouri, gave a new impetus to the industry. By 1840, the exports of tobacco equalled those of 1790, and from 1850 to 1860, the production increased 115 per cent. In 1860, over 370,000,000 pounds were produced, of which about 50 per cent was exported, mainly to England. This increase in tobacco production came chiefly from the newer Southern States. In fact, between 1840 and 1860, the old tobacco lands of the Tidewater region were so exhausted and the negro population had become such a burden that the economist, George Tucker, of the University of Virginia, predicted that the planters in this region would progressively free their slaves.

**Rice.** In several respects this crop was unique among the agricultural staples of the ante-bellum South. Of the several crops raised by the plantation method directly for

---

[18] UNITED STATES CENSUS (1880), p. 38.

a market, and with the exception of a limited cultivation of sugar cane, rice was the only food crop. Its production, on account of the need for a suitable temperature and a copious supply of water, necessarily was limited to a very narrow locale. Generally the slaves on rice plantations were more cruelly treated than those on any other type of plantation in the South, because such plantations, usually owned by absentee planters who feared the malaria of the lowlands, were operated almost entirely by overseers who desired to make a good showing by increasing production to a maximum. At one time it was believed that it was cheaper to replace slaves in the rice fields than to lighten their tasks and to increase their cost of maintenance. Despite this fact, however, some of the rice planters became the leading agriculturists of the South in the use of scientific methods, such as the rotation of crops and the use of fertilizer.

Prior to 1850, over 50 per cent of the rice crop of the United States was produced in South Carolina alone, and about 80 per cent came from the coastal regions of South Carolina and Georgia. The culture of rice in the antebellum South reached its highest total in 1850, when over 245,000,000 pounds were grown: over 159,000,000 pounds, in South Carolina; and nearly 39,000,000, in Georgia. During the decade 1850–1860, the production of rice in the South declined considerably, as indicated by the table on page 262.[19]

In 1840, about 72 per cent of the crop was exported to foreign lands and to many points in the Northern States. However, as time went on, the exports of rice increased absolutely but declined relatively to the increased total crop. The market price received was far above the actual expense of production; and, as a result, the planters grew rich, built beautiful and spacious homes, and educated their children in the best American and European schools.

---

[19] Compiled from UNITED STATES CENSUS (1850 and 1860), *Reports*.

### PRODUCTION OF RICE IN THE SOUTH

| State | 1850 | 1860 |
|---|---|---|
| Alabama | 2,312,252 lbs. | 493,465 lbs. |
| Arkansas | 63,179 | 16,831 |
| Florida | 1,075,090 | 223,704 |
| Georgia | 38,950,691 | 52,507,652 |
| Louisiana | 4,425,349 | 6,331,257 |
| Mississippi | 2,709,856 | 809,082 |
| North Carolina | 5,465,868 | 7,593,976 |
| South Carolina | 159,930,613 | 119,100,528 |
| Tennessee | 258,854 | 40,572 |
| Texas | 88,203 | 26,031 |
| TOTAL | 245,289,955 lbs. | 187,143,098 lbs. |
| VALUE OF ENTIRE CROP | $8,585,148 | $7,485,723 |

**Indigo.** In the colonial period, indigo was grown both in South Carolina and in Georgia on the higher lands of the seaboard, and was often cultivated on the same plantation with rice. After the Revolutionary War, though large quantities of accumulated stock were exported, the production of indigo quickly declined. John Davis, writing about the year 1799, stated: [20] "The culture of indigo [in South Carolina] is nearly relinquished. It attains more perfection in the *East Indies,* which can amply supply the markets of *Europe.*"

Three causes contributed to this result. First, the Revolutionary War caused the planters to lose the British bounty that had artificially stimulated indigo culture in colonial days. Second, cotton could be produced on the same kind of land as, and far more easily than, indigo. Third, there was the disutility in processing indigo for the market, for a very unpleasant vapor arose from the vats and drying sheds, which was injurious to the health of planters and laborers. As late as 1845, about 35,000 pounds of indigo were produced annually in Orangeburg County, South Carolina, on land that would have been submarginal for cotton culture.

---

[20] John Davis, *Travels of Four Years and a Half in the United States of America,* p. 84.

**Cane sugar.** As early as 1751, Jesuits brought some cane from Santo Domingo and planted it on their Louisiana plantation, which was located just above Canal Street in New Orleans. Ever since that time, sugar cane has been grown in Louisiana. For about fifty years, it had practically no commercial value and was grown only in small patches "for chewing" or for making "syrup" and "tafia," because no way had been found to manufacture "cane sugar." In the meantime several ineffectual attempts had been made to find a satisfactory process of granulating the syrup, but this was not discovered until 1795. In that year, Etienne de Bore proved that cane juice could be crystallized into sugar at a profit. According to Gayarre, De Bore began to plant and make preparations for manufacture in 1794 and, in 1795, made a crop of sugar which sold for $12,000—a good price at that time. An impatient crowd watched the concentration of the juice and when the announcement "It granulates!" was made, "the wonderful tidings flowed from mouth to mouth and went dying in the distance as if a hundred glad echoes were telling it to another." [21]

The unexpected success of De Bore's experiment turned attention to the production of cane sugar, but the emulation of his example was slow because of the high cost of the apparatus and the necessity of waiting several years while the seed cane was being propagated on the plantation. In 1818, the total production of sugar was only about 25,000 hogsheads, and in 1822, when steam power was introduced for crushing the cane, only about 30,000 hogsheads of a thousand pounds each were being produced. Apparently the introduction of the steam engine gave the industry a new impetus, for from 1822 to 1827, sugar production more than doubled. In 1827, there were in Louisiana 308 sugar cane plantations, utilizing over 21,000 slaves. Thereafter, sugar production fluctuated from year to year

---

[21] Charles Gayarre, *History of Louisiana.*

without extraordinary expansion until 1844. In that year, production again doubled over the preceding annual quantities, and the number of sugar cane plantations in Louisiana rose to 762, and the number of slaves utilized thereon, to over 51,000. The production of sugar during the entire period prior to 1860 was erratic; one year the quantity produced would be more than twice that produced in the preceding year, only to fall subsequently to a low figure. This variation was due to the fact that either sugar cane or cotton could be grown on the same plantation. Thus, in 1835, when sugar fell to 6 cents a pound, which was below the cost of production, many planters the next year abandoned cane and planted cotton.

Seven years later, the shift from sugar to cotton production was reversed. The price of cotton fell, and under the provisions of the new Tariff Act of 1842, a duty of 2½ cents per pound was to be imposed upon brown sugar. As a result, many planters turned from cotton culture to the cultivation of sugar cane. The expansion of sugar production was rapid and spread beyond the limits of Louisiana. In 1848, Colonel Jeremiah Austill, of Alabama, made as much as 2,500 pounds of "superior sugar finely granulated and of good color." About the same time there were thirty-five plantations in Texas yielding over 10,000 hogsheads of sugar. In 1849, 113 new sugar houses, including a few in Mississippi, were erected.

In 1850, the price of cotton had risen enough to check further expansion of sugar production in the South. Many planters returned to cotton on account of a fall of sugar prices in 1854. The see-saw shifting between cotton and sugar greatly affected the supply of the latter for the domestic market. Various tariff levies were imposed from time to time, in an effort to stimulate production. At other times the duty was lowered to insure a supply of sugar in the domestic market. But good crops simultaneously in Louisiana and in Cuba tended to make the protective duties ineffective in stabilizing sugar prices, while the short crops of sugar caused the price to rise in spite of the low tariff. Politicians made much of the effectiveness of the tariff in stabilizing sugar production in Louisiana, and there are writers who still maintain that its production in the ante-bellum South was contingent upon such protection.

In the production of the staple crops, cotton, tobacco, rice, indigo, and cane sugar, the planters were confronted with the problems inherent in the system of slave labor. Slavery prevented the mobilization of labor from where it was overabundant to where it was most needed. Olmsted found that in the Red River cotton plantations much cotton was allowed to waste because there was no extra supply of labor.[22] Slaves were inefficient and careless, and their average daily output was amazingly small. "Slave labor in each individual case and for each small measure of time," wrote Edmund Ruffin, of Virginia, "is more slow and inefficient than the labor of a free man."[23]

## Food Crops and Livestock

In addition to the staple money crops, the ante-bellum South produced a few food crops for local consumption. On the plantations such crops supplemented the staples, while on the small farms, especially in the Highland region, they were usually the principal crops. The great prominence of cotton has tended to overshadow the importance of these lesser crops, and has caused some writers immediately prior to 1860 to assume that the South was wholly dependent upon the North for provisions. Thus, Kettel, writing in 1860, quoted the following from the daily press as expressing a common belief at that time:[24] "Such is the mutual dependence of the South and the North that, were it not that the latter supplies to the former its provisions, clothing, and agricultural implements, the South

---

[22] F. L. Olmsted, *Journey in the Black Country*, p. 346.
[23] Quoted from U. B. Phillips, *American Negro Slavery*, p. 352.
[24] Thomas P. Kettel, *Southern Wealth and Northern Profits*, p. 43.

would not be able to supply any cotton for export, but
could scarcely supply home demand." Then Kettel, by
citing statistics from the Federal Census reports, goes on
to demonstrate the "fallacy" of this statement. The truth
seems to be that certain regions of the ante-bellum South
were much less dependent than others upon Northern sections of the country not only for food but even for producer's goods.

Corn. This product was grown on practically every
farm and plantation in the ante-bellum South. In 1849,
the per capita yield was about 37 bushels, and the total
crop was about 60 per cent of that raised in the United
States. A decade later, the total yield for the section rose
about 20 per cent, but fell relatively, because it was only
52 per cent of the total crop of the United States. It is to
be noted, however, that Kentucky, Tennessee, and Virginia
were the chief corn-producing states of the South.[25]

### YIELD IN BUSHELS OF CORN IN THE ANTE-BELLUM SOUTH

| State | 1849 | 1859 |
|---|---|---|
| Maryland | 10,749,858 bu. | 13,444,922 bu. |
| Virginia | 35,254,319 | 38,319,999 |
| North Carolina | 27,941,051 | 30,078,564 |
| South Carolina | 16,271,454 | 15,065,606 |
| Georgia | 30,080,099 | 30,776,293 |
| Florida | 1,996,809 | 2,884,391 |
| Alabama | 28,754,048 | 33,226,282 |
| Mississippi | 22,446,552 | 29,057,682 |
| Louisiana | 10,266,373 | 16,853,745 |
| Texas | 6,028,876 | 16,500,702 |
| Arkansas | 8,893,939 | 17,823,588 |
| Missouri | 36,214,537 | 72,892,157 |
| Kentucky | 58,672,591 | 64,043,633 |
| Tennessee | 52,276,223 | 52,089,926 |
| TOTAL | 355,846,729 bu. | 433,067,490 bu. |
| UNITED STATES | 592,071,104 bu. | 838,992,742 bu. |

As a matter of fact, corn, or maize, has been peculiarly
identified with the entire development of the South. Not

[25] Compiled from *Reports* of the UNITED STATES CENSUS (Seventh and
Eighth).

only was it commonly cultivated in every community and fed to domestic animals, but it usually entered into the diet of the Southern people, both black and white, as a most important element. Indeed, "hoecakes," "corn pone," "grits," "mush," and hominy were important items on menus from the Potomac to the Rio Grande.

**Wheat.** In 1849, 27 per cent of the total wheat crop of the Nation and, in 1850, 22 per cent, were raised in the South. Production, however, was limited mainly to the northern and more elevated portions of the South. Thus, in 1859, Maryland, Virginia, North Carolina, Tennessee, Kentucky, and Missouri, together, produced approximately 83 per cent of the South's total crop of about 49,000,000 bushels.

**Other cereal crops.** In 1859, the Southern States were producing 19 per cent of the total rye crop in the United States, and 5 per cent of the total crops of buckwheat and barley, respectively. Like wheat, each of these crops was produced in the northern and more elevated regions of the South. Buckwheat, which, contrary to popular legends, has always been a minor crop in the South, was at this time produced almost solely in the Appalachian region.

**Vegetables.** Of these the most important was the sweet potato, a plant almost peculiar to the South. In 1850, the crop amounted to about 30,000,000 bushels. The industry had assumed little commercial importance, for nearly all of this quantity was required to feed the resident population. No wonder, therefore, the novelists of Southern life seldom fail to mention the sweet potato, as a touch of local color in their stories!

The Irish potato also held an important place on the menu of the South. In 1850, this crop amounted to about 12,000,000 bushels, and like sweet potatoes, this quantity was consumed by the resident population. Nor must peas and beans, especially cowpeas, be overlooked. The latter have long been one of the chief vegetable foods of the poor whites and the negroes throughout the lower South.

Although several different vegetables were grown on practically every Southern farm and plantation, the variety was by no means so great as in recent years. Nor was there so much demand for vegetables in the diet of the population, for science had not yet emphasized the virtues of a vegetable diet. No trucking area was devoted exclusively to the growing of vegetables for market, because nearly every home maintained its own garden. The vegetable and fruit growing of the ante-bellum South was of no commercial importance, and the great vegetable and fruit industries which now characterize some of the Southern States were to be developed after slavery was abolished and urbanization had begun in earnest.

**Miscellaneous crops.** Prior to the census report in 1840, there are scarcely any records of the hay crop of the United States. At that time the hay crop of the state of New York was about four times that of the entire South. Perhaps this lack of hay may be accounted for by the fact that pasturage was climatically possible longer in the South than in the North. What is more probable is that land was valued more highly for producing staples than for growing hay. As a result of the situation, the South began to depend for hay largely upon the markets of the North. In other words, land came to have a specialized use: in the North, hay had to be produced for the winter; in the South, staple crops could be produced more profitably than hay.

Besides the foregoing crops, mention should perhaps be made of two or three crops which were a kind of survival of the agricultural system of colonial days. These were flax, hemp, and hops. In 1860, Kentucky produced 39,409 tons of hemp and 340 tons of flax; and Missouri, 19,267 tons of hemp and 50 tons of flax. Other Southern States producing much smaller amounts of hemp and flax were North Carolina, Tennessee, and Arkansas. In 1850, 33,780 pounds of hops were produced in the South.

**Livestock.** In 1840, the total number of livestock in the South was 31,055,189, as compared with 30,864,814 in the North. A decade later, the difference was greater, but to the advantage of the South.

Although "niggers and mules" were generally considered inseparable on cotton plantations, the South, during the two decades before 1860, was raising four or five times as many horses as mules. In addition, draught horses were raised, and the American saddle horse must be regarded as almost exclusively a Kentucky product. Not only Kentucky, but also Virginia, Missouri, Tennessee, and South Carolina were noted in ante-bellum days for fine horses and horsemanship.

The statistics for 1860 show Missouri first among the Southern States in the raising of horses, with Kentucky, Texas, and Virginia close behind. Kentucky led in the number of mules, while Tennessee, Alabama, and Georgia produced only a few less.

In 1783, a Maryland firm, by the name of "Miller & Gough," imported into Virginia a few shorthorn cattle from Europe. This was the beginning of a valuable cattle industry in the northerly and more elevated regions of the South. The admission of Texas into the Union was of great economic importance to the cattle industry, for throughout the western portion of the state vast herds of long-horned cattle roamed almost wild. The Federal Census of 1860 shows that there were over 3,000,000 head of cattle in Texas, a number three times as great as that in either Missouri, Virginia, or Georgia, the other most important cattle-raising states of the ante-bellum South.

In Maryland, Kentucky, Missouri, and, to a certain extent, Tennessee, the sheep industry developed rapidly on account of the introduction of the Merino breed. Each of the Southern States raised enough sheep to supply the wool and mutton required for home use. Throughout the South, especially in the hilly regions, considerable numbers of goats were raised also. Although the Sultan of Turkey, about 1849, sent a few Angora goats into South Carolina, most of the Southern goats were of the short-haired type, and were used for food and not for milking purposes, as in some European regions.

Hog meat was one of the most important items in the diet of the Southern population. Everywhere swine were raised in large numbers. The razorback, made famous by humorists, roamed the woods and lived upon acorns and wild legumes. His chief characteristics were a long snout, an indefatigable energy for rooting, and a high-geared speed necessary to escape the negroes who, when chance afforded, went foraging for bigger quests than "massa's" chickens or watermelons. Kentucky took the lead in introducing improved breeds, and the well-known Hampshire seems to have been developed largely in that state. At any rate, the Kentucky "Thin-Rinds" were a race of hogs superior to the proletariat razorbacks.

Two other products of Southern agriculture must be mentioned—poultry and bees. For the former there are no statistics, but there is sufficient reason to believe that practically every home produced enough poultry for its own requirements. Likewise, bees were common and were peculiarly suited to the South, where nectar-laden flowers filled the springtime with fragrance. Indeed, the South had a prosperous bee industry, for in 1850, the statistics show a total production of 7,964,760 pounds of honey and wax, valued at $1,194,714.

If one compares the yield of the North with that of the South and at the same time remembers that about two thirds of the population of the Nation lived in the North, it becomes plainly evident that the South produced its share, and sometimes more than its share, of general agricultural produce and livestock. Thus, in 1860, the South produced nearly one fourth of the wheat, over one half of the corn, about nine tenths of the sweet potatoes, nearly one half of the horses, about nine tenths of the mules and asses, over one third of the sheep, and nearly two thirds of the swine. A decade earlier, the statistics would have been even more favorable to the South, for the rapid development of the Northwest more than offset that of the Southwest, and as a result the South lost proportionately in corn and wheat production.

## Agricultural Specialization

There has been a general impression that the ante-bellum South was so specialized in the production of a few staple crops, especially cotton, that it was necessary to import most of the food supply from other states. In the face of facts, this generalization must be modified.

The South, loosely described, consisted of three agricultural zones. The border states and the more elevated regions, engaged mainly in raising food crops and livestock, comprised one zone, which produced not only enough food for the resident population, but also a considerable surplus for market. The Cotton Belt extended from the Atlantic coastal region into Texas. This was the zone that had to import much food and livestock, though practically every planter produced some of both. The regions producing tobacco, rice, and sugar cane may be considered as a kind of peripheral zone around the coast from Maryland to Texas. In this zone a few planters, here and there, produced practically all their own food, but a great many of them were almost wholly dependent upon imports from other regions. The states in 1860 that produced the smallest per capita amount of foods, such as wheat, corn, and pork, were: South Carolina, Florida, and Louisiana.

Although there are no statistics indicating the exact amount of food and livestock bought in any given year by the importing states of the South, there is enough evidence to show that most of the supply came from the border states of the South and from the West. Most of the foodstuffs were sent down the Mississippi River from Ohio, Kentucky, Missouri, and Tennessee. Levi Woodbury, writing in 1833 of his trip down the Mississippi, said: "At every village we find from ten to twenty flat-bottom boats, which besides corn on the ear, pork, bacon, whiskey, cattle, and fowls, have a great assortment of notions from Cincinnati and elsewhere. Among them are brooms, cabinet-furniture, cider, plows, apples, and cordage. They remain in one place until all is sold out, if the demand be brisk; if not, they move farther down. After all is sold they dispose of their boat and return with the crews by the steamers to their homes."

The nature and origin of some of the trade is indicated by De Bow in his *Resources of the Southern and Western States*, published in 1853.[26]

SOUTHERN DESTINATION OF ARTICLES SHIPPED
FROM THE POST OF CINCINNATI, 1850–1851

| Commodity | To New Orleans | To Other Down-River Ports |
|---|---|---|
| Beef, barrels............... | 19,319 | 68 |
| Butter, firkins and kegs....... | 35,200 | 959 |
| Cheese.................... | 69,258 | 48,432 |
| Candles, boxes.............. | 76,245 | 20,272 |
| Flour, barrels.............. | 281,609 | 95,943 |
| Lard, barrels.............. | 22,854 | 117 |
| Pork, barrels.............. | 112,622 | 1,055 |
| Lard, kegs................. | 56,380 | 5,358 |
| Pork, pounds.............. | 1,345,860 | 755,860 |
| Whiskey, barrels........... | 140,661 | 56,164 |

Besides shipments down the Mississippi, horses and mules from Kentucky and Tennessee, like slaves from Virginia, were generally driven overland into the cotton states and then sold at retail.

Practically all the importation of food and livestock into the Southern States rested upon the principle of *comparative advantage*. As long as the planters were receiving a profitable price for their cotton, they believed that specialization was to their advantage. As soon as the price of cotton fell, the system of an unbalanced agricultural economy began to impinge upon them, and their reaction

---

[26] See J. D. B. De Bow, *Resources of the Southern and Western States*, Vol. I, p. 212.

was often expressed in verbal protest, though seldom in a change of practice.

For example, Edward Ingle attributes the following statement to a Mississippian in 1853: [27] "Let the cotton planters for three years dare to make their own corn, pork, beef, mutton, wool, and they will see cotton at a certain price of twelve cents, and see good corn-houses, full barns, fine pastures, thrift, and all else indicative of prosperity. In lieu of which, what did you see in your last summer's tour? Did you see any little twelve by six log cribs covered with four-feet board? Any fodder-stacks, with the Mississippi mud? A pasture for calves without grass or water? Sheep with one-half without food? Fences as if the rails had fallen from above and happened to light upon each other? Men riding with rope bridle-reins? It boots not what I am, whether the one thing or the other. Are these things true or false? Has the age of false prophets and bad counselors passed?"

## Efforts to Promote Scientific Agriculture

Agriculture in the ante-bellum South, both on the plantations and on the farms, was characterized by a simplicity of method. However, there were a few noteworthy experiments in farming and a few attempts to disseminate scientific knowledge among the agriculturists.

After the colonial period, George Washington was the first conspicuous Southerner to advocate scientific agricultural methods. He was followed by Edmund Ruffin, of Petersburg, Virginia, who aroused some interest in the study of soils. But the farmer and planter, as long as land was virgin soil and crop prices were high, regarded all such efforts as unnecessary innovations.

Eventually, various organizations and periodicals, intended to stimulate attention in the possibilities of an im-

---

[27] Edward Ingle, *Southern Sidelights* (1896), p. 57. Reprinted by permission of Thomas Y. Crowell Company, New York.

proved system of agriculture, came into existence, and, as time went on and land became exhausted, these may have had some slight influence upon the South. In 1819, *The American Farmer,* always considered the pioneer agricultural paper, was established at Baltimore. It was devoted mainly to general agriculture from the Southern viewpoint, and numbered among its contributors most of the men who were important in the agricultural development of the Southeastern States.

Other periodicals of considerable importance were: *The Southern Agriculturist,* of Charleston, South Carolina; *The Farmers' Register,* of Petersburg, Virginia; *The Southern Planter,* of Richmond, Virginia; *The Southern Cultivator,* of Augusta, Georgia; *The Tennessee Agriculturist* and *The Southwestern Farmer,* of Raymond, Mississippi; *The Alabama Planter, The Carolina Planter,* and *The Countryman,* of Eatonton, Georgia; and *De Bow's Commercial Review,* of New Orleans. All were published during the two or three decades before 1860, and contributed much information to the agriculturists, although a great deal of the printed matter was comprised of propaganda of one sort or another, mainly of a political nature.

Of most importance, however, was *The American Cotton Planter,* for this paper was ably edited. Among other things advocated was diversification. For example, in January 1853, the following exhortation appeared in its pages: "We are . . . paying $18 to $20 per barrel for pork, say $9 to $10 per hundred, when we can, to a certainty, cultivate 30 acres of corn per hand, which at only 20 bushels, will make 600 bushels of corn to feed hogs. . . . Are we to lose all advantage of our climate?"

In the South the first agencies formed to promote the study of natural resources were the agricultural societies. Of these the first was founded in South Carolina as early as 1784. Yet it was not until the middle of the nineteenth century that such organizations became general throughout the South, but these societies perhaps contributed more to the social life of the states than to the dissemination of scientific knowledge.

Agricultural fairs and expositions ought also to be mentioned. By 1860, practically every Southern State was holding an annual fair. On these occasions premiums of all sorts were offered. For instance, a notice of a fair to be held in Alabama in 1851, in the Greensboro *Alabama Beacon,* listed prizes for corn, cotton, wheat, rice, sugar cane, field peas, Irish potatoes, sweet potatoes, and oats; for cattle, horses, poultry, cakes, preserves, needle work of several kinds; and for wine and other things. In addition to the premiums, there was to be an "orator of the day." These fairs were of more social than scientific value, and frequently, according to the reporters, some prominent lady proved to be "the bright, particular star, the observed of all observers." [28]

Prior to 1860, the South did not feel keenly the need for scientific knowledge, and therefore moved very slowly in the direction of agricultural betterment. As De Bow pointed out in 1847: "It is a common complaint, founded also upon too melancholy a truth, that the Southern States have been content to prosecute agriculture with little regard to system, economy, or the dictates of liberal science."

### Bibliographical Note

Agriculture in the ante-bellum South can best be approached through the works of U. B. Phillips. His *American Negro Slavery* (Boston, 1918) and *Life and Labor in the Old South* (Boston, 1929) are well drawn pictures of a vanished civilization. He has also edited the first two volumes of *Documentary History of American Industrial Society,* ten volumes (Cleveland, Ohio, 1910–1911), which present valuable source material on the plantation system. In Volume V, pages 152–275, of THE SOUTH IN THE BUILDING OF THE NATION, thirteen volumes (Richmond, 1909–1913), there are several short articles

---

[28] For a detailed description of such occasions in the social life of that period, see Minnie Clare Boyd, *Alabama in the Fifties.*

which give a disjointed but informative description of agriculture in the ante-bellum South.

A few very good sectional studies have been made of Southern slavery. To be mentioned are: John S. Bassett, *History of Slavery in North Carolina* (Baltimore, 1899); H. A. Trexler, *Slavery in Missouri, 1804–1865* (Baltimore, 1914); I. E. McDougall, *Slavery in Kentucky, 1792–1865* (Washington, 1918); R. H. Taylor, *Slave Holding in North Carolina: An Economic View* (Chapel Hill, N. C., 1926); and C. H. Wesley, *Negro Labor in the United States, 1850–1925* (New York, 1927), which pays particular attention to plantation slavery. On the slave trade, the best treatment is Frederic Bancroft, *Slave-Trading in the Old South* (Baltimore, 1931). Well worth consulting also is W. E. B. Du Bois, *Suppression of the African Slave-Trade to the United States, 1638–1870* (New York, 1896).

The best contemporary descriptions of the ante-bellum South are: F. L. Olmsted, *Journeys and Explorations in the Cotton Kingdom,* two volumes (New York, 1861); and J. D. B. De Bow, *Industrial Resources etc. of the Southern and Western States,* three volumes (New Orleans, 1852–1853).

A rather unsympathetic study of Southern agriculture is M. B. Hammond, *Cotton Industry: An Essay in American Economic History* (New York, 1897). An interesting study is W. E. Dodd, *Cotton Kingdom* (New Haven, Conn., 1921); and the best elementary sketch of cotton in the South is E. C. Brooks, *Story of Cotton and the Development of the Cotton States* (Chicago, 1911). Robert L. De Coin, *History and Cultivation of Cotton and Tobacco* (London, 1864), contains some interesting information, though this study has been superseded by more scholarly and comprehensive works. For a brief contribution to the study of marketing cotton, see Alfred H. Stone, "The Cotton Factorage System of the Southern States," in the *American Historical Review* for April 1915, pages 779–797.

*Tobacco Industry in the United States* (New York, 1907), by Meyer Jacobstein, contains a brief treatment of the ante-bellum period of tobacco production in the South.

The only satisfactory study yet made of the plantation overseer is that by John Spencer Bassett, *Southern Plantation Overseer as Revealed in His Letters* (Northampton, Mass., 1925). F. P. Gaines, *Southern Plantation: A Study in the De-*

*velopment and Accuracy of a Tradition* (New York, 1924), is an effort to check the popular conception of the old plantation system with authentic material on the plantation as it actually existed. Of greater literary charm, but less authoritative, is Thomas Nelson Page, *Old South* (New York, 1892).

Of the great number of brief sketches and essays on ante-bellum agriculture, two are of special interest: F. J. Turner, "The South, 1820–1830," in the *American Historical Review*, April 1906, pages 559–573; and William M. Brewer, "Some Effects of the Plantation System upon the Ante-bellum South," *Georgia Historical Quarterly*, September 1927, pages 250–273.

W. T. Hutchinson, *Cyrus Hall McCormick: Seed Time, 1809–1856* (New York, 1930), contains some interesting material on agricultural improvements; and A. O. Craven, *Edmund Ruffin, Southerner* (Chicago, 1932), brings scholarly and new research to the study of this important leader in the movement for scientific methods in Southern agriculture.

# CHAPTER X

# Industry in the Ante-Bellum South, 1783–1860

AS IN the colonial period, manufacturing in the ante-bellum South was still of secondary importance. Planting was generally considered the quickest road to fortune and to social distinction. In the cotton states the planters invested their surplus capital in land and negroes to make "more cotton to buy more negroes, to raise more cotton to buy more negroes." The planters as a class, "like the haughty Greek and Roman," looked down upon "the trading and manufacturing spirit as essentially servile." [1]

## Development of Industry

In spite of an agrarian predominance, however, manufacturing continued to increase absolutely in the South, especially in the Piedmont and the Highland regions, until, by 1860, the South had almost as much capital invested in manufacturing as there had been invested in similar industries in New England a decade before. The South possessed nearly one fifth of the manufacturing establishments of the Nation.

### LUMBER INDUSTRY

Of industries dependent on forest reserves, the most important was lumbering, because of the increasing market demand for timber, especially after 1834. By that time, yellow pine had been introduced in the North for ship-building. This industry required inexpensive equipment

---

[1] *De Bow's Review,* Vol. XII, p. 556.

and unskilled labor only. In Virginia, from 1810 to 1860, the number of sawmills increased from 112 to 779, and, according to Olmsted, that state was engaged also in an extensive manufacture of cypress shingles and had even raised for that purpose the sunken timber of the Dismal Swamp.[2] In 1834, a Maine company had acquired 700,000 acres of timber in Georgia and was operating 4 mills and 18 saws in the neighborhood of Savannah. Toward the middle of the century, North Carolina lumbermen migrated from their stumped-out state to Alabama and western Florida, and began to fell trees for lumber. By 1855, Mobile and Wilmington were each exporting annually about 18,000,000 feet of lumber, over one third of which went to foreign ports. In Louisiana, in 1800, 30 sawmills were producing lumber for sugar boxes. Some of the first steam engines in the Southwest ran sawmills on the lower Mississippi. In fact, the production of lumber during the decade prior to 1860 increased more rapidly in the South than it did for the United States as a whole:[3]

VALUE OF LUMBER PRODUCTION IN THE SOUTH, 1839–1859

| State | 1839 | 1849 | 1859 |
|---|---|---|---|
| Virginia...................... | $538,092 | $  977,412 | $2,201,187 |
| Maryland and Dist. of Columbia. | 226,977 | 614,168 | 626,989 |
| North Carolina............... | 506,766 | 985,075 | 1,074,003 |
| South Carolina............... | 537,684 | 1,108,880 | 1,124,440 |
| Georgia...................... | 114,050 | 923,403 | 2,412,996 |
| Florida...................... | 20,346 | 391,034 | 1,476,645 |
| Alabama..................... | 169,008 | 1,103,481 | 1,873,484 |
| Mississippi.................. | 192,794 | 913,197 | 1,823,627 |
| Louisiana.................... | 66,106 | 1,129,677 | 1,575,995 |
| Texas....................... | ---------- | 466,012 | 1,735,454 |
| Kentucky.................... | 130,329 | 1,502,434 | 2,463,085 |
| Tennessee................... | 217,606 | 725,387 | 2,199,703 |
| Arkansas.................... | 176,617 | 122,918 | 1,155,902 |
| Oklahoma.................... | ---------- | ---------- | ---------- |
| Missouri.................... | 70,355 | 1,479,124 | 3,074,226 |
| TOTAL SOUTH........... | $2,966,730 | $12,442,202 | $24,817,736 |
| UNITED STATES......... | $12,943,507 | $58,521,976 | $93,338,606 |

[2] F. L. Olmsted, *Seaboard Slave States*, p. 150.

[3] Compiled from statistics of the United States Forest Service.

Naval stores—that is, spirits of turpentine, tar, and rosin —which in the colonial period were produced in all of the Southern colonies, subsequently became a special product of the pine forests of the Carolinas, Georgia, Florida, and the eastern Gulf States. For a few years the production of turpentine was especially carried on in North Carolina. But in 1834, the process of distillation was greatly simplified by the introduction of the copper still, and as a result more attention was given to the turpentine industry in other regions of the South. By 1842, rectified spirits of turpentine (camphene), though a rather dangerous explosive, had become popular as an illuminant. This product was manufactured at Mobile. Such large quantities of spirits of turpentine were manufactured in the South that rosin, the residuary product, was greatly overproduced and the stills had to be moved away from the seaports into the forests to prevent unnecessary transportation. In 1860, the value of the turpentine produced in the South was $7,400,000.

After the Revolutionary War, shipbuilding in the South, except in Maryland, was of minor importance. In 1810, Baltimore ranked second among American ports in the ownership of merchant vessels, and these vessels were largely the product of its own yards. During the war with Great Britain, 209 vessels were sent out as privateers from this port, and subsequently Chesapeake builders maintained an enviable reputation for the quality and speed of their sailing vessels.

Although most of the shipyards were north of Virginia, there were sporadic attempts at shipbuilding south of that state and along the Gulf coast. In 1850, according to newspaper reports, there was a movement on foot to build a large steamboat at Mobile. Two years later, a company prepared to build a "large merchant ship," and the *Cotton Planter*, in 1853, boasted that this ship, the *William Jones Jr.*, was the first ever entirely built and furnished in the vicinity of Mobile. Alabama began to offer state bounties upon tonnage built within the state, and in 1852, the Louisiana Legislature offered a bonus of $5 a ton for every vessel of more than 1,000 tons built in the state. The industry in either state could not compete with the more highly subsidized shipbuilding industry in the North and the better built ships at Baltimore. River boats and steamboats were produced at St. Louis and Louisville, but both were soon surpassed by Cincinnati in the production of river vessels.

The value of vessels built in the United States in 1840 was $7,069,094, of which only $684,032 belonged to the Southern States. In 1860, the South built only 236 vessels, having a total tonnage of 39,478; while the North built 835 vessels, having a total tonnage of 173,414. It is also interesting to note that, in 1850, the distribution of ships built in the South was as follows: [4]

SHIPBUILDING IN THE SOUTH, 1850

| State | Number of Ships |
|---|---|
| Maryland | 68 |
| Virginia | 32 |
| North Carolina | 8 |
| Louisiana | 7 |
| Kentucky | 7 |
| Missouri | 4 |
| Florida | 4 |
| Texas | 3 |
| Georgia | 2 |
| Tennessee | 1 |
| TOTAL FOR SOUTH | 136 |
| TOTAL FOR UNITED STATES | 892 |

In 1840, the South was producing nearly 16 per cent of the furniture manufactured in the United States. By 1850, there was a slight absolute increase for the section, but a relative decline in comparison with the rapidly increasing manufacture of furniture in the North Atlantic States. By 1860, the South was producing less furniture than twenty

---

[4] Compiled from UNITED STATES CENSUS (1850), *Report*.

years before, and only about 5 per cent of the total for the United States. Prior to 1860, Baltimore and St. Louis were the chief centers of furniture manufacturing in the South. As early as 1816, Baltimore had extensive "cabinet-shops," one of which is said to have produced about $100,000 worth of furniture annually. In St. Louis were factories that made ordinary chairs, beds, and tables. Furniture was made also by local cabinet-makers throughout the South. A great deal of furniture of all kinds was imported from the North, and some of the finer grades were brought in even from Europe.

Paper was manufactured from wood and rags. The mills were small-scale local establishments and were found in several regions of the South prior to 1860. As early as 1787, Kentucky had a paper mill, and by 1810, Virginia had four.

In various parts of the South, there were made by local craftsmen many kinds of wooden products, including carriages, wagons, doors, sashes, blinds, boxes, spokes, hubs, felloes, staves, heading and hoops, brooms, and coffins. Nearly every community had its coffin maker, and much folklore grew up around that trade. Perhaps no superstition was more generally believed than that the coffin maker was usually forewarned by a mysterious rattling of his tools the night before he received an order!

### Textile Manufactures

Before the Revolutionary War, two types of economic organization in the Southern colonies were evolving: the plantation system, and the small farm. On the Coastal Plain the large planters carried on little household manufacturing in comparison with that done by the small farmers of the Piedmont and the Great Valley. This difference was the original basis for the subsequent agrarianism and industrialization of the South. Thus, when cotton culture became the chief concern of the planter class, the small farmers, using their own free labor, could not, or would not, compete with slave labor. At the same time there was an abundance of water power in the Piedmont. Hence, motivated by the anticipation of profits to be had without slaves and with small capital, the Piedmontese turned more and more to the development of textile industries, especially cotton mills.

**Cotton.** To understand the development of cotton manufactures in the ante-bellum South, it is necessary to note briefly the most important facts concerning the development of the industry in the United States as a whole, because there were certain external economies as well as certain problems which were by no means localized in the South.

Prior to 1800, cotton manufacturing passed through a period of experimentation from which there evolved two types of mills: the jenny mill, and the Arkwright power mill. The first jenny mill in this country was established in Philadelphia in 1787. In 1790, Slater set up an Arkwright mill at Pawtucket, and it is from this date that the real factory system of the United States has its beginning. By 1800, one jenny mill and eight Arkwright mills constituted the entire cotton industry of the United States.

The Embargo of 1807 and the War of 1812, by cutting off foreign supplies of cloth and by diverting capital from commerce to manufacturing, imparted an artificial stimulus to the industry. It was during this period that a few mill builders migrated from the North into the Piedmont region of the South and, with local help, established small yarn factories in the Carolinas, Georgia, Tennessee, and Kentucky. Following the War of 1812, the industry was confronted with a severe depression and a market flooded with European goods. As a result, few cotton mills in the United States survived without reorganization. By 1820, the production of cotton goods was only about half as large as that of 1815, though the number of spindles was practically double the number in 1810.

During the decade following 1820, there was a rapid

expansion of the industry. The number of spindles quadrupled, and the number of looms increased tenfold. The cylindrical printing machine was introduced, and calico with "big flowers" became the vogue. About this time the Southern people, enraged at the North on account of the tariff and resenting their economic dependence on that section, started a rather effective agitation to erect larger and more complete cotton factories. From 1840 to 1860, the number of spindles in the cotton industry grew nearly twice as fast as the increase in the population of the Nation. In the South immediately before 1850, factory development began spontaneously at several points, and, according to Victor S. Clark, "had not two financial crises and a war checked its progress, we should probably date from this time the beginning of the modern epoch of cotton manufacturing in the South." [5]

Prior to 1820, mills in the South for manufacturing cotton were for the most part merely yarn plants equipped with spindles for the production of coarse yarn, which was used by local household looms. A few mills were equipped with looms, and yarn was traded by these mills for homespun linen warp, which was then used with the cotton yarn in weaving coarse cloth for country use. Few of the mills were large, and they were generally operated by water power, though Lexington, as early as 1815, had a "steam cotton factory." The typical early cotton mills in the South, however, were scarcely more than expanded plantation spinning houses, driven by power and producing mainly for a local market.

According to the official reports of 1810, there were only 6 spinning frames in Maryland, 17 in Virginia, 56 in North Carolina, and 91 in Georgia; but the 6 frames in Maryland carried more spindles than all the frames in Georgia. A decade later, a rough estimate shows 9 cotton mills in

---

[5] P. 319, Vol. V of THE SOUTH IN THE BUILDING OF THE NATION. Reprinted by permission of the author and the publishers, the College of William and Mary, Williamsburg, Va.

Maryland, with a total of about 11,000 spindles; and 21 mills in Kentucky, with about 7,000 spindles. Yet, very few Southern mills were large, the average number of spindles per mill in Virginia, the Carolinas, and Georgia being only about 1,300.

By 1840, cotton mills in the South had gained greater importance. The application of power to the plants and the development of transportation which opened up more distant markets, imparted a new stimulus to the industry. As Clark points out:[6] "This conjunction of cotton, water wheel, and steamboat now began to influence the localization of Southern industry. The James, the Savannah, the Chattahoochee, the Alabama, and the Tennessee were the principal streams of the cotton states that afforded both power and transit to distant markets. Near the head of navigation, upon those rivers, at Richmond and Petersburg in Virginia, at Augusta and Columbus in Georgia, at Huntsville, Florence, and the mill villages near Montgomery in Alabama, arose the first Southern factory centers to feed the larger commerce of the country."

In 1855, the Secretary of the Treasury of the United States authorized R. C. Morgan and W. A. Shannon to report the manufactures in each state from 1790 to 1850. Although this report is admittedly inaccurate in many details, it shows that, in 1840, Maryland was the chief cotton-manufacturing state in the South. Baltimore was the leading center for the manufacture of cotton duck, for which the shipyards furnished a ready market.

In 1840, Virginia had 22 cotton mills, capitalized at $1,300,000 and producing annually $450,000 worth of yarn and coarse cloth. In that state, Petersburg and Richmond were the centers of cotton manufacturing. In 1835, Petersburg had 3 mills, two of which had about 7,000 spindles but no looms; by 1842, this city had about 25,000 spindles and 724 looms. In 1835, Richmond had 2 mills, with 6,000

---

[6] *Ibid.,* p. 322.

spindles and 80 looms; by 1842, this city had 3 mills, with 14,000 spindles and 263 looms. At Lynchburg, there was one mill; at Wheeling, 2 mills.

In North Carolina, the textile center at that time was at Fayetteville, on the Cape Fear River. In 1836, this town had only one small cotton mill, but in 1841, there were 6 in operation and 2 under construction. The state as a whole had about 20 cotton mills, most of which were located at the Fall Line.

In South Carolina, cotton manufacturing developed slowly. In 1833, the Vancluse mills were organized, and for a few years they were the only incorporated factory south of Baltimore. But the directors held only two meetings: one to organize the enterprise, the other to sell their property when the undertaking failed. In 1834, the Saluda Company was organized, and in 1838, the De Kalb factory was established; however, both of these enterprises were small affairs, and the De Kalb factory is worthy of note only because it was one of a few factories that owned slaves. Both factories soon failed. Strange to say, Charleston, in 1836, enacted a law prohibiting the establishment of a steam mill of any description within the corporate limits, except with the consent of the city council. This action of course retarded the establishment of cotton factories in the city. In 1847, William Gregg established a cotton factory at Graniteville, which, prior to 1860, was the largest in the South and had nearly 9,000 spindles and 300 looms. This factory was driven by a 116 horse power turbine and was devoted almost exclusively to the production of sheetings and "nigger cloth."

In 1840, Georgia had less cotton manufacturing than either Virginia or the Carolinas. At Athens, there were 3 mills, with a total of 4,000 spindles and 100 looms; and at Augusta, there were 2 mills, with a total of about 2,000 spindles. In Upson County, there were 3 mills, with about 4,000 spindles and 50 looms. In Muscogee and Carroll Counties, there were also 5 or 6 mills. The state at that time had about 19 cotton factories, but the output from them averaged approximately only $300,000 annually. By 1850, on account of a phenomenal increase, however, Georgia became the leading cotton-manufacturing state in the ante-bellum South.

In Alabama in 1850, a cotton mill capitalized at $107,000 was established at Autaugaville. This mill had a capacity of 1,200 bales of cotton annually and became a pronounced success. By 1860, Alabama had 14 cotton mills, with a total of 35,700 spindles and 623 looms, and a capital investment estimated at $1,316,000. In 1820, Kentucky had more spindles than Maine or Vermont, and was producing more cotton yarn than any other Southern State. By 1850, however, this state had lost its relative position in the industry and was of minor importance as a cotton-manufacturing state.

As early as 1795, there was a small cotton factory established in Sumner County, Tennessee, but it supplied only a local market. By 1830, a larger and more successful cotton factory was in operation at Mount Pleasant, and by 1839, mills had been established in each of the natural divisions of the state, though mainly in middle Tennessee. In Adams County, Mississippi, and at Van Buren, Arkansas, and even in Florida and Missouri, there were sporadic attempts at cotton manufacturing. By 1855, Louisiana and Texas were the only Southern States in which cotton spinning was not carried on.

Yet, despite the apparent rise of cotton manufacturing in the South, there was by 1860 only one spindle in the section to every fourteen in New England. Furthermore, there were fewer mills in the South in 1860 than a decade before, although the units of production had become much larger. The following table plainly indicates the extent of the development of cotton manufacturing in the ante-bellum South as compared with that in the North.[7]

---

[7] Compiled from UNITED STATES CENSUS (1840, 1850, and 1860), *Reports*.

COTTON FACTORIES IN THE UNITED STATES, 1840–1860

| | Number of Factories | Capital | Value of Product |
|---|---|---|---|
| **1840** | | | |
| South | 280 | $ 5,965,978 | $ 3,724,789 |
| North | 960 | 45,136,381 | 42,625,664 |
| TOTAL | 1,240 | $51,102,359 | $46,350,453 |
| **1850** | | | |
| South | 205 | $10,859,156 | $ 9,366,331 |
| North | 869 | 63,641,775 | 52,502,853 |
| TOTAL | 1,074 | $74,500,931 | $61,869,184 |
| **1860** | | | |
| South | 181 | $12,407,421 | $ 11,360,173 |
| North | 734 | 87,144,044 | 103,777,753 |
| TOTAL | 951 | $99,551,465 | $115,137,926 |

It is important in this connection to consider two sets of problems created by the new type of industry—namely, problems concerning the entrepreneur, such as: availability of capital, market demand, and net earnings; and problems concerning the community, such as: wages, hours of labor, and possible benefits to employees.

The first problem confronted by a promoter of a cotton mill was that of obtaining capital. As a rule, planters invested their surplus in land and slaves, and these were practically non-fluid. The persons in the ante-bellum South who had considerable capital were the *factors*. They, in many instances, supplied the money for producing crops, marketed the crops, and finally imported much of the merchandise sold to the planters. In this way they had a triple grip on the planters that yielded them an almost certain profit. The factors were unwilling to transfer their funds to an industry having a higher risk.

The amount of capital required for a mill was usually raised by small commitments from local business men, merchants, bankers, and even professional men. For example, the Vaucluse mills were capitalized at $45,000, and this amount was furnished by seven business men. In

1833, in about two hours on the streets of Petersburg, $120,000 was raised to build a mill. Occasionally one individual furnished the entire capital for an enterprise. In a few instances a relatively large amount of capital for those days was utilized in a single plant. As early as 1812, there was within the borders of Maryland one textile mill with an invested capital of $400,000.

The Southern cotton manufacturers had to face peculiar limitations of their market. Although some of the yarn and cloth was sold in New York and Philadelphia, most of it had to be sold locally or in Charleston, Richmond, and Savannah. Goods, especially the better grades, imported from the North and from England came into competition with the Southern products in the Southern market and, in spite of the element of distance, sold for the same price as the locally manufactured goods. Southern merchants frequently went North, moreover, to buy their quality goods, because the prices were lower and because there was a strong prejudice in the South against any homemade style of goods. Thus, according to a writer in *De Bow's Review:* "Almost every country merchant who visits Charleston has a through ticket to New York in his pocket." [8] To combat this situation, Southern mill owners sometimes marked their products with misleading trademarks and sold them as imported goods. As a general result, the Southern cotton manufacturer was relegated to the humble role of supplying lower grade products, such as coarse yarns, cotton bagging, and "nigger cloth."

Managerial ability varied from mill to mill, and several mills soon went into bankruptcy. From fragmentary records it appears, however, that some of the Southern mills prior to 1860, in spite of handicaps, made what may be termed a good return upon the capital invested. The Union Manufacturing Company, of Baltimore, in 1813, earned 6.75 per cent on its paid-in capital of $400,000; in

---

[8] *De Bow's Review,* Vol. XXIX, p. 776.

1814, 9.25 per cent; and in 1815, 8.25 per cent. In 1839, two mills in Petersburg earned 16 per cent and 18 per cent, respectively. In 1846, six mills in North Carolina earned 14 per cent; and in the same year, mills in Georgia earned from 16 per cent to 25 per cent. Gregg's factory, at Graniteville, declared an average dividend of 7 per cent for the first five years; in 1852, the net earnings rose to 8 per cent; in 1853, they were 11½ per cent; and by 1854, they were 18 per cent. In Georgia, the Macon Manufacturing Company, by 1855, had accumulated a reserve of $37,000 and declared a dividend of 10 per cent.

One of the reasons, if not the chief one, for the large net earnings of cotton mills in the ante-bellum South was the low wages paid for labor. As has been too frequently true of the textile industry in the South, these early mills succeeded, not so much on account of superior managerial ability, as by means of the exploitation of labor, which was comprised mainly of women and children. Here and there a few slaves were employed in cotton factories, but this type of labor was the exception rather than the rule. The De Kalb factory and the Saluda Company, in South Carolina, and a mill at Athens, Georgia, employed Negro slaves. They were never satisfactory, however, and the greater number of employees were women and children who ranged from ten to sixteen years of age.[9] White men were employed as clerks and engineers. The wages of children varied in different mills and averaged from 10 to 20 cents a day; those of women ran as high as 40 to 50 cents a day. In 1849, the Vancluse mills employed 94 hands averaging 37.85 cents a day. Of these employees, 11 were men, 50 or 60 were girls, and the rest were boys. A mill at Augusta, Georgia, employed 300 whites, mostly women and young children, at an average wage of $3.05 a week. The famous factory at Prattsville, Alabama, paid the fabulous salary of $8.00 a month to women and children. At Columbus,

---

[9] See Raymond Pinchbeck's *Negro Artisan in Virginia,* for a complete discussion of the negro in industry.

Georgia, a mill employed 100 white hands, aged twelve years and up, at a wage of about 12 cents a day.

This situation, however, seemed to be entirely commendable from the Northern viewpoint at that time. In 1860, a writer on the *New York Herald,* in describing Georgia cotton mills, expressed himself as follows: "The operatives in all these factories are white people, chiefly girls and boys from twelve to twenty years of age. On an average they are better paid, and worked easier than is usually the case in the North. Country girls from the pine forests, as green and awkward as it is possible to find them, soon become skilful operatives, and ere they have been in the mills a year are able to earn from four to six dollars a week."

In fact, Northerners who had an eye to establishing more cotton mills in the South—several plants were already operated by Northern men—spoke sympathetically of the "ignorant, half-fed, ill-clothed" Southern people whose suffering could be alleviated only when some benefactor established cotton mills. At the same time, the pay was at, or even below, a subsistence wage and the day's work in the mills, even for children, was from daylight until dark. In rejection of both the facts and the propaganda of this kind for industrialization of the South, a Southern writer declared the "increasing host who live by toil in factories, the paupers who belong to the State, and still greater numbers who drag out a wretched existence in the crowded haunts of want and vice in their great cities, form more than an offset to anything that can be said of negro slavery." [10]

Occasionally there was an isolated example of paternalism. Such was Gregg's factory, at Graniteville, South Carolina. The factory was built of white granite. Ornamental cottages, each costing about $400, were provided for the employees' families. A savings bank was established and, in 1855, had over $8,000 on deposit. Liquor

---

[10] *De Bow's Review,* Vol. XIX, p. 46.

was prohibited. Churches were established, and religious education was given to the children of the community. Children under twelve years of age were required to attend school; after they had passed that age, they were employed in the factory, while their mothers kept house and their fathers worked in gardens.

**Wool.** In addition to the cotton factories, there were several woolen mills in the South. For three decades following the close of the Revolutionary War, one of the chief household industries was the spinning and weaving of wool. In 1791, Hamilton, in his report on manufactures, estimated that in certain parts of the country about four fifths of the clothing of the resident population was made at home. Tenche Coxe concluded from the same survey that the interior counties of Maryland, Virginia, the Carolinas, and Georgia produced at home sufficient clothing for their needs. In 1810, Gallatin made a somewhat similar report on the manufactures of the South.

Gradually, however, there was a transition from the household production of woolen cloth to a factory system. The Embargo of 1807 and the War of 1812, as well as new technical devices for spinning, weaving, and fulling, were mainly responsible for the change, but of no slight effect was the introduction of Merino sheep. In 1800, the best wool sheep in the world were the Merino flocks of Spain. In 1801, M. Du Pont de Nemours, of Wilmington, Delaware, imported a famous Merino ram named "Don Pedro" and valued at $1,000. After that time increasing numbers were imported, especially through the American Minister to Spain, who sent over several thousand in 1810, when the flocks of Spanish nobles were confiscated during that year. The craze for Merino sheep became so general that there was a decided increase in sheep raising and a larger production of fine, long-fibered wool suitable for manufacturing.

As early as 1812, several small woolen mills had been erected in Cecil County, Maryland, and somewhat later, small factories were established in Virginia and Kentucky.

Before 1840, there were in Maryland and Virginia a few carpet factories, which presumably were profitable enterprises, because the coarsest wool could be utilized for their product, and because, at that time, carpets, like automobiles today, were the standard by which the prosperity of a household was adjudged.   A popular ditty of the period referred to the social distinction conferred by a carpet:

"I had a girl in Baltimore,
Brussels carpet on the floor,
Horse cars running by the door,
What could a fellow wish for more."

The most extensive development of wool manufacturing in the ante-bellum South occurred from 1840 to 1860. During that period, the Southern wool clip was about 24 per cent of the total for the United States, and Southern wool establishments, including fulling mills, more than doubled in number.   The amount of capital invested in the woolen industry in the South increased from 3.3 per cent to about 18 per cent of the total capital invested in that industry in the United States, and the value of the products multiplied nearly seven times.   In 1845, the number of sets of woolen machinery in the South was 66. Maryland had 29; Virginia, 18; Kentucky, 10; Georgia, 3; Tennessee, 2; and North Carolina, South Carolina, Louisiana, and Missouri, one each.   The chief wool-manufacturing states of the South were Maryland, Virginia, and Kentucky.

As compared with the North, the South lagged far behind in the manufacture of wool.   This fact is shown plainly by the table on page 294. [11]

In the ante-bellum South there were a few other textile industries besides cotton and woolen factories.   Throughout the period in the upland regions, flax and hemp continued to be produced in large quantities, much of which

[11] Compiled from UNITED STATES CENSUS (1840, 1850, and 1860), *Reports*.

OUTPUT OF WOOLEN FACTORIES IN THE
UNITED STATES, 1840–1860

| | Number of Factories | Capital | Hands Employed (Male) | (Female) | Value of Products |
|---|---|---|---|---|---|
| **1840** | | | | | |
| South...... | 153 | $ 519,780 | 720[a] | 241 | $ 672,578 |
| North..... | 1,267 | 15,245,124 | 11,444 | 8,937 | 20,024,421 |
| TOTAL... | 1,420 | $15,764,904 | 12,164 | 9,178 | $20,696,999 |
| **1850** | | | | | |
| South...... | 203 | $ 1,150,560 | 1,209 | 439 | $ 1,898,182 |
| North..... | 1,356 | 27,968,090 | 21,469 | 16,135 | 41,309,363 |
| TOTAL... | 1,559 | $29,118,650 | 22,678 | 16,574 | $43,207,545 |
| **1860** | | | | | |
| South...... | 449 | $ 6,561,825 | 2,191 | 706 | $ 4,596,094 |
| North..... | 1,460 | 28,958,702 | 26,589 | 19,414 | 64,269,869 |
| TOTAL... | 1,909 | $35,520,527 | 28,780 | 20,120 | $68,865,963 |

[a]Estimates for 1840.

was used in household industry. In 1810, Virginia—mainly the western counties—produced nearly 5,000,000 yards of flaxen homespuns. At the same time, 128,484 spinning wheels and 40,978 looms were reported in use in North Carolina; 20,058 spinning wheels and 13,290 looms, in Georgia; and 23,559 looms, in Kentucky. From Maryland to Alabama, flax and hemp production was common in nearly all the households of small farmers and even on some of the large plantations.

However, this household industry, as in the case of wool, gradually gave way to the factory or the mill. As early as 1789, Kentucky began, by means of lotteries, to build linen factories, and by 1802, 65 hemp manufacturers petitioned the Federal Government for a protective tariff on the industry. Missouri later became interested in growing and manufacturing hemp and, by 1850, was the most important competitor of Kentucky in that industry. The manufacture of hempen cordage was of considerable significance. In 1810, Virginia had five ropewalks and produced cordage to the value of $162,412. At the same time, Maryland produced cordage valued at $561,800, and Kentucky's production amounted to $398,400.

An effort to manufacture silk also was made in the South. In the decades between 1810 and 1840, silk mills were established at Baltimore and at Nashville, and at Mount Pleasant, South Carolina. These mills were unsuccessful, however, and the industry eventually became localized in the North.

**Secondary textiles.**  Besides the primary textile industries in the South, there were secondary industries established here and there for the manufacture of articles of clothing.  For example, in Montgomery, Alabama, Churchill & Company was organized for the manufacture of "silk, cassimere and soft hats."  By 1860, there were seven establishments in that state for making hats and caps. Usually clothing was made in the homes of the Southern people; ready-to-wear clothing was not generally sold in the Southern States during the ante-bellum period.

## OTHER MANUFACTURES

**Flour mills.**  In the South at this time, flour and meal exceeded in value those products derived from other raw materials.  Throughout the section the old, overslung water wheel slowly ground meal, which carried a peculiarly delicious flavor.  Perhaps no industry in those days was more closely identified with the various communities.  One of the most picturesque and common sights was that of a man astride a horse or mule carrying grist to a mill.  While he and his neighbors waited in turn for the miller to do the grinding, the mill itself often became a veritable open forum for the discussion of social, economic, political, and religious topics.

At the same mills, wheat was ground, but on a different set of millstones or "burrs," from those provided for the manufacture of corn meal.  As time went on, however, separate flour mills were established.  Prior to 1860, Virginia was the leading flour-manufacturing state in the

South. As early as 1810, this state had 441 flour mills and was producing over 750,000 barrels of flour. Between 1834 and 1850, according to Victor S. Clark, "the largest grain mills in the world were at Richmond, Virginia, the capacity of a single establishment approaching 1,000 barrels daily and enabling the city to ship nearly 30,000 barrels of flour a month to Brazil."[12] By 1860, the state had 1,383 flour mills, having a total invested capital of nearly $6,000,000 and employing 2,241 hands. North Carolina, by 1847, had 323 flour mills and 2,033 gristmills. Even the cotton-growing states, though they imported most of their flour, had a few grain-manufacturing establishments. Colonel John G. Winter had an important mill at Montgomery, Alabama. In 1855, a disastrous fire occurred in this mill and destroyed 2,500 bushels of corn, a great quantity of wheat, and numerous sacks of flour—making a total damage of about $50,000.[13]

During the two decades before the Civil War, the South, as measured by value of product, was producing approximately one third as much flour and meal as the North.[14]

FLOUR AND MEAL MANUFACTURES IN THE
UNITED STATES, 1850–1860

| 1850 | Value of Product | 1860 | Value of Product |
|---|---|---|---|
| South | $ 31,111,765 | South | $ 55,848,921 |
| North | 104,786,041 | North | 167,295,388 |
| TOTAL | $135,897,806 | TOTAL | $223,144,309 |

**Tobacco.** Tobacco manufacturing in the South showed very little activity prior to 1850. In 1840, Virginia alone was producing approximately one third of the American crop, and manufacturing almost two fifths of it. About 1850, there was a revival in the industry. This was due not only to a general increase in population and prosperity, but also to the accidental discovery in North Carolina of bright

---

[12] P. 327, Vol. V of THE SOUTH IN THE BUILDING OF THE NATION.

[13] *Montgomery Advertiser*, May 12, 1855.

[14] Compiled from UNITED STATES CENSUS (1850 and 1860), *Reports*.

yellow tobacco, which stimulated tobacco consumption considerably.

Prior to 1860, most of the tobacco manufactured in the South was pipe tobacco. The cigar market was still too narrow to attract many investors. Cigars were expensive and were usually smoked only by those who considered their use a mark of social distinction.

The chief centers of tobacco manufacturing in the South were Richmond, Lynchburg, Petersburg, Louisville, and New Orleans. By 1858, tobacco manufacturing had been started at Durham, North Carolina, but that city's phenomenal rise in the industry had to await the passing of the Civil War. By 1860, the Southern manufacture of tobacco was valued at $19,200,000.

**Leather.** In the leading cattle-raising states of the South, local tanneries and small leather factories were not uncommon. The total value of leather produced in the South was practically the same for 1850 and 1860. In the latter year, production reached $6,942,050, or about 12 per cent of the total for the United States.

The most important leather-using manufacture was that of boots and shoes. There were several of these factories in the South prior to 1860. Even as early as 1796, 2 shoe factories in Lexington were large enough to advertise for 7 or 8 operatives at a time. In 1860, Virginia had 258 boot and shoe factories, with a total capital investment of $258,622 and an organization of 1,032 hands. At the same time, the total value of boots and shoes manufactured in the South was $5,964,307, about 7 per cent of the total value of boots and shoes manufactured in the United States. There were local harness shops, but this industry still was mainly in the handicraft stage throughout the South.

**Liquor.** If measured by the money value of the product, there was more whiskey made in the ante-bellum South than there were boots and shoes. Everywhere in the grain district were small neighborhood distilleries; and in Maryland, Virginia, and Kentucky there was an extensive commercial manufacture of whiskey. Moreover, large quantities of malt liquor were made, valued in 1860 at about $2,700,000. As compared with the North, the South's output of liquor appeared as follows: [15]

GALLONS OF LIQUOR DISTILLED IN THE
UNITED STATES, 1860

South...........................  7,244,414
North........................ 80,758,574
                              _____
TOTAL.................... 88,002,988

In other words, in 1860, the per capita production of liquor for the white population of the South was only about 0.9 of a gallon, while that for the North was 4.2 gallons.

**Cottonseed oil.** This product was also being manufactured in the South before the Civil War. This industry began in 1804 at New Orleans, and subsequently the oil was manufactured commercially, not only in that city, but also at Natchez, Mobile, and Petersburg.

## IRON INDUSTRY

The iron industry in the ante-bellum South was characterized both by development in the production of raw iron by means of smelting and refining, and by the erection of plants, foundries, and machine shops for the manufacture of iron.

The production of raw iron was developed considerably by the use of magnetic iron ore instead of bog iron, which had been commonly used until the close of the Revolutionary War, and by the introduction in 1840 of anthracite coal for smelting. The building of railroads prior to 1860 also stimulated the production of iron. After the Revolutionary War, the production of iron in the South took a fresh start, and by 1860, that section was producing $2,743,454 worth of pig iron and $3,353,371 worth of wrought iron, or a total of $6,096,825 worth of raw iron. This amount, however,

---

[15] Compiled from UNITED STATES CENSUS (1860), *Report.*

was only about 14 per cent of the value of the total output in the United States.

One of the important iron regions of the South was northeastern Maryland. In Frederick County, several iron enterprises were established before the close of the Revolution. The Catoctin furnace, built in 1774 by James Johnson & Company, may be mentioned as important, because it was subsequently rebuilt several times and was still in blast in 1880. In Washington County, there were several iron enterprises of an early date. The Mount Etna furnace, near Hagerstown, during the Revolutionary War cast the first Maryland cannon made. In the extreme western part of the state near Friendsville, the Yohogany Ironworks, consisting of a furnace and two forges to use charcoal, was erected in 1828 and 1829. Subsequently, other furnaces were erected in the same region. In 1840, the Mount Savage Iron Company erected two large blast furnaces, to use coke, near Cumberland. Six years later, a furnace was built at Cumberland. In his *Report on the Manufacture of Iron,* addressed to the governor of Maryland in 1840, J. H. Alexander said that there was on the eastern shore of Maryland a furnace built in 1830 to use bog ore yielding only 28 per cent of iron, and that the annual production of the furnace in 1834 was 700 tons. By 1850, Maryland ranked third in the production of pig iron in the United States.

According to Jefferson's *Notes on the State of Virginia,* written in 1781 and 1782, the iron industry in Virginia at that time was not extensive. Other records show that, about 1790, the iron industry in the state began a noticeable expansion, especially in the Valley of Virginia. About 1800, a furnace was built in Loudon County, and its owner "cut a canal through the end of Catoctin Mountain, 500 feet through solid rock and 60 feet beneath the surface to obtain water for his furnace and mill." About the same time iron furnaces were erected in Craig, Grayson, Wythe, Washington, Carroll, and other southwestern counties.

Most of these furnaces used charcoal and were operated by "rule of thumb." Near Richmond, there was erected during the Revolution "an excellent air furnace" which "used bituminous coal from the mines of Chesterfield County." This furnace was said to have been destroyed by Benedict Arnold in 1781. Later, several furnaces and forges were built at Lynchburg and at other points in the James River Valley. Prior to 1856, there were no less than 88 charcoal furnaces built in Virginia.

North Carolina also had several iron furnaces. In 1795, a furnace of considerable importance was built by Perkins & Taylor on Snow Creek. Five years later, one was built on Big Creek. Other furnaces were erected at early dates on Tom's Creek and on Troublesome Creek, and at other points in Lincoln, Rockingham, and Burke Counties. After 1800, the iron industry in North Carolina was still further developed, and by 1840, according to the census, there were 8 furnaces in that state, which produced during the year 968 gross tons of cast iron, including both pig iron and castings.

Not long after the Revolutionary War, furnaces were erected in South Carolina, mainly on creeks flowing into the Catawba River. In 1840, there were 4 furnaces in the state. In 1856, there were 81 in York County, one in Union County, and 6 in Spartansburg County, but only 4 were in actual operation. Georgia had no colonial iron industry; a furnace built in 1832 near Clarksville was probably the first in the state. This, however, was abandoned five years later. Other furnaces, subsequently built in Cass County, were also abandoned. Still others were erected in Walker, Polk, Floyd, and Dade Counties. All used charcoal, and most of them were abandoned before the Civil War.

According to Thomas Jefferson, there were iron mines "on Kentucky, between the Cumberland and Barren Rivers" and also "between Cumberland and Tanissee" before the Revolution closed. The first ironworks in Kentucky of which there is a specific record was Burbon, better known as "State furnace," in Bath County, erected in 1791. In 1810, Tenche Coxe mentioned 4 furnaces in that state. After this date numerous furnaces were built in Greenup, Carter, and Boyd Counties, and elsewhere; by 1850, Kentucky ranked fourth among the states in pig iron production.

About 1795, an iron furnace was built in Sullivan County, Tennessee, at the junction of the North and South forks of the Holston River, near the Virginia line, on "the great road from Knoxville to Philadelphia." In 1792, the Cumberland furnace was built in Dickson County. By 1850, Tennessee ranked fifth in the United States in the production of pig iron.

As early as 1818, an iron furnace was built in Alabama a few miles from Russellville. This furnace was abandoned in 1827, and presumably no other furnace was erected in the state until 1843, when one was built at Polksville, in Calhoun County. Five years later, one was built in Shelby County, and another at Round Mountain, Cherokee County, in 1853. These were all charcoal furnaces and, so far as available records show, were the only ones in the state prior to 1856. The development of the Birmingham district came at a much later date.

In 1840, Missouri had only 2 furnaces, but during the next two decades, several others were established. In 1846, a furnace was built at the base of Little Iron Mountain, and within the next eight years, 2 others were built at the same place. Between 1849 and 1855, 2 furnaces were built on Pilot Knob, and in 1859, one was built at Irondale, Washington County. The one at Moselle, Franklin County, had been started in 1846. St. Louis had no blast furnace until 1863.

Prior to 1860, Texas had only one blast furnace, which was in the extreme northeastern part of Cass County. During the Civil War, 2 or 3 other furnaces were built: one "on Horton's headright just west of Springdale," in Cass County, and another near Jacksonville.

Each of the Southern States, except Florida, Mississippi, and Louisiana, had iron furnaces during the ante-bellum period. The states of chief importance in the production of iron in the section were Maryland, Kentucky, Tennessee, and Virginia; these ranked in importance in the order named.

Although plants for the fabrication of iron—such as forges, rolling mills, machine shops, and the like—did not necessarily seek the same localities as iron furnaces, they were usually established in the same vicinity.

In Maryland, shortly after the erection of the Catoctin furnace, the Bush Creek forge was built in the same vicinity and was in operation until 1810. James Johnson & Company built a rolling and slitting mill at a spot known three decades later as "Reel's Mill." In Washington County, the Johnsons also built Lick Creek Forge; and later on another company built a small rolling mill and nail factory in the neighborhood of Antietam. As early as 1778, a slitting mill was established at or near Baltimore. After the Revolution one of the most successful rolling mills in the state was the Avalon Ironworks—near Realy House, on the Baltimore & Ohio Railroad—which produced nails and bar iron and, about 1848, was also rolling rails. Another rolling mill was built near Elkton, and still another, near Port Deposit. In 1843, the Mount Savage mill was built especially to roll iron rails and, in 1844, rolled the first rails in America that were not "strap rails." These were of the U-shaped type.

In Virginia, several forges were built about 1800: one near Waynesborough, two in Rockbridge County, and one in Rockingham County. Most of the forges were located near the furnaces in the Valley of Virginia. Household pots and other moulded articles were made by these local forges. Nails remained for a longer time a household industry. Thomas Jefferson had twelve young slaves making nails for him, and it is said that "they made about a ton of nails a month at a considerable profit." The site of this old nail shop can still be seen at Monticello. According to *Cramer's Pittsburg Almanack* for 1813, the first rolling mill established west of the Allegheny Mountains was located in West Virginia—then a part of Virginia. This mill rolled only sheet iron, which was used for salt pans, domestic utensils, and nail plates. Prior to 1860, Wheeling was the center of the rolling mill industry in Virginia, although there were in the state at that time other mills of importance, especially the four at Richmond. Locomotives were built upon order at Richmond. According to available records, there were in Virginia before 1856 at least 59 forges and bloomeries,[16] and about 12 rolling mills. The forges were located in twenty-five counties.

In 1810, North Carolina, according to Tenche Coxe, had 6 bloomeries, 2 rolling and slitting mills, and 2 naileries in Lincoln County; one bloomery in Iredell County; 6 bloomeries and one trip-hammer in Burke County; and 5 bloomeries in Surry County—or a total of 18 bloomeries. In 1840, the state had 43 bloomeries, forges, and rolling mills, which produced 963 tons of bar iron. During the next two decades, a few additional bloomeries were erected, but there was no great increase in the number of forges and other fabrication plants.

In 1810, Tenche Coxe reported 9 bloomeries in South Carolina. In 1815, Scrivenor described the iron industry in the state as follows: "On Allison's Creek, in York district there are a forge, a furnace, a rolling mill for making sheet iron, and a nail manufactory. On Middle Tiger River are iron works on a small scale; also on the Enoree River and Rudy River, on the north fork of Saluda River, on George's Creek, and on Twenty-six Mile Creek. In 1802 an air furnace was erected on a neck of land between Cooper and Ashley Rivers, where good castings are made."

---

[16] A *bloomery* is an establishment which is equipped for reducing crude steel to some general shape, as that of heavy bars or slabs.

By 1856, there were in the state 3 small rolling mills and 2 bloomeries.

In 1859, Georgia had 2 rolling mills and a nail and spike factory. By that time, a dozen or more forges had been built in Kentucky, and also 8 rolling mills. In 1856, Tennessee had 75 forges and bloomeries, and 4 rolling mills. Most of these were in east Tennessee. According to the Census of 1840, Missouri had 3 forges in Crawford County and one in Washington County. These presumably were within the vicinity of the furnaces in those counties. By 1850, the iron industry of St. Louis was just beginning and only one rolling mill had been built; but by the end of the decade, there were 5 rolling mills in that locality. Prior to 1860, very little fabrication of iron was carried on in Texas. During the Civil War, however, considerable quantities of guns and munitions were produced in the state.

Although it appears from the foregoing survey that the iron industry was diffused rather widely over the ante-bellum South, it must be remembered that all of these enterprises were relatively small and that many of them were of very short duration. In fact, besides the manufacture of household pots and pans, and nails and iron bars for local blacksmith shops, there was not much manufacturing of machinery. In 1860, the value of machinery made in the South was only $6,751,050, while the value for the entire United States was $47,118,550.

## OTHER INDUSTRIES

**Coal.** While iron was the chief mineral industry in the ante-bellum South, a few other minerals were being exploited on a small scale. Prior to 1860, coal was being produced in six of the Southern States. As early as 1784, coal was discovered in Maryland, and two decades later, the western Maryland coal basin was opened. In 1820, a shipment of coal—probably the first—from Allegheny County was sent down the Potomac in boats. During that year, coal mining in the state increased to about 3,000 tons. In 1832, the annual shipment of coal down the Potomac was approximately 300,000 bushels. This coal was sold at Georgetown for 20 cents a bushel. It was not until after the Baltimore & Ohio Railroad (1842) and the Chesapeake & Ohio Canal (1850) were extended to Cumberland that the coal industry in Maryland began to grow rapidly. Prior to 1842, the coal region of the state had probably yielded a total of not more than 75,000 tons. From that time until 1860, the increase in annual production was constant, except during the general depression of 1857.

As already noted, the Virginia coal mines were possibly the first worked in America. Virginia coal was used extensively during the Revolutionary War in the manufacture of shot and shell. Both before and after the Revolution, it was exported to various cities on the Atlantic coast. In 1789, Virginia coal was selling in Philadelphia at 1s. 6d. per bushel. In 1822, the export tonnage from the state was 42,000 tons, and by 1828, the production from the several coal fields of the state (then including West Virginia) had increased to 100,000 tons per year. In 1833, the peak year, the exports of coal amounted to 142,000 tons, but about a decade later, the shipments fell to 65,000 tons.

In North Carolina, there was some coal produced during the Civil War, but prior to that time there appears to have been only 3 tons produced in 1840. In Alabama, coal was probably used at Birmingham as early as 1836; however, the first actual mining of coal in the state did not begin until about 1850. Even then, most of the operations were carried on for local blacksmith shops. The beds worked were in Marshall County and at Tuscaloosa. When the Civil War broke out, the coal industry in Alabama had just begun.

In Missouri, coal production grew rapidly. In 1840, the state had an output of less than 10,000 tons, but a quarter of a century later, it produced forty-two times as much and

had become one of the ten leading coal-producing states of
the Nation.  In 1828, Kentucky was producing 328 tons
of coal annually; by 1860, the tonnage had risen to 285,760.
The coal fields of Kentucky, however, though rather well
known at an earlier date, were not made readily accessible
before 1880, and as a result their most rapid development
has been in more recent years.

Coal mining in Tennessee was unimportant during the
first half of the nineteenth century.  In 1842, the annual
production did not exceed 1,000 tons.  In 1860, the industry
had developed until the annual tonnage was over 165,000.

Thus, it appears that, by 1860, coal was being mined in
Alabama, Kentucky, Maryland, Missouri, Tennessee, and
Virginia (including West Virginia).  Moreover, the aggregate output for the five-year period, 1856–1860, was about
8,500,000 tons.

**Lead.**  Prior to 1860, lead was being produced in five
Southern States.  In Virginia, lead mining began with the
discovery of deposits in Wythe County by Colonel Chiswell
before the Revolutionary War.  During the first quarter of
the nineteenth century, the product was hauled by wagons
to Baltimore, which was the chief market for Virginia lead
at that time.  During the next quarter of the century, over
11,000 tons of pig lead were produced in the Virginia region.
Then, since these works were the principal source of lead
for the Confederate Army, they were destroyed in 1864 by
Federal troops.  Lead was also found in Davidson County,
North Carolina, in 1836, and was mined continually until
the war.  In Tennessee, deposits were worked at Lead Mine
Bend, in the eastern part of the state.  In Arkansas, in
1851, a furnace was established for smelting lead, but the
enterprise soon proved unprofitable.

The most important center of lead production, as well as
the only important place for zinc production, in the South
was Missouri.  From the days of French exploration in that
region lead was an important attraction.  In 1720, Rinault,
with 200 artisans and 500 slaves, began working the La

Motte Mine.  Subsequently other richer mines were opened. In 1819, there were 45 lead mines in Missouri, and 27 of these were employing 1,130 men.  The annual production was nearly 1,900 tons.  This increased during the next two decades to 3,600 tons.  In 1852, developments began in the famous Joplin district, in southwest Missouri, but the development in this district, because of lack of transportation facilities, was very slow until after the construction of the Iron Mountain Railway in 1858.

PRODUCTION OF SALT IN THE
UNITED STATES, 1860[17]

| | |
|---|---|
| South...................... | 2,246,178 bu: |
| North...................... | 9,944,775 bu: |
| TOTAL.................. | 12,190,953 bu. |

**Salt.**  Prior to 1860, there were three major sources of salt manufacture in the South: the Holston Valley, in the vicinity of Saltville, Virginia; the region of the Great Kanawha, about Charleston (now West Virginia); and the deposits of Petit Anse and the salt lakes in the northwestern part of Louisiana.  All of the earlier production of these regions was obtained by a process of evaporation. Rock salt was not discovered until 1840 in Virginia, and 1862, in Louisiana.  The Holston Valley district produced annually from 100,000 to 200,000 barrels of salt.  At one time during the Civil War the output was said to have been over 2,000 barrels daily.  The area about Charleston (West Virginia) was one of the most important sources for salt in the United States.  As early as 1817, coal was used for evaporating the brines.  Ten years later, steam pumps were introduced for pumping up the brine, and after 1835, steam evaporation became common.  By 1846, this region was producing nearly 650,000 barrels of salt annually.  In Louisiana, the salt deposits of Petit Anse were worked commercially, especially during the first year or two of the Civil War.  The salt licks of northwestern Louisiana were

---

[17] Compiled from UNITED STATES CENSUS (1860), *Report.*

used by the settlers, who went there annually to boil their own supplies of salt. These salt licks were eventually almost deserted on account of the weakness of the brines.

**Copper.** Prior to the Civil War the only important source of copper production was in Tennessee, although deposits of that metal were discovered in Maryland and North Carolina. Copper sheeting for the dome of the Federal Capitol, in Washington, came from Maryland. Sporadic attempts were made at mining copper in Virginia, and in 1855, there were probably as many as 8 mines producing ore in the southwestern part of the state.

A small slate industry was established about 1850 in Maryland and Virginia by slate-makers from Wales.

**Gold.** Both in the colonial days and immediately after the Revolution, flecks, grains, and nuggets of gold had been found here and there at different times along the eastern side of the mountains from Vermont to Virginia. Such occasional finds created little excitement, but in 1804, when larger deposits were discovered in North Carolina, a search for gold began all through the South, and in 1830, when rich finds were made in Georgia, the first wave of the "gold fever" swept over the United States. Indeed, within a short period 6,000 or 7,000 miners were prospecting for gold in the lower South. The territory of Georgia became a veritable "free-for-all mining camp." In 1830, Governor Gilmer wrote to the Attorney General of the United States: [18] "I am in doubt as to what ought to be done with the gold diggers. They, with their various attendants, foragers, and suppliers, make up between six and ten thousand persons. They occupy the country between the Chestatee and Etowah Rivers, near the mountains, gold being found in the greatest quantity deposited in small streams, which flow into these rivers." In spite of the governor's proclamations prohibiting gold digging—"paper bullets," as he described them—and in spite of the fact

---

[18] See *Bulletin No. 4* of GEOLOGICAL SURVEY OF GEORGIA.

that he sent soldiers into the area, many of the miners continued their prospecting. From 1804 to 1827, North Carolina furnished all the gold supply for the Federal Government. This amounted to $110,000. In 1830, Georgia furnished $212,000. In 1838, branch mints were established at Charlotte, North Carolina, and at Dahlonega, Georgia. Small quantities of gold were also found in Maryland, Virginia, South Carolina, Alabama, and Tennessee.

The total production of gold in the South was negligible as compared with that of California in later years. Nevertheless, the Southern "gold boom" had an economic effect upon the region concerned. Population was brought into a section which was sparsely settled. After the first rush was over, some seekers left the region, but many remained to become permanent residents. "When gold was not found [in Georgia]," says George G. Smith, "and there was no indication of it, the lands were very cheap; from $10.00 to $20.00 was the price of a single lot, and many a man bought a small farm for the price of an Indian pony. The cheapness of the lands led to rapid and thick settlement. The county was soon filled up with enterprising young people, and numbers who became substantial farmers on large farms began life in one of these Cherokee counties on forty acres of poor land." [19] It must, however, be added that many became, not "substantial farmers," but the sires of a posterity still belonging to a class termed in the South *poor whites*.

**Minor industries.** Besides the industries already described, there were others more or less common in different regions of the South. Most of these were of a local nature or belong to the category of household industries. Their importance in 1860 is roughly indicated by their approximate values, which were as follows: [20]

---

[19] George Gillam Smith, *Story of Georgia and of Georgia People, 1730 to 1860*, pp. 423–424.

[20] Compiled from UNITED STATES CENSUS (1860), *Report*.

MINOR INDUSTRIES IN THE SOUTH, 1860

| Industry | Value |
|---|---|
| Blacksmithing | $3,700,000 |
| Brickmaking | 2,800,000 |
| Packing and canning | 8,100,000 |
| Fisheries | 516,176 |

The Southern fisheries were of slight importance as compared with those of the North. In 1860, the value of the product from fisheries in the North was estimated at $13,768,229.

## General Analysis of the Industrial Situation

Since the historical development and the diffusion of specific industries in the ante-bellum South have been described, a more general analysis of the industrial situation as it appeared in 1860 will be attempted.

As noted in Chapter I, certain regions of the South have always had an abundance of natural resources suitable for industrial utilization. Some of these resources, however, were unknown in 1860; others were practically inaccessible on account of lack of transportation facilities. Technological inventions had already begun to revolutionize industry, but capital and labor for industrial development were scarce in the section. As a result, the ante-bellum industries of the South were comprised of small local units. Such establishments as were built must not be considered comparable with those of modern times; instead, the factories of those days were small, old-fashioned mills, located usually on the bank of some stream and driven frequently by lumbering water wheels, though occasionally a steam engine was installed.

The average number of persons employed in an establishment was only 6, and the amount of capital invested in manufacturing per capita of free population in the section was as follows: [21]

---

[21] Compiled from UNITED STATES CENSUS (1860), Report.

CAPITAL INVESTED IN INDUSTRY, 1860

| State | Amount Per Capita of Free Population |
|-------|-------------------------------------|
| Maryland | $34.80 |
| Virginia | 24.30 |
| Florida | 23.80 |
| South Carolina | 23.00 |
| Kentucky | 21.00 |
| Louisiana | 19.00 |
| Missouri | 18.70 |
| Georgia | 18.30 |
| Tennessee | 17.70 |
| Alabama | 17.00 |
| North Carolina | 14.60 |
| Mississippi | 13.30 |
| Texas | 7.70 |
| Arkansas | 4.00 |

The South in 1860 had roughly the same per capita investment in industry as the states of Michigan, Ohio, Wisconsin, Illinois, Indiana, Minnesota, and Iowa. The South and the West in 1860 ranked about equal in the per capita investment in industry. Total capital and total labor in industry in the South were only about 16 per cent and 20 per cent, respectively, of those applied in industry in the North. The investment per worker in the South was $885, or $140 more than the investment per worker in the North. This represents a meager amount when compared with $5,000, the average investment per worker in the United States in 1920.

According to computations made from census reports, industry in the South and the North in 1860 appeared as follows:

INDUSTRY IN THE UNITED STATES, 1860

|  | South | North | Total |
|--|-------|-------|-------|
| Establishments | 31,365 | 109,068 | 140,433 |
| Capital Invested | $167,855,315 | $842,000,400 | $1,009,855,715 |
| Cost of Raw Material | $167,095,962 | $864,509,130 | $1,031,605,092 |
| Persons Employed | 189,532 | 1,131,614 | 1,321,246 |
| Cost of Labor | $51,606,773 | $327,272,193 | $378,878,966 |
| Value of Products | $291,375,413 | $1,594,486,263 | $1,885,861,676 |

## Efforts to Encourage Industrialization

As the ante-bellum period drew to a close, a significant movement began in the South—a movement to encourage industrialization. So long as cotton prices were considered good and imported articles could be bought more cheaply than those manufactured locally, there was no necessity for the development of Southern manufactures. The world-wide panic of 1837 and the succeeding depression showed with cruel emphasis how dependent the South was upon the outside world. In 1840, cotton was selling at a disastrously low price. In 1845, when the bottom of the depression was reached, cotton on the New York market was averaging only 5.63 cents per pound, and the farmers were getting one or two cents less.

Because of these conditions Southern thinkers—supported by political demagogues, social uplifters, reformers, and intellectual camp followers—began to advocate industrialization as a remedy. The whole theory of the subsequent movement was succinctly stated in the early forties by a writer in the *Southern Quarterly Review*. He said: [22] "An exclusively agricultural people in the present age of the world will always be poor. They want a home market. They want cities and towns, they want diversity of employment." Indeed, the press of the South during these years was filled with the doctrine of industrialization. "As long as we are tributaries," said a writer in the *Charleston Mercury*, "dependent on foreign labor and skill for food, clothing and countless necessaries of life, we are in thraldom." [23] The Prospectus of the *Cotton Planter* for January 1853 pleaded for Southern industry, and called attention to the time when the cotton gin was first introduced into South Carolina; and *Hunt's Merchants' Magazine*, which was a Northern publication, was surprisingly active in urging industrialization upon the South.

[22] Quoted in Broadus Mitchell's *Life of William Gregg*, p. 15.
[23] *Charleston Mercury* (undated), quoted in *Niles' Weekly Register*, April 19, 1845.

Between the years 1837 and 1860, more than twelve commercial conventions were held in the Southern States. Between 1837 and 1839, meetings were held at Macon, Augusta, and Charleston.  In the latter city, six of the Southern States were represented by 219 delegates, Georgia sending 33 and South Carolina, 170.  The primary purpose of these gatherings was to arouse interest in the commercial independence of the South.  It was urged by elaborate arguments that European capital should be attracted, that banks should aid the merchants, and that direct trade with Europe should be stimulated by opening up the interior of the South to the trade of the Southern ports.  Nothing practical was achieved by these early conventions.

Between 1845 and 1852, meetings were held in Memphis and New Orleans.  At these conventions, speakers argued for the construction of railroads and other internal improvements by the help of the Federal Government.  John C. Calhoun proposed that, since the joint effort of states and individuals could not complete such projects of internal improvements, the Federal Government should contribute aid by granting, to roads proposing to pass through them, alternate portions of unoccupied lands.  At the convention held in New Orleans in January 1852, over 600 delegates were present from eleven Southern States.  Among the plans considered was the building of a railroad from Washington to New Orleans.

Between 1852 and 1860, commercial conventions assembled annually at various Southern cities for the purpose of taking steps to maintain and improve the South's position in the Union.  At first, questions concerning manufacturing and education were brought before the conventions, but later, politics crept into the discussions and the border states failed to send delegates.  In 1858, politicians assumed control of the meeting at Montgomery and reduced it to a debating society.  In 1859, the subject of paramount importance was free trade, because its advocates thought that they saw in the policy a means of reversing the conditions that had operated against the South. By this time, however, sectional hatred had come to dominate both commercial conventions and agricultural society meetings in the South. In September 1859, F. F. Worley, chairman of the Darlington Agricultural Society, at its annual meeting read a paper on "The Importance to the South of Manufacturing her own Staple-Cotton." [24] In this paper he expressed as follows the more or less general feeling toward the North: "We have afforded material for the building of Northern cities, the construction of Northern ships, the erection of Northern palaces, and the realization of Northern fortunes; and what have we received in return? For thanks, we have received wrongs and indignities, and acknowledgements of indebtedness have come to us in the shape of supercilious threats."

### Bibliographical Note

Some invaluable notes on the industry of the ante-bellum South may be collected from the following general works: V. S. Clark, *History of Manufactures in the United States, 1607–1860* (Washington, 1916); J. L. Bishop, *History of American Manufactures from 1608 to 1860–1866*, three volumes (Philadelphia and London, 1868); and Malcolm Keir, *Manufacturing* (New York, 1928). Edward Ingle's *Southern Sidelights* (Baltimore, 1896), Chapter III, contains a brief summary of industry in the ante-bellum South; and G. White, *Statistics of Georgia* (Atlanta, 1849), gives some interesting figures on industry in that state before the Civil War. T. P. Kettel, *Southern Wealth and Northern Profits; As Exhibited in Statistical Facts and Official Figures* (New York, 1860), while not entirely reliable and frequently prejudiced, contains some interesting comparisons of Southern and Northern industry and commerce.

Of contemporary reports, the most comprehensive are: *De Bow's Commercial Review of the South and West*, thirty-nine volumes (New Orleans, 1846–1870); and *Niles' Weekly Register*, seventy-six volumes (Baltimore, 1811–1849). These periodicals contain more general data about this period of the South's economic development than any other sources.

---

[24] *American Cotton Planter,* December 1859, pp. 361–362.

For the iron industry in the ante-bellum period, see: Kath-leen Bruce, *Virginia Iron Manufacture in the Slave Era* (New York, 1930); and L. J. Cappon, "Trend of the Southern Iron Industry under the Plantation System," in the *Journal of Economic and Business History*, Volume II, pages 353–381. Also, some information may be had from J. P. Lesley, *Iron Manufacturers' Guide* (New York, 1859).

The most comprehensive study of the cotton industry for the ante-bellum period is found in M. B. Hammond's *Cotton Industry* (New York, 1897). A. Kohn, *Cotton Mills of South Carolina* (Columbia, S. C., 1907), describes briefly the ante-bellum period in that state. The most complete study of an individual cotton mill owner is Broadus Mitchell, *William Gregg, Factory Master of the Old South* (Chapel Hill, N. C., 1928).

The movement toward industrialization in the ante-bellum South is well analyzed by Herbert Wender in his *Southern Commercial Conventions, 1837–1859*, Volume XLVIII of the JOHNS HOPKINS UNIVERSITY STUDIES IN HISTORICAL AND POLITICAL SCIENCE.

# CHAPTER XI

# Transportation in the Ante-Bellum South, 1783–1860

I N the ante-bellum South, transportation was a problem of vital importance. The staple crops had to be brought to the seaports for shipment to outside markets. Large quantities of food and manufactures, especially in the staple-producing areas, had to be brought in from beyond the limits of the buying regions. There was a movement of trade in opposite directions, which required both ocean shipping and internal transportation. Having little desire to possess a carrying trade, the South concerned itself chiefly with developing a system of internal transportation.

The South physiographically presents both natural facilities for and pronounced obstacles to transportation. In the tobacco-growing region of the ante-bellum South, the transportation problem was simply that of getting products to the navigable rivers and the Chesapeake Bay. In the rice-growing region, there were a multitude of shallow waterways on which to transport crops to the deep-water ports along the coast. In the Piedmont region, however, a different problem was encountered. The outer edge of the region could be reached by navigable streams, but within the section, the streams were too swift for easy transportation. Therefore it became necessary to supplement the waterways with other forms of transportation. In the Coastal Plain and the Mississippi embayment, long reaches of navigable rivers extended to nearly every district where there were large plantations. Although Kentucky, middle

Tennessee, and Missouri had outlets by way of the Ohio, the Cumberland, and the Mississippi Rivers, these regions had no direct water route to the Atlantic seaboard.  In comparison with the other regions of the South, the Highland region presented the most pronounced obstacles and by far the most difficult problems for carrying on trade. Where there were no navigable rivers or few mountain gaps, communities were practically isolated from one another, until railroads pierced the mountains or by circuitous routes facilitated contact between such communities.  In this region more than in any other of the South, physical geography dictated the routes of trade and travel.[a]

Along the coast were the seaports, with access to the outside world; the most important of them were Baltimore, Norfolk, Wilmington, Charleston, Savannah, Mobile, New Orleans, and, potentially, Galveston.  The lesser ports included Beaufort, North Carolina; Beaufort, South Carolina; Brunswick, Georgia; and St. Augustine and Pensacola, Florida, all of which were practically cut off from the hinterland by the pine barrens.  Moreover, there were along the coast a few towns with river connections into the interior, but these had no harbors; for example, Georgetown, South Carolina; Darien, Georgia; and Appalachicola, Florida.  Nevertheless, all the seacoast towns may be conceived as the center of commerce in the ante-bellum South.

The next circle of trade may be outlined by connecting the Fall Line on the larger rivers, at which points pack trains and wagons met the boats coming up the rivers to the Fall Line, since they seldom could navigate further into the interior.  Here, towns grew up as collecting centers for produce going out and supplies coming in.  On the Atlantic coast, such towns were Alexandria, Fredericksburg, Richmond, Petersburg, Fayetteville, Columbia, Augusta, Milledgeville, and Macon.  On the rivers flowing into the

---

[a] The approach taken in this chapter is based upon the analysis made by Ulrich B. Phillips in *A History of Transportation in the Eastern Cotton Belt to 1860.*

Gulf, the Fall Line towns were Columbus, Montgomery, Shreveport, Nashville, and Knoxville.

Another circle may be drawn through those localities on the larger rivers, not at the Fall Line, but which were more or less physiographic centers of given regions. Such were Natchez, Vicksburg, Memphis, St. Louis, and Louisville. Finally, there were several towns which owed their origin to the "penetration of the mountain barriers" and "their growth to the development of direct trade in food supplies." The most notable of these were Atlanta and Chattanooga.

With the location of the centers of commerce in the ante-bellum South thus visualized, it is now possible to consider the development of a system of transportation the purposes of which were: first, to connect the interior points, so far as possible, with the seaports; and second, to connect the interior centers of trade with one another.

### Transportation Facilities

The development of internal transportation in the ante-bellum South may be considered under three heads: waterways, roads, and railroads.

#### WATERWAYS

In the early colonization of the South, transportation by water was of paramount importance. Since streams were the safest and easiest means of travel, all of the first settlements were made along their banks. Even as late as the middle of the eighteenth century, when the danger of Indians along the coast had been minimized, there were still in the colonies no roads that did not become impassable in bad weather. Settlements in Florida and along the Gulf clung to the waterways, and trade was carried on exclusively along the rivers. Thus, in 1712, a river trade was opened between Quebec, Canada, and Louisiana and Mobile Bay. Although the French, Spanish, and British in pre-Revolutionary days navigated the Mississippi, it was not until 1795 that Spain granted the United States by treaty the free navigation of that great river, with the right of deposit at New Orleans. The purchase of Louisiana in 1803 gave the South the port of New Orleans, and the United States, control over the Mississippi.

After the Louisiana Purchase, Southerners, as well as many inhabitants of other sections, began to urge that Congress provide aid for the construction of roads and canals, because it was evident that great areas of the Nation were practically isolated. Neither the report of Albert Gallatin in 1808 nor similar recommendations made by John C. Calhoun a decade later received the favorable consideration of Congress. Consequently the states themselves undertook to make some of the most immediately essential internal improvements.

Even in the colonial period, there had been a few notable attempts to improve the waterways. Among these was the improvement of the Potomac River, undertaken by a private company in whose management George Washington was active. At the close of the Revolutionary War, the legislatures chartered several private corporations for the improvement of rivers and the construction of canals. Maryland chartered a company to cut a canal between Chesapeake Bay and the Delaware River. Virginia and North Carolina authorized the incorporation of a company to construct a canal through the Dismal Swamp, in order to furnish navigable communication between Chesapeake Bay and Albemarle Sound. In South Carolina, the Santee Canal was built to connect the Santee River with Cooper's Creek.

Most of these early projects were undertaken by private corporations, but the total cost of the improvements was beyond the resources of such corporations. In these early years, investments in trade yielding large direct returns were more attractive than long-time investments with uncertain profits. Hence it became necessary to provide funds for these corporations by some other means than the issuing of bonds. One method was to authorize the corporations to conduct lotteries, and the state frequently subscribed the capital stock of such corporations. Occasionally direct appropriations were made.

Prior to the War of 1812, power was denied Congress to grant direct aid for internal improvements within a state. No constitutional objection could be raised against appropriations for improvements within territories, however, and small appropriations were made for a few internal improvements, chiefly roads.

In the South, internal improvements were not undertaken in earnest until 1817, when Virginia created a special fund for internal improvements and vested the handling of the funds in a *board of public works*. The fund was to consist of bonuses received from the incorporation of new banks, and of shares held by the state in turnpike, canal, and river improvement companies, and in the Bank of Virginia. By 1819, similar steps had been taken in North Carolina; the practice was followed a little later by other Southern States.

Nearly all state aid then took the form of subscriptions to the stock of private companies. In the decade prior to 1825, South Carolina expended $1,500,000 on public works. Tennessee and Kentucky made surveys for improving important rivers. Kentucky provided that $40,000 of the state's dividend from the Bank of Kentucky should be appropriated annually for improving river transportation.

The strict constructionists of the Federal Constitution were gradually weakened politically, and the protagonists for empowering Congress to grant Federal aid for internal improvements within the states eventually gained control. As a result, between 1825 and 1830, Congress authorized subscriptions to the shares of four canal companies in the South. Moreover, between 1830 and 1860, Congress appropriated over $5,000,000 for river improvements, and more than $350,000 for the construction of canals. Of these appropriations a large part, but by no means an equal proportion, was devoted to internal improvements in the

Southern States. Relatively speaking, before the Civil War very little was actually accomplished in improving waterways in the South, because the advent of railroad building caused attention to be diverted from canal building and river improvements.

Various craft—known as *arks, Durham boats, flats, keel boats, Kentucky boats,* and the like—were most commonly used in river and canal transportation. Of these craft, perhaps the *flatboats* were the most typical. Usually they consisted of only two slabs of well-seasoned timber, upon which a strong floor of roughhewn timber, called "puncheons," was securely fastened and calked with tar to render it waterproof. A rude shelter was then built, to protect the crew, and at one end there was a rough helm. Oars were added, in order to pass over shoals in the streams. These boats were generally used in carrying heavy freight, like cotton and coal. On arriving at their destination, the crew sold the timber in their boat and returned to their starting point on packet boats, or they "hit the gravel train," as they phrased it, for their homes, to build another boat in which to repeat the trip. This system was so generally used that, even twenty years after the introduction of steamboats, at least four thousand flatboats still descended the Mississippi River annually.

In 1807, steamboat transportation was made commercially successful by Robert Fulton, who built the *Clermont,* which made the trip from New York to Albany in thirty-two hours. Four years later, Fulton, Livingston, and Nicholas Roosevelt introduced the steamboat to western waters, when the *New Orleans* descended the Ohio and the Mississippi Rivers. The *New Orleans* had a carrying capacity of one hundred tons and had cost $38,000. In 1812, this boat entered the regular service between Natchez and New Orleans and, in that year, earned $20,000 on her investment. Furthermore the investors had secured a monopoly grant from Louisiana. In 1815. despite the general belief that vessels could never "buck" the current above

Natchez, the *Enterprise* reached Louisville after a trip of twenty-five days up the river from New Orleans. The following year, another boat, the *Washington,* a large vessel built by Captain Henry M. Screve, also ascended the Mississippi. This boat defied the monopoly granted to Livingston and Fulton by Louisiana, and the case was before the courts when the decision in Gibbons *vs.* Ogden freed all navigable rivers in the United States. By 1816, sixty steamboats were in active service on the Mississippi; by 1825, this number had been increased to one hundred and twenty-five; and until the Civil War, steamboats were the chief means of transportation on the Mississippi and its tributaries. Moreover, steamboats soon came into active service on every other navigable river in the South. Thus, during the fifties of the last century, the steamboat *Eastport,* with a capacity of four thousand bales of cotton, and the *Cherokee,* of three thousand bales capacity, regularly plied from Florence, Alabama, to New Orleans. Other steamboats were running regularly from Florence to Louisville. Through the use of steamboats, the Tennessee River in Alabama had become a veritable artery of trade.

Unfortunately, steamboats frequently struck snags and shoals in the rivers, destroying not only vessels and cargoes, but sometimes even crews. Notices of such occurrences were, indeed, a regular thing in the newspapers of the period. A news item in the *Mobile Herald and Tribune* for November 27, 1850, stated: "The *Antoinette Douglas* hung upon the Traits' Shoals [in the Alabama River] . . . 25 or 30 lives lost . . . boiler burst."

### ROADS

Prior to the eighteenth century most of the roads in the Southern colonies were little more than Indian trails. Historically, the first American road of which there is a record was at Jamestown. Roads are said to have been built in Maryland as early as 1625, but all of these early roads were simply paths from plantations to river landings. In 1632, road laws were enacted in Virginia, and in 1657, the county courts in the colony were given control over roads. It was not until five years later that surveyors were appointed to establish roads. In 1666, systematic road building began in Maryland. County commissioners were empowered to appoint road overseers and to levy road taxes. Sixteen years later, South Carolina passed its first road law and fixed a labor tax. In Alabama as early as 1702, the French had built roads, and in later years these were used as mail routes. In 1735, at the time of the settlement of Augusta, Georgia built its first road. During the next two or three decades, roads were gradually extended into the interior of these colonial areas. In Maryland in 1739, the Monocacy Road was laid out between Maryland and Philadelphia, the first wagon road in America. In Virginia about 1750, a road was opened across the Appalachian Mountains, but it was nothing more than a portage path between the Potomac and the Monongahela Rivers. The Wilderness Road, through the Cumberland Gap in Virginia, was established by Daniel Boone in 1775. In 1785, a road ten feet wide was built in Tennessee from Nashville to the lower end of Clinch Mountain. In Mississippi, one of the earliest projects of the territorial government was to establish roads connecting that region with other parts of the South. In 1801, the Natchez Trace was built in Mississippi, and in the same year, the Federal Government undertook to construct two roads in Alabama, one of which extended to Natchez. In 1804, the Tennessee Legislature authorized the construction of roads in that state. In 1807, a similar step was taken by the Legislature of Mississippi. In Texas prior to 1832, practically no roads had been built; and Missouri, Arkansas, and Oklahoma were still inhabited mainly by Indians.

The most important ante-bellum roads were *turnpikes*— so termed because long, piked poles mounted on posts were constructed at the places where tolls were to be collected, and, when travelers came up, the piked poles were swung across the road until the toll was paid.

Before 1800, the Alexandria Turnpike was established in Virginia, and by the beginning of the nineteenth century, several companies had been incorporated in Maryland for the purpose of building turnpikes. In Alabama, a few years later, companies were organized to build such roads, and a law was enacted authorizing the companies to establish toll gates at intervals of five miles. The tolls were never to exceed 25 per cent nor to fall below 12½ per cent annually on the capital invested. In Tennessee, upon the founding of the Bank of Tennessee, the state was authorized to subscribe to one half of the stock in turnpike companies, the total subscription being limited to $4,000,-000. The amount of the bonds actually issued under this act was $1,500,000.

Of the several turnpikes established in the ante-bellum South, by far the most important was the National Road, or the "Cumberland Road" as it was first called. This road was built from Cumberland, Maryland, to Wheeling (now West Virginia), by the Federal Government, the intention being to establish a road as far as St. Louis. The road was, for those days, an excellent thoroughfare. The rivers and creeks were spanned by stone bridges. The distances were indexed by iron mileposts, and the toll houses were equipped with strong iron gates.

The construction of the first section of the National Road was authorized by an act of Congress in 1806, appropriating $30,000. Henry Clay and Henry Beeson, a former Congressman, were the chief supporters of the project. So enthusiastic was Beeson that he argued, on account of the number of horseshoes and the number of nails necessitated by such a road, it would be better adapted than a railroad to promote trade. It was not until 1820 that the actual work of surveying and locating the road was begun through Ohio, Indiana, and Illinois; and not until 1825—after a national political campaign had been fought, in part, over the question of the constitutionality of authorizing Federal aid for internal improvement—that large appropriations were made for completing the entire road.  By 1836, it was completed as far as Vandalia.  The cost and maintenance expense to that date were $6,812,000.

From Cumberland to Baltimore, the road was mainly built by certain banks of Maryland, which were rechartered in 1816 on condition that they complete the work.  This undertaking, however, far from being a burden to the banks, for several years yielded as much as 20 per cent upon their investment.

Upon the completion of the road to Vandalia in 1836, Congress, partly on account of a controversy between Alton and St. Louis as to where the road should cross the Mississippi, and partly because of a continual need for repairs, turned over to the states that part of the road built by the Federal Government.

The National Road had far-reaching effects upon the South.  Before its construction, eight days were required to travel from Baltimore to Wheeling, but soon after its completion, the time was reduced to three days.  According to Professor F. J. Turner, the road reduced the freight rates to half the amount charged in 1815.  The growth of Wheeling was greatly stimulated.  Villages sprang up along the road and nearby property rose in value.  The road operated as a powerful factor in westward migration and in the establishment of new settlements.  It greatly shortened and improved the old Monongahela Route to the Ohio and became, during the second quarter of the nineteenth century, one of the greatest highways between the East and the West.

No other post road in the United States at that time did so much business.  Wagons were so numerous, according to one account, that the leaders of one team had their noses in the trough at the end of the wagon ahead.  "As many as twenty four-horse coaches have been connected in a line at one time on the road, and large broad-wheeled wagons, covered with white canvas stretched over bows, laden with merchandise and drawn by six Conestoga horses, were visible all day long at every point, and many times until late in the evening, besides innumerable caravans of horses, mules, cattle, hogs, and sheep. It looked more like the leading avenue of a great city than a road through rural districts." [1] Every mile of the road had its tavern, and every tavern had "its pretty maid or jovial host. The eating was the cream of the earth." The charge for meals was only 25 cents, and "the whiskey at five cents a glass, was never known to be associated with a headache."

This great road was a veritable stream of life, which undoubtedly affected the growth of the population of the Southern highlands and increased the settlements in Kentucky. At the same time, many of the mountain settlers, as well as inhabitants from the Atlantic coast, joined the westward tide and left the South forever.

Toward the middle of the nineteenth century, there arose a great clamor for the construction of *plank roads,* and some of the Southern States enacted laws authorizing the formation of plank road companies. In Alabama, there were twenty-four such roads chartered by the legislature during the session of 1848–1850. Plank roads were introduced in North Carolina, Georgia, and a few other Southern States. In Kentucky, the legislature fixed such high tolls that plank roads never became popular.

The chief purpose of plank roads was to connect localities with the nearest railroad centers. In general it was argued that such roads were superior to macadam roads and that they could be constructed more cheaply, especially in localities possessing plenty of timber. The method used in constructing a plank road was quite simple. Parallel rows of sleepers, or sills, were imbedded in the road at intervals of three or four feet. Across these were laid, side by side, planks about eight or ten feet long and three or four inches

---

[1] Thomas B. Searight, *Old Pike,* p. 16.

thick.  On each side of the road, ditches were dug for the purpose of drainage, and occasionally gravel was scattered on top of the boards where there were slippery grades. However, plank roads were too new for promoters to have authoritative statistics upon maintenance expense and the number of years such a structure could be expected to last. Tolls were high, in order to attract investors into plank road companies.  Hence, such roads soon went out of existence on account of the heavy cost of maintenance and the prohibitive rate of toll.

In 1854, the *Montgomery Mail* described the South Plank Road, in Alabama:  "If it is as bad out of town as in, it is little short of a nuisance.  The part in town is badly out of repair; the idea of charging the double tolls that are now taken upon it has no foundation in justice. Four cents a mile for buggies!  More than railroad rates and the traveler furnishing his own conveyance. . . . A portion of the plank road stockholders are quite willing to vest their rights in the country, if it can be done legally, under a contract to commute with planters for road service; the money to be applied to keeping up the road." [2]

## RAILROADS

On account of the expansion of agriculture and the simultaneous decline in crop prices during the early decades of the nineteenth century, planters and merchants in the South were faced with the problem of developing, as well as reducing costs of, transportation. Waterways in some localities were improved, steamboats were introduced on navigable streams, and roads of various types were constructed.  Nevertheless, the transportation of crops and supplies remained expensive and burdensome, especially in the interior.  The greatest need of the early ante-bellum South was some invention that would solve this transportation problem.  The invention was steam locomotion, which

---

[2] *Montgomery Mail*, September 28, 1854.

came at the right moment to make railroads an integral and an indispensable factor in the development not only of the South but of the whole Nation.

The growth of railways in the ante-bellum South falls roughly into three periods: from 1830 to 1843; from 1843 to 1853; and from 1853 to 1860.

**1830–1843.** The first period was characterized by ambitious and optimistic projects initiated by a few towns which were the trade centers. The railroads actually built during this period were seldom more than a few miles in length. In 1835, the South had 458 miles of railways, or about 42 per cent of the total mileage of the Nation. By 1840, this had been increased to 849 miles, or 30 per cent of the total mileage of the United States—other regions, especially Pennsylvania, having more rapidly extended their lines.

In the building of early railroads on the North American Continent, the South took the lead, and the section was the birthplace of railroad transportation in the United States. Although a small stone-quarry railroad at Quincy, Massachusetts, and a coal-mine railroad at Honesdale, Pennsylvania, were the first lines in America, neither was a common carrier. The first real railroad in the United States was the Baltimore & Ohio. In 1826, a group of capitalists were granted a charter by the state of Maryland for a corporation organized to build a railroad from Baltimore to the Ohio River. The next year, as the contemplated extension of this road across the Allegheny Mountains was likely to be made within the bounds of Virginia, a charter was also obtained in that state. Then, on July 4, 1828, at the same time that John Quincy Adams turned the first shovelful of dirt for the Baltimore & Ohio Canal, Charles Carroll, the only surviving signer of the Declaration of Independence, placed the first stone of the track of the Baltimore & Ohio Railroad. Within six months, 14 miles of the road were completed. In 1832, the road extended 73 miles west of Baltimore, but not until 1853 did it reach the Ohio River.

The next railroad company in the United States was organized at Charleston, South Carolina, in May 1828. Funds were raised, and by the autumn of 1833, the Charleston & Hamburg Line—later called the "South Carolina Railroad"—was completed. This line extended 136 miles from Charleston to Hamburg, South Carolina, on the Savannah River opposite Augusta, Georgia, and was at that time the longest railroad in the world.

The third railroad in the United States was a line, 20 miles long, built in 1832 to connect Woodville, Mississippi, with St. Francisville, Louisiana, a convenient shipping point on the Mississippi River.

Numerous other short railways were built in the South. In Virginia, the Petersburg Railroad Company was incorporated during February 1830, and in North Carolina, about a year later. By the end of 1832, track had been laid from Petersburg to Emporia, Virginia, a distance of 41 miles. The following year, the road was completed from Emporia, Virginia, to Weldon, North Carolina, a distance of 20 miles, or a total of 61 miles of track connecting Petersburg with Weldon. On April 8, 1831, the Winchester & Potomac Railroad was incorporated. Construction began in 1833 and continued until 1835, when the entire line of about 31 miles was completed from Winchester, Virginia, to Harpers Ferry. The Portsmouth & Roanoke Railroad Company was incorporated in Virginia during March 1832, and in North Carolina, the first of the next year. This company built in Virginia between 1833 and 1836 approximately 61 miles of railroad extending from Portsmouth to the Virginia-North Carolina state line. In 1834, the Richmond, Fredericksburg & Potomac Railroad Company was incorporated, and by the end of 1836, it had completed its line from Richmond to Hazel Run, a distance of 60 miles. In 1834, the Greenville & Roanoke Railroad Company was incorporated in Virginia and in

North Carolina, to build 18 miles of railroad, connecting Greenville with the Roanoke River.

During 1836, Virginia witnessed great activity in railroad building. In that year, two important companies were incorporated: the Richmond & Petersburg Railroad Company, which by 1840 completed a line of about 35 miles; and the City Point Railroad Company, which constructed about 9 miles of railroad, from Petersburg to City Point. Virginia inaugurated a vigorous program of railroad construction during the thirties and, by 1839, had a little over 10 per cent of the railroad mileage of the United States.

In Maryland, the Annapolis & Elk Ridge Railroad Company was chartered in 1837 and, three years later, began operating a line about 20 miles long from Annapolis to Annapolis Junction. In North Carolina, the Wilmington & Raleigh Railroad Company, chartered in 1833, had by 1840 completed a line of 162 miles from Wilmington to Weldon. In Georgia during one year, 1833, there were chartered: the Georgia, the Central of Georgia, and the Monroe Railroad Companies. By 1838, the latter road had been completed from Monroe to Forsyth. By 1839, the Central of Georgia Railroad extended 76 miles. By 1840, the Georgia Railroad Company had completed 105 miles of its proposed line. In north Alabama, a company was chartered in 1830 and built a railroad for about 40 miles along Muscle Shoals, to serve as a portage between the upper and lower reaches of the Tennessee River. In Mississippi during 1836, a railroad was begun to connect Jackson and Vicksburg, a distance of 46 miles. The road was completed in 1840. At about the same time, a short line was built in that state between Port Gibson and Grand Gulf.

Other early railroad projects were undertaken in several regions of the South, as for example, the Tuscumbia & Decatur Railroad, in Alabama; the Memphis & Lagrange Railroad; and a New Orleans' project to build a railroad to Nashville.  But these, as well as others less pretentious, were utterly wrecked by the panic of 1837.

In the Southwest prior to the late forties and the early fifties, there were no railroad projects, because the trade from the upper Mississippi Valley, the Tennessee region especially, had not yet been diverted from Memphis and New Orleans by overland transportation to the Southwest.

1843–1853.  The second period of railway construction in the South was characterized by the linking of the early short lines into intercity systems.  During this period the mileage of Southern railroads more than doubled, but relative to the total mileage of the United States, it declined from approximately 30 per cent to about 20 per cent.

By 1853, the Baltimore & Ohio Railroad had completed its line to Wheeling.  In 1840, the Charleston & Hamburg Railroad had completed its Columbia branch of 68 miles; in 1843, the Camden branch of 38 miles was completed under a separate charter; and in 1844, all three roads— the Charleston & Hamburg, and the Camden and the Columbia branches—were merged under the charter of the South Carolina Railroad.  In 1845, the Georgia Railroad, having built branches to Macon (74 miles), to Athens (40 miles), and to Washington, Georgia (about 18 miles), completed its line of 171 miles from Augusta to Atlanta.  In 1850, the Western & Atlantic Railway finished its line of 138 miles connecting Atlanta and Chattanooga.  In 1845, the Nashville & Chattanooga Railroad was chartered and, when it was opened a year later, formed a connection with the river and rail system of the Northwest and at the same time made Atlanta the "gate city" of the South.  In 1850, the Louisa Railroad Company, in Virginia, changed its name to the "Virginia Central Railroad Company," and vigorously pushed its construction work to join certain Virginia towns.  Before the end of 1850, the line from Shadwell to Charlottesville was completed, a distance of about 5 miles.  The following year, the road from Doswell to Richmond was completed, adding about 26 miles; and

during the same year, the road was extended from Char-
lottesville to Ivy, and in 1852, from Ivy to Meechum's
River.  Two years later, the line from Waynesboro to
Staunton was completed.  In 1851, the Seaboard & Roanoke
Railroad Company began operating its entire line from
Portsmouth, Virginia, to Weldon, North Carolina.

Besides the extension of established railroads, several
new lines were projected.  In 1845, the Southwestern
Company, of Georgia, began building railroads from
Macon westward and southwestward to Columbus, Ameri-
cus, Albany, and other small towns.  The Atlanta & West
Point, and the Montgomery & West Point Companies,
allied with each other, began building from Atlanta to
Montgomery.  The Charlotte & South Carolina and the
Greenville & Columbia, both projected in 1845–1846, became the two main lines of the Piedmont region.  In Virginia from 1846 to 1849, eleven new railroad companies
were organized.  In 1850, the Manassas Gap Railroad
Company was incorporated, and by 1854, it had constructed
a railroad from Manassas to Strasburg, a distance of nearly
62 miles.

But it must be noted that, even in 1850, all of the
railroad mileage in the South, except 200 or 300 miles,
lay eastward of Alabama and the Appalachian Mountains.

**1853–1860.**  The third period of railway construction in
the South was one of rapid expansion, stimulated by a
desire for through routes reaching to the trade centers
of other sections.  By 1853, the stage was set for a period
of active railroad construction in the United States, and
the South shared the enthusiasm characteristic of the
country at large.  The depression following the panic of
1837 had been followed by conditions of general business
prosperity.  Agriculture, industry, and commerce were
expanding rapidly and creating an urgent demand for
increased transportation facilities.  In 1850, the total extent of railroads in the South was 2,068 miles.  In 1860,

the mileage had increased to 10,386, of which about one half lay in the transmontane and southwest regions.

In the eastern half of the South, several roads were extended and a few new ones built. By 1853, the Baltimore & Ohio Railroad had been extended to the Ohio River. By 1859, the Virginia Central had completed its line from Richmond to the Jackson River; and the Southside Railroad and the North Carolina Central had extended their lines. Roads were being built from Wilmington, North Carolina, through Florence, to Charleston; from Charleston to Savannah; from Savannah to southwest Georgia; and from Jacksonville to Tallahassee and St. Marks.

In the Highland, or middle, region of the South, the Virginia & Tennessee Railroad Company pushed its line with great vigor, and in 1852, that road was in operation to Big Lick (Roanoke). In 1859, it ran from Lynchburg to Bristol, a distance of about 205 miles. This road, connected at one end with the East Tennessee & Georgia, and at the other end, with the Southside Railroad, thus formed a long, intramontane line almost parallel with the coast.

In the region between the Ohio River and the Gulf of Mexico, several important lines were established during this period. Running northeastward from Memphis was the Memphis & Chicago. Farther eastward was the Louisville & Nashville. The Tennessee & Alabama was built southward from Nashville. The Alabama & Mississippi—or the "Southern Railroad," as it was afterwards called for a short time—was constructed to fill in the gaps between Montgomery and Vicksburg. The Mississippi Central—or the later "Memphis & New Orleans"—extended the line of the New Orleans, Jackson & Northern to Memphis. The New Orleans, Jackson & Northern opened a line from New Orleans to Canton in 1859. Finally, in 1859, the Mobile & Ohio, chartered in 1848, opened its line of about 483 miles from Mobile to Cairo. In addition to these main lines, by 1860, the South had several dozen minor railroads scattered through different regions and serving as feeders to the main lines or, in some instances, to the waterways.

Beyond the Mississippi River, Missouri had a total of 547 miles of railroad, a continuous line running across the state and roads radiating from St. Louis. In Texas after 1850, an enthusiasm for railroads spread rapidly. Many companies were formed for the purpose of building roads from the Gulf ports into northern Texas or even to the Pacific Ocean. But few of these companies could obtain enough capital, and only the Buffalo, Bayou, Brazos & Colorado was able to actually begin building a line by 1852. Since the companies could not get help from Northern capitalists on account of the high risk of building railroads through this sparsely settled region, it was urged that Texas should give aid. In 1852, a provision was made that the new railroad companies should receive eight sections of land for every mile of road constructed and approved by the state engineer. By the end of 1860, eleven roads were under construction, with a total mileage of 492.

Thus, by 1860, the skeleton of the South's railroad system had been planned, and during the Civil War, it was completed. The unfinished gaps of the eastern through route—from Richmond to New Orleans; from Danville to Greensboro; and from Selma, Alabama, to Meridian, Mississippi—were built, and a spur was thrust into Florida.

During the first period of railway construction, there was much uncertainty in the minds of civil engineers regarding the relative value of canals and railroads. The promoters of the Baltimore & Ohio Railroad were immediately confronted with this problem when they requested from the General Assembly of Virginia a charter to allow them the privilege of selecting a route through that state. Professor Charles C. Wright, who has made a thorough study of the early development of railroad transportation in Virginia, says:[3] "In the report of the Principal Engineer of Virginia for 1830 the Question was raised whether a railroad (The Baltimore and Ohio) would be a successful and valuable substitute for the navigation of the river (the James), on its whole line or in part. He held that a railroad 'might' be expedient only in the upper section, in connection with the crossing of the Allegheny, but not otherwise, or elsewhere, because frequent translation of goods should be avoided. Particularly below the mountains the railway would be less desirable on account of its cost and inconvenience. 'And, what would be strongly objected to, the formation of a straight line would necessarily cut in many places, through the valuable James river bottoms. The improvement would, thus occasion even greater complaints; and proportionate damages, than a canal which can be made to wind closer to the hills.' "

It was pointed out that the canal could receive small streams, while a railway required that every stream, however small, be bridged; also, that high expensive embankments would need to be constructed to keep the railroad free from the danger of high water. Other points in favor of a canal were mentioned as follows:[4]

"(1) The railroad would accommodate only one side of the river while a canal would accommodate both. . . .

"(2) 'The expense of fencing, so onerous on the canal, would be increased here, as likewise the difficulty of keeping the work in order, where it would be crossed at so many points in farms belonging to the same owner on both sides of the road, which will generally divide the buildings from the fields.' . . . The late performances of locomotive engines, the account continues, 'have greatly enhanced the advantages of railways, though we should not be deceived by the accounts of the great speed they have proved capable of; this being obtained evidently at a greater expense of

[3] Charles Conrad Wright, *Development of Railroad Transportation in Virginia* (Ph.D. Thesis, University of Virginia), p. 11.
[4] *Ibid.*, pp. 11–12.

power or diminution of weight transported, is not applicable to the most favorable transportation of goods, and is objectionable on the score of prudence; nor is their ascent up certain inclined planes, a criterion of their usefulness in that respect, as what they do alone, they could not perform with a load; and it would not require a steep rise to make them inferior even to horses.' . . . After enumerating other advantages and disadvantages of this project, the engineer concluded by saying, 'These considerations are so decisive in favor of the railroad that it would be useless to mention its advantages as regards its easier ultimate connection with the head of the Holston.' "

The early railroad projects come into competition not only with the building of canals, but also with turnpike and plank road enterprises. By the end of the first period of railway construction in the South, however, public sentiment as a general rule had come to favor railroads.

Many difficult problems were encountered in the raising of sufficient funds to construct the necessary 10,000 miles of railroad in the ante-bellum South. Local private capital was scarce, and there was always the fundamental difficulty inherent in financing railroads in sparsely settled regions, where an adequate return on the investment was contingent upon the subsequent economic development of such regions. Yet by 1860, over $325,000,000 had been invested in railway construction in the South, or nearly 29 per cent of the capital invested in railway construction in the Nation as a whole.

The railroads in the ante-bellum South were built in part by bonds sold to foreign and Northern capitalists, in part by governmental aid—especially by money paid from the state for shares—and in part by people along the lines who paid money for shares and took an active part in the management of the roads. Before the Civil War, Southern railroads were run to pay dividends and not to make speculative fortunes; and their capitalization, as a rule, approximated rather closely the actual cost of the lines and equipment.

Few Southern railroads had large bonded debts, except where state aid had been granted. Thus, in 1847, the Georgia Railroad had a capital stock of $2,289,200, but no bonded debt. By 1860, it had increased its line to 231 miles and its capital stock to $4,156,000; its bonded debt, moreover, was only $312,500, and that amount was offset by $1,003,500 in securities which the company owned in other roads. At the same time, the Southwestern Railroad, with a line 206 miles long, had a capital stock of $3,318,279, but a bonded debt of only $396,500. In 1860, the Macon & Western Railroad, with a line of 103 miles and a capital stock of $1,500,000, had no bonded debt. The capital structure of these railroads seems to have been planned with remarkable foresight.

There are no reliable statistics as to the original cost of construction of the early railroads in the South. The combination of sandy soil, easy grades, cheap lumber, and cheap labor in the Coastal Plains evidently resulted in reduced cost of construction, and presumably a few of the early roads cost less than $15,000 a mile. In spite of this fact, according to *Poor's Manual,* large sums of money were expended upon some of these early lines without adequate returns. Therefore, when the demand for railroads in the South became more urgent, the people turned to the states, and even the Federal Government, for assistance in carrying out their plans.

In 1828, Maryland had subscribed $500,000 of the stock of the Baltimore & Ohio, and in 1836, $3,000,000. By 1836, Virginia was pretty well committed to the policy of aiding railroad construction through the purchase of a part of the capital stock, generally the last two fifths. The amount subscribed by Virginia to stock of various railroads up to 1838 was as follows: [5]

---

[5] *Ibid.*, p. 401. Statistics compiled from a report of the Virginia State Board of Public Works (1838).

RAILROAD SUBSCRIPTIONS BY VIRGINIA ASSEMBLY

| *Railroad Company* | *Amount Subscribed* |
|---|---|
| Petersburg Railroad Company................$ | 80,000 |
| Winchester & Potomac Railroad Company..... | 120,000 |
| Portsmouth & Roanoke Railroad Company..... | 240,000 |
| Richmond, Fredericksburg & Potomac Railroad Company................................ | 206,800 |
| City Point Railroad Company................ | 60,000 |
| Louisa Railroad Company.................... | 120,000 |
| Richmond & Petersburg Railroad Company.... | 200,000 |
| TOTAL.............................. | $1,026,800 |

By 1838, some of the other Southern States had invested in railroads as follows: Alabama, $3,000,000; Kentucky, $350,000; Louisiana, $50,000; Maryland, $5,500,000; South Carolina, $2,000,000; and Tennessee, $3,730,000. All of the Southern States, moreover, by 1838, had assisted railroad construction to the extent of over $41,-000,000.

The panic of 1837, which halted the work of internal improvements in the United States, had two very definite effects on railroad financing in the South. It was practically impossible to get individuals to subscribe to stock in newly organized railroad companies; and in many cases, it was impossible to collect outstanding subscriptions. For several years after 1837, there appeared in Southern newspapers notices begging and urging subscribers to railroad stocks to pay their overdue subscriptions.

With the return of prosperity, railway construction was renewed with great vigor. Not only did the states give further assistance, but Georgia even went so far as to build a railroad. As early as 1836, that state, by an act of the legislature had committed herself to a project of building a railroad, but it was not completed until 1851. The road was the Western & Atlantic and, as Professor Ulrich B. Phillips says, "is of large historical concern in two regards: it was the perfecting member in the well-devised railway system which made Georgia the keystone state of the South, and Atlanta the gate city from the northwest to the eastern cotton belt; and it furnishes the most important example in American history, thus far, of the state ownership and operation of railroads."[6]  The legislative appropriations for this railroad were as follows:[7]

LEGISLATIVE APPROPRIATIONS FOR THE WESTERN & ATLANTIC

| Year | Amount |
|---|---|
| 1836–1837 | $ 350,000 |
| 1837–1838 | 500,000 |
| 1838–1839 | 1,500,000 |
| 1847–1848 | 375,000 |
| 1851–1852 | 525,000 |
| TOTAL | $3,250,000 |

Another notable example in state assistance on an extreme scale was in Virginia in 1856.  In that year, the General Assembly authorized the board of public works to subscribe, on behalf of the state, to $1,200,000 of the capital stock of the Alexandria, London & Hampshire Railroad Company, or in the proportion of three shares to every two subscribed by individuals.

In Tennessee at the end of 1859, according to a legislative report, there were ten railroads having a total length of 1,180 miles.  The aggregate cost of equipment was $2,149,350.  The total capital stock, all paid in, amounted to $11,390,606.  The bonded debt amounted to $11,050,449, but $8,979,000 of this amount was state aid from Tennessee, and $2,961,000 additional state aid had been provided by Tennessee for the completion of roads under construction.

In Alabama, there appears to have been a fund accumulated from 5 per cent of the proceeds from public land sales.  Three per cent of this fund had been invested and lost in the state bank, but in 1859, the legislature agreed

---

[6] *History of Transportation in the Eastern Cotton Belt to 1860* (1908), p. 303. Reprinted by permission of the Columbia University Press, New York.

[7] *Ibid.* Table compiled from statistics found in Phillips.

that it owed the fund $858,498.  This money was loaned to various railroad companies in the state.

Aside from state aid, a few railroads in the South before 1860 were assisted through Federal land grants.  In 1850, Senator Stephen A. Douglas succeeded in getting Congress to pass a railroad act which initiated the system of Federal aid that prevailed through the decade.  According to this system, alternate sections of public land were to be granted to the railroads.  The following railroads benefited as indicated: [8]

FEDERAL LAND GRANTS TO SOUTHERN
RAILROADS, BEFORE 1860

| Railroad | Grant |
| --- | --- |
| Mobile & Ohio | 413,528.44 acres |
| Alabama & Florida | 309,022.84 acres |
| Alabama-Tennessee | 858,515.98 acres |
| Alabama & Chattanooga | 652,966.66 acres |
| South & North Alabama | 445,158.78 acres |
| Mobile & Girard | 302,181.16 acres |
| TOTAL | 2,981,373.86 acres |

During the decade before the Civil War, Congress granted land, in aid of railways, to Mississippi, Missouri, Arkansas, Florida, and Louisiana—the Southern States which, at that time, were least able to bear the burden of railway construction.

Of almost equal importance with the financial problems were the construction and the maintenance of the tracks, the technological changes in equipment, and the actual operation of the roads.

As a rule, roadbeds were poorly constructed.  No bridges were made of iron; most of them were wood, but a few were creditable pieces of construction.  The first tracks were built by laying either wood or crossties with longitudinal wooden rails, on which were then spiked flat, iron rails about two and a half inches wide and from one half to five

---

[8] Compiled from W. E. Martin, *Early History of Internal Improvements in Alabama*, p. 64.

eighths of an inch thick.  This sort of track, however, proved to be a dangerous type of construction, because, after the track had been used for a time, the end of a rail would occasionally come loose, curve upwards, break through the floor of a car, and cause injury to either freight or passengers.  These upturned ends of rails were termed "snake heads," and the accidents caused by them, "acts of God"—for which the railroad could not be held legally liable.  In a few instances iron rails were secured directly to stone blocks, laid longitudinally without crossties.

Until the Civil War there were at least twelve different railway gauges in the United States.  In the South, the Charleston & Hamburg Railroad had adopted a gauge of five feet.  This became a precedent for nearly every important railroad in the section and thereby facilitated through traffic until connections had to be made with roads of different gauges reaching into other sections.

The first engines used were of the vertical type, without cabs.  Operatives knew very little about the principle of steam locomotives.  In 1830, the Charleston & Hamburg Railroad purchased one of the first locomotives built in this country.  It was called the *Best Friend*.  One day, after having operated this engine for about a year, the negro fireman became annoyed at the continuous hissing of the steam valve.  Forthwith he sat down upon the lever governing the valve, stopped the noise, and blew up the boiler.  The first engines burned wood instead of coal, and the sparks from the dry pine fuel frequently burned holes in the passengers' clothing and often set fire to the forests along the line.  The first passenger cars were little more than bodies of stagecoaches mounted upon wheels adapted to the rails.  The brakes were the same as those used on wagons.

Although the speed of these trains was considered marvelous at that time, it was seldom more than ten or twelve miles an hour.  In 1840, an advertisement appeared: [9]

---

[9] Seymour Dunbar, *History of Travel in America*, Vol. III, p. 961.

"The United States' Mail Line!
The Only Line
Carrying the Great Mail!
Daily to the South,
Via, Baltimore, Washington, Fredericksburg,
Richmond, Petersburg, Weldon, Wilmington and
Charleston (S. C.).
Whole time from Philadelphia to Charleston (all Stoppages
Included) 60 Hours, or nearly 12 miles per Hour! ! ! !"

At night, trains ran at slower speed and the risk of accident was increased. The annual report of the Richmond, Fredericksburg & Potomac Railroad Company, for 1839, contains the interesting statement:[10] "The difficulties of performing transportation in the night on a railway cannot be well understood or appreciated by persons inexperienced in this kind of business, such as keeping the engine in repair, the influence of dew and frost on the track."

Even during the decade of the fifties, the air brake, the automatic coupler, the block system of signals, scientifically constructed roadbeds, and high-speed engines were still unknown. Furthermore, the rolling stock of the Southern roads was scant, and nearly all companies were dependent upon importations from the North and abroad.

It is interesting to note some of the "Rules for Safe Travel," promulgated during the fifties. For example, "Express trains are more dangerous, never use them except when necessary; in case of accident, causing irregular stoppage, it is better to quit the train; select carriages near the center of the train if possible; and travel by day, if possible, not in foggy weather." In spite of all precautions, a railroad passenger in those days literally took his life in his hands when he began his journey. During the

---

[10] Charles C. Wright, *Development of Railroad Transportation in Virginia*, p. 27.

decade before the Civil War, the number of accidents became appalling; they were due principally to increased traffic, to the effort to get speed, to depreciated and obsolete equipment, and to the rotting of wooden trestles along the line.

Another problem that had to be worked out was that of through tickets. In 1843, attention was called to "a matter of injustice" to the Virginia railroads "in the matter of through fares." [11] It was pointed out that in distributing the receipts from through fares among the different lines furnishing the transportation from centers in the South, through Virginia, to Baltimore, the Baltimore & Ohio Railroad received $2.50 for 38 miles, the regular fare, while the Virginia roads got only $5.78 for 161 miles. All the loss from reduced through fares was thus thrown on the Virginia roads. This problem was more involved than is at first apparent, especially on long routes. A person going from Baltimore to New Orleans, approximately 1,460 miles, in 1846, was compelled to use five railroads, two stagecoaches, and two steamboats. His fare was $62.50. Was he to buy nine separate tickets, or one through ticket? If the latter, how was his total fare to be allocated among the several transportation agencies? Under the circumstances at that time, it was usually more desirable that he buy separate tickets.

Despite all the problems confronting them, the railroads of the ante-bellum South, had there been no Civil War, would not have found themselves in serious distress. In Maryland, the 572 miles of railroad in 1857 had net earnings of $2,470,594; in Virginia, several roads were earning about 6 per cent; and in Alabama, in 1855, the Montgomery & West Point Railroad earned 8 per cent on its capital stock.[12] Even the panic of 1857, which sent so

---

[11] *Ibid.*, p. 47.

[12] *Ibid.*, Chap. III. See also: Henry V. Poor, *History of the Railroads and Canals of the United States of America* (published in New York City in 1860); and *Montgomery Advertiser and State Gazette*, April 10, 1855.

many Northern railroads into the hands of receivers, seems to have had little effect on Southern roads.

## Telegraphic Communication

The first telegraph line in America was established in 1844 between Baltimore and Washington. Because of its success, telegraph companies were quickly formed in the East and the South. In 1846, the Washington & New Orleans Telegraph Company was opened, with a subsequent large business. In 1856, this company was leased to the Magnetic Telegraph Company, which had been started by Morse and Kendall, under a charter granted by the Maryland Legislature. As early as 1847, the South had 120 miles of telegraph line; and $275,000 in stock had been taken by Southerners in the line connecting Washington and New Orleans. In 1860, the principal telegraph companies in the South were: the Washington & New Orleans Telegraph Company, with lines extending from Washington to Atlanta, via Richmond, Lynchburg, Bristol, Knoxville, and Chattanooga; the People's Telegraph Company, with lines from Louisville to New Orleans, via Nashville, Memphis, Columbus, and Jackson; and the New Orleans & Ohio Telegraph Company, via Wheeling, Lexington, Natchez, and Vicksburg. During the Civil War, all the Southern telegraph companies were combined into two systems: the American Telegraph Company; and the New Orleans & Ohio, usually termed the "Southwestern Telegraph Company." By 1867, the American Company had absorbed the Southwestern and had itself passed into the control of the Western Union.

## Effects of Transportation and Communication Developments

The development of systems of transportation and communication in the ante-bellum South enhanced real estate values, reduced marketing costs, and made possible a kind of sectional solidarity. Just before the Civil War numerous statistics were published showing to what extent real estate values had advanced where railroads had been constructed in Southern States.  One of these tables gave the following comparative figures: [13]

### COMPARATIVE FIGURES ON REAL ESTATE VALUES AND RAILROAD EXPENDITURES

| State | Real Estate Value, 1850 | Expended on Railroads | Real Estate Values |
|---|---|---|---|
| Missouri | $ 66,802,223 | $30,871,363 | $235,892,792 (1858) |
| Texas | 28,149,671 | 5,000,000 | 86,539,306 (1856) |
| Kentucky | 177,013,407 | 13,314,059 | 270,960,818 (1859) |
| Arkansas | 17,372,524 | 7,978,298 | 141,747,536 (1857) |
| Tennessee | 107,981,793 | 26,337,427 | 166,417,907 (1856) |
| Virginia | 252,105,824 | 42,607,674 | 374,989,888 (1859) |

Obviously, railroads alone were not wholly responsible for these extraordinary increases in land values.  Other causes were also operating, such as, increased population and, especially, after 1848, the rapidly rising, general price level in the United States.  Nevertheless, the construction of railroads, as well as the building of canals and highways, enhanced the value of land by increasing its availability, and sometimes even caused booms in the development of localities formerly inaccessible to outside markets.

As compared with the earlier means of transportation, steamboats and railroads in the ante-bellum South not only facilitated travel and the movement of goods and crops, but greatly reduced the expense of transportation.  Passenger fares and freight rates varied widely, however, throughout the section.  For transporting passengers, a number of railroads had two rates of fare, first class and second class, with a charge from 3 to 6 cents per mile for first class, and from 2 to 5 cents for second class.  In 1848, the first class passenger rates from Baltimore to Cumberland were 3.91 cents per mile; from Baltimore to Washington, 4 cents per mile; from Washington to Richmond, including portage, 4.13 cents per mile; from Augusta to

---

[13] Compiled from Edward Ingle, *Southern Sidelights*, p. 101.

Atlanta, 4 cents per mile; and from Vicksburg to Jackson, 6 cents per mile.

Nearly all of the roads had some simple classification of freight: several roads divided freight into four classes, with a different rate for each class; a few applied commodity rates on wheat, cotton, and plaster.

Freight rates varied more than passenger fares—from one and a half cents per ton per mile for the class of freight taking the lowest rate to over 15 cents per ton per mile for first class freight. In 1849, the cost for freight taking the lowest rate on the Baltimore & Ohio was 1.182 cents per ton per mile, and on the Central of Georgia it was 1.679 cents per ton per mile. The cost of transportation by waterways also varied, and often included such items as river and fire insurance and the cost of weighing. Thus, in 1852, the total cost of sending a 450-pound bale of cotton from Huntsville, Alabama, to New Orleans was $6.17; to send the same quantity to Charleston would have cost $6.68.

Yet, in spite of the fact that there was little uniformity in steamboat and railway rates, the relatively lower expenses of transportation were particularly effective in stimulating agriculture at a time when market prices for export staples were declining to a point that would have curtailed production if the earlier transportation costs had continued. Of no less importance was the fact that the transportation and communication facilities established in the ante-bellum South tied together remote areas and contributed immeasurably to its solidarity as a homogeneous section of the Nation.

### Bibliographical Note

Transportation in the ante-bellum South has received considerable treatment. *History of Transportation in the United States before 1860*, prepared, under the editorship of B. H. Meyer, by Caroline E. MacGill (Washington, 1917), contains valuable notes on the ante-bellum period of transportation. Seymour Dunbar's *History of Travel in America*, four volumes

(Indianapolis, Ind., 1915), is written in a popular style, but contains much original material and several early illustrations of transportation facilities in this country. The best treatment of transportation in the region west of the Alleghenies is C. H. Ambler, *Transportation in the Ohio Valley* (Cleveland, Ohio, 1931). A. B. Hulbert, *Historic Highways of America*, fifteen volumes (Cleveland, Ohio, 1902–1905), gives interesting descriptions of trails, roads, and canals. T. B. Searight's *Old Pike: A History of the National Road* (Uniontown, Pa., 1894) is an anecdotal history of that thoroughfare. The history of several individual projects is summarized in J. A. Durrenburger, *Turnpikes, A Study of the Toll Road Movement in the Middle Atlantic States and Maryland* (Valdosta, Ga., 1931).

A fundamental study of canal building is H. S. Tanner, *Description of the Canals and Railroads of the United States; Comprehending Notices of all the Works of Internal Improvements Throughout the Several States* (New York, 1840). W. F. Dunaway, *History of the James River and Kanawha Company* (New York, 1922), is a detailed account of that project.

An approach to steamboat navigation may be had through H. H. Morrison, *History of American Steam Navigation* (Brooklyn, N. Y., 1903). The best brief account of navigation of the Mississippi during the ante-bellum period is to be found in F. H. Dixon, *Traffic History of the Mississippi River System*, National Waterway Commission, Document No. II (Washington, 1909). To be noted also is A. B. Hulbert's article, "Western Ship-Building," in the *American Historical Review*, Volume XX, pages 720–733. Entertaining but superficial accounts of travel on the Mississippi may be found in: Herbert and Edward Quick, *Mississippi Steamboatin'* (Boston, 1926); G. L. Eskew, *Pageant of the Packets* (Boston, 1929); and Mark Twain, *Life on the Mississippi* (New York, 1883).

U. B. Phillips, *History of Railroad Transportation in the Eastern Cotton Belt to 1860* (New York, 1908), is the most accurate treatment of railroad history in the ante-bellum South. Another source of information is H. V. Poor, *History of the Railroads and Canals of the United States* (New York, 1860). Although C. F. Adams' *Railroads: Their Origin and Problems* (New York, 1878), has been superseded by more scholarly and interesting studies, it contains several valuable bits of information found nowhere else except in rare first sources. L. H. Haney, *Congressional History of Railways in the United States to 1850* (Madison, Wis., 1910), is a summary of national aid and policy. R. S. Cotterell, "Southern Railroads 1850–1860," in the *Mississippi Valley Historical Review*, Volume 10, page 396 *et seq.*, contains some interesting details. C. K. Brown, *State Movement in Railroad Development* (Chapel Hill, N. C., 1928), treats the early development of railroads in South Carolina. There are many histories of the different railroads in the South. Of these, four may be mentioned because they contain original materials: Milton Riezenstein, *Economic History of the Baltimore and Ohio Railroad 1827–1853* (New York, 1897); Edward Hungerford, *Story of the Baltimore and Ohio Railroad 1827–1927*, two volumes (New York, 1928); H. D. Dozier, *History of the Atlantic Coast Line Railroad* (New York, 1920); and S. M. Derrick, *Centennial History of South Carolina Railroad* (Columbia, S. C., 1930).

The most important works dealing with state aid for internal improvements in the ante-bellum South are: J. W. Milton, *Aid to Railways in Missouri* (Chicago, 1896); and R. L. Morton, "The Virginia State Debt and Internal Improvements 1820–1838," in the *Journal of Political Economy*, Volume XXV, pages 339–373.

Studies of transportation in the various states include: C. C. Weaver, *Internal Improvements in North Carolina* (Baltimore, 1903); W. E. Martin, *Early History of Internal Improvements in Alabama* (Baltimore, 1902); and Charles W. Ramsdell, "Internal Improvements in Texas," in the *Proceedings of the Mississippi Valley Historical Association* (1915–1918), Vol. 9. Several theses on the history of transportation in the different Southern States have been written by graduate students in Southern universities, but as yet few of these have been published.

# CHAPTER XII

# Finance in the Ante-Bellum South, 1783–1860

THE development of banking in the South before 1860 was largely determined by the nature of the credit requirements of agriculture. Extension of the plantation system called for increasing amounts of money and credit. The planters had no money till their crops were sold, and most of what they received had to be used to pay debts made in anticipation of the harvest. There was consequently a demand on the part of planters for money to be employed as working capital.

## Banking

The Southern colonies, as already noted, attempted to supply the demand for money and credit by declaring certain metals, articles, and commodities legal tender, and by issuing paper currency. Upon the adoption of the Federal Constitution, according to Article I, Section 10, it was provided that: "No State shall . . . coin money; emit Bills of Credit; make anything but gold and silver coin a tender in payment of debts. . . ."

In 1791, at the recommendation of Alexander Hamilton, the *First Bank of the United States* was established at Philadelphia. This was a large central bank, branches of which were eventually established in Boston, New York, Baltimore, Norfolk, Charleston, Savannah, Washington, and New Orleans. With its branches, this bank was empowered to receive deposits, to issue notes, and to act as the fiscal agent of the Government. It attempted to conduct the domestic exchange of the country. At the time the First Bank of the United States was chartered, there was in existence in the South only one state bank—the Bank of Maryland, chartered in 1790. By the time the charter of the First Bank expired, in 1811, state banks had been established in Virginia, North Carolina, and Kentucky.

In 1816, a bill was introduced in Congress for the purpose of establishing the *Second Bank of the United States,* on practically the same principles as the First Bank. John C. Calhoun supported the measure and made a violent attack on state banks, which, he said, circulated $170,000,000 in bank notes and had only $15,000,000 in specie to redeem them. Henry Clay, who had opposed the creation of the First Bank, now favored the Second Bank, because the state banks were in such wretched condition. John Randolph opposed the bank, specifically because it would become an "engine of irresistible power in the hands of any administration." According to his argument, "it was as much swindling to issue notes with the intent not to pay as it was burglary to break into a house"; but, he continued, "a man might as well go to Constantinople to preach Christianity as to get up here and preach against banks." [1] Largely because of the efforts of Calhoun, who was at that time a loose constructionist and an ardent nationalist, the bill finally passed the House and Senate by a close vote, and on April 10, 1816, it was approved by President Madison. The Second Bank provided the mechanism by which several millions of dollars of loanable funds were drawn from other sections of the Nation and invested in the agricultural development of the South. In 1836, the bank was liquidated, and the Government deposits which had been kept in it were distributed among the state banks, including banks in Baltimore, Richmond, Raleigh, Charleston, Savannah, Augusta, Mobile, New Orleans, Louisville, Nashville, St. Louis, and Natchez.

Meanwhile several state banks had been established in

---

[1] Reprinted in D. R. Dewey, *Financial History of the United States,* p. 149.

the South, and, after the Second Bank ceased to function, a phenomenal expansion of banking occurred in all parts of the United States. In the South, as in the West, banking practices too frequently became wild and reckless, and ended in inevitable disaster. Of the banks established in the ante-bellum South, there were two outstanding types: *state banks,* and *property banks.*

## STATE BANKS

By 1860, practically every Southern State had entered into banking. As Professor J. Laurence Laughlin says: [2] "The states entered more or less into banking, largely under the belief that banks would afford such great profits as to lighten the expenses of the state, or to provide a fiscal agent, or by sale of bonds to contribute to the capital of banks, thereby sharing in their management. . . . Also, the states furnished the entire capital of what might be directly called state banks and controlled their management."

**Maryland.** In 1790, the legislature of this state chartered the Bank of Maryland. This bank was established at Baltimore and proved to be of great assistance to commerce and trade.

**Virginia.** To assist the city of Alexandria in her competition with Baltimore, the Virginia Legislature, in 1792, granted a charter to the Bank of Alexandria, which was the first bank chartered in the state. With a capital of only $150,000, this little bank evidently was successful, for within two years after its establishment, its stock sold for 100 per cent above par. In 1801, when the Federal Government accepted from Virginia the grant of territory, ten miles square, for the National Capital, the Bank of Alexandria passed from Virginia jurisdiction, and did not

---

[2] J. Laurence Laughlin, *New Exposition of Money, Credit and Prices* (1931), Vol. II, pp. 284–285. Reprinted by permission of the University of Chicago Press, Chicago.

return to state control until 1847, when Alexandria itself was retroceded to Virginia.

The Virginia banking system was reëstablished in 1804, when the legislature chartered the Bank of Virginia. "In accordance with the provisions of the charter," says Dr. George T. Starnes, "the Bank of Virginia was to be located at Richmond with branches at Norfolk, Fredericksburg, and Petersburg." [3] The capital stock of $1,500,000, of which the state reserved the right to subscribe $300,000, was apportioned among the districts of the state. The bank was permitted to hold real estate and other effects to the value of $3,500,000, including its capital stock, and could not charge over 6 per cent interest.

In 1812, a second mother bank, with a capital of $2,-000,000, was chartered. This, the Farmers' Bank of Virginia, was empowered to establish branches at Norfolk, Lynchburg, Winchester, Petersburg, and Fredericksburg. Of the shares in this bank, 3,334 were to be given to the state and were to be paid for out of the dividends of the bank itself. Five years later, the legislature provided for the incorporation of two new mother banks, with branches. The capital stock of each was to be no less than $400,000 nor more than $600,000. In addition to the capital stock, there was to be issued, in the name of the state, shares of stock up to 15 per cent of the stock actually subscribed. One of these banks—located at Wheeling and termed the "Northwestern Bank of Virginia"—at the first meeting of its stockholders was authorized to establish branches at Wellsburg, Morgantown, and Clarksburg, each with a capital of not less than $100,000. The other bank—located at Winchester, and termed the "Bank of the Valley of Virginia"—was likewise authorized to establish branches: one in London, or Fauquier, and another in Jefferson, Berkeley, Hampshire, or Hardy County, as the stockholders might determine. The minimum capital for each of these branches was $100,000. In 1834, the Merchants and

---

[3] George T. Starnes, *Sixty Years of Branch Banking in Virginia*, p. 29.

Mechanics' Bank at Wheeling was established; and in 1837, an act was passed by the legislature for the purpose of establishing at Norfolk the Exchange Bank of Virginia, with branches to be located at Richmond, Petersburg, and Clarksville. In all, Virginia, prior to 1860, established six mother banks, with a total of forty-six branches.

Although this system resembled the Scotch system in that heavy capitalization was a feature, yet few restrictions were placed upon the institutions. Like other banks throughout the country, they could issue notes in excess of capital and there was no requirement as to reserves. Consequently they kept only that amount of specie which they found by experience was necessary to redeem their notes. Directors were liable for loans in excess of issue. The state subscribed for stock, and therefore elected its share of the directors. Despite the severe panic of 1837, which caused some embarrassment to the banks, there were very few losses; and on the whole, as Dr. Starnes concludes, "there is abundant reason for believing that the Virginia banking system was one of the most successful of the period under consideration." [4]

**Kentucky.** In 1802, this state made a bad beginning in her banking experience by permitting the Kentucky Insurance Company to circulate promissory notes received by assignment in the course of business, and later by granting it the privilege of issuing notes. This company was empowered with banking privileges as follows: "And every bond, bill obligatory, or note in writing given by the said president and directors in behalf of the said Insurance Company shall be assignable by endorsement thereon, in like manner and with the like effect as foreign bills of exchange now are; and such of the notes as are payable to bearer shall be negotiable and assignable by delivery only." The company was given, also, the privilege to deal in exchange and to loan its money at 6 per cent interest,

---

[4] *Ibid.*, p. 127.

and unlimited power to issue any amount of circulating medium upon which it might determine. However, in 1804, the legislature restricted the note issue to the aggregate of the debts due the company, including both good and bad debts, money on hand, and personal and real property, together with the amount of capital stock. Within the limits of this provision it was possible to issue $300,000, or over, in notes without any provision to redeem them.

Obviously the results of this vicious system of banking could have been nothing less than inflation, speculation, and apparent prosperity. In 1806, the state entered into the banking business by subscribing to the capital stock of the Bank of Kentucky. Strange to say, this bank had a nominal capital of $1,000,000 and shares of $100 each were to be issued, but it was authorized to begin business when only $20,000 was paid in. The legislature had the power to elect the president and a majority of the directors. The bank's funds were handled recklessly, and loans were made freely to all political friends. In 1814, the bank had to suspend operation, but opened again in 1815 with an increased capitalization of $3,000,000. In the meantime there was a rising tide of resentment against the unscrupulous use of the monopolistic privileges of this bank, and as a reactionary step, in 1818, forty-six independent banks were established by the state with a capital of nearly $9,000,000. Bank failures in great numbers resulted, and these banks, which had been permitted to issue notes, were now permitted to redeem them in the notes of the Bank of Kentucky.

In 1820, the legislature chartered another bank, called the "Bank of the Commonwealth of Kentucky," and authorized it to issue notes to the amount of $3,000,000, based on "public credit." These notes were to be apportioned to different sections of the state, and were to be used in loans, not exceeding $2,000, to needy debtors for the payment of "just debts." The notes, though issued without assets or cash reserves, were legal tender for public debt and were issued in denominations as low as 12½ cents. As a result of all these issues of local paper money, prices rose and debtors temporarily benefited. But by 1822, the notes of the Bank of the Commonwealth depreciated over 50 per cent and the question of their constitutionality had been raised. In 1830, this bank was ordered to close its unprofitable branches, and seven years later, it was ordered to redeem its notes in specie. In the meantime the bank had obtained large amounts of land, and politicians had continually used the bank to enrich themselves.

**North Carolina.** Following the example of Virginia's banking system, North Carolina chartered two mother banks in 1804 and a third in 1810. The first two banks, the Bank of New Berne and the Bank of Cape Fear, were authorized to have a capital of $800,000 to be paid in gold or silver. The third bank, the State Bank of North Carolina, was incorporated with a capital of $1,600,000. These banks were poorly managed from the very beginning. The capital was paid in stock notes given by subscribers, instead of in money. By 1818, notes had been issued at the rate of twelve dollars to one dollar of specie reserves. The banks encouraged the depreciation of their note issues, in order to show a large profit by buying the notes up at a discount. So disastrous were the banks to the whole fiscal system of the state that the legislature, in 1828, determined to liquidate them as quickly as possible. Then, in 1835, the legislature changed its policy, and the state sold bonds to reorganize the Bank of the State of North Carolina.

**South Carolina.** Between 1792 and 1812, five banks were established in Charleston. These banks, which were private corporations, were successfully managed, and not a dollar of their deposits was lost until the Civil War. In 1812, the South Carolina Legislature chartered the Bank of the State of South Carolina. The capital of this bank was not distributed among private stockholders, but was held exclusively by the state. The bank was authorized to transact a regular banking business: to receive deposits, to discount eligible notes, to make loans, and to issue notes. The charter also provided that, "the total amount of debts which the bank shall at any time owe, including the monies actually deposited in the bank for safe keeping, shall not exceed in the aggregate the sum of two million four hundred thousand dollars." Loans were made on real estate, but the amount loaned was limited to $2,000 to a person. As a whole the bank was successful. In 1843, the average profit of the bank was 7 per cent, and in 1848, it was reported that the bank had received and paid out for the state $28,000,000, without loss, and that it had never suspended specie payments.

**Mississippi.** In 1809, the Territorial Commissioners of Mississippi chartered the Bank of Mississippi at Natchez. Its capital stock was $100,000; besides its regular banking functions, it was permitted to issue notes up to three times its capital. In 1817, when Mississippi was admitted into the Union, the state constitution provided that at least one fourth of the capital of any bank must be reserved for state subscription. This action definitely put the state into the banking business. The next year, the bank at Natchez was made a state bank. Its capital was increased to $3,000,000, of which the state was to subscribe $750,000. This bank was similar to most of the other state banks already described in that it was authorized to do commercial banking and to issue notes. In 1830, the bank was placed in liquidation and the Planters' Bank was established in its place. By the sale of bonds, the state subscribed one half of the $4,000,000 capital of this new bank, which was permitted to issue notes recklessly, keeping only about a 5 per cent reserve in specie. Consequently, when the panic came, the bank failed, and the liability for outstanding bonds fell upon the state.

**Alabama.** The first bank in this state was the Planters and Mechanics' (afterwards Merchants') Bank, established at Huntsville in 1816. As authorized by the Alabama Territorial Legislature, the charter of this bank provided that the capital stock should not exceed $500,000, divided into 5,000 shares of $100 each. The bank was permitted to issue notes, but the amount was limited to three times the capital stock actually paid in and the directors were made liable for any excess issue. In 1818, similar acts were passed for the establishment of two banks, at St. Stephens and at Mobile. By 1823, the notes issued by the bank at Huntsville had become practically irredeemable, and in that year, two of the three banks closed.

When Alabama was admitted into the Union in 1819, attention was immediately directed toward the establishment of a state bank, but to insure the state against any group monopoly of the banking privilege, there were written into the constitution specific provisions for establishing and operating a state bank. In accordance with the constitution, the General Assembly at its first session enacted a law "to incorporate the subscribers to the Bank of the State of Alabama." The authorized capital was limited to $2,000,000, two fifths of which was reserved for the state. The necessary capital could not be raised, and the bank never commenced business.

Notwithstanding the failure of the first effort to establish a state bank, the legislature in 1823 enacted another law to establish the Bank of the State of Alabama. This new act, instead of requiring a subscription of actual money for its stock, as in the case of the first proposal, provided that the capital should be furnished by the general credit—that is to say, by the state, and without specific limit. The state was to derive the capital from the sale of public lands and from bond issues limited to $100,000. According to a report in *Niles' Weekly Register*,[5] it appears that the stock of this new bank was sold at par in New York, and that $100,000 in specie was shipped to Mobile. This step was merely the beginning of the acquisition of capital.

[5] *Niles' Weekly Register,* 1825.

The original plan of selling bonds was continued until $14,000,000 was issued, and the total available capital for this bank amounted to $15,859,420. Branches were established at Decatur, Huntsville, Mobile, and Montgomery.

For the first three years, the bank maintained its solvency, but by 1837, of the bills discounted $6,300,000 were found to be bad debts. Consequently, in that year, $7,500,000 of additional state bonds had to be issued to cover the deficit. This situation arose on account of political favoritism. The president and the directors of the bank had complete and unsupervised control over its management; they were responsible only to the General Assembly, who elected them annually. Hence, in order to insure reëlection, each member of the legislature received whatever loans he desired for himself and also for his constituents. The positions of president and directors of the bank virtually were sold to the highest bidder—that is to say, to those men who would promise the members of the legislature the largest amount of loans.

The candidates for the directorships were always very liberal in their treatment of the legislators. On one occasion during the campaign for election, a member of the house of representatives died. Each member of the house, as was the custom, wore crepe on his left arm for thirty days. This emblem of mourning was an indication that the wearer was eligible for bank honors, such as loans. Consequently, when a backwoodsman in Tuscaloosa put crepe on his arm, he was, for several days before his identity was suspected, feasted royally by the elite of the city.

In Tuscaloosa a hotel keeper believed that if he were a director of the state bank, he could make his hotel the most popular in town. He eventually secured his election. Immediately thereafter his hotel became crowded. The other hotel keepers suffered temporarily, but in time discovered the secret of their competitor's success. Soon all five of the hotel keepers in Tuscaloosa were advertising the fact that they were members of the board of directors of the State Bank of Alabama—a group that became known as the "Culinary Sanhedrin." Moreover, like the fabled "Knights of the Round Table," they met frequently around the board of directors' table, clincked their glasses, and drank to the success of the State Bank of Alabama.

By 1841, the rumors of bank fraud became alarming and the legislature ordered an investigation. The joint committee reported: "They found and discovered the existence of a disgraceful league to plunder the banks and to swindle the people of the state." [6] The governor subsequently ordered the state bank, with its branches, to be placed in gradual liquidation. Upon the liquidation of these banks, there was left on the state a burden of indebtedness of $14,000,000, on which interest to the amount of $16,000,000 had been paid before the liquidation of the banks. In addition to these amounts, there had been absorbed property of the schools and the state university to the amount of $1,600,000. These amounts and other miscellaneous losses brought the total loss of the state to approximately $35,000,000.

**Louisiana.** In this state, three banks were established during the first eleven years of the nineteenth century. In 1824, the legislature chartered the Bank of the State of Louisiana, with a capital of $4,000,000, one half of which the state was to subscribe by the sale of bonds. The other half of the capital was to be loaned on real estate mortgages. It is interesting to note that the state provided her funds by the issue of bonds at the rate of $100 in bonds for $83⅓ of stock, and the bank itself acted as the agent in selling the bonds. By 1827, besides property banks—to be discussed later—there were eleven banks in New Orleans, with a total paid-in capital of approximately $40,000,000, about one half of which had been borrowed in Europe and about $7,000,000 of which had been loaned from investors in other states than Louisiana. A large

---

[6] *House Journal of Alabama* (1842–1843).

number of these banks were eliminated by the panic of 1837.

**Georgia.** Several banks, including the state bank, were chartered in Georgia before 1819. The state took stock in nearly all of these banks. Most of them failed during the crisis of 1818–1819.

In 1828, the state organized the Central Bank of Georgia to supersede the earlier state bank. Its capital was based on the state's holdings in other banks, as well as various cash claims of the state. The purposes of the bank were to act as fiscal agent of the state, and to furnish small loans up to $2,500. The bank was authorized to issue notes to the amount it possessed of the notes of other chartered banks in the state, plus its United States bank notes and specie. This bank was poorly managed, because it was used to further political ends. At one time the legislature ordered it to lend $750,000 to needy citizens. The bank failed in 1841.

**Tennessee.** As in Georgia, several banks in Tennessee were chartered before 1819. The Nashville Bank was chartered in 1807 and was the first institution of its kind to be established in the state. In 1811, the Bank of the State of Tennessee was formed in Knoxville. The business transacted by these banks was small, and under a policy of inflation they were ruined by the crisis of 1818–1819. The legislature then established the Bank of Tennessee, the capital being supplied from state funds, state land, and the sale of bonds. Branches were established in the three geographical divisions of the state, and loans were apportioned among the counties according to the taxes paid in each. Creditors refusing to accept notes issued by this bank were required to wait two years for their money, according to a measure known as the "Stay Law." However, in 1821, the Tennessee State Supreme Court declared this law unconstitutional. In 1822, the cashier defaulted in the sum of $140,000, and in 1830, the institution, popularly dubbed the "Saddle-Bags Bank," failed. The next year, a new bank was projected by the legislature, but no action was taken until 1832, when the organization was chartered as the "Union Bank." The state was authorized to take $500,000 of the capital stock and to issue bonds in payment. Branches were established, and business was carried on according to the usual methods of the times, until the panic of 1837 proved disastrous and the legislature then reëstablished the Bank of Tennessee.

**Arkansas.** The first constitution of Arkansas, adopted in 1836, provided that a state bank might be established for the purposes of being "a repository of the funds to or under the control of the state," and lending such funds "in every county in proportion to the population." As chartered by the legislature in the fall of 1836, the State Bank of Arkansas was patterned somewhat closely after the state banks of Alabama, Georgia, and South Carolina. The capital was $1,000,000, to be obtained by selling state bonds, and as soon as $50,000 was paid in specie, the bank could open for business. The bank was ordered to open a branch for each additional $50,000 of its capital actually received in coin. It was permitted to issue up to three times its capital notes in denominations of $5 and over; it could make loans to individuals up to $10,000; and it could charge from 6 to 8 per cent interest according to the duration of the loan. In 1837, when the bank began to operate, the paid-in capital was $400,000, and of this amount one fourth had been raised from the sale of bonds, a small amount from land and miscellaneous sources, and the remainder from the surplus Federal revenue distributed to the states. Part of the amount received from the Federal Government, however, was never collected, because it was paid in notes upon other state banks which failed. As in the neighboring states, this state bank was poorly managed, the directors of a branch having borrowed in one instance over 80 per cent of its capital. The bank failed within six years after its organization and threw upon the state the entire burden of outstanding bonds.

**Missouri.** The Bank of St. Louis was chartered in 1813 and failed six years later; the Bank of Missouri was chartered in 1817 and failed five years later. Upon its admission into the Union in 1821, Missouri adopted a constitution which explicitly provided that the General Assembly could create only one bank. The legislature did not create even this bank—termed the "State Bank of Missouri"—until fourteen years later. This delay, no doubt, as Dr. Leonard C. Helderman says, was due to "the facts that much Mexican silver came from Sante Fe; that a branch of the United States Bank existed at St. Louis; and that Thomas Hart Benton, formerly a director but now no friend of banks, was a dominant figure in Missouri politics." [7]

The Bank of the State of Missouri had an authorized capital of $5,000,000, one half of which was reserved to the state, and it had five branches. Its note issue was limited to equal its capital during the first five years of the bank's existence, with the privilege of doubling the amount of issue thereafter. As a whole the bank was conservatively managed; it proved stable and enjoyed the general public confidence. Yet in 1857, a reaction arose against this bank, and the Missouri Legislature became prodigal in chartering new banks, though a law was enacted regulating the general operation of all banks and requiring them to keep $33\frac{1}{3}$ per cent reserve against note circulation.

**Texas.** In this state, before it had become a part of the United States, numerous corporations had been chartered with banking privileges. But upon entering the Union in 1845, Texas adopted a constitution which specifically provided that "no corporate body shall hereafter be created, renewed or extended, with banking or discounting privileges." Notes were circulated by private firms, however, and apparently were permitted by the state.

---

[7] Leonard C. Helderman, *National and State Banks,* p. 63.

## Property Banks

*Property banks* were peculiar to the South. They were state institutions established for the purpose of attracting foreign capital into agriculture and internal developments, by the issue and sale of bonds secured by real estate. They had the privilege of issuing notes and performing the ordinary functions of commercial banks.

Louisiana took the lead in establishing these banks. In 1827, the legislature incorporated the Consolidated Association of the Planters of Louisiana. This bank was to have a capital of $2,000,000, to be obtained from the sale of 5 per cent bonds secured by real estate mortgages. The company alone could not sell these bonds. Hence, the legislature authorized the state to issue $2,000,000 in bonds to the company in exchange for $2,500,000 in mortgages, which the company might obtain from individual borrowers. The state bonds were to be sold wherever possible. For this loan of the state's credit to the company, the state was to receive a bonus of $1,000,000 of the company's stock whenever the bonds were all paid.

During the next decade, the bank got into difficulties. It undertook to redeem nearly $500,000 of the bonds issued, but by doing so, impaired its capital. Furthermore, since it had issued notes without adequate specie reserves and could not redeem them, its failure in 1842 was inevitable. In 1832, another property bank was established; it was called the "Union Bank." This bank was to have a capital of $7,000,000. Subscribers to the stock were the borrowers, who pledged their subscriptions by mortgages and, in turn, assigned these mortgages—as in the case of the Planters' Bank—to the state as security for state bonds. There were to be eight branches. The bank was authorized to make loans upon real estate, especially on property in New Orleans. It also could issue notes up to three times its capital. The bank soon tied up its capital in frozen assets, issued too many notes, and went into liquidation along with the Planters' Bank.

In 1833, the legislature chartered a third property bank, called the "Citizens' Bank of Louisiana." This bank was to have a capital of $12,000,000, and powers and privileges similar to the Union Bank. According to the *Report of the Joint Committee on Finance of the Senate and House of Representatives in Louisiana,* in 1837, property banks in the state up to that time had borrowed foreign capital to the amount of $25,400,000 and had taken mortgages of $40,000,000 on local property. Added to this were the liabilities incurred by note issues. As a result, when the panic came in 1837, these banks were too weak to bear the strain, and drastic action was imperative.

In 1842, the whole banking policy of the state was changed by what was perhaps the most constructive piece of banking legislation in the entire South before the Civil War. Horace White summarized it as follows:[8]  "The principal features of this law were the requirements (1) of a specie reserve equal to one-third of all its liabilities to the public; (2) the other two-thirds of its liabilities to be represented by commercial paper having not more than ninety days to run; (3) all commercial paper to be paid at maturity; and if not paid, or if an extension is asked for, the account of the party to be closed and his name to be sent to the other banks as a delinquent; (4) all banks to be examined by a board of state officers quarterly or oftener; (5) bank directors to be individually *liable* for all loans or investments made in violation of the law, unless they could show that they had voted against the same if present; (6) no bank to have less than fifty shareholders having at least thirty shares each; (7) any director going out of the state for more than thirty days, or absenting himself from five successive meetings of the board, to be deemed to have resigned, and the vacancy to be filled at

---

[8] Horace White, *Sound Currency,* Vol. II, pp. 209–210.

once; (8) no bank to pay out any notes but its own; (9) all banks to pay their balance to each other [in] specie every Saturday, under penalty of being immediately put in liquidation; (10) no bank to purchase its own shares or lend on its own shares more than thirty per cent of the market value thereof."

Florida in 1833, while yet a territory, chartered the Union Bank, which somewhat resembled the Union Bank of Louisiana. Its capital of $3,000,000 was to be raised by bonds issued to the bank by the territory for mortgages on real estate and slaves of borrowers or stockholders. Most of these bonds were sold in Europe. This sale was accomplished by paying the interest on one series from the proceeds from the next series. A clique of eighty planters acquired all the stock of the bank, inflated the currency by an overissue of notes, and, with the bank's funds, recklessly speculated in land. The bank failed in 1842, and when Florida became a state, the bonds were repudiated by the legislature.

The Real Estate Bank of Arkansas was chartered in 1836; it was modeled upon the Union Bank of Louisiana. Its capital was to be $2,000,000, to be obtained from the sale of state bonds based on $2,250,000 in mortgages subscribed by stockholders or borrowers. Demand for shares became so great that over $4,000,000 in mortgages was subscribed. Over 2,000 bonds were issued, of which about 500 were put up as collateral with a New York bank for a loan that actually amounted to only about $120,000. By 1838, branches of the bank were established at Columbus, Helena, Van Buren, and Washington. Loans were made recklessly; notes were issued almost at will; specie payment soon had to be suspended; and interest defaulted on the bonds. Within six years from its opening, the bank had to be put in liquidation.

In 1837, Mississippi chartered the Union Bank, which one writer has correctly termed the "Mississippi Bubble." [9]

---

[9] Leonard C. Helderman, *National and State Banks*, p. 69.

With an authorized capital of $15,500,000, this bank was planned to become the most gigantic property bank in the South. Its capital was to be obtained in the same manner as the capital for the Union Bank of Louisiana: state bonds based upon mortgages of stockholders or borrowers were to be issued and these bonds were to be sold to Eastern and European investors. Two thirds of all loans made by the bank were to be on mortgages and payable on an eight-year amortization plan. The debt of the bank was not to exceed twice the capital paid in, and notes were not to be issued for less than $10 each. In 1838, the charter was amended and the state, by taking $5,000,000 of the stock, became an active partner in the bank. The mother bank was located at Jackson, and branches were established in specially designated districts. The bank, however, soon became involved in legal disputes with its bondholders, and in general was poorly managed. In 1841, it had a suspended debt in suit of $2,600,000, a debt in suit of $1,700,-000, immediate liabilities of $3,000,000, and frozen assets of about $8,000,000. Accordingly the bank was put in liquidation, and eventually the bonds were repudiated by the state.

Several other Southern States established property banks. In Texas, the Commercial and Agricultural Bank of Galveston had been chartered by Mexico; and, when Texas entered the Union, the state attempted to abolish it, in accordance with the general provision of the state constitution prohibiting all banking. The Texas State Supreme Court upheld the validity of the bank's charter. Consequently this bank enjoyed a virtual monopoly both in commercial banking and in real estate financing. In Maryland, one property bank was attempted in Baltimore and another, in Frederick. The former was to have a capital of $5,000,000, and the latter, of $2,000,000; but neither of these banks was finally organized. Alabama also attempted various schemes for financing land, but like her state bank, these proved futile.

It may be noted that nearly all of the state and property banks in the ante-bellum South, with the exception of the state banks in Virginia and South Carolina, failed about 1841. This trend was due mainly to a prolonged depression, from 1837 to 1843, in the United States and in England.[10] In 1838–1839, there was a widely heralded bull market in cotton, led by Nicholas Biddle and his bank in Philadelphia. This caused many Southern banks, particularly in the Cotton Belt, to lend extensively on cotton at approximately 14 cents per pound. Planters, believing that cotton would continue to rise, decided to keep their crop off the market and borrowed all they could. By the spring of 1840, the price of middling cotton had declined to about 7 cents per pound. The next year, the price declined still further. Finally, when the time of settlement came, the planters could not redeem their notes. Mortgages which fell due on land could not be collected without severe losses, because the land hypothecated as security had greatly depreciated, since land was now capitalized on the low yield from cotton prices. Bank failures were inevitable, especially in cases where the banks had borrowed their capital and could no longer meet their interest requirements.

The situation was well described by W. H. Willis, of North Carolina, in a diary written in 1840:[11] "Speculation, speculation, has been making poor men rich and rich men princes; men of no capital, in three years have become wealthy, and those of some have grown to hundreds of thousands—But as great as are the resources of Miss.; and as valuable as are her lands, yet there were limits to both and these limits have been passed, lost sight of and forgotten as things having no existence. A revulsion has taken place, Miss. is ruined, her rich men are poor and her poor men beggars.

"Millions on millions have been speculated on and gam-

---

[10] See Wesley C. Mitchell, *Business Cycles, The Problem and Its Setting*, p. 426.

[11] SOUTHERN HISTORY ASSOCIATION PUBLICATIONS, Vol. 8, p. 35.

bled away by banking, by luxury, and too much prosperity, until of all the states in the Union she has become much the worst. We have seen hard times in North Carolina; hard times in the east, hard times everywhere, but Miss. exceeds them all. Some of the finest lands in Madison and Hinds Counties may now be had for comparatively nothing. Those that once commanded from thirty to fifty dollars per acre may now be bought for three or five dollars and that with considerable improvements, while many have been sold at sherrs. [sheriffs'] sales at fifty cents that were considered worth ten to twenty doll. . . . So great is the panic and so dreadful the distress that there are a great many farms prepared to receive crops and some of them actually planted, and yet deserted, not a human being to be found upon them."

When prosperity returned, the states began to tighten their regulations on banking and to adopt better banking systems. This practice was especially true of Louisiana, Tennessee, and Virginia, where, after 1850, there was established a free banking system, copied after that of New York.

## Fiscal Systems

During the ante-bellum period, without going beyond the limitations on state and local tax powers set by the Federal Constitution,[12] each Southern State developed a fiscal

---

[12] As summarized by William J. Shultz, these limitations are: "(1) The states may not levy import or export duties; (2) the states may not levy tonnage taxes without the consent of Congress; (3) federal treaties are part of the supreme law of the land; (4) the states may not pass laws impairing the obligation of contracts; (5) the citizens of each state are entitled to all privileges and immunities of citizens in the several states; (6) no state shall deprive any person of life, liberty or property without due process of law; (7) no state shall deny to any person within its jurisdiction the equal protection of the laws; (8) the states may not tax property or instrumentalities of the federal government; and (9) the states may not tax interstate commerce."—*American Public Finance and Taxation*, p. 261. Published by Prentice-Hall, Inc., New York.

system in its own way. As a result, each system differed from the others in numerous details. An analysis of the whole group shows that each system developed along the same general directions, however, and embodied the same general principles.

At first, each state resorted to a specific tax system—that is to say, levies were laid per unit of taxable objects and not according to their values. When the classes of property became more numerous, the specific tax system became unwieldy to administer and quite impracticable. To remedy the situation, the states swept together the varying rates and levies into a general property tax. Furthermore, by 1860, nearly every Southern State had incurred a heavy bonded debt for establishing banks and for making internal improvements. As time went on, there was a tendency in each state toward broadening the scope of its tax system by the inclusion of new tax forms.

The fiscal machinery was always organized in the form of a pyramid. Standing at the bottom were the local tax officials—assessors, tax collectors, or, in a few instances, sheriffs, who functioned as tax officials. At the apex were the state agents—state treasurer and auditor, or officers having similar functions.

## STATE TAXATION SYSTEMS

**Virginia.** Since the right to lay impost duties was surrendered by the states upon their adoption of the Federal Constitution, freer use was necessarily made of other forms of taxes, especially land and specific property taxes. Until 1850, land outside of towns was taxed at a given rate on each one hundred dollars of its assessed value, and town lots, including houses, were taxed entirely upon their rental value. Personal property was assessed by the *listing method* and taxed by a system of specific levies. For example, some specific property taxes for 1849 appeared as follows: [13]

---

[13] Auditor's *Report* (Virginia, 1849), p. 24.

## SPECIFIC PROPERTY TAXES, 1849

| | |
|---|---:|
| 253,609 Slaves at 32 cents | $ 81,154 |
| 311,884 horses, mules, asses, colts at 10 cents | 31,188 |
| 10,705 Gold watches at one dollar | 10,705 |
| 5,002 patent lever & Lepine silver watches at 50 cents | 2,501 |
| 13,175 Silver & Metallic Watches (other than above) at twenty-five cents | 3,293 |
| 33,168 brass and other metallic clocks at twenty-five cents each | 8,292 |
| 36,290 other clocks at 12½ cents | 4,536 |
| 15,456 riding or pleasure carriages 1½% in value | 23,766 |
| 77 stage coaches 1½% in value | 285 |
| 2,034 jersey wagons & carryalls 1½% in value | 1,472 |
| 3,288 gigs 1½% in value | 1,593 |
| 4,745 pianos 1½% in value | 8,616 |
| 21 harps 1½% value | 82 |
| gold and silver plate | 2,454 |
| TOTAL | $179,839 |

The poll tax was repealed in 1787 and not again levied until 1792, and then only at a very nominal rate on "all male persons above sixteen years of age," except a few specially exempted persons. Thereafter, it appears that the poll upon white males was practically discarded and that it became almost exclusively a discriminatory tax against free negroes either to drive them from the state or to coerce them again into slavery because of failure to pay the tax. According to Dr. T. R. Snavely: [14] "The number of free Negroes had increased constantly since 1782, and the problem assumed such proportions by 1800 that a movement for colonization was started," and "new and un-usually stringent measures for keeping watch over and controlling the actions of free Negroes were enacted." In 1815, the poll tax on free negroes was raised to $2.50, while in 1853, the poll tax on white males was 40 cents.

By the middle of the nineteenth century, the principle of ability had been recognized and applied in a limited way to the Virginia tax system. Thus, several licenses were levied at a progressive rate in proportion to the capitaliza-tion of the business or, in some instances, in proportion to

---

[14] Tipton Ray Snavely, *Taxation of Negroes in Virginia,* p. 12.

the population of the town or city in which the taxable business operated.

An income tax law was enacted in 1843, and it was the first income tax law enacted by any Southern State. This law, however, merely supplemented and did not supersede the existing forms of taxation, for it was regarded as an experiment in the theory of ability to pay. Its introduction apparently was due to a desire to attain greater justice in the distribution of the increasing tax burdens, especially since the depression of 1837 and the westward migration had caused a noticeable readjustment in the taxable wealth of the state. The exemption allowed was $400 for money incomes, but no exemptions were allowed on interest, profits, or rents. The rates and bases of the tax were as follows:

VIRGINIA INCOME TAX, 1843

| Rate | Base |
|------|------|
| 1%   | Money Income |
| 2½%  | Interest |
| 1½%  | Profits and Rent |

Subsequently a few minor changes were made in the law. The highest yield of this tax in any one year was only $20,160, or 2.9 per cent of the total tax for the state.

In 1842, dividends on bank stocks were made taxable, and in 1844, a collateral inheritance tax was first adopted by the General Assembly. The latter required that estates valued at $250 or more, passing to persons other than the decedent's father, mother, husband, wife, brothers, sisters, or lineal descendants, should be subjected to a tax at the rate of 2 per cent. But, as Professor Charles J. Bullock has observed of early inheritance taxes, the law was merely a "fiscal curiosity," [15] and a feeble effort to extend the taxing power of the state.

The period from 1789 to 1850 was characterized both by the widening of the tax scheme and by the recognition of a more rational principle of taxation—namely the prin-

---

[15] Quoted in H. L. Lutz, *Public Finance*, p. 471.

ciple of "ability to pay," which, in addition to its manifesta-
tion in the license taxes and the income tax, was
responsible for the decline in the significance of the poll tax.

ENTRY IN ALBERMARLE COUNTY LAND BOOK, SHOWING
TAXES PAID BY THOMAS JEFFERSON IN 1820[16]

| Dr. | THOMAS JEFFERSON | | | Cr. |
|---|---|---|---|---|
| June | Rev. on 4,899 | | Oct. | By Draft |
| | Acres of Land........$100.64 | | 13th | on |
| | Rev. on 57 | | | Bernard |
| | slaves, 13 | | | Peyton.....$197.21 |
| | horses & 1 | | | |
| | coache at | | | |
| | $350................ | 47.74 | | |
| | C. & P. L. | | | |
| | on 1 white | | | |
| | & 53 Blacks.......... | 33.73 | | |
| | Ticket............... | 10.60 | | |
| | | $192.71 | | |
| | Ticket............... | 2.00 | | |
| | Ticket............... | 2.50 | | |
| | | $197.21 | | |

The "rule of uniformity" was written into the new constitution of 1851. This rule, sweeping together the taxes
on realty, on "land" and "lots," and over one hundred
specific property taxes, established the general property tax.
In 1852, the rate was fixed at 18 cents on every hundred
dollars of the assessed valuation of property; in 1853, at 20
cents; and finally, in 1856, at 40 cents.

Another provision of the new constitution was: "Every
slave who has attained the age of twelve years shall be
assessed with a tax equal to and not exceeding that assessed
on land of the value of three hundred dollars. Slaves under
that age shall not be subject to taxation." In 1856, the
rate of this tax was $1.20 upon each taxable slave.

Of all the taxes levied, however, the general property
tax became the most important. In 1853, it yielded 90.4

---

[16] Original in University of Virginia Library.

per cent of the total state tax, and for fifty years, it remained supreme as a fiscal expedient in Virginia.

During the ante-bellum period certain changes were effected in the state offices of both the treasurer and the auditor.  In 1792, an act was passed which reduced the number of auditors from three to one, and required that the appointee should thereafter receive his position only by the joint vote of the legislature.  The same act placed both the treasurer and the auditor under the direct supervision of the governor.  The most noteworthy change was an act, passed in 1814, which made it the duty of the treasurer to recommend new taxes.  As in earlier periods, the local tax officials, assessors, and collectors were appointed by the county courts.

In 1842, Virginia had a state debt of $6,994,307, of which $458,107 had been incurred for internal improvements.  In 1860, the bonded debt had reached $33,000,000.  To offset this amount, there were assets of a face value of $43,000,000, consisting principally of stocks and bonds in canal and railway companies.  On the whole the fiscal status and future prospects of Virginia in 1860 appeared to be satisfactory.

**Alabama.**  The first constitution of Alabama, adopted July 5, 1819, provided that: "All lands liable to taxation in this state shall be taxed in proportion to their value." This was the basis for the ad valorem tax on land, but personalty during the period was taxable according to a schedule of specific rates.

Although, at first, the rates both of ad valorem and specific taxes were nominal, the revenue collected met the meager needs of a simple economy.  It was not long, however, until the state took up the idea of establishing a state bank with branches.  Pursuant to a series of acts dating from 1823 to 1826, the state not only invested $8,000,000 in bank stock, but even put a portion of this stock into the state school and university funds as compensation for Federal land grants for educational purposes.  For a time the banks prospered to such an extent that a great part of the expenses of the state were paid by the earnings of such stock; and in 1836, the legislature went so far as to abolish most of the direct taxes.

Then, caught in the crisis of 1837, the banks had to suspend specie payment and finally had to be liquidated in 1842, and the state was left heavily in debt. To meet interest requirements and to maintain credit, not only were the rates of the tax levies raised, but, within the decade following the bank disaster, the state endeavored also to tap entirely new sources of revenue.

In 1843, the legislature enacted an income tax law, of one half of one per cent on the incomes of certain professional and salaried men. In 1848, the rate was raised to one per cent and the scope extended. Finally, by 1862, the income tax included a 5 per cent tax on "net profits" of several forms of business, and a 10 per cent tax on wages and salaries of men exempt from military service. In 1848, the state enacted an inheritance tax law imposing a tax of 2 per cent on every bequest of personal property and devise of real estate made in favor of any person or corporation other than the testator's wife, children, grandchildren, brothers, or sisters. By the next session of the legislature, the list of exempt relatives was made to include the husband, parents, or adopted children, and subsequently, acts further restricted the law until it came to be a levy on legacies. The rate of this tax during the Civil War was raised to 10 per cent, but soon thereafter, was reduced to one-half per cent in cases where letters testamentary were taken out in Alabama. The tax was finally abolished in 1868, after being imposed in some form or other for twenty years.

As the state's requirements for revenue steadily increased on account of the bonded debt and the expanding governmental activities, the legislature was compelled to broaden the scope of the specific taxes and to increase the tax rates horizontally. For example, the act of 1843 imposed the following rates on slaves:

TAX RATES ON SLAVES, 1843

Slaves under 10 years........................$0.10
Slaves between 10 and 50 years................ .50
Free negroes and mulattoes between 20 and 60... 1.00
Female slaves exempt

By 1852, the following rates prevailed:

TAX RATES ON SLAVES, 1852

Slaves under 5 years........................$0.25
Slaves from  5 to 10 years.................... .45
Slaves from 10 to 15 years.................... .80
Slaves from 15 to 30 years.·.................. 1.10
Slaves from 30 to 40 years.................... .80
Slaves from 40 to 50 years.................... .50
Slaves from 50 to 60 years.................... .20
Each slave working as a mechanic............. 2.00
Male free negroes between 21 and 45........... 2.00
Female free negroes between 21 and 45......... 1.00

Likewise, the rate of taxation was increased upon neat cattle, horses, jewelry, and household articles too numerous to mention.

In addition to the various taxes already noted, there existed poll taxes, license taxes, and taxes on money lent at interest. Thus, by the time the war began, Alabama had already evolved a tax system comprised in the main of an ad valorem tax on land, specific taxes on personal property, license taxes, poll taxes, an inheritance tax, and an income tax.

When Alabama was admitted into the Union in 1819, the fiscal machinery, established under the territorial government and similar to that of Virginia, was continued without any great change.

Before the Civil War the bonded debt of the state was incurred mainly for the purpose of providing capital for the State Bank of Alabama. The total bond issues authorized from 1823 to 1837 amounted to $15,940,000, but of this amount only $10,959,566 in bonds were actually sold. In 1842, the total bonded debt of the state was

$15,400,000. However, after the state bank was placed in liquidation, its remaining assets were applied to the reduction of the bonded debt, and by 1860, the amount had been scaled down to only $3,445,000.

**Other Southern States.** The fiscal systems of the other Southern States differed from those of Virginia and Alabama mainly in details, such as, the rate of levy, the amount of debt, and the number of officials in charge of the fiscal machinery.

In Maryland, in addition to various license and excise taxes, an income tax and a general property tax were levied. The income tax was only of short duration. The general property tax was first enacted in 1777; thereafter it was levied at intervals in small amounts and for specific purposes. The power of assessing property and of levying taxes was placed in elected boards of county commissioners; otherwise, the fiscal machinery was organized practically as in Virginia. In 1842, Maryland had a bonded debt of $15,214,761, of which about 92 per cent had been incurred for internal improvements.

In North Carolina, during the first four decades of the nineteenth century, tax receipts were derived mainly from land, polls, and licenses. During the forties, the fiscal requirements of the state for internal improvements were much increased. As a result the tax system had to be widened in scope. In 1847, an inheritance tax of one per cent was authorized. The next year, the state began the taxation of jewelry, plate, and certain other kinds of personalty. In 1849, an income tax was levied on interest and profits. Thereafter the license taxes were extended, until, by the Civil War, they were levied upon twenty or more occupations. In 1860, the state had a bonded debt of about $12,000,000.

During the ante-bellum period, South Carolina derived her revenues from taxes on lands, negroes, securities, and licenses on businesses and professions. In 1842, the bonded debt of the state was $5,691,234, but by 1856, this amount had been reduced to $2,693,276.

In Georgia, land was divided into classes and each class taxed upon its valuation per acre. Free white males and slaves paid a poll tax of 37½ cents, and free negroes, 50 cents. In 1805, banks were taxed by the state; this was the first instance of a bank tax in the United States. The tax was levied upon the capital and note issues. · In 1850, a tax was also levied upon railroads. Besides these taxes, there appeared an increasing number of license taxes common to other Southern States. In 1842, the state had a bonded debt of $1,309,000, incurred for internal improvements; in 1860, the state debt amounted to $2,670,750.

In 1855, Florida adopted a general property tax, which was levied at slightly less than 2 mills on the dollar. Besides this tax, there appeared the usual poll tax and licenses. White males, however, were assessed a poll tax of only 50 cents, while free negroes paid $3. As a rule local taxes were assessed upon the same bases and collected in the same manner as the state taxes. By 1850, Florida had a bonded indebtedness of $4,000,000, practically all of which had been incurred for establishing banks.

During the ante-bellum period the tax system of Mississippi was several times widened in scope. While Mississippi was still a territory, land was taxed according to a system of classification, and annual income was used as the measure of its taxable value. Upon entering the Union, the state abolished this tax and established the method of assessment of land according to its "actual value," as sworn to by the owner or person in charge. The personal property tax, moreover, became as important as this new ad valorem tax on land. The personal property list was extended to include, not only slaves, carriages, and bank stock, but also gold and silver plate, pianos, clocks, money loaned at interest, brokers' capital, weapons, cattle, and horses. Later the personal property tax was supplemented by a license-privilege system of taxes. The main sources

of revenue in the state were taxes on real and personal
property, licenses, and the sale of public lands. The organization of the fiscal machinery was almost identical
with that in Virginia. In 1842, the state debt incurred for
banking was $7,000,000. Because of the corrupt political
management of the banks, the people turned against them,
with the result that the entire $7,000,000 was repudiated.
From 1830 to 1840, Mississippi's public debt was about
$12,000,000, but practically none of this was ever paid.

Like most of the other Southern States, Louisiana derived its revenue from an ad valorem tax on land, from
specific taxes upon slaves, livestock, and vehicles, and from
licenses upon certain businesses and professions. The
bonded debt of the state in 1839 was $19,139,000. Three
years later, it was $23,985,000, of which over $20,000,000
had been incurred on account of state banking.

In Texas, according to Dr. E. T. Miller, who has made
a comprehensive and scholarly study of the entire fiscal
history of that state: [17] "The general property tax, occupation, and poll taxes were concurrently levied down to 1861.
In no year, however, were the receipts from taxes adequate
to meet the ordinary expenditures. The *ad valorem* rate
of state taxation never exceeded one-fifth of one per cent,
and for the greater part of the period was less. The
enormous extent of nonresident land holding, and the im-
perfections in the laws resulted in the undervaluation of
land and in its escape from assessment. From 1852 to 1858,
nine-tenths of the proceeds of the state taxes were relinquished to the counties to be used for building court houses,
jails, etc." Although William M. Gouge, writing in
1851,[18] recorded the state debt of Texas at that time as
$12,436,991, it appears from available evidence that the

---

[17] E. T. Miller, *Financial History of Texas* (1907), p. 54. Reprinted
by permission of the University of Texas, Austin, Texas. See Miller also
for a more detailed discussion of taxation in this frontier state prior
to 1860.

[18] William M. Gouge, *Fiscal History of Texas,* p. 289.

state entered the Civil War free of obligations, except for a small floating debt.

In Arkansas, the principal sources of state revenue were the ad valorem tax on land, levied at the rate of one fourth of one per cent on the assessed value; specific taxes on certain kinds of personalty, including slaves; and license taxes on Indian traders, peddlers, and keepers of saloons, billiard rooms, and nine-pin galleries. Unlike the other Southern States, Arkansas in her constitution prohibited the poll tax. The most important tax official was the sheriff, who administered the local taxes and collected the state revenues. In 1860, Arkansas had a state debt of $4,036,952.

In Missouri, the constitution of 1820 abolished specific taxes and established the "rule of uniformity" as the basis for a general property tax. At an early date a special tax was levied upon bachelors, but in 1822, this was changed to a poll tax upon adult white males. License taxes were continually expanded. The shares of corporations were taxed, and for a time a discriminatory tax was laid upon merchandise. Tax laws were administered as elsewhere in the South. By 1859, when the railroads began to default in their payments of interest, the state had invested borrowed money in them to the extent of $23,701,000.

In Kentucky, the real property tax was the chief source of revenue. At first, this was a specific tax per acre levied according to the different classes of land. In 1815, the ad valorem system was adopted for the taxation of lands, houses, and slaves. The state debt, on account of fraud and corrupt politicians, at various times greatly embarrassed the legislature, but by 1857, the amount had been reduced to $3,592,412.

Tennessee inherited its early tax system from North Carolina. At first, a specific land tax, as well as other specific taxes was levied. In 1834, a new constitution substituted an ad valorem tax for the specific tax on land. As in other Southern States, there was a poll tax and several kinds of licenses. Tennessee created a public debt by issuing bonds to establish banks and to make internal improvements; in 1842, this debt amounted to $3,198,166, but by 1862, it had risen to nearly $20,000,000.

The state fiscal systems in the ante-bellum South had a fundamental homogeneity, because they were evolved to meet changes in economic development common to the entire section.

### Bibliographical Note

A few works on the history of banking in the United States contain brief discussions of banking in the ante-bellum South. The most serviceable of these are: D. R. Dewey, *History of State Banking before the Civil War* (Washington, 1910); John Jay Knox, *History of Banking in the United States* (New York, 1920); W. G. Sumner, *History of Banking in the United States* (New York, 1896); C. F. Dunbar, *Theory and History of Banking* (New York, 1891); and A. O. Eliason, *Rise of Commercial Banking Institutions in the United States* (Minneapolis, 1901). A brief summary of the theoretical views about banking in those days may be found in George Tucker's article entitled "Banks or No Banks," in *Hunt's Merchants' Magazine* (New York, 1839–1870), Volume 38, pages 147–157.

George T. Starnes, *Sixty Years of Branch Banking in Virginia* (New York, 1931), is an excellent piece of research, and shows clearly the underlying theory of banking in Virginia prior to the Civil War. Of less value but containing some interesting facts is W. L. Royall, *History of Virginia Banks and Banking Prior to the Civil War* (Washington, 1907). The only authoritative treatment of ante-bellum banking in Maryland is A. C. Bryan's *History of State Banking in Maryland* (Baltimore, 1899). For Tennessee, the only treatment of importance is Thomas P. Abernethy, "The Early Development of Commerce and Banking in Tennessee," in the *Mississippi Valley Historical Review*, Volume 14, page 311 *et seq.* For Kentucky, see B. W. Duke, *History of the Bank of Kentucky, 1792–1895* (Louisville, 1895); and E. C. Griffith, "Early Banking in Kentucky," in the *Proceedings of the Mississippi Valley Historical Association*, Volume II, page 168 *et seq.* W. O. Scroggs,

*Financial History of Alabama* (Ph.D. Thesis, Harvard University, 1907); and J. H. Fitts, "History of Banks and Banking in Alabama," in the *Proceedings of the Alabama Bankers Association* (1891), pages 8–33, are the only satisfactory treatments of the ante-bellum period of banking in Alabama. A brief sketch of banking in Mississippi may be found in C. H. Brough, *History of Banking in Mississippi*, Volume III of the PUBLICATIONS OF THE MISSISSIPPI STATE HISTORICAL SOCIETY, pages 317–340.

Brief sketches of the history of taxation in the Southern States may be found in Volume V, pages 498–546, of THE SOUTH IN THE BUILDING OF THE NATION (Richmond, 1909); this volume is edited by J. C. Ballagh. *Studies in State Taxation* (Baltimore), which is the volume for 1900 in the JOHNS HOPKINS UNIVERSITY STUDIES IN HISTORICAL AND POLITICAL SCIENCE, contains brief sketches of the ante-bellum period of taxation in Maryland, North Carolina, and Georgia. T. R. Snavely, *Taxation of Negroes in Virginia* (Charlottesville, Va., 1917), is a complete treatment of that aspect of taxation in Virginia, and incidentally touches most of the other forms of taxes levied in the state. For Maryland, see H. S. Hanna, *Financial History of Maryland, 1789–1848* (Baltimore, 1907). E. Q. Hawk, *Taxation in Alabama*, in the BULLETIN OF BIRMINGHAM-SOUTHERN COLLEGE (Birmingham, Ala., 1930), contains a brief summary of that subject during the ante-bellum period. E. T. Miller, *Financial History of Texas*, in the BULLETIN OF THE UNIVERSITY OF TEXAS (Austin, Texas, 1916), is a scholarly and complete treatment of taxation and public debt in Texas.

There is need for exhaustive studies in the fiscal history of most of the Southern States for the ante-bellum period.

# CHAPTER XIII

# Causes of the Civil War

FROM the foregoing survey it appears that the economic set-up of the South by 1860 was still relatively simple. Mainly on account of the physiographic background, agriculture—which began at Jamestown as an experiment—had, with the acquisition of new land, spread until it was the chief occupation of the entire section. In the border states, grain crops and livestock were produced; in the rest of the South, the staple crops predominated, and of these cotton was king. A few industries had been established here and there, especially in the Piedmont region, but they were small and manufactured articles almost solely for local markets. The skeleton of a transportation system, comprised of waterways, roads, and railways, had been established. To supply funds for such internal improvements and for agriculture, nearly every Southern State had organized a banking system, but failure had resulted in all the states except Virginia and South Carolina, where more conservative practices had been maintained by legal restrictions. Furthermore, each Southern State had evolved an elementary fiscal system, and each had incurred a public debt ranging from less than $1,000,000 to more than $20,000,000. By 1860, the population of the section had increased to 12,315,374, of which 261,918 were free negroes and 3,953,593, or 32 per cent, were negro slaves.

Much has been written about the political developments which culminated in secession and war; but to assume that political issues were paramount as causes of the Civil War is far from true, as an examination of economic conditions will show.

## Economic Causes

### SLAVERY

One of the most provoking questions in the history of the United States is why the North, in colonial days, was so busily engaged in importing African slaves into the South and then, two generations later, became determined to emancipate them. Was it because Northern men had developed a higher sense of morality and human freedom than their Puritanical grandfathers? Or was it due to the operation of economic causes which they veneered with moral doctrines?

It is well known that the slave trade in colonial times was highly profitable to New England shipping interests. But when slavery became unprofitable in the tobacco-growing regions of the South and planters in that section could supply the Cotton Belt with their excess of slaves, a great demand no longer existed for imported slaves from Africa. This fact within itself tended to destroy any further importation of slaves by the North.

Foreign white immigrants poured into the North rather than into the South, because they could not, as free labor, compete with slave labor. Hence there was a fundamental antagonism to the South on the part of this new Northern population. To crystallize their attitude, growing out of an economic cause, it was easy to turn from rationalizing to advocating high moral principles.

Many persons were for moral reasons sincerely opposed to slavery, and some of the leaders of the antislavery movement were honest fanatics who believed that they were engaged in a great moral crusade. In 1831, William Lloyd Garrison published in Boston the first issue of the *Liberator*, in which he announced that slavery was "a crime—a damning crime," that slaveholders were criminals, and that he would "strenuously contend for the immediate enfranchisement of our slave population. . . ." Moreover, he affirmed: "I am in earnest. . . . I will not equivocate. . . .

I will not excuse. . . . I will not retreat a single inch . . . and I will be heard." To him the Constitution itself was a "slave-owners' document . . . a covenant with death and an agreement with hell."

Around Garrison's banner there formed a band of radical, antislavery adherents. Among these the most distinguished were Wendell Phillips, John Greenleaf Whittier, James Russell Lowell, Ralph Waldo Emerson, and Harriet Beecher Stowe. Every known method of arousing public sentiment was used by the agitators. Antislavery societies were formed; propaganda was printed and circulated; petitions were drawn up; speeches were made; and pressure was brought upon Northern members of Congress. Mobs were organized for the rescue of fugitive slaves, and, in a few instances, agitators were sent into the South to stir up slave revolts. The "underground railroad"—an elaborate network of secret routes—was used deliberately to steal thousands of slaves from their owners, and to spirit them away to Canada. In short, the agitators flouted courts, laws, and the Constitution by stealing negroes, who, by courts, laws, and the Constitution, had been recognized as property.

The South was just as determined to keep slavery, and rallied to its defense on economic, moral, and even religious grounds. In 1860, J. B. De Bow, editor of *De Bow's Review,* pointed out that the prosperity not only of the slave owners but of the independent farmer as well depended largely upon slavery. "The non-slaveholder knows that as soon as his savings will admit, he can become a slaveholder, and thus relieve his wife from the necessities of the kitchen and the laundry, and his children from the labors of the field." [1]

When the slavery question was debated in the Federal Convention of 1787, Georgia and South Carolina were the only states that wished to continue the slave trade in the

---

[1] J. B. De Bow, "The Interest in Slavery of the Southern Non-Slaveholders," *Association Tract No. 5* (Pamphlet 9).

United States. At the time New England needed more votes in order to give the Federal Government control over foreign commerce. As a result, a political deal was arranged whereby Georgia and South Carolina voted for Federal control of commerce, and Connecticut, New Hampshire, and Massachusetts voted for a continuance of the slave trade for twenty years. When this compromise was effected, slavery was generally regarded as a decaying institution. With the rise of cotton planting, however, slavery expanded and became an integral part of the economic organization of the staple-crop regions of the South.

Although, at the beginning, antislavery sentiment in the North was divided into two groups—the movement to prohibit the expansion of slavery into new territory, and the movement for abolition at any cost—both movements eventually merged into each other. Northern politicians struggled in Congress to express the will of their constituency. Upon the entrance of Missouri as a state into the Union, it became necessary to decide the question whether slavery should be permitted "to overflow into the vast territory obtained through the Louisiana Purchase of 1803." [2] In 1820, after a heated controversy, the so-called "Missouri Compromise" was effected, admitting Missouri as a slave state and Maine as a free state, but prohibiting slavery in the rest of the Louisiana Purchase north of 36 degrees 30 minutes north latitude. According to Professor E. L. Bogart: [3] "This must have seemed a good bargain to the non-slaveholding whites, for it pushed the line very far south and left to slavery little territory which was not already considered as belonging to it. The planting interests were willing to make this concession for the sake of peace, for as yet cotton had not become the dominant Southern interest."

In 1848, gold was discovered in California, and caused a great rush of immigrants into that region. As President

---

[2] Harold U. Faulkner, *American Economic History,* p. 396.

[3] E. L. Bogart, *Economic History of the American People,* p. 476.

Zachary Taylor pointed out, it became imperative "to substitute the rule of law and order there for the bowie-knife
and revolvers." In the territory known as "New Mexico,"
there was only slightly less need for organized government.
President Taylor advised the people of both territories to
frame constitutions and to seek immediate admission to
the Union. In 1849, California adopted a constitution prohibiting slavery; in 1850, New Mexico accepted a free-soil
constitution.

These constitutions were ratified, subject to the consent
of Congress, and immediately brought up the problem concerning the status of slavery in the territory acquired as a
result of the Mexican War. For over a year, there raged
in Congress a battle led by Calhoun, Clay, and Webster.
Calhoun demanded more representation for the South in
Congress, the return of fugitive slaves, and a cessation of
agitation and legislation unfriendly to the South. William
H. Seward, the antislavery leader from New York, hotly
rejected Calhoun's demands, and asserted that for antislavery men "there is a higher law than the Constitution."
The breach threatened to widen into disunion, when Henry
Clay came forward with a compromise in which he proposed that California should be admitted as a free state;
that territorial governments should be established in the
remainder of the Mexican cessions, but that Congress
should take no action for the introduction or the exclusion
of slavery there; that slave trade, but not slavery, should
be abolished in the District of Columbia; and that Congress
should enact a more effective fugitive-slave law. Clay was
ably supported by Webster. These measures passed Congress and, in September 1850, became laws with President
Fillmore's signature.[4]

These acts, known as the "Compromise of 1850," established a "business man's peace." Northern men who had
large investments in the South feared disunion and tried

---

[4] President Taylor died July 9, 1850, and was succeeded by Fillmore,
who, unlike Taylor, favored the compromise.

to get behind Seward to prevent war. In Boston and New York a large sum of money was raised for printing and circulating Webster's speech supporting the compromise, and over 200,000 copies were distributed.

By the Compromise of 1850, it was hoped that the status of slavery had been definitely fixed for the whole country, but in 1854, Congress passed the Kansas-Nebraska Act, setting aside the Compromise of 1850 and repealing the Missouri Compromise. The Kansas-Nebraska Act established the Cass-Douglas principle, which permitted settlers in new territories to decide for themselves whether or not slavery should be allowed within their jurisdictions. As a result of this act and the consequent battle over "Bleeding Kansas," the Republican Party was organized in the North to check any further extension of the slave system into western territory. In 1857 in the Dred Scott decision, the United States Supreme Court held that legally a slave was property and, as such, was not a citizen; and that a slave owner had the right under the Constitution to take his property (slaves) wherever he pleased. This decision proved intolerable to the Republicans. They not only denounced the Supreme Court, but began preaching the doctrine of a "higher law," which demanded that the further extension of slavery be prevented.

In 1860, the Democratic Party split into two factions over Douglas' interpretation of squatter sovereignty. Douglas, in the face of the Dred Scott decision, held that in theory slavery might exist in a territory, but in practice it could be destroyed by legislative "local police regulation." On the other hand, Jefferson Davis, in February 1860, presented in the Senate a resolution in which he denounced Douglas' doctrine by declaring that "neither Congress nor a territorial legislature, by direct or indirect legislation, has the power to annul or impair the Constitutional right of any citizen to take his slave property into the common territories and there hold and enjoy the same while the territorial condition remains." Davis demanded Federal protection for slavery in the territories.

This split in the Democratic Party made possible the election of Abraham Lincoln, a Republican, who was a minority President with practically no support in the South. He was pledged to prevent the further spread of slavery in the United States.[5] At the time Southern men had become embittered not only because of antislavery legislation, but also on account of the violent denunciations of the antislavery agitators. During the Lincoln Presidential campaign, the voters of South Carolina declared: "The irrepressible conflict is about to be visited upon us through the Black Republican nominee and his fanatical, diabolical Republican party." In the North, moreover, large financial interests, fearing that secession would derange business, opposed the Republicans; and William B. Astor and other wealthy men are said to have spent $2,000,000 in an effort to prevent Lincoln from carrying New York state.

It is incorrect to say that the South was wholly proslavery or that the North was wholly antislavery. In the South many of the poor whites opposed slavery. One of the most widely distributed books attacking slavery was *The Impending Crisis of the South,* written by Hinton R. Helper, a poor white of North Carolina. He fortified his statements by facts gleaned from United States Census reports; and after a bold argument that the slavery system had plunged the South "into a state of comparative imbecility and obscurity," he concluded with the threat that "in concert with the intelligent free voters of the North, we, the non-slaveholding whites of the South, expect to elevate John C. Frémont, Cassius M. Clay, James G. Birney, or some other Southern non-slaveholder, to the

---

[5] According to C. W. Ramsdell, "The Natural Limits of Slavery Expansion," in the *Mississippi Valley Historical Review,* Vol. 16, pp. 151–171, both Davis and Lincoln were fighting over straw issues in 1860, and neither showed an intelligent grasp of the laws of economic evolution. He stated further that "slavery had about reached its zenith by 1860," and there would have been practically no further spread westward.

Presidency in 1860; and that the patriot thus elevated to that dignified station will, through our cordial coöperation, be succeeded by William H. Seward, Charles Sumner, John McLean, or some other non-slaveholder of the North;— and furthermore, that if, in these or in any other similar cases, the oligarchs do not quietly submit to the will of a constitutional majority of the people, as expressed at the ballot-box, the first battle between freedom and slavery will be fought at home and may God defend the right!" [6] The South possibly never would have resisted the emancipation of slaves to the extent of a war, had abolitionists in the North refrained from the dissemination of a propaganda of hate, and had slavery alone been the sole issue at stake between the two sections.

## Land Policy of the Federal Government

In the South, the plantation system was expansive and required plenty of land. In the North, manufacturing required the concentration of both population and capital. The South wanted more land; the North wanted cheap labor. The acquisition of the Louisiana Purchase and the opening of the West were advantageous to the South because they made available new land; but they were not so for the North, because the westward drain of population kept wages high. Out of this situation arose a bitter political issue—namely, what should be the land policy of the Federal Government?

How far apart the North and the South were on this question became evident in the debate in the Senate in 1830, between Haynes of South Carolina and Webster of Massachusetts. Haynes argued that the Federal Government should adopt a policy of selling large tracts of land at low prices; that to interfere with land sales would check the growth of the agricultural states; and that through a liberal land policy a great home market could be built up

---

[6] Hinton R. Helper, *Impending Crisis*, p. 413.

for the benefit of the manufacturing states. Webster, taking the New England view, advocated a policy of selling smaller tracts at higher prices and of using the revenue thus derived for the construction of internal improvements. The debate marked the beginning of a great, constitutional struggle between the two sections over the nature of the Union—a struggle that lasted until 1860.

By 1860, however, the attitude of the two sections had changed. The North and the West, eager to attract settlers to the prairie regions, in general favored the homestead policy, which implied free lands to actual settlers. The South, on the other hand, persistently blocked homestead legislation, largely because it feared such a policy would attract millions of immigrants to the Northwest and thus further distort the balance of population between the North and the South. It was not until after the Southern Congressmen had left Washington that the Republican Party succeeded in passing its homestead legislation.

## THE TARIFF

From 1807 to 1815, when the United States was partly cut off from European imports, there was a rapid increase in the establishment of new manufactures, particularly in the North. By 1816, the protection afforded by the war had passed and these infant industries were jeopardized by an influx of the accumulated products of European manufacturers. Then Madison, Jefferson, Calhoun, and other Southern political leaders championed a protective tariff, because, as they argued, the United States ought to become a self-sufficient nation, independent of Europe.

After 1816, the South began to realize its mistake, and the section soon became a unit against protection. The South was a seller of cotton, tobacco, and other staples in the world market, and was a buyer of manufactured goods in a protected market. The West, however, favored protection, because it was interested, as it believed, in the development of a home market and wanted a surplus revenue for the construction of internal improvements. Therefore, in 1824, 1828, and 1832, it voted almost solidly for an increase in protective duties. In 1846, because of the influence of the South as its chief market, the West voted for the Walker Tariff, which was practically an act for "revenue only." The Middle Atlantic States, because of their manufacturing interests, as a rule voted for protection. At first New England was hesitant, because conditions made it necessary to recognize the influence of shipping interests as well as that of manufacturers; in fact, New England cast a majority of its votes against both the Tariff Act of 1824 and that of 1828. As soon as the manufacturing interests became predominant, however, New England became enthusiastic for a protective tariff policy. Daniel Webster, the chief spokesman, in 1824, had argued manfully *against* protection, but four years later, he argued even more ardently *for* protection.

The Tariff Act of 1828 was the first high-water mark of the early protectionist movement. The bill was framed largely for political purposes, and the duties were intentionally made so high that it was hoped even New England would object to the bill. According to Professor F. W. Taussig: [7] "The Southern members openly said that they meant to make the tariff so bitter a pill that no New England member would be able to swallow it." As conceived by the Jackson men, the plan was to draw a tariff bill which would satisfy the protective demands of the West and which, at the same time, would be so obnoxious to New England on account of the high duties on raw materials that this section, in combination with the South, would defeat the bill and thereby allow the followers of Andrew Jackson, without having offended the South, to pose as the friends of infant industries. As John Randolph declared, this bill, "referred to manufactures of no sort or kind, except the manufacture of a President of the United States." Although the bill met with strong opposition

---

[7] F. W. Taussig, *Tariff History of the United States,* p. 97.

from the South, New England, after modifications in the
Senate, supported it in the final vote, and this act, known
as the "Tariff of Abominations," became the law of the
land for four years.

In the meantime, there was on the part of the South a
growing opposition which became so extreme that Congress, in 1832, decided the best policy was to enact a more
moderate tariff. This compromise failed to appease the
Southern leaders; they feared that by such tactics the
North was attempting to fasten a protective system permanently upon them. Calhoun, who was now the Southern leader in Congress, determined to oppose the new act,
and chose as his weapon the doctrine of nullification, which
had been suggested by Kentucky against the Alien and
Sedition Acts, and by New England in opposing the second
war with England. In November 1832, the South Carolina Legislature called a convention which passed the
famous "Nullification Act," asserting that, in so far as this
state was concerned, the Tariff Laws of 1828 and 1832 were
null and void, and could not be enforced after February
1, 1833. President Andrew Jackson declared that the law
would be enforced at all costs.

Out of this situation came the so-called "Compromise
Tariff of 1833," which provided for a gradual reduction
of duties over a period of ten years, until the general level
of 20 per cent was reached. After this time, except for
the period 1842–1846, when the duties were raised to the
level of the 1832 act, the protective tariff controversy was
dormant until 1860, and duties were extraordinarily low
from 1846 to 1860. Nevertheless, the experiences of the
past still rankled the South, and the dependence of the
section upon Northern manufactures certainly did not
lessen the fear of a recurrence of the protective policy. In
1860, the *Boston Post,* in commenting on the extent of
trade between New England and the South, pointed out:
"The aggregate value of the merchandise sold to the South
annually we estimate at some $60,000,000. The basis of

the estimate is, first, the estimated amount of boots and shoes sold, which intelligent merchants place at from $20,-000,000 to $30,000,000, including a limited amount that are manufactured with us and sold in New York. In the next place, we know from merchants in the trade, that the amount of dry-goods sold South yearly is many millions of dollars, and that the amount is second only to that of the sales of boots and shoes. In the third place, we learn from careful inquiry, and from the best sources, that the fish of various kinds sold realize $3,000,000, or in that neighborhood. Upwards of $1,000,000 is received for furniture sold in the South each year. The Southern States are much better markets than the Western for this article."

Obviously, the tariff did not benefit the South, since its main money crops were exports and its purchases had to be made in a protected market. What the North desired in the South was a market protected from foreign competition.

## State Rights

The doctrine of *State rights* in itself was not a cause of the Civil War; it was, rather, a political weapon of the minority, the Southern States. When Alexander Hamilton championed the theory of a strong central government, Thomas Jefferson argued for the sovereign power of the separate states and the limitation of the Federal Government to safeguarding such individual sovereignty. In fact, these two political theories persisted from the beginning of the National Government, and State rights had been invoked several times by minority groups even before the fifties. As time went on, it became more evident that the South was a minority and, as such, was outvoted in Congress by the North, especially upon the allocation of public revenues for internal improvements and pensions. Upon analyzing the political relationship of the South to the North, a Southern Senator, in Congress in 1856, concluded: [8] "We are in a minority in the Senate where the states are represented; we are in a minority in the other branch where the people are represented numerically; and we are in a minority in the electoral college."

The only political weapon, therefore, that the South had with which to oppose the abolition of slavery, an unfavorable land policy, a protective tariff, and the exploitation of Federal revenues for the benefit of the North, was the doctrine of State rights. For ten years, the argument for State rights had led to compromises in Congress, but with the election of Lincoln, the end of conciliation had come. A Southern Congressman announced: [9] "The argument is exhausted. All hope of relief in the Union through the agencies of committees, Congressional legislation, or constitutional amendments, is extinguished, and we trust the South will not be deceived by appearances or the pretense of new guarantees. . . . We are satisfied that the honor, safety, and independence of the Southern People are to be found only in a Southern Confederacy . . . and that the sole and primary aim of each slaveholding state ought to be its speedy and absolute separation from an unnatural and hostile union."

## Secession

By 1860, the political relationship between the North and the South, fundamentally because of economic causes, had reached an *impasse*. There was a growing belief in the South that England, in the event of a war between the states, would support the Southern cause rather than permit her textile industry to perish for lack of cotton. Thus, embittered against the North and inspired with the hope of foreign aid, the Southern States began to secede. Four days after Lincoln's election, the South Carolina Legisla-

---

[8] Remarks in the Senate, May 20, 1856. Appendix to the *Congressional Globe, 34 Congressional Session*, p. 546.

[9] Ulrich B. Phillips, *Life of Toombs* (1913), p. 205. Reprinted by permission of the Macmillan Company, New York.

ture, which had remained in session for the express purpose, called for a convention of the state to meet December 17 at Charleston. On December 20, 1860, that body, by a unanimous vote of its 169 members, "dissolved" the "union now subsisting between South Carolina and other states, under the name of the 'United States of America.' " Within a month, five other states followed: Florida, Georgia, Alabama, Mississippi, and Louisiana. In February 1861, Texas seceded; in April, Virginia; and in May, North Carolina, Arkansas, and Tennessee. Almost simultaneously with secession, these states formed a union under a new constitution, and termed their government the *Confederate States of America.*

### Bibliographical Note

Of the political histories which pay some attention to the economic causes of the Civil War, A. M. Schlesinger, *Political and Social History of the United States, 1829–1925* (New York, 1925), is perhaps the best. J. F. Rhodes, *History of the United States,* Volume I (New York, 1892), contains a detailed discussion of the Compromise of 1850. Of some interest from an economic viewpoint is William G. Brown, *Lower South in American History* (New York, 1902). Some valuable notes may be collected from W. J. White, *Secession Movement in the United States, 1847–1852* (New York, 1916); C. W. Harris, *Sectional Struggle* (Philadelphia, 1902); and C. W. Loring, *Nullification and Secession* (New York, 1893). A more satisfactory treatment of the subject is to be found in R. R. Russell, *Economic Aspects of Southern Sectionalism, 1840–1861* (Urbana, Ill., 1923); this work is Volume XI, Numbers 1–2, in the UNIVERSITY OF ILLINOIS STUDIES IN THE SOCIAL SCIENCES. Some material of a general economic nature may be found in T. P. Kettel, *Southern Wealth and Northern Profits* (New York, 1860); Edward Ingle, *Southern Sidelights* (New York, 1896), Chapter III; and G. S. Callender, *Selections from the Economic History of the United States, 1765–1860* (Boston, 1900).

The most searching study yet made of the extension of slavery into the Southwest is Charles W. Ramsdell, "The Natural Limits of Slavery Expansion," in the *Mississippi Valley Historical Re-*

*view*, Volume 16, pages 151–171. Contemporary arguments for and against slavery are to be found in: *Pro-Slavery Argument* (Philadelphia, 1852), by Thomas R. Dew; and *Impending Crisis of the South* (New York, 1857), by H. R. Helper. The best discussion of the enforcement of the fugitive slave law is W. H. Siebert, *Underground Railroad from Slavery to Freedom* (New York, 1898).

The standard treatment of the tariff is F. W. Taussig, *Tariff History of the United States*, Eighth Edition (New York, 1931).

Special studies of this period have been made for some of the Southern States: R. H. Shryock, *Georgia and the Union in 1850* (Durham, N. C., 1926); J. C. McGregory, *Disruption of Virginia* (New York, 1922); H. M. Wagstaff, *State Rights and Political Parties in North Carolina, 1776–1861* (Baltimore, 1906); J. G. Van Deusen, *Economic Bases of Disunion in South Carolina* (New York, 1928); and C. S. Boucher, *Nullification Controversy in South Carolina* (Chicago, 1916). An interesting contrast in interpretation may be found in C. H. Ambler, *Sectionalism in Virginia from 1776 to 1861* (Chicago, 1910), and U. B. Phillips, "Georgia and State Rights," in Volume II, pages 3–224 of the *American Historical Association Annual Report* (1901).

An excellent survey of political leadership against an economic background is William E. Dodd, *Statesmen of the Old South* (New York, 1911).

# CHAPTER XIV

# The Civil War

A T the beginning of the Civil War, the attitude of the borderland, including Maryland, Western Virginia, Kentucky, Missouri, and Delaware, was extremely doubtful, because its location made it commercially dependent upon both the North and the lower South. As the war progressed, this region, primarily because of Lincoln's skillful tactics, remained in the Union. Nevertheless, it furnished many volunteers for the Confederate Army, and at no time was its attitude wholly in sympathy with that of the North.

Because of the location of the National Capital, Federal possession of Maryland had to be maintained at all costs. Almost from the outset, the Northern press demanded that Baltimore be laid in ashes. This procedure was not followed, but the city was put under the control of a Provost-Marshal and the entire city governmental machinery was superseded by a military force. Despite this fact, and enraged at the ruthless and arbitrary conduct of the Lincoln administration, thousands of Marylanders crossed the Potomac and joined the Confederate Army.

Nature had already divided Virginia: eastern and western Virginia were not only different physiographically, but the people of the two regions had never been homogeneous. In western Virginia, grain farming predominated and the number of slaves was far less than in any other part of the South. A chain of mountains divided the two regions geographically and effectually cut off communication. The Civil War furnished the occasion for the division of the state politically. As a result, in 1862, West Virginia was

397

formed out of fifty Virginia counties, embracing practically 24,000 square miles of territory. This step was an irreparable economic loss to Virginia, for in that region was her greatest potential wealth in coal and timber.

In January 1861, the Legislature of Kentucky, by the adoption of two resolutions, expressed plainly the attitude of the state at that time. The first resolution declared the General Assembly had heard with profound regret that New York, Ohio, Maine, and Massachusetts had tendered to President Lincoln men and money for coercing the South. The second resolution expressed the threat that, when those states undertook to carry through this purpose, "the people of Kentucky, uniting with their brethren of the South, will as one man resist such invasion to the last extremity." Again, in April, when the Secretary of War of the Federal Government called upon the state to furnish troops, Governor Magoffin replied: "I say emphatically that Kentucky will furnish no troops for the wicked purpose of subduing her sister states." But Lincoln was unwilling to permit Kentucky to remain neutral, for, as he said:[1] "At a stroke it would take all the trouble off of the hands of secession, except only what proceeds from the external blockade. It would do for the disunionists that which, of all things they most desire—feed them well, and give them disunion without a struggle of their own." Therefore, the administration planned to send envoys of the Washington Government into the state secretly to organize troops for the Federal Army.

Lieutenant William Nelson, of the United States Navy, a native Kentuckian, came to the state on this mission and, after conferring with the local leaders of the Union Party, was ordered by Lincoln to enlist in the state five regiments of infantry and two of cavalry. Having started a movement from the inside to organize Kentucky for the Union, the next step was to trick the Confederacy into

---

[1] *Complete Works,* Vol. VI, p. 307; quoted in Edward C. Smith, *Borderland in the Civil War,* p. 277.

violating the neutrality of the state and thereby to give the Federal Government an excuse for invasion. This step was easily accomplished. General Grant threatened to seize Columbus, Kentucky, by moving in that direction on the Missouri side of the Mississippi River. General Polk, who was at Memphis, presumably unaware of the trap set for the Confederacy, moved north and occupied Columbus first—exactly what Lincoln had hoped for—and in a short time the Federal element within the state, which had secretly been organizing both whites and negroes, threw off its disguise and seized control of Kentucky for the Union.

Apparently Missouri believed that she would gain more by remaining in the Union than by fighting for the Confederacy. Of the $360,000,000 of taxable property in the state, only about 12 per cent was made up of the assessed value of slaves. To offset the loss of slave property should emancipation be proclaimed, Missouri business men felt they would benefit from a transcontinental railroad that might be projected by the Federal Government. After a bitter struggle in which the German element proved decisive, Missouri remained in the Union. This state then suffered more from internal disorder than any of the border states. Beginning with the anomalous theory of "armed neutrality," it was at the end of the Civil War devastated by no less than one thousand battles, both great and small; guerillas, comprised of deserters from both armies, stole and destroyed property and upon the slightest pretext killed peaceful citizens. During the four years of war, Missouri furnished about 60,000 soldiers to the Confederate Army, and the Congress at Richmond voted to admit Missouri as the twelfth state and Kentucky as the thirteenth in the Confederacy. It was believed in the South that a majority of the people both in Missouri and in Kentucky preferred the doctrine of State rights to the Union policy of coercion.[2]

[2] See Edward C. Smith, *Borderland in the Civil War*, p. 356 *et seq.*

The map on page 401 indicates the territorial limits of the Southern Confederacy and the strategic position of the border states between the North and the Confederacy. Although the South has a longer coast line than the North, it had few ships; hence it was easily blockaded from the outside world. Indeed, the superior sea power of the North probably was the decisive factor in determining the result of the war.

From its inception the Southern Confederacy was engaged in a struggle for existence. An army had to be mustered, equipped, trained, and fed; and industrial resources had to be mobilized for the purposes of war. Yet, of all the problems confronting the Confederate Government and each state in the Confederacy, the most difficult and, at the same time, the most vitally important was the financial problem.

## Finances of the Confederate Government

### ORGANIZATION

The fiscal machinery then organized by the Confederate Government was almost identical with that of the Federal Government. A Treasury Department with several divisions was perfected on the system devised by Alexander Hamilton. At the head of this Department was the Secretary of the Treasury, and under him were assistant treasurers, a comptroller, auditors, and a register. The first Secretary of the Treasury was C. G. Memminger, who had been a member of the ways and means committee in the South Carolina Legislature during the crises of 1837 and 1857 and, therefore, had had some experience with the problems of banking and public finance. Several officials associated with Memminger were not without practical experience in financial matters; some had served in the United States Treasury and had resigned to offer their services to the "new Government." Assistant treasurers were stationed at central points throughout the Confed-

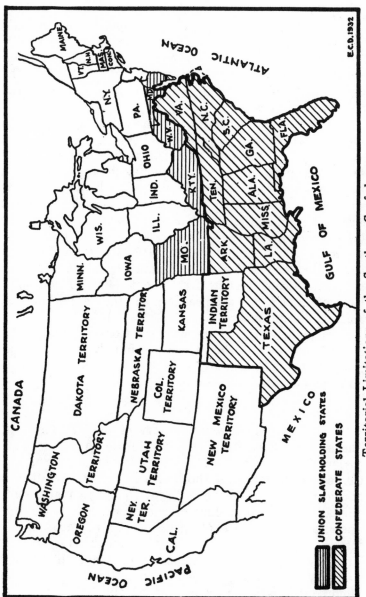

Territorial Limitations of the Southern Confederacy

E.C.D. 1932

eracy, and at one time numbered nearly three hundred. They served as the fiscal agents of the Government, collecting taxes, selling bonds, and making the necessary disbursements. When, at first, custom collectors were stationed at the ports, all the United States Collectors who joined the Confederate Government were given their original powers and salaries.

The Confederate Constitution was nearly identical with the Federal Constitution in regard to the power to coin money and to regulate its value; to authorize paper money as legal tender; and to borrow money upon public credit. But the "new Government" had no funds, and the next step was to seize the United States funds at the Southern custom houses and mints. The first actual money came to the Confederate Treasury on March 14, 1861, through the seizure of the Bullion Fund of $389,267, at the New Orleans mint, and $147,519, the balance from custom duties at New Orleans. Thereafter, about $460,000 additional United States funds were confiscated; they were, however, an insignificant amount.

During the course of the war, the Confederate Government, in an effort to meet the continually increasing demands for funds, had to resort to loans, to the issue of paper money, and to taxation.

## LOANS

While Memminger was Secretary of the Treasury, emphasis was put on loans, and very little effort was made to levy taxes. On the last day of February, 1861, the Confederate Congress authorized a loan of $15,000,000, in ten-year bonds, bearing 8 per cent coupons payable semi-annually. An export duty of one eighth of one per cent upon raw cotton was pledged for the payment of the interest. In March, the Treasury issued $1,000,000 in Treasury notes, and in August, a like amount. These were payable in one year; bore $3.65 interest on every one hundred dollars, and were made receivable both for custom duties and for taxes, but not for export duty on cotton. Although these loans were placed mainly in the banks in Charleston, Savannah, Mobile, and New Orleans, the banks each merely furnished notes for the deposits on the loan and again paid them out on the Confederate Treasurer's draft, since all of the banks, except those at New Orleans and Mobile, had suspended specie payments.

By May 1861, the "new Government," in estimating its probable expenditures, calculated that by the end of the year it would have a deficit of about $38,000,000, in spite of the bond issue, the $1,000,000 note issue, and the amount seized from the United States funds in the South. Ordinary financing could not meet this emergency. Several plans were presented, including a tariff of 12½ per cent, but obviously the impending curtailment of foreign trade by the possible success of the Northern blockade made the tariff highly precarious as a source of revenue. On May 16, 1861, the Confederate Congress authorized the joint issue of $50,000,000 in bonds at 8 per cent, payable in twenty years; of this issue it decided that $20,000,000 might be two-year Treasury notes. On August 19, 1861, a loan of $100,000,000 was authorized. These bonds were also for twenty years, bearing 8 per cent interest, and the shorter-term bonds authorized in May were revoked in favor of the new issue. The bonds were to be issued for funding Treasury notes—in exchange for the proceeds of the sale of agricultural produce—and for purchasing war supplies. This loan was accompanied by the first tax levy of the Confederate Government.

By the end of 1861, the actual expenditure amounted to $165,000,000, while the estimates had been only $72,-000,000. Memminger was worried: "Our Treasury cannot be guided by experience, since history furnishes no parallel of circumstances. It must feel its way." Subsequently there was adopted a system of funding whereby a smaller issue was taken up by a larger, new bond issue, and thus a surplus was left for the Treasury.

On April 12, 1862, Congress authorized an issue of $165,-
000,000 in ten-thirty bonds at 8 per cent, and $50,000,000
in additional notes.  But bonds of the Confederate Government no longer found many direct purchasers, for they
were allowed to be sold only above par.  In fact, after
July 1862, bonds were not thrown open to general bids.
The intention of the Treasury had been to give bonds
either in exchange for Treasury notes, which were being
circulated as paper money, or in exchange for produce for
the Army.  Since the planters preferred notes, the $100,-
000,000 bond issue of August 1861 had not been exhausted
and the bonds of the new loan of April 12, 1862, were not
even issued.

By the fall of 1862, the public credit of the Confederacy
was exhausted.  The Government had financed its purchases in Europe by the use of letters of credit and bills
of exchange.  To redeem these, gold coin was drained out
of the country, because of the South's unfavorable balance
of trade.  The situation had resulted from an embargo
upon the export of cotton, whereby it was hoped that
England would be forced to intervene in behalf of the
Confederacy before she would allow her textile industry to
perish.  This hope, however, proved futile, because England was more vitally dependent upon Northern wheat
than upon Southern cotton.[3]

Without gold or exports, letters of credit could not be
bought, and the purchase of foreign supplies had to stop.
In these circumstances a new plan of making loans was
adopted.  The Government had already experimented with
produce loans—that is, bonds given in exchange for agricultural products.  By 1862, the Government had obtained
about 400,000 bales of cotton, because planters, unable to
export their cotton, were quite willing to exchange it for
bonds or notes.  The Government, however, could neither
export cotton, on account of the blockade, nor use it to

---

[3] For a detailed account of the foreign relations of the Confederate
States, see Frank L. Owsley, *King Cotton Diplomacy*.

feed or equip the Army. It was mainly on account of this predicament that the *Richmond Examiner*, of April 11, 1862, declared that the "Produce Loan" was a sham and a delusion, but that if all the cotton was delivered to the Government and formed the basis of a *bona fide* loan of money value, it would be "more desirable than gold or silver" and "more valuable after the blockade."

Although the method of exchanging bonds for produce had put no actual money in the Treasury, it gave effective form to the effort to place a foreign loan. The new plan was to hypothecate cotton as collateral for a foreign loan. "The Confederacy would pay interest and commission and 'would place in the hands of the agent of such house on this side such numbers of bales of cotton as might be agreed to be sufficient to cover the advance . . . the cotton to remain on this side until the blockade is raised.' . . . The cotton would, of course, be stored and insured at the expense of the Government at any convenient point designated, but not in a cotton port, during the existing blockade." [4]

At first this plan was rejected by European bankers, but toward the close of 1862, Emile Erlanger, the great French banker, was induced to float a loan for the Confederate Government. According to his plan, the Government was to give him bonds secured by cotton, and he would underwrite the bonds, credit the proceeds of their sale to the Confederate agents, and then wait for the cotton until it could successfully run the blockade or until after the war. Negotiations were carried on secretly; a contract between the Secretary of the Treasury and Jules Beeri, for Emile Erlanger et Compagnie, was signed January 3, 1863. By the end of the month, a secret issue of Confederate bonds for $15,000,000 was authorized. These were twenty-year bonds with interest, at 7 per cent, payable half yearly—one fortieth of the face value of the loan

---

[4] *Ibid.*, p. 386. See also *O. R. Ser.* 4, Vol. I, pp. 845–846.

being redeemable at half-yearly drawings beginning the following March.

The loans were issued in denominations of £100 to £1,000, and the £100 bond was made convertible into 4,000 pounds of cotton at 6d. per pound, but not later than six months after peace. Furthermore, the conditions of the contract fixed the price of the bonds at 77 per cent. The bankers were to receive 5 per cent commission on their sales and were allowed all profit in excess of 77 per cent. These bonds were floated in Paris, Frankfurt, Amsterdam, and London, and the full amount was subscribed at 90 per cent. Cotton was then selling at 21d. and 300,000 bales were said to have been hypothecated as collateral for this loan. Within thirty days, however, the price of cotton began to drop and the subscribers began to refuse to pay further installments upon the bonds. Erlanger then authorized the Confederate agent to support the bonds by buying back part of them; but this bull market was only temporary and, when the repurchased stock was placed on the market again, £704,000 remained unsold.

The net receipts from this loan to the Confederacy amounted to only about $6,550,000. Apparently, then, the loan was a wild speculation in buying Southern cotton at 6d. per pound, in order to sell it at a much higher price in Europe if it could run the blockade or if the Confederacy should win. Actually, the loan strengthened the foreign credit of the Confederacy, because the Confederacy lived up to its contract. The *London Index*, of September 15, 1864, explained that the Confederate cotton bonds were quoted at 73 per cent while those of the United States were quoted at 41 per cent, because the Confederate cotton loan derived its strength from the broad substratum of hypothecated cotton.

Although Erlanger et Compagnie offered to make a new loan of £5,000,000 for the Confederate Government, Secretary Memminger did not advise it, since the first loan had yielded only about 50 per cent of its value.

During the remaining years of the war, the financial problems of the Confederacy became rapidly more distressing. Treasury notes were issued in such large amounts that the inevitable inflation almost undermined the whole fiscal system. In order to prevent such a catastrophe, desperate efforts were made from time to time by funding these notes in bonds, as well as by attempting to borrow specie wherever possible.

## PAPER MONEY

One of the chief concerns of the Confederate Treasury was the establishing of a system of national currency. The Treasury pronounced gold a commodity of merchandise and not a true standard of measure unless it circulated freely. Hence, new currency had to be devised for the "new Government." The plan adopted was to issue Treasury notes, as already mentioned. The first issue of these notes was authorized under the act of March 4, 1861; the notes bore interest and fell due in one year; the smallest denomination was $50; and the amount issued did not exceed $1,000,000. In the fall of 1861, this issue was doubled; moreover, it was not long until the Government drifted into the easy habit of issuing Treasury notes, which actually were fiat money. Thus by the act of May 16, 1861, the Treasury issued $20,000,000 in non-interest-bearing notes, redeemable in two years and in denominations as low as $5. In August, $100,000,000 more of these notes were issued, redeemable six months after the ratification of peace.

Although the first issues of Treasury notes were fundable in bonds, they remained in circulation. The next issues were, obviously, paper money, because they bore no interest, and the last issue mentioned was redeemable only at some indefinite future time. Thereafter the issues of Treasury notes—fiat money—rapidly increased. It appears the theory prevailed during the earlier years of the war that it was impossible for too much paper money to be afloat. The Confederate presses groaned under their steady output of Treasury notes, and the Register and the Secretary of the Treasury were reduced to the extremity of hiring men to sign the almost innumerable bills.

The Treasury issued, in April 1862, $5,000,000 and, a little later, $10,000,000 in one- and two-dollar notes; and a year later, it issued a large amount of fractional currency. In September 1863, no limit was put on the issue of notes, and throughout the remainder of the war, the amount in circulation was continually increased. Obviously the issues of notes had become excessive.

Hence, in March 1863, the Confederate Congress passed a compulsory funding act, intended to remedy the situation. This act provided that non-interest-bearing notes dated before December 1, 1862, were fundable in 8 per cent bonds till April 22, 1863. Thereafter, till August 1, 1863, they were fundable in 7 per cent bonds, but after that date, they were non-fundable, though receivable for dues. Non-interest-bearing notes dated between December 1, 1862, and April 6, 1863, were fundable in 7 per cent bonds until August 1, 1863, and thereafter, in 4 per cent bonds. Although this act was intended to reduce the outstanding notes by funding them into bonds up to $200,000,000, it defeated its purpose by permitting the Treasury at the same time to issue notes monthly up to $50,000,000.

By the act of February 17, 1864, another and more desperate attempt was made to reduce the quantity of circulating notes. In fact, this act was heralded as "marking an epoch in the monetary department of modern polity." According to the previous funding act, of March 1863, notes were divided into three classes with reference to the date of issue, and each class was to be refunded at different times and rates. This new act divided the notes on the basis of their denominations and demoralized portions of them by the application of a progressive tax. For example, all notes, above $5, belonging to the twenty-year 4 per cent bond issue, were allowed, east of the Mississippi, to circulate until April 1, and west of the Mississippi, until July 1. After that date, they were to be taxed at the rate of 33⅓ per cent, but could be exchanged before January 1865 for 4 per cent bonds. Moreover, taxes were to be paid, not in the interest coupons of special bond issues, but in 4 per cent certificates, which were supposed to be the funded representative of the redundant notes being retired. To administer this law, one hundred and twelve new depositaries were appointed and quartermasters in the Army were ordered to function in similar capacities. When the notes were collected by refunding, they were to be canceled by being cut into pieces and beaten with a hammer.

This new act caused a panic in business. Sellers of goods demanded of buyers not only the notes but the proposed tax in addition. Such action obviously sent prices skyward. Governor Brown, of Georgia, declared: "The act has shaken confidence in the justice and competence of Congress. The country was prepared to pay cheerfully a heavy tax, but it did not expect repudiation and bad faith." Indeed, it was a fatal act, and Secretary Memminger was forced to resign in June, "to be succeeded by some individual of proper ability as a financier and more likely to command public confidence."

G. A. Trenholm, of Charleston, became the new Secretary of the Treasury. Among other things he proposed a multiple standard of value, founded on the agricultural staples of cotton, corn, and wheat; his argument was that this standard would bring stability into the financial reckoning, which, he asserted, was convulsed by the variableness of gold. Despite his efforts, Confederate finances went from bad to worse, and at last, in spite of the pledge of February 17, 1864, not to issue more notes, the act of March 18, 1865, was passed over the President's veto and $80,000,000 in notes were issued to pay the soldiers. As a result of this reckless policy of issuing paper money—

Treasury notes—there was outstanding by the end of the war a total amount of over $1,000,000,000.

## TAXATION

Although the Confederate Government relied as far as possible upon bonds and Treasury notes to finance the war, it became necessary, especially during the last two years, to resort to taxation as a supplementary measure. Altogether, the Confederate Government enacted four different tax laws.

The Confederate Congress, acting mainly upon the advice and information given by the Secretary of the Treasury, included with the Loan Act of August 19, 1861, a provision for a direct war tax, as follows: "A War tax shall be assessed and levied of fifty cents upon each $100 in value of the following property in the Confederate States; real estate of all kinds; slaves; merchandise; bank stock; railroad and other corporation stock; money at interest, or invested by individuals in the purchase of bills; notes, and other securities for money, except bonds of the Confederate States; cattle, horses, and mules; gold watches; gold and silver plate, pianos and pleasure carriages; provided that taxable property enumerated of any head of a family is of a value not less than $500." Moreover, this provision allowed each state to anticipate the amount of taxes assessed upon its citizens and to pay the sum minus a 10 per cent rebate into the Confederate Treasury at any time before April 1, 1862. This procedure was unfortunate, for it made each state, instead of the Central Government, a borrower.

On April 24, 1863, the Confederate Congress, acting upon the insistence of the Secretary of the Treasury and the press, passed a new tax measure, which was far more stringent than the first. This law provided the following taxes:

(1) A property tax of 8 per cent, to be levied on the value of all naval stores, salt, wines and liquors, tobacco, cotton and wool, sugar, molasses and syrup, and on all

other agricultural products except those necessary for home consumption; on all kinds of money and currency on hand or on deposit; and the reduced rate of only one per cent on all credits.

(2) A license tax, to be imposed as follows: bankers, $500; auctioneers, retail dealers, tobacconists, peddlers, jewelrymen, apothecaries, photographers, and confectioners, each $50 plus 2½ per cent on gross sales; wholesale dealers in liquors, $200 plus 5 per cent on gross sales; retail dealers in liquor, $100 plus 10 per cent on gross sales; wholesale dealers, $200 plus 2½ per cent on gross sales; pawnbrokers, $200; distillers, $200 plus 20 per cent on gross sales; hotels, from $30, for the fifth class, to $500, for the first class; brokers, $200; theaters, $500 plus 50 per cent on gross receipts; circuses, jugglers, bowling alleys, livery stables, lawyers, physicians, surgeons, and dentists, from $40 to $50 each.

(3) A tax to be imposed on earnings, according to the following arrangement: (a) Salaries of $1,500 and less, one per cent; those above that amount, the same plus 2 per cent on the excess. Salaries less than $1,000 and those derived from military and naval service were to be exempt. (b) Net income from sources other than salaries: $500 to $1,500, 5 per cent; $1,500 to $3,000, 5 per cent on $1,500, and 10 per cent on the excess; $3,000 to $5,000, 10 per cent; $5,000 to $10,000, 12½ per cent; $10,000 and above, 15 per cent.

(4) A separate 10 per cent tax, to be levied during 1863 upon profits derived from the sale of provisions or any food products, iron, shoes, blankets, and cotton cloth.

(5) A tax in kind, of one tenth of the agricultural produce during the year 1863. This tithe was to be delivered by the farmers to the post-quartermasters not later than March 1, 1864.

By April 1864, to satisfy the requirements imposed by these tax levies, Georgia had paid $22,000,000; Virginia, $21,500,000; South Carolina, $12,500,000; North Carolina,

$10,000,000; Alabama, $9,500,000; Texas, about $3,000,-000; Mississippi, $2,000,000; Florida, $1,000,000; Louisiana, $200,000; and Tennessee, $140,000. Arkansas, however, had paid nothing.[5]

The next year, the Confederate Congress, once more relying upon the advice of the Secretary of the Treasury and the public press, not only reënacted the law of 1863, but made taxation heavier by additional levies. These comprised 10 per cent on the value of gold and silver plate; 5 per cent on all property not otherwise taxed by the act; 5 per cent on all solvent credits, on currency other than Confederate notes and not employed in business already taxed, on coin and bullion, and on all shares in corporations; and an additional 10 per cent tax on profits from any business, and 25 per cent from any concern on profits in excess of 25 per cent.

In June of the same year, all the rates contained in this act were raised horizontally by one fifth; the proceeds were to go to the "soldiers' fund." The receipts from such levies, for example, when applied to Virginia, were itemized as indicated on page 413.[6]

Finally, in March 1865, realizing the almost hopeless condition of the revenue system, the Confederate Congress enacted the most extreme tax rates of the war—upon objects already taxed by previous laws. The tax in kind was not only continued but could not be paid in money; the taxes on incomes and salaries were continued; specie and foreign credits were taxed at the rate of 20 per cent; 5 per cent was levied on all other credits, except state and Confederate bonds, the interest from which in lieu of the principal was taxed as income; profits from slaves were taxed at the rate of 10 per cent, in addition to the tax upon profits as income; profits in excess of 25 per cent

---

[5] *Confederate Archives:* Report of Register to Secretary Memminger, April 29, 1864.

[6] Commissioner of Taxes of the Confederate States, *Report* (October 28, 1864). Original in Virginia State Library, Richmond.

## TAXES PAID BY VIRGINIA TO THE CONFEDERATE GOVERNMENT, 1864

| | | |
|---|---:|---:|
| Total value of real and personal property in the state of Virginia subject to taxation under the Act of February 17, 1864, on the basis of valuation established by said Act.............................. | | $531,941,083 |
| Estimated Tax thereon at 5%................. | $26,597,054 | |
| Jewelry, plate and Watches $3,000,000.......... | 150,000 | |
| | $26,747,054 | |
| 5% additional.  Deduct this amt. on account partial occupation by public enemy............ | 4,497,054 | |
| | $22,250,000 | |
| Estimated property tax under Act of Feb. 17, 1864.  Deduct this amt. on account Credit tax in kind $15,250,000.  Deduct this amt. on account Credit income tax $2,555,000.......... | $17,800,000 | |
| Estimated net proceeds property tax....... | | $   4,450,000 |
| Estimated amt. of all other taxes under Act 24th April, 1863, less estimated amt. assessed under 1st section said Act now repealed............................. | | $ 15,000,000 |
| Estimated amount of 30% tax, Sec. 6, Act June 14, 1864......................... | | 200,000 |
| Aggregate amount of taxes for 1864........ | | $ 19,650,000 |

Act April 24, 1863, Feb. 17, 1864, June, 1864.
Soldiers' Fund Tax.

| | | | |
|---|---:|---:|---:|
| one-fifth.....................$22,250,000 | $4,450,000 | | |
| one-fifth..................... 15,000,000 | 3,000,000 | | |
| one-fifth..................... 200,000 | 40,000 | 7,490,000 | |
| TOTAL................. | | | $ 27,140,000 |

were taxed 25 per cent; all other property was taxed at the rate of 8 per cent upon its 1860 valuation; and in addition to all these rates, a horizontal increase was levied to provide for the "soldiers' fund."

The total receipts and expenditures of the Confederate Government during the Civil War were as follows: [7]

---

[7] Compiled from *Reports* of the Secretaries of the Confederate Treasury (Memminger and Trenholm).

## TOTAL RECEIPTS OF CONFEDERATE GOVERNMENT DURING CIVIL WAR

| | Feb. 18, 1861 to Feb. 18, 1862 | Feb. 18, 1862 to Jan. 1, 1863 | Jan. 1, 1863 to Oct. 1, 1863 | Oct. 1, 1863 to Oct. 1, 1864 | Totals |
|---|---|---|---|---|---|
| Bonds............ | $ 31,152,660 | $ 47,773,572 | $154,840,600 | $312,404,900 | $ 546,171,732 |
| Call Certificates... | ............... | 59,742,796 | 23,475,100 | 61,128,660 | 144,346,556 |
| Notes........... | 95,790,250 | 329,294,885 | 391,623,530 | 543,264,878 | 1,359,973,543 |
| Bank Loans....... | 9,813,545 | 2,539,799 | ............... | ............... | 12,353,344 |
| Customs......... | 1,270,875 | 668,566 | 942,900 | 518,750 | 3,401,091 |
| Taxes........... | ............... | 16,664,513 | 4,128,988 | 101,701,038 | 122,494,539 |
| Sequestration..... | ............... | ............... | 1,862,500 | 4,539,490 | 6,401,990 |
| Patent Funds..... | ............... | 13,920 | 10,794 | 26,957 | 51,671 |
| Repayments...... | ............... | 3,865,851 | 24,638,428 | 62,891,596 | 91,395,875 |
| Miscellaneous..... | 1,022,673 | 2,291,812 | ............... | 6,964,383 | 10,278,868 |
| Tax on Notes..... | ............... | ............... | ............... | 14,440,567 | 14,440,567 |
| **TOTAL RECEIPTS** | **$139,050,003** | **$462,855,714** | **$601,522,840** | **$1,107,881,219** | **$2,311,309,776** |

## TOTAL EXPENDITURES OF CONFEDERATE GOVERNMENT DURING CIVIL WAR

| | Feb. 18, 1861 to Feb. 18, 1862 | Feb. 18, 1862 to Jan. 1, 1863 | Jan. 1, 1863 to Oct. 1, 1863 | Oct. 1, 1863 to Oct. 1, 1864 | Totals |
|---|---|---|---|---|---|
| War............ | $152,844,430 | $341,011,754 | $377,988,244 | $484,939,816 | $1,356,784,244 |
| Navy........... | 7,600,485 | 20,599,283 | 38,437,661 | 26,408,525 | 93,045,954 |
| Civil........... | 5,045,660 | 13,673,376 | 11,629,278 | 16,038,973 | 46,387,287 |
| Debt Service...... | ............... | 41,727,320 | 91,256,739 | 470,607,163 | 603,591,222 |
| **TOTAL EXPENDITURES......** | **$165,490,575** | **$417,011,733** | **$519,311,922** | **$997,994,477** | **$2,099,808,707** |

The greater part of the total receipts were derived from loans and not from taxes. Even toward the end of the war, tax receipts were still relatively insignificant. Such a condition obviously was in violation of the principle that "at the outbreak of war more has to be raised by loans than by taxes, but as the war proceeds the proportion of expenditure from revenue must increase." [8] The situation could not have been avoided under the circumstances, however, because of the general stagnation of business and the destruction of property by the Union Army; but the Confederate Government, by putting an embargo on cotton, did make a fundamental mistake. Had the Government during the first year of the war proceeded to sell cotton to Europe or to float a foreign loan secured by cotton, and had it, with the proceeds, bought ships and kept its ports open, in all probability its financial problems never would

[8] G. Findlay Shirras, *Science of Public Finance*, p. 95.

have reached such an *impasse*. The plan adopted in order to force England to intervene in behalf of the South, moreover, not only failed, but also made the blockade possible and finally put cotton into the hands of speculators who used it largely to enhance their own profits, even to the extent of a large cotton trade between the lines.

### State Finances

Like the Confederate Central Government, each state, driven to extremes in meeting financial needs, relied more upon loans and the issue of paper money than upon taxation.

**Virginia.** This state did not attempt, at first, to raise her quota of the Confederate war tax by means of taxation. Instead, in order to relieve her citizens of the immediate burden, she issued state bonds to the banks, which advanced the necessary sum. This expedient was not sufficient, however, because the bonded debt of $33,000,000, already incurred for "improvements," had practically exhausted the credit of the state.

Far more important was the issue of state treasury notes. Beginning in March 1861, the sum of $1,000,000 was issued. In April, this amount was doubled; in June, it reached $4,000,000. In December, another $4,000,000 was issued, and in the following March, $1,300,000. Consequently, during the first two years of the war, Virginia issued a total of $9,300,000 in state treasury notes. Nor was this all. Certain cities at the same time freely issued municipal treasury notes to serve as a circulating medium. In 1863, complaint was made that the $500,000 in notes issued by Richmond were entirely insufficient for the needs of that city.

The banks, authorized by the state convention, as early as 1861 also began issuing notes of small denominations in amounts up to 5 per cent of their own capital. Thus by May 1862, the banks of Virginia reported a circulation of $12,000,000 and specie of only $3,000,000.

Inevitably the circulating medium became redundant.

The *Richmond Examiner* declared,[9] "The banks have more money than they know what to do with. Some of their branches in the interior have had no applications for loans for three months. Capitalists and men of business are all alike plethoric of funds."

On the other hand, the ample revenue provided by these issues of bonds and notes made it temporarily unnecessary for the state to increase the tax burden. In 1863, the act raising the rates to one per cent on property, $2.00 on polls, and 2½ per cent on incomes in excess of $500, was suspended for one year. There was a general feeling that the state levies should vary inversely with the Confederate levies, and that this condition could be made possible only by the issue of bonds and notes.

Practically no changes occurred in the tax scheme except in the rates of different levies. These were somewhat raised in 1862; but the increases made in 1863 were repealed, and in 1864, the rate of the property tax was actually lowered. Clearly these changes were of little fiscal significance, not only because of the inflation of prices, but also because of a general laxity in assessing and levying the taxes.

**Other Confederate States.** Practically the same fiscal methods were adopted in the other Confederate States as in Virginia. As a rule, taxes were raised, and notes were issued and made receivable for the taxes. In North Carolina by 1864, $8,500,000 in notes had been issued, many in small denominations. During the war, a large part of the taxable property of South Carolina was destroyed, and as elsewhere in the South, land depreciated in value. In spite of this fact, every available source of income within the state was drawn upon by increased levies. Bonds were issued, and Charleston alone issued $800,000 in notes (fiat money). By 1864, Georgia had issued nearly $18,000,000 in notes. By 1866, her debt, after the repudiation of the Confederate debt, was still $5,706,500; whereas in 1860, it

---

[9] *Richmond Examiner,* January 17, 1862.

had been only $2,670,750. By 1864, Florida had issued $1,650,000 in notes and Pensacola had a considerable amount in circulation.

As in some other Southern States, the exigencies of the war forced Alabama to raise tax rates to ridiculous heights, especially toward the close, when prices had become excessively inflated. No significant changes were made in the structure of the tax system itself until a decade later. In 1865, Alabama's public debt stood at $16,439,732. Of this amount $13,094,732 had been added during the war.

In 1861, the Constitutional Convention in Mississippi, not only renounced that state's allegiance to the Union, but at the same time passed "an Ordinance to Raise Means for the Defense of the State." This ordinance provided for the collection from each taxpayer of an additional special levy of 50 per cent on the regular state tax, and also a tax upon "every inhabitant of $\frac{3}{10}$ per centum on all money owned or controlled by such inhabitant"; the money thus collected was to constitute a "military fund." Subsequently the rates of the existing taxes were raised higher and higher. Finally, in 1865, to provide for the families of soldiers, a direct tax in kind was imposed on the gross amount of corn produced in excess of 100 bushels; of wheat, in excess of 25 bushels; and of bacon, in excess of 100 pounds; and a similar tax was levied on the tolls from all grain mills, on the gross profit from leather, and on all woolen and cotton fabrics manufactured for sale.[10] Certain localities also were empowered to levy a similar tax. In 1861, the Mississippi Legislature authorized the issue of $1,000,000 in state treasury notes and $5,000,000 in cotton notes; by 1864, the state issued $16,301,581 in notes and bonds.

At the end of 1865, the total state debt of Louisiana amounted to $11,182, 377. About $7,000,000 in notes (fiat money) had been issued before the capture of New Orleans.

---

[10] *Mississippi Laws* (February and March 1865), pp. 3–10.

According to Professor E. T. Miller,[11] Texas, although she had entered the war practically out of debt, had incurred by October 30, 1865, a debt of $7,989,897. Of this amount, $981,140 was funded, $2,208,047 was in the form of state treasury notes and cotton certificates, $1,455,914 was due to soldiers' funds and war supplies, and the balance was miscellaneous. At the close of the war, the state had a money balance on hand of $3,368,510: of this amount only $15,397 was in specie; the remainder was state treasury notes.

By 1865, the expenses of the state government in Arkansas had fallen to about $150,000, while the state debt had increased to about $6,500,000, of which approximately $2,000,000 had been incurred on account of the war. In Tennessee, as in other Confederate States, tax levies were raised, and bonds and notes issued in increasing amounts.

Finally, it must be noted that even railroads were granted banking privileges in Florida, Georgia, and Mississippi, and in many regions of the South, other corporations, as well as private individuals, issued paper money. In Virginia, Florida, Alabama, Mississippi, Arkansas, and Louisiana, an effort was made to prevent individuals from issuing notes, but in the turmoil of war the law was easily violated. Everywhere, counterfeiting was carried on, and Northerners joined in the game, which became an easy practice since every man who could hire a printing press could copy the ordinary state or Confederate notes, and such counterfeits were generally received without challenge.

## Economic Demoralization

During the Civil War the South was demoralized both by the system of financing the war and by the military operations.

In 1860, the crops of the South had been good. The Southern banks had about 33 per cent of the banking capital of the Nation and held approximately 46 per cent

---

[11] THE SOUTH IN THE BUILDING OF THE NATION, Vol. V, p. 539.

of the specie. As a rule, banking in the South had become more conservative, especially in the case of the New Orleans banks, which now held about one third of the

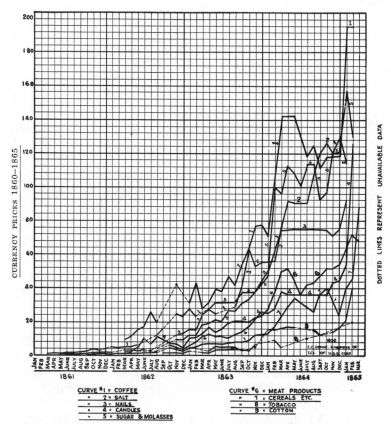

Currency Prices of Commodities in the Confederate States, 1861–1865. Figures from J. C. Schwab, *Confederate States of America, 1861–1865,* Appendix 1.

specie in the South. Upon the insistence of the Secretary of the Confederate Treasury, as well as through necessity, every bank within the territorial limits of the Confederacy soon suspended specie payments. In fact, the deluge of

fiat money issued by the Confederate Government, the
states, and individuals caused gold and silver coin to disappear, either by leaving the country entirely or by being
hoarded in secret places.

The Treasury notes (fiat money)—being mere promises
to pay a stipulated sum at the expiration of a specified
period, usually "after the ratification of a treaty of peace"
—fluctuated in value according to the quantity of their
issue and the fortunes of the Confederate Army. Of course,
other factors than this inconvertible paper, which constituted the larger part of the monetary mechanism of the
Confederacy, affected the general course of prices. There
were the effects of the curtailment of production on account
of the Northern invasions and seizures, the smuggling of
goods, and reckless speculation. Nevertheless, it is perhaps correct to say that the superabundant issues of fiat
money were mainly responsible for the extraordinary rise
in prices, which, along with the military destruction of life
and property, completely demoralized the economic life
of the South.

J. C. Schwab has prepared a partial table of costs of
articles of general consumption according to prices quoted
in Confederate currency from early in 1861 to February
1865.[12] The chart on page 419 shows the movement of
these prices. Articles increased in price at different rates,
because other factors than inflation entered into the equa-
tion. For example, substitutes could be had for sugar,
whereas coffee, being an import, had to run the blockade
at great risk.

Schwab's figures give only a general notion of the rising
prices toward the end of the war. At that time prices for
the same commodities varied widely between cities and
rural districts and between different regions. Moreover,
statistics alone can never measure the privations and hardships caused by the rapidly depreciating currency during

---

[12] *Confederate States of America, 1861–1865,* Appendix I.

the last bitter months of the war. In front of the hungry, footsore, shivering Confederate soldiers, there was death at the cannon's mouth; in the rear, there was starvation. In March 1863, flour sold for $25 a barrel; in January 1864, for $95 a barrel; and in January 1865, for $1,000 a barrel. As one writer has described the situation: [13] "Side by side with reports of battles and the records of peace commissions, congresses, and legislatures, the blurred columns of the Confederate press were wont to teem with domestic recipes for cheap dishes, directions for raising and utilizing various vegetable products, instructions for making much of little in matters pertaining to every phase of household life. Hard by a list of dead and wounded would stand a recipe for tanning dog-skins for gloves; while the paragraphs just succeeding the closing column of the description of a naval engagement off Hampton Roads were directions for the use of boneset as a substitute for quinine."

Even more impressive than a whole column of price statistics were news items like the one that appeared in Virginia newspapers early in January 1865 (*Richmond Dispatch, Richmond Whig,* and various others): "Thompson Taylor, Esq., who had charge of the cooking of the New Year's dinner for the soldiers of General Lee's army, sold the surplus grease from the meats cooked to one of the railroad companies for seven dollars per pound."

In those tragic days of scarcity and depreciated currency, all kinds of makeshifts had to be used in the diet of the South. Raspberry leaves and the roots of sassafras were used for tea. Beer, known as "possum toddy," was made of persimmons. Rye was used for coffee. Sorghum came to take the place of sugar. "Corn pone" took the place of wheat bread. Practically all the cattle and hogs in several localities were taken by Northern troops and recon-

---

[13] *Century Magazine* (September 1888), Vol. XIV, p. 764. A. C. Gordon's article, entitled "Hardtimes in the Confederacy."

noitering parties, as well as by local thieves. Bacon and beefsteak became a luxury in Southern homes.

In August 1864, a private citizen's coat and vest, made of five yards of coarse homespun cloth, cost $230, exclusive of the charge for making them—the tailor's price for his services being $50. In January 1865, the material in a woman's dress which before the war would have cost $10 at that time cost $500.

In February 1864, it was announced officially that two hundred soldiers of the Stonewall Brigade were without shoes. Because of the scarcity of leather, shoes were made with wooden bottoms. Everywhere, as in colonial days, household industries were put in operation to help supply the needs of the Army, the families, and the slaves.

In addition to all the hardships caused by depreciated currency, the civilian population also suffered desperately on account of the pillage and wanton destruction of personal property by Northern troops. No statistics could be kept of such losses. The following quotations, however, taken from a diary kept by James Oliver Sessions, an aged planter in Mississippi, give a glimpse of the ruthless exploitation of civilians: [14] "July 13, 1863: Today the Federal boats some 12 or 15 in number came up the river, for the purpose as I suppose of attacking Yazoo City. There was but one gun boat amongst them. They proceeded on up the river and about ½ past 2 in the afternoon firing commenced and continued about ½ hour; whether there was a fight or not I don't know. Later in the afternoon some of the boats came down and landed here, and crowds of men came to the yard and destroyed all our chickens, vegetables, meat, milk, butter, bee hives, etc., both at the house and in the quarters. They did not come into the house, however, and nothing was taken from it. The day has been a dark drizzly one but there has

---

[14] This diary is now in the possession of Hardaman Meade, Birmingham, Alabama.

been no hard rains. The sick are doing pretty well but the number of them is increasing.

"July 14, 1863: This morning I find that 4 of the negroes, viz. Tom, Jasper, Joe Butter and Josiah are missing. The two Joes went in the boats. Tom and Jasper with the land forces. No work today. The stock, what is left is in the field and of course the crop will be destroyed. God's will be done. I have not been able to attend to the sick but believe all are doing as well as could be expected.

"July 21st, 1863: The Yankee boats went down the river and took off about 2,500 or 3,000 negroes as was supposed. Fifteen (15) of mine, besides the 2 who left on Monday."

A few days later he wrote: "4 Boats came up again the first week in August and left on Tuesday the 11th taking off this time Tom and Horace both prime hands. Thus making 19 (negroes) I have lost besides Cotton who is with the Confederate army I suppose. All of them with the exception of 4 children valuable hands. From the time they first came viz. the 21st of July until the present [August 23d] no work of consequence has been done on the place, and there is not much prospect that any will be done soon. Those who are left consider themselves free and work or not as they think proper."

### Bibliographical Note

E. C. Smith, *Borderland in the Civil War* (New York, 1927), is an excellent discussion of the influence of the border states on the conduct and outcome of the Civil War. J. R. Robertson, "Sectionalism in Kentucky, 1855–1865," in the *Mississippi Valley Historical Review*, June 1917, pages 46–63, touches some important aspects of that state's economic importance in the struggle.

The standard treatment of the financial history of the Confederacy is J. C. Schwab, *Confederate States of America, 1861–1865: A Financial and Industrial History of the South during the Civil War* (New York, 1901). A more detailed account of the Confederate Treasury may be found in E. A. Smith, *History of the Confederate Treasury* (Richmond, 1901). *Life and Times of C. G. Memminger*, by H. D. Capers (Richmond, 1894), contains some enlightening facts, but there is need for a new appraisal of Memminger's suggested methods for financing the Confederacy.

By far the best treatment of the Confederacy's reliance for help upon Europe is F. L. Owsley, *King Cotton Diplomacy* (Chicago, 1931). Other works dealing somewhat differently with the same subject are: Jordan and Pratt, *Europe and the American Civil War* (New York, 1931); A. B. Scherer, *Cotton as a World Power, a Study in the Economic Interpretation of History* (New York, 1916); and Francis B. C. Brandlee, *Blockade Running During the Civil War and the Effect of Land and Water Transportation on the Confederacy* (Salem, Mass., 1925).

Dealing with the conduct of the war in different Southern States are: W. L. Fleming, *Civil War and Reconstruction in Alabama* (New York, 1905); E. M. Coulter, *Civil War and Reconstruction in Kentucky* (Chapel Hill, N. C., 1926); and W. W. Davis, *Civil War and Readjustment in Florida* (New York, 1913).

# CHAPTER XV

# The Aftermath

THE Civil War uprooted the economic life of the South and, for nearly two decades, left it helpless in the hands of unscrupulous politicians. Even the very thoughts and purposes of the people were changed. As Woodrow Wilson truly said of the entire Nation:[1] "An old age had passed away, a new age had come in, with the sweep of that stupendous storm."

## The South's Economic Losses During the Civil War

When the Civil War was over, land and personal property throughout the South had greatly declined in taxable value.

Virginia—the strategic battleground of the war—had been continually invaded, and great areas of her territory had actually been devastated. In the eastern part of the state, a whole series of battles had been fought and agriculture had been completely disrupted. In the Shenandoah Valley, "the granary of the Confederacy," the Northern troops had destroyed homes, barns, fences, agricultural implements, cattle, horses, and grain. As described in the eloquent language of a contemporary of that time, at the close of the war, "large quantities of the state's most productive lands were lying waste and uncultivated; for fortifications and graves of soldiers marked the place where fences and forests had stood."[2] During the decade from 1860 to 1870, the total assessed valuation of all property subject to ad valorem taxation in the state had decreased

---

[1] Woodrow Wilson, *History of the American People,* Vol. VI, p. 265.
[2] Charles W. Williams, *Present Financial Status of Virginia* (1877), p. 2.

from \$657,021,336 to \$292,351,934, or from a per capita assessment of \$411 to only \$238.

In South Carolina, Columbia was looted and burned. Charleston was in ruins; as estimated by Sidney Andrews, \$5,000,000 would not have restored that city. In describing the general devastation in South Carolina, Andrews added: [3] "It would seem that it is not clearly understood how thoroughly Sherman's Army destroyed everything in its line of march—destroyed it without questioning who suffered by the action. . . . The values and the bases of values were nearly all destroyed. Many lost about everything but honor. The cotton with which they meant to pay their debts has been burned, and they are without other means."

General Sherman said: "I estimate the damage done to the state of Georgia and its military resources at \$100,-000,000, at least \$20,000,000 of which has inured to our advantage and the remainder is simply waste and destruction."

Not only had Alabama lost more than 25,000 men, which was about 20 per cent of her white male population, but thousands of helpless women and children were left without means of livelihood in the midst of a paralyzing wreckage. In 1860, the estimated true value of all property in Alabama had been \$725,000,000; in 1866, it was only \$123,-000,000.

In Arkansas, homes were without furniture. Fencing had been destroyed, fields laid waste, and livestock taken away. The state was a general picture of utter impoverishment.

Nor were conditions much different elsewhere in the South, as indicated by the following statistics: [4]

---

[3] Sidney Andrews, *The South Since the War*, p. 11.

[4] Compiled from William A. Scott, *Repudiation of State Debts*, Appendix IIB.

ASSESSED VALUATION OF PROPERTY

| State | 1860 | 1870 | Per Cent of Decrease |
|-------|------|------|----------------------|
| North Carolina....... | $292,297,602 | $130,378,190 | 55.4 |
| Florida.............. | 68,929,685 | 32,480,843 | 52.9 |
| Mississippi.......... | 509,472,917 | 177,278,890 | 65.5 |
| Louisiana............ | 435,787,265 | 253,371,890 | 41.9 |
| Tennessee............ | 382,495,200 | 253,782,161 | 33.7 |

Investments in internal improvement companies had become almost, if not entirely, worthless.

In Virginia, the great system of public works, once the pride of the state, was in utter ruin. The canal "lay a great gash across the heart of the Commonwealth," and the railroads had become "mere streaks of rust." Not only had their bridges in many instances been destroyed by Federal troops, but not even had the worn-out rolling stock been replaced. The property of the Manassas Gap Railroad Company had been entirely wrecked, and its rails and rolling stock removed for use in other parts of the state where they could better facilitate the movement of troops and war supplies. The road of the Roanoke Valley Railroad Company was entirely dismantled; the rails and rolling stock were confiscated by the Confederate Government and turned over to the Richmond & Danville Railroad Company. During the last months of the war, the Richmond & Petersburg Railroad was in the zone of terrific fighting. "When the Confederate Army abandoned Richmond on April 3, 1865, it burned the long bridge over the James River and the depot at Richmond. The treasurer of the railroad company was wounded in an attempt to secure the books and records, all of which were consequently burned with the depot and workshops, though the sheds and most of the rolling stock were saved. The purely physical loss was estimated at $254,318, nearly a third of the capitalization of the road." [5] No railroads in

---

[5] H. D. Dozier, *History of the Atlantic Coast Line Railroad* (1920), p. 103. Reprinted by permission of the Houghton Mifflin Company, New York.

Virginia, except those about Lynchburg, escaped tremendous losses.

In North Carolina, the eastern railroads were practically worthless. Of the 281 miles of track owned by the Central of Georgia Company—the line extending between Savannah and Macon, and with branches to Augusta and Eatonton—Sherman's army destroyed 136 miles of the main line, including bridges and depots. In many places Sherman's troops piled up the crossties, threw the rails on top of them, and then set fire to the heap so that the heat would twist the rails out of shape for further use.[6] In South Carolina, the railroads in the central part of the state were in ruins. In Alabama, slightly less damage had been done, particularly to the rolling stock. In Florida, Mississippi, and Louisiana, what few miles of railroads had been built before the war were now practically worthless. In Tennessee, few lines—except the railroad between Knoxville and Chattanooga—escaped complete destruction. A Northern historian has said that probably upon no complete road in the South did the iron rest intact during the war.[7] Often, for scores of miles the crossties had been torn up and used for fuel. In several places the roadbeds—as for example, that of the Memphis & Little Rock—had been washed out by floods. Hundreds of depots had been burned, and rolling stock destroyed, worn out, or lost. According to an incomplete report made by Colonel S. R. Hamil, on September 30, 1867, the estimated loss of twenty-one railroads in the South, not including those that suffered most, was $28,187,404.[8] No doubt a complete estimate would have shown that the South had lost during the war two thirds of the railroads that she had in 1861.

The South's entire banking capital, including that circulated by the banks, had practically passed out of existence as money.

---

[6] See J. F. Rhodes, *United States*, Vol. V, pp. 21 and 87.

[7] *Ibid.*, p. 87.

[8] *Ex. Doc. 73*, 40th Cong., 2d sess., p. 56.

Enormously significant as were all the other losses, the effects of the abolition of slavery were more immediately disastrous, for they meant, not only the loss of taxable property, the slaves themselves, and the disarrangement of the system of labor based upon slavery, but in many instances the breaking up of the great estates.

The negroes, as a rule, desired to test the reality of freedom by roving about enjoying new amusements and leisure. Attracted by the *Freedmen's Bureau*, large numbers of them flocked to towns. Nor did the negroes who remained on the plantations after 1865 take kindly to white supervision. They objected to overseers, drivers, and plantation bells as remnants of slavery. Cotton fields were planted and then neglected in cultivation; or the crop was left unpicked in the field, for lack of laborers.

In 1866, the cotton crop actually picked was less than a million bales, and not until 1879, did the South produce a crop so large as that in 1860. Immediately after the war, planters borrowed what capital they could and tried out hired labor; but in spite of the high prices of cotton,[9] its cultivation on large plantations was unprofitable, because of the debts that had to be incurred, the heavy burden of taxation under *"carpetbag"* rule, and the lack of a dependable supply of labor.

In the decade 1860–1870, the total value of farm property in the ex-Confederate States declined 48 per cent, and plantations which had sold for $150,000 fell in value to $10,000. At nearly every county seat, mortgage sales were monthly events throughout almost the entire reconstruction period. In Virginia, large planters sold off pieces

[9] The table below lists some of the cotton prices:

AVERAGE NEW YORK PRICE OF COTTON

| Year | Maximum in Cents per lb. | Minimum in Cents per lb. |
|------|--------------------------|--------------------------|
| 1866 | 43.20 | 23.98 |
| 1872 | 20.48 | 15.00 |
| 1876 | 13.00 | 10.38 |

of their estates and mortgaged the balance at high rates of interest until, by the end of the reconstruction era, they had begun to repair the losses from war and to equip their remaining acreage with improved implements. By this process the number of farms increased to 44,668, an increase of 60 per cent. In Mississippi in 1865, there were only 412 farms of less than 10,000 acres, but three years later, there were 10,003. In the ex-Confederate States from 1860 to 1870, the number of farms of less than 100 acres increased 55 per cent, and the average size of farms fell from 401.7 acres to 229.8 acres.

Mainly by means of promissory notes, many poor whites and, in a few instances, some ex-slaves, got possession of the pieces of land that were either sold by the large planters or foreclosed to satisfy mortgages, and established themselves as *independent farmers*.

In the Cotton Belt the most difficult problem confronting the planters was how to utilize ex-slaves. White labor was not available, for the surplus was moving west to take up lands under the terms of the Homestead Act of 1862, and the "carpetbaggers," who swarmed down from the North, were not interested in working in the cotton fields. Planters tried to induce foreign immigrants to come to the cotton region. Georgia, South Carolina, and Alabama established labor bureaus and advertised for foreign immigrants; but these efforts all proved futile because the foreign immigrant preferred the opportunity to acquire land elsewhere in the United States, and did not relish competition with black labor. The planters, believing that freed negroes might work better for Northern men, then tried the experiment of employing Northern managers. This plan failed utterly, because such managers were quite unfamiliar with negro habits. In the end the cotton planters were forced to work out a new system for utilizing what resources they had; namely, plantations equipped with worn-out implements, and worked by freed negroes.

The statement that the Civil War completely crushed

the South is a mere platitude, because neither words nor statistics can truly describe the total economic and other losses of the war. The plantation system was uprooted, the banking system was ruined, the transportation system had been practically destroyed, the slaves were freed and indoctrinated with a propaganda of hate for their former masters, and the sorrow of death, like a pall, hung over nearly every home.

Even today, one is struck by the simple but crushing report adopted by the Virginia House of Delegates in 1877. This report estimated in terms of money all the losses to that state during the war and the reconstruction period. They were as follows: [10] Personal property, $116,000,000; realty, $121,000,000; internal improvements, $26,000,000; banking capital, $15,000,000; circulation, $12,000,000; state's interest in banks, $4,000,000; and slaves and other property, $163,000,000. Viewed as a whole, Virginia's property losses amounted to $457,000,000.

## Reconstruction

As soon as the war was over, a horde of demagogues, self-seekers, and unscrupulous politicians, as well as honest Northerners, swept down upon the South and, backed by the authority of the Federal Government, attempted to "reconstruct" the section. Unmindful of all economic losses and actual conditions, and rallying to themselves the negroes and the "mud-sills of society" in general, they proceeded to set up new political machinery in the defeated states and to incur as fast as possible state debts for the purpose of reckless expenditures.

The political aspects of this reconstruction period are familiar to most readers, and need be reiterated here only in outline to form a background for the economic study.

Lincoln, according to the plan for reconstruction embodied in his Proclamation of 1863, proposed to recognize

---

[10] *House Journal*, January 13, 1877.

any Southern State in which 10 per cent of the voters of 1860 organized as a political group and took an oath of allegiance to the Union. At Lincoln's death, Johnson became President and undertook to carry out this plan with slight modifications. He met with complete failure, because of his conflict with a radical Republican Congress.

In 1867, the Congressional plan of reconstruction was adopted over the President's veto. In January of the same year, unconditional negro suffrage was imposed on all the ex-Confederate States except Tennessee, which had been readmitted in 1866 under the Fourteenth Amendment. The Reconstruction Act declared that no legal government existed in the South, and divided the entire section into five military districts. Martial law was to be enforced in each district, but any Southern State might set up a constitutional civil government whenever it was willing to grant to the negroes full suffrage and completely to disfranchise the citizens who had participated in the "rebellion." In the same year, Ohio rejected, by over 50,000 votes, the proposition to give negroes suffrage in that state.

When the Southern States indicated that they preferred martial law to negro government, Congress, in March of 1867, passed another act directing the military authorities to register as voters the negroes in the South but to exclude the leading white inhabitants. Elections were then to be held for delegates to a Constitutional Convention, which was to frame amendments to the Federal Constitution that, in turn, were to be submitted for ratification to the same list of voters, for every person who had held any civil office under the Confederacy or had been in the Confederate Army was disfranchised. The negroes were organized into secret political societies known as *Union Leagues,* in which they were indoctrinated with the propaganda that their former masters were their worst enemies and would re-enslave them at the first opportunity.

Between 1867 and 1870, the "carpetbag," Southern "scalawag," and negro domination of the South was nearly

absolute. Generally, new state constitutions were adopted
mainly with the support of negro votes, because many of
the whites were disfranchised. By the same method, negroes were elected to the legislatures and thieves made
themselves governors.

In Virginia, a new constitution was adopted in 1867, and,
as C. C. Pearsons says, "had these Radicals been allowed
to carry out the terms of this constitution, rampant democracy would unquestionably have had full play for years to
come, and one can only conjecture the extremes to which
it would have gone." [11] Notwithstanding the gradual check
against this movement by the conservatives, the results
were extremely damaging to the entire fiscal system of the
state. In 1870, the legislature had 27 negroes as senators
and representatives.[12] Practically all the others were
"carpetbaggers."

As summarized by John Skelton Williams, the situation
was as follows: [13] "After the fighting there came upon us
from the North some misty and honest dreamers, some
sincere fanatics, many camp followers, plunderers, and adventurers, villainously intent on the robbery of a rich land
and a helpless and crushed people, with legislatures composed of cornfield Negroes and controlled by the scum of
the armies and the bright criminals of many Northern
communities. The ghosts and shadows and suggestions of
railroads of the Southern States were used as means for
robbery under forms of law. State bonds for railroad extension and development were issued recklessly by millions
and sold for what they would bring, and the proceeds were
audaciously stolen, without even pretenses of use for the
purposes for which they were alleged to be intended."

In North Carolina, political events followed a similar

[11] C. C. Pearsons, *Readjuster Movement in Virginia*, p. 19.

[12] *Richmond Dispatch, Richmond Whig, Richmond Enquirer,* October
5–12, 1869.

[13] "Railroad Progress in the South." Speech delivered at a dinner given
by the Harvard alumni at Richmond, 1909.

course. In 1868, a new constitution was adopted, and in the legislature which first met under this document, 19 of the Republican members were negroes.

In South Carolina, the legislature for the session 1868–1872 was comprised mainly of negroes and poor whites. Only 22 of the entire legislature of 155 could read and write. Several members could write only their names; 41, moreover, had to sign by making an "X" mark. There were 98 negro members. Of these, one paid $83 in taxes, 30 together paid only $60, and 67 paid none. Of the 57 white members, 33 together paid only $491 in taxes, and the rest paid none.[14]

In 1868, a new constitution was ratified in Georgia, and Atlanta was selected as the capital of the state. In the same year, 28 negroes were elected to the legislature. Similarly in Alabama, a new constitution was adopted, negroes were made members of the legislature, and William H. Smith, a Confederate deserter, was elected governor. In Mississippi, the legislature of 1870 was made up of "carpetbaggers" and 35 negroes, 5 in the senate and 30 in the house. A negro was made secretary of state, and one was elected Senator of the United States.

In 1868, a new constitution was established in Louisiana. Henry Clay Warmoth, a native of Illinois, who had been dismissed from the Union Army by Grant, and who, having gone to Texas in 1865, had been indicted there for the embezzlement of Government cotton, was made governor. Oscar J. Dunn, a negro, was elected lieutenant governor. In his recently written, attempted vindication of many of his official acts, Warmoth points out that the legislature elected in 1868 had "six colored men in the Senate out of its thirty-six members; and though the House of Representatives had more colored men in it than did the Senate

---

[14] For a group picture of this legislature, see Walter L. Fleming, *Documentary History of Reconstruction*, Vol. I, Frontispiece.

they never constituted more than one-third of the membership." [15]

The "carpetbaggers" declared that they intended to "squeeze Arkansas as dry as a sucked orange," and proceeded to do so by the same methods used by "carpetbaggers" elsewhere in the South. Although Florida and Texas experienced many difficulties in reconstruction, they were not so ruthlessly exploited. In 1866, Tennessee without delay ratified the Fourteenth Amendment of the Federal Constitution. By doing this, she obtained representation in Congress, and escaped the worst evils of "carpetbag" rule.

In its entirety the so-called "reconstruction of the South" was, as John W. Burgess has truly said, "the most soul-sickening spectacle that Americans had ever been called upon to behold. Every principle of the old American polity was here reversed. In place of government by the most intelligent and virtuous part of the people for the benefit of the governed, here was government by the most ignorant and vicious part of the population for the benefit, the vulgar, materialistic, brutal benefit of the governing set." [16]

Under this vicious political regime, debts and tax levies were piled upon the Southern people.

The dominating political machine in Virginia made a desperate effort to shift the tax burden upon the large land-owners in order to break up the plantations which had fostered slavery. In 1868, Tianiah, a negro, introduced a bill in the legislature instructing the committee on finance and taxation to incorporate in the report a provision that no land should be assessed for taxation at a rate less than $2 per acre.[17] By 1871, realty was paying 59 per cent of the

[15] Henry Clay Warmoth, *War, Politics and Reconstruction,* p. xii of Introduction.

[16] John W. Burgess, *Reconstruction and the Constitution, 1866–1876* (1902), pp. 263–264. Reprinted by permission of Charles Scribner's Sons, New York.

[17] *Richmond Dispatch,* January 13, 1868.

total taxes of the state, and in 1872, the *Richmond Whig Daily* alleged that real property of the state was assessed at least three or four times its market value. On the other hand, the negroes, though they had been granted suffrage, would seldom pay poll taxes.

The situation was described by Sheriff W. H. Custis, of Hampton, in the following letter written to the governor in 1867:[18] "In reply to an order of the Court of the County of Elizabeth City (concerning which I wrote you some time since) about the Freedmen not paying the revenue, you desired me if I was resisted in the performance of my duty to call on you for assistance. I have been resisted and my life threatened, and it is impossible for me to collect it unless I get aid either from the state or military authorities. I have applied to General Scofield through the Freedmen's Bureau, as well as General Burten at the Fort, but neither of them will assist me. The auditor tells me that the Revenue must be collected, but it is quite an impossibility. A short time since one Matthew Ashby (colored) openly resisted and assaulted me when I asked of him his taxes and I was powerless.

"There are between 8,000 and 12,000 negroes in this county and many of them armed. I must have a military guard before I can perform my duties, and I ask you that you will take steps to procure it for me."

In 1871, the question of settling the Virginia state debt, which, with accrued interest, amounted to $45,660,348, was considered. One third was assigned to West Virginia, and the remainder was funded into new bonds bearing interest at 5 and 6 per cent. The coupons were made receivable for taxes; and temporarily, disastrous effects upon the tax system followed.

In North Carolina within four months after the "carpetbag" government became operative, bond issues were au-

---

[18] *Calendar of Virginia State Papers*, Vol. II, p. 497.

thorized to the extent of $25,350,000. Of this amount about $12,000,000 in bonds were actually issued, but the bonds were gambled away and the interest was never paid. Although the purpose of the issue was to aid railroads within the state, not a mile of railroad was built with the proceeds. Taxes became confiscatory, and by 1870, land had fallen over 50 per cent in value as compared with the preceding decade. By the end of the "carpetbag" regime, the state debt of North Carolina had been increased from about $16,000,000 to $42,000,000.

In 1867, the bonded debt of South Carolina was $5,800,-000; five years later, it was approximately $24,000,000, while current debts were so numerous that they were not even estimated in the aggregate. This situation was the result of some of the most reckless expenditures by state officials in the history of American public finance. The state house was refurnished; $5 clocks were replaced by some costing $600; $4 looking-glasses, by $600 mirrors; $2 window curtains, by curtains costing from $600 to $1,500; $4 benches, by $200 sofas; $1 chairs, by $60 chairs; 40 cent spittoons, by $14 cuspidors; and each legislator was provided with a $25 *Webster's Unabridged Dictionary* and a $10 gold pen. (Compare with literacy statistics on page 434 of text.) Forty bedrooms were furnished, and each legislator was permitted at the end of the session to take home all his furnishings. F. J. Moses, Jr., speaker of the house, lost $1,000 on a horse race; and the next day, the house voted him $1,000 as a "gratuity."

Bills incurred by officials and legislators and paid by the state reveal a queer medley of legislative expenditures! In 1873, "Mr. J. Woodruff for the Senate" bought of George Symmers the following: [19]

---

[19] *Report on Public Frauds in South Carolina, 1868–1873* (Columbia, S. C., 1868), p. 7. Part of this official document is reprinted in Walter L. Fleming, *Documentary History of Reconstruction*, Vol. II, pp. 65–68.

Jan. 29   1 gallon whiskey, $7  
          1 case Champagne, $45...................$ 52.00  
Jan. 29   Cheese, $3.50  
          4 dozen quarts lager, $7—$28............ 31.50  
Jan. 30   1 box cigars, $10  
          1 case wine, $45........................ 55.00  
Jan. 31   4 dozen Bass ale, $3.50—$14.00  
          Matches, 50¢.......................... 14.50  
Feb. 1   6 boxes cigars, $10—$60.00  
          Cheese, $1.25; crackers, $1.25............. 62.50  
Feb. 1   1 dozen ale, $3.50  
          1 dozen porter, $3.50  
          1 jar ginger, $3.00 (Green)................ 10.00  
Feb. 1   ½ gallon c. whiskey, $1.50  
          1 bottle wine, $2.00...................... 3.50  
Feb. 1   3 bottles wine, $6.00  
          1 box cigars, $9.00 (Robertson)........... 15.00  
Feb. 4   4 dozen ale, $3.50—$14.00  
          1 gallon c. whiskey, $3.00................ 17.00  
Feb. 4   Matches, 40¢  
          1 gallon c. whiskey, $3.00................ 3.40  
Feb. 5   1 pineapple cheese, $2.50  
          5 pounds crackers, $1.25................. 3.75  
Feb. 5   3 boxes cigars, $10.00—$30.00  
          6 one-gallon whiskey, $7.00.............. 37.00  
Feb. 5   1 pineapple cheese, $2.50  
          6 boxes sardines, $1.80.................. 4.30  
Feb. 5   2 boxes cigars, $10.00.................... 20.00  
Feb. 7   Bill of merchandise to December........... 284.29  
Feb. 7   1 gallon whiskey, $7.00  
          1 gallon c. whiskey, $3.00  
          1 cheese, $2.50......................... 12.50  
Feb. 7   2 bottles champagne..................... 7.00  
Feb. 8   1 box 6 pounds candles, $2.40  
          1 gallon c. whiskey, $3.00................ 5.40  
Feb. 8   1 cheese, $1.75  
          5 pounds crackers, $1.25................. 3.00  
Feb. 8   1 box cigars, $10.00  
          3 doz. ale, $3.50—$10.50................. 20.50  
Feb. 10   3 gallons whiskey, $7.00—$21.00  
          2 gallons sherry, $14.00.................. 35.00  
Feb. 10   2 boxes cigars, $20.00  
          1 gallon whiskey, $7.00.................. 27.00  
Feb. 11   1 gallon whiskey, $7.00  
          6 pounds cheese, $1.63  
          crackers, $1.25.......................... 9.88  
Feb. 11   2 dozen porter, $7.00  
          3 bottles Maraschino, $4.00—$12.00  
          (Robertson).......................... 19.00

| Feb. 11 | 3 bottles curaçao, $12.00 | |
| | 1 case champagne, $45.00 (Robertson)......$ | 57.00 |
| Feb. 12 | 1 gallon whiskey, $7.00 | |
| | 1 dozen boxes matches, 40¢.............. | 7.40 |
| Feb. 12 | 1 cask, 8 dozen porter, $3.50 (Lee)......... | 28.00 |
| Feb. 13 | 1 gallon c. whiskey, $3.00 | |
| | 10 pounds of crackers, 25¢—$2.50.......... | 5.50 |
| Feb. 13 | 6 boxes sardines, $1.80 | |
| | 6 pounds cheese, 25¢—$1.50.............. | 3.30 |
| Feb. 13 | 3 pounds Schwitzer cheese, 40¢—$1.20 | |
| | 14 one-gallon whiskey, $7.00.............. | 8.20 |
| | | $862.42 |

This account was paid by the state treasurer.

Other accounts paid out of the state treasury show the purchase of hams, oysters, rice, flour, lard, coffee, tea, sugar, linen-bosomed shirts, suspenders, cravats, palpitators, embroidered ginghams, silks, stockings, chemises, garters, gowns, diamond rings and earrings, gold watches and chains, valises, combs, brushes, blankets, towels, a baby's swinging cradle, and even a metallic coffin.

Not only was ostentatious consumption carried on by the members of the legislature at the expense of the state, but large sums were actually stolen. To satisfy the negroes, who were clamoring for their promised "forty acres and a mule," the legislature appropriated $700,000 with which to buy land; only about $50,000 was ever expended for that purpose and the rest went into the pockets of the "inner ring." To redeem $500,000 in bank notes, the legislature appropriated $1,250,000, and the securities belonging to the educational fund were sold.

At the end of the fiscal year 1866, Georgia had a bonded debt, including accrued interest, of only $828,802; by 1871, however, the debt had been increased to nearly $18,000,000. Of this amount $6,923,400 was incurred through a reckless endorsement of railroad bonds.

Even Florida suffered from the increased burdens of taxation and indebtedness. State bonds during the "carpetbag" regime were authorized to the amount of $1,850,000, and the state expenditures were more than doubled.

In Alabama, the exploitation was appalling. Under the confiscation laws of the Federal Government, as disclosed by a Federal Grand Jury at Mobile in 1865, Federal agents had stolen for themselves 125,000 bales of cotton in the state. Aside from the actual theft of the cotton, the Federal Government imposed a cotton tax of 2½ cents per pound in 1865; 3 cents per pound in 1866; and 2½ cents per pound in 1867. The total tax thus collected on cotton before it left the state was $10,388,072. Like other Southern States, Alabama was compelled to incur a deficit annually during the "carpetbag" government. For the fiscal year of 1866, the total state receipts were only $62,967, whereas the total disbursements were $606,494. In 1867, while her income increased to $691,048, her disbursements rose to $819,434. An added difficulty was the rapidly growing state debt, which, by 1866, exclusive of the educational and university fund, amounted to $4,550,862. Nevertheless, in 1867, the legislature passed an act which authorized the state to indorse railroad bonds to the amount of $12,000 per mile, and in 1868, the indorsement was raised to $16,000 per mile. The railroad companies of the state forthwith increased their bonded indebtedness. By 1873, the state had indorsed over $10,000,000 in these bonds. No sooner had this occurred than the railroad companies defaulted, and left the state responsible for the interest on the whole debt. By 1874, the state debt stood at $30,037,564, which, together with some $12,000,000 in city and county debts, amounted to about 65 per cent of the value of all the farm land in the state. In 1873, the legislature passed an act increasing the rate of taxation 50 per cent. It must not be overlooked that all these enormous increases in tax rates took place during a period of rapidly declining property values, and consequently the tax yielded in reality a smaller amount proportionately than that acquired under the lower rates levied upon higher property valuations.

In Mississippi, the total state receipts for 1870 were only

$436,000, but the total expenditures were $1,061,294—more than half of which consisted of the expenses of the legislative session during that year. By the end of the reconstruction period, the state debt had been more than doubled and reached a total of $3,197,036. In this state, as in others, the main burden thrown upon the people was increased taxes. The state and local rates at one time ran as high as $1.85 on each $100 of assessed valuation of land and personalty. In 1875, about 19,600,000 acres of land were assessed to owners at $82,000,000; and about 3,700,-000 acres, at an assessed value of approximately $12,000,-000, were held for delinquent taxes. In other words, about one fifth of the taxable area of the state had to be forfeited for delinquent taxes.

The state debt of Louisiana, on December 1, 1865, was $11,182,377; by the end of 1870, it amounted to $22,-589,628. Since, as in Alabama, railroad bonds were endorsed by the state, by January 1, 1872, the total actual and contingent debt of Louisiana had reached $41,194,474. In addition, a local debt of about $30,000,000 had been incurred. The cost of the four years and five months of the "carpetbagger" Warmoth's administration as governor of Louisiana was as follows:

| | |
|---|---:|
| Money actually expended by the state | $26,394,572 |
| By local bodies (conservatively estimated) | 25,300,000 |
| Increase in debt (state and local) | 54,000,000 |
| TOTAL | $105,694,572 |

At the end of Warmoth's governorship, there was practically nothing to show for these extravagant expenditures, except corruption. Even Warmoth denounced the legislature for bribery and said that he himself had been offered $50,000 to sign a bill. In 1871, the expenses of the senate were $191,763 and of the house, $767,192, or an average of $113 a day for each member of the legislature.

In comparison with the other Confederate States, Texas suffered little during the reconstruction period. Although expenditures were increased beyond the state's ability to pay, they were increased through extravagance rather than corruption. Slight changes were made in the tax rates, but Texas escaped from this period with a funded debt of only $643,800 and a floating debt of $1,455,148. The railroads had been granted land instead of a bond subsidy.

In Arkansas, the reconstruction government plunged the state in debt to the extent of $17,260,362. Property was assessed nearly 50 per cent above its cash value in 1868, and the total tax rate, local and state, was equivalent to about 8 per cent.

By the end of the reconstruction period, Tennessee had a debt, including accrued interest, of nearly $42,000,000. This debt consisted of the state debt proper, amounting to $3,844,000; the Brownlow debts, which were created by this ecclesiastic who had gone into politics as a reconstructionist, and which amounted to $20,363,406; and the "state aid" debt, which comprised the remainder and which was incurred mainly in aid of railroads. When the state finally enforced the liens against the railroads, it lost $13,804,000 of the debt.

As already stated, practically every Southern State had before the Civil War a bonded debt ranging from $1,000,000 to over $20,000,000. During the war, eleven of these states, together with the Confederate Government, had incurred a tremendous debt. This war debt of the South was declared "null and void" by the Federal Government, and the holders of these bonds suffered the total loss. In spite of this fact, during the reconstruction period, the state debts of the eleven ex-Confederate States were increased, if conservatively estimated, by a total of $131,000,000. Most of the funds represented by this debt were either extravagantly wasted or stolen.

### Overthrow of Carpetbag and Negro Domination

Several factors contributed mightily to the final overthrow of the carpetbag and negro domination of the South:

the Ku Klux Klan; the panic of 1873; and a more intelligent attitude on the part of the North, as evidenced by the Liberal Republican Revolt of 1872, and the passage of the General Amnesty Act.

## ORGANIZATIONS

Although most of the ex-slaves remained quiet, "carpetbaggers" and ambitious Southern "scalawags," encouraged by some Northern leaders, undertook to arouse the negroes against the planter class. One method was the formation of organizations called *Union Leagues,* which were societies composed mainly of negroes who became members by taking an oath that they would support the new political order. Members of these organizations resorted to a certain amount of violence toward their old masters; sometimes they burned houses and barns, stole personal property, and even waylaid Southern white men. An effective method was soon found for counteracting the organizations.

The Ku Klux Klan was a secret order founded at Pulaski, Tennessee, in 1866. The organization may originally have been formed for the purpose of amusement, but soon it became evident that the grotesque and mysterious ceremonies could be used effectively as a means of social control over the credulous and ignorant negroes who had been influenced against their former masters by designing "carpetbaggers" and "scalawags." Consequently, the order soon spread over the entire South, the total membership being over 500,000.[20] It became an "invisible government" to rid the South of "carpetbag" and negro misrule. According to its constitution, the objects of this order were:

"*First:* To protect the weak, the innocent, and the defenseless, from the indignities, wrongs, and outrages of the

---

[20] Northerners applied the term *Ku Klux Klan* to all secret movements of terrorism in the South. In reality, however, there were several underground organizations—such as the *White Camelia,* the *Pale Faces,* and the *White Brotherhood*—which differed slightly from one another in details of organization and method of carrying out their common purpose.

lawless, the violent, and the brutal; to relieve the injured and oppressed; to succor the suffering and unfortunate and especially the widows and orphans of Confederate soldiers.

"*Second:* To protect and defend the Constitution of the United States and all laws passed in conformity thereto, and to protect the states and the people thereof from all invasion from any source whatever.

"*Third:* To aid and assist in the execution of all constitutional laws, and to protect the people from unlawful seizure and from trial except by their peers in conformity to the laws of the land." [21]

It is interesting to note the methods used by this organization. "A few nights ago," says a writer in the *Planter's Banner,* "a K.K.K. alighted in front of a cabin and gave four raps on the door. The colored head of the family made his appearance.

" 'Any carpetbaggers in this neighborhood?' said the frowning ghost.

" 'No, Sah,' said the negro.

" 'Any yellow tickets in this cabin?'

" 'No, Sah,' was the reply.

"Taking off his head, and handing it to the colored gentleman, the ghost said: 'Please hold my head while I tighten this cork leg; I lost one leg when I was killed at Shiloh.'

"The negro fainted and has not yet come to his senses." [22]

The most familiar method used on the "carpetbagger" was "tarring and feathering." That is to say, a group of Klansmen would capture a "carpetbagger," strip him of his clothes, cover him with a coat of tar, and then sprinkle feathers over his body. This treatment usually was sufficient to rid the community of his presence. If not, other violence was imposed. In 1869, the Klan was dissolved by order of General Nathan B. Forrest, its Imperial Wizard; and thereafter many of the local "Dens," having lost their

[21] See original *Constitution of the Ku Klux Klan,* p. 3.
[22] *Planter's Banner,* May 23, 1868.

conservative members, degenerated into turbulent groups for the purpose of loot or personal vengeance. However, the Klan, while in the hands of responsible leaders, was a powerful disintegrating force, operating in the very midst of the "carpetbag" organization.

## PANIC OF 1873

During the Civil War, the North had experienced a period of rising prices and unprecedented prosperity. With the Federal Army absorbing many laborers from industry, such a condition tended to force up the wages of those who remained in the factories. To meet the demand for war supplies, industrial activity had been greatly accelerated.

When the war closed, this artificial stimulation stopped and the South, which, prior to 1860, had been the North's chief market, was practically bankrupt. Borrowers, in anticipation of greater profits, paid high rates of interest to develop new enterprises and went heavily in debt. From 1867 to 1873, an enormous amount of capital was invested in building railroads through the sparsely settled West. Altogether, no less than 32,000 miles of new railroads, at a cost of over $2,000,000,000, were built in the Nation during these years. Because the large sums invested in such railroads could not bring immediate returns, scores of railroads could not meet the interest on their bonded debt. Between 1861 and 1868, the United States had borrowed abroad, on her national, state, municipal, railway, and other securities, an amount estimated at $1,500,000,000.

Then, in 1873, a world depression set in. It was evident first at Vienna in May, then rapidly spread through Europe, and finally reached the United States. In September, Jay Cooke & Company, a large American brokerage firm engaged in the building of the Northern Pacific Railroad, failed. This event precipitated the panic, which was the severest that this Nation had ever experienced.

As in every severe business depression, the veneer which

ordinarily covers speculators and exploiters was ruthlessly broken away. The North saw corruption at Washington, and in the South, and became acutely aware of the demoralization of its former market by the "carpetbag" regime. The business cycle and the political cycle almost coincided; and as a result, in 1874, the Republican political machine, which apparently had a stranglehold on the Federal Government and was responsible for the hidecus situation in the South, was defeated by one of the most overwhelming votes in the history of the United States.

Already the South had been slowly relieving itself of Black Republican rule, but the national election hastened the event. Rutherford B. Hayes, who was seated as President, in 1877, withdrew the Federal troops from the South, and Democratic government was again established in the Southern States. When the state governments returned to the hands of the Southern people, committees were appointed in nearly every state legislature to investigate the bonded debts of the states. As a result of such investigations, the debts contracted under the "carpetbag" regime and, in a few states, the bonds of defunct banks and internal improvement companies of ante-bellum days were either repudiated or scaled down. The debts made by the Confederate Government and the Southern States for carrying on the war had been repudiated by the Fourteenth Amendment of the Federal Constitution.[23] The creditors of the South were thus compelled through both Federal and state laws to accept enormous losses.

The following table, taken from R. P. Porter's article "State Debts and Repudiation," in the *International Review* for November 1880, indicates the growth of their indebtedness and the amounts scaled down or repudiated in the Southern States that had especially suffered from reconstruction:

---

[23] See *Constitution of the United States*, Amendment XIV, Section 4.

## STATE DEBTS AND REPUDIATION, 1860-1880

| State | 1860 | 1870 | Highest Point Reached | 1880 | Amount of Debt Repudiated and Scaled Down Between Highest Period and June 1880 |
|---|---|---|---|---|---|
| Virginia | $31,779,062 | $47,390,839 | $47,390,839 | $29,345,238 | $18,045,613 |
| North Carolina | 9,699,000 | 29,900,045 | 29,900,045 | 3,629,511 | 26,270,534 |
| South Carolina | 4,046,540 | 7,665,909 | 24,782,906 | 7,175,454 | 17,607,452 |
| Georgia | 2,670,750 | 6,544,500 | 20,197,500 | 10,334,000 | 9,863,500 |
| Florida | 4,120,000 | 1,288,697 | 5,512,268 | 1,391,357 | 4,120,911 |
| Alabama | 6,700,000 | 8,478,018 | 31,952,000 | 11,613,670 | 20,338,330 |
| Mississippi | None | 1,796,230 | 3,226,847 | 379,485 | 2,847,362 |
| Louisiana | 4,561,109 | 25,021,734 | 40,416,734 | 12,635,810 | 27,780,924 |
| Arkansas | 3,092,623 | 3,459,537 | 18,287,233 | 5,813,627 | 12,473,646 |
| Tennessee | 20,898,606 | 38,539,802 | 41,863,406 | 25,685,822 | 16,177,584 |

Notwithstanding the bad effects that such repudiation had upon public credit, a new generation was rising to utilize the natural resources of the section and to build out of the political and economic wreckage of the past a *New South.*

### Bibliographical Note

Some of the most important source material on the economic conditions of the South during the reconstruction period may be found in W. L. Fleming's *Documentary History of Reconstruction,* two volumes (Cleveland, Ohio, 1906–1907).

A colorful and partisan account may be found in C. G. Bowers, *Tragic Era* (New York, 1929). The general accounts include: W. A. Dunning, *Reconstruction, Political and Economic, 1865–1877* (New York, 1907); P. J. Hamilton, *Reconstruction Period* (Philadelphia, 1906); Holland Thompson, *New South,* Volume XLII in the CHRONICLES OF AMERICA (New York, 1910); W. L. Fleming and others, Volume VI of THE SOUTH IN THE BUILDING OF THE NATION (Richmond, 1865–1909); and P. A. Bruce, *Rise of the New South,* Volume XVII in THE HISTORY OF NORTH AMERICA (Philadelphia, 1905).

The operation of reconstruction in different Southern States is given by a series of monograph studies: W. L. Fleming, *Civil War and Reconstruction in Alabama* (New York, 1905); T. S. Staples, *Reconstruction in Arkansas,* Volume CIX in the COLUMBIA UNIVERSITY STUDIES (New York, 1923); Powell Clayton, *Aftermath of the Civil War in Arkansas* (New York, 1915); W. W. Davis, *Civil War and Reconstruction in Florida,* Volume LIII in the COLUMBIA UNIVERSITY STUDIES (New York, 1913);

C. Mildred Thompson, *Reconstruction in Georgia*, Volume LXIV, Number 1 in the COLUMBIA UNIVERSITY STUDIES (New York, 1915); E. M. Coulter, *Civil War and Readjustment in Kentucky* (Chapel Hill, N. C., 1926); J. R. Flicklen, *History of Reconstruction in Louisiana (through 1868)*, Volume XXVIII, Number 1 in the JOHNS HOPKINS UNIVERSITY STUDIES IN HISTORICAL AND POLITICAL SCIENCE (Baltimore, 1910); Ella Lonn, *Reconstruction in Louisiana After 1868* (New York, 1918); H. C. Warmoth, *War, Politics and Reconstruction* (New York, 1930); J. W. Garner, *Reconstruction in Mississippi* (New York, 1901); J. G. de R. Hamilton, *Reconstruction in North Carolina*, Volume LVIII in the COLUMBIA UNIVERSITY STUDIES (New York, 1914); F. B. Simkins and R. H. Woody, *South Carolina During the Reconstruction* (Chapel Hill, N. C., 1932); J. S. Reynolds, *Reconstruction in South Carolina* (Columbia, S. C., 1905); J. W. Fertig, *Secession and Reconstruction of Tennessee* (Chicago, 1898); and C. W. Ramsdell, *Reconstruction in Texas*, Volume XXXVI, Number 1 in the COLUMBIA UNIVERSITY STUDIES (New York, 1910).

The best treatment of the Ku Klux Klan is J. C. Lester and D. L. Wilson, *Ku Klux Klan, Its Origin, Growth and Disbandment* (Washington, 1905). For short sketches of the Ku Klux Klan, see: W. G. Brown, *Lower South in American History* (New York, 1902); and E. P. Oberholtzer, *History of the United States*, Volume II (New York, 1922). A comprehensive study of negroes in the South during this period is P. S. Pierce, *Freedmen's Bureau*, Volume III, Number 1 in the UNIVERSITY OF IOWA STUDIES (Iowa City, Iowa, 1904).

Some interesting notes on the effect of reconstruction on landholdings may be found in R. P. Brooks, *Agrarian Revolution in Georgia, 1865–1912*, Number 639 of the UNIVERSITY OF WISCONSIN BULLETIN (Madison, Wis., 1915). A brief treatment of the railroads in the South during this period is C. R. Fish, *Reconstruction of the Southern Railroads*, Number 2 in the UNIVERSITY OF WISCONSIN STUDIES IN HISTORY AND SOCIAL SCIENCES (Madison, Wis., 1919).

Thomas Nelson Page's *Red Rock* (New York, 1912), is a novel dealing with reconstruction, and may be read profitably for its touches of realism.

# CHAPTER XVI

# Economic Progress in the South After 1880

FOR two decades, from 1860 to 1880, the South was submerged by war and its aftermath. During the first decade, the estimated true value of all property in the section declined by nearly $2,000,000,000, while that in the rest of the Nation increased by $15,400,000,000. During the second decade, the estimated true value of all property in the South increased by only $1,172,000,000 over the census figures for 1870, while that in the rest of the Nation increased by $26,310,000,000. During the Civil War, the South lost several hundred thousand of its best man power; since that time, migration has been a further drain upon its population.

In spite of such enormous losses, which have been irreparable, the economic development of the South after 1880, which roughly marks the end of the reconstruction period, has been rapid and compares favorably with that of the entire United States. The estimated true value of all property in the South and the total for the United States are listed in the table on page 450.[1]

## Agriculture

Since the reconstruction period the South's chief money crop, cotton, has repeatedly gone through the rounds of expansion and depression.

---

[1] Compilation based upon statistics of U. S. Department of Commerce, *Wealth, Public Debt and Taxation* (1922), p. 25 *et seq.*: "Estimated National Wealth."

PROPERTY VALUES IN THE SOUTH AND
IN THE UNITED STATES

| Year | Value in Thousands of Dollars | | Percentage of Increase over Preceding Estimates | |
|------|------|------|------|------|
| | South | United States | South | United States |
| 1880............ | $ 8,847,000 | $ 43,642,000 | ........ | ........ |
| 1890............ | 13,412,988 | 65,037,091 | 51.3 | 49.0 |
| 1900............ | 16,991,447 | 88,517,307 | 26.6 | 36.1 |
| 1904............ | 20,478,304 | 107,104,194 | 20.5 | 20.9 |
| 1912............ | 39,460,701 | 186,299,664 | 92.8 | 73.8 |
| 1922............ | 69,678,097 | 320,803,862 | 76.5 | 72.2 |

## COTTON

In 1878, the cotton crop equalled that of 1860, and in 1879, it reached 5,475,000 bales, the largest up to that time. Production had greatly increased in Texas and Arkansas, and some cotton was being raised in Oklahoma, then termed "Indian Territory." With the exception of Alabama and Louisiana, all the cotton states produced more bales in 1879 than in 1859. From 1880 to 1890, cotton planters in the South were in a fairly prosperous condition. There was an increasing demand for cotton both in Europe, especially on the Continent, and in the United States, especially in the South, where cotton mills increased rapidly after 1870. Cotton exchanges had been established, and the increasing practice of purchasing cotton for future delivery was apparently a steadying influence on the price. The development of improved means of transportation in the South and the growing use of commercial fertilizers also favored expansion of the crop, and in 1890, production reached 8,562,000 bales.

During the last decade of the nineteenth century, Southern cotton growers experienced a severe depression. Through the years 1889 to 1893, the average price per pound paid for upland cotton fell from 11.5 cents to 7.5 cents. In 1894, production reached 10,025,000 bales and the price fell to 5.9 cents per pound. During the next two years, production decreased and prices rose to 7 cents and

8 cents per pound. This condition was a direct incentive to expansion. In 1897, production reached 10,985,000 bales, but the price fell to 5.6 cents per pound. The next year, production reached 11,435,000 bales and the price fell to 4.9 cents per pound. In many instances the price paid for cotton did not cover the cost of production. According to a report of the Senate Committee on Agriculture and Forestry in 1893: "It is the general concensus of opinion that cotton cannot except under the most favorable circumstances be raised profitably at less than 8 cents a pound, nor without loss under 7 cents." [2]

Many of the cotton growers were heavily in debt. In 1890, according to the United States Census, the farms in the leading cotton-growing states were mortgaged to 44.1 per cent of their value. The losses incurred by cotton growers, on account of the low prices received for their cotton, increased their already heavy burden of indebtedness and forced many of them to forfeit their land. From 1880 to 1900, the number of landowners who resided on plantations decreased considerably, and the *tenant system* increased accordingly. Much of the land fell into the hands of the merchants, the manufacturers, and various corporations.

No doubt the expansion of production contributed to the fall of cotton prices in the years 1894, 1897, and 1898, but the general decline in cotton prices during the major part of the decade must be attributed to the world-wide business depression. In 1893, the United States experienced a panic which was "one of the longest and severest crises in American business history." [3] This was followed

---

[2] See (U. S. Senate) Committee on Agriculture and Forestry, *Report on Conditions of Cotton Growers in the United States, the Present Price of Cotton, and the Remedy*, 53d Cong., 3d Sess., Report 986, Vols. I and II.

[3] See Wesley C. Mitchell, *Business Cycles, The Problem and Its Setting*, pp. 355 and 429.

by the "submerged cycle" of 1894–1897. In England, beginning in 1891, a severe depression continued for nearly four years; and on the Continent, France, Germany, Italy, and other nations likewise suffered from a business depression more or less severe. Even Russia, Japan, and China were affected adversely by the widespread stagnation of business. Obviously, Southern cotton growers could not escape the effects of the general decline in commodity prices. In the field of party politics, many expressed their discontent by affiliation with the Populist Revolt.

Between 1899 and 1909, the total acreage in cotton increased 32 per cent. This increase continued until the outbreak of the World War in 1914. In 1900, almost 25,-000,000 acres of cotton were planted, and in 1913, 37,000,000 acres. The acreage increase was particularly marked in the new regions of Texas and Oklahoma. Cotton production, except for seasonal fluctuations, showed from 1900 to 1913 a steady increase from 10,102,000 bales to 13,982,000 bales. During the same period, the average annual price at New York varied from 9 cents to 14 cents per pound.

During the first years of the new century, the boll weevil became the most significant handicap to cotton production. This pest first made its appearance in Mexico about 1862. Thirty years later, it crossed the Rio Grande River at Brownsville, Texas, and spread eastward and northward at the rate of forty or fifty miles a year. In 1902 mainly because of the ravages of this insect, Texas sustained an estimated loss of over 940,000 bales. By 1913, the boll weevil had spread over the entire Cotton Belt, except the part in the Atlantic Coastal Plain. During that year, as estimated by the Bureau of Agricultural Economics, the loss of cotton on account of this insect was 6.69 per cent "of the estimated crop in absence of the boll weevil." [4]

This pest, however, was not the only problem confront-

---

[4] See U. S. Department of Agriculture, *Yearbook* (1930), p. 198.

ing Southern cotton growers. Cotton production by
irrigation was begun in Arizona and southern California,
and at the same time competition from foreign countries
increased. On the other hand, progress was made with
efforts in the South to produce better grades of cotton and
higher yields. Cottonseed became a valuable item in the
way of by-products; for cottonseed, which had been waste
in 1860, fertilizer in 1870, and cattle food in 1880, now
became "table food and many things else." [5]

In 1914, cotton production reached 16,134,000 bales.
This amount was four times the crop of 1860, but the marketing of so large a crop when commerce was greatly disturbed on account of the outbreak of war in Europe caused
the average price to fall from 12.5 cents to 7.3 cents per
pound. In 1915, the cotton crop was 5,000,000 bales less
than the year before, and the price rose to 12 cents. For
the next five years, the crop neither rose above 12,000,000
bales nor fell below 11,000,000 bales, but in 1919, the price
at New York had climbed to 38 cents per pound. The next
year, production reached 13,440,000 bales and the price
fell to 18 cents. In 1928, the crop yielded 14,478,000 bales,
but the price rose to 20 cents. In 1931, the crop increased
to 17,095,000 bales, and the price fell below 7 cents per
pound. Again, Southern cotton growers were caught in the
grip of a world-wide depression.

Cotton continued to spread westward, until, in 1931,
Texas and Oklahoma were producing 38.5 per cent of the
Nation's crop. In Arkansas, Georgia, North Carolina, and
South Carolina, the use of commercial fertilizers opened
new areas of production. The following table indicates
the expansion of cotton westward and northward in the
fifty-two years from 1879 to 1931: [6]

---

[5] F. G. Mathers, "Waste Products: Cotton-seed Oil," *Popular Science
Monthly*, May 1894, p. 104.

[6] Compiled from U. S. Department of Commerce, *Reports*.

PRODUCTION OF COTTON IN LEADING
COTTON-GROWING STATES

(BALES OF LINT, 500-POUNDS GROSS WEIGHT)

| State | 1879 | 1899 | 1919 | 1931 |
|---|---|---|---|---|
| Mississippi | 963,000 | 1,286,000 | 957,000 | 1,761,000 |
| Georgia | 814,000 | 1,232,000 | 1,681,000 | 1,392,000 |
| Texas | 805,000 | 2,584,000 | 2,971,000 | 5,322,000 |
| Alabama | 699,000 | 1,093,000 | 718,000 | 1,419,000 |
| Arkansas | 608,000 | 705,000 | 869,000 | 1,906,000 |
| South Carolina | 522,000 | 843,000 | 1,476,000 | 1,004,000 |
| Louisana | 508,000 | 699,000 | 306,000 | 899,000 |
| North Carolina | 389,000 | 433,000 | 858,000 | 756,000 |
| Tennessee | 330,000 | 235,000 | 306,000 | 594,000 |
| Oklahoma | ............ | 227,000 | 1,006,000 | 1,261,000 |
| Others | 117,000 | 107,000 | 228,000 | 781,000 |
| UNITED STATES | 5,755,000 | 9,444,000 | 11,376,000 | 17,095,000 |

There were specific reasons for the westward expansion of cotton. During the first decade of the twentieth century, the boll weevil destroyed large areas of cotton in the more moist regions of the eastern Black Belt and forced cotton growers to seek the drier climate of the Panhandle and the region of the upper Mississippi Delta. During the Great War, the high price paid for cotton was a further incentive to westward expansion. In fact, the premium on cotton became so high that it caused growers to utilize the submarginal lands of the Southwest. Furthermore, in recent years the rise of industry in the Piedmont and Highland regions of the South attracted many cotton-field negroes in the South Atlantic States away from agriculture and forced the abandonment of cotton acreage in these states on account of lack of labor. On the other hand, in the newer Trans-Mississippi regions, there could be acquired tracts of land sufficiently large to warrant capital expenditures for machinery, such as tractors, sleds for picking, and other devices, the use of which minimized the need for cotton-field laborers.

Before the Great War, the South was producing more than 60 per cent of the world's cotton crop; in 1929, it produced 55 per cent. In 1900, 66 per cent of the South's crop was exported, and in 1928, 55 per cent. In 1929,

Southern cotton exports comprised 43 per cent of the value of all agricultural exports from the United States.

Hence, for more than a century, the South has held a monopoly of cotton production. However, since the Great War, Southern cotton has had to meet increasing competition in the world market. In 1929, the world's consumption of Indian cotton was 10,000,000 bales, as compared to the South's crop of 14,500,000 bales. In recent years, cotton production has been expanded in Egyptian Sudan, Uganda, Asiatic Turkey, and Asiatic Russia. Within five years following 1923, Russia increased her cotton crop from 196,000 bales to 1,232,000 bales, and threatened to become in a short time a dangerous competitor in the world market. The South may eventually lose its monopoly of cotton supply unless industrial improvements and cheaper credit are made available to reduce the cost of production so as to undersell the other countries of the world.

The cost of producing cotton depends upon both the yield per acre and the amount of capital and labor employed in effective cultivation. On account of the great variety of soil, the yield per acre in the cotton-growing states has never been uniform. In 1879, Louisiana raised 294 pounds per acre, the highest yield of all the Southern States. At the same time, Florida raised only 112 pounds per acre, the lowest yield. If equal amounts of capital and labor per acre were applied in the two states, it is evident that the cost of production in Florida was far above that in Louisiana. The table on page 456 indicates the yield per acre in the leading cotton-growing states during the fifty years from 1879 to 1929.[7]

In 1923, when the price of cotton passed 35 cents per pound, it was contended that growers could not produce it profitably for less than 25 cents or 30 cents per pound.[8] In the regions where the boll weevil reduced the yield to

---

[7] Compiled from U. S. Department of Agriculture, *Yearbooks*.

[8] W. R. Cooper and C. R. Hawley, *Cost of Producing Field Crops, 1923*, published in 1925 by the U. S. Department of Agriculture, Circular 340.

NUMBER OF POUNDS OF LINT COTTON PER ACRE

| State | 1879 | 1909 | 1929 |
|---|---|---|---|
| Louisiana | 294 | 156 | 189 |
| Arkansas | 292 | 162 | 186 |
| Oklahoma | 243 | 162 | 128 |
| Mississippi | 229 | 168 | 225 |
| North Carolina | 218 | 240 | 197 |
| South Carolina | 191 | 234 | 185 |
| Texas | 185 | 132 | 106 |
| Georgia | 156 | 204 | 170 |
| Alabama | 150 | 153 | 178 |
| Florida | 112 | 133 | 145 |

one tenth of a bale per acre, the growers spent considerable sums in an effort to combat the pest, and the cost of production rose to an extraordinary degree. On the other hand, full production, due to favorable seasons, usually caused the cost of production to drop materially. For the season 1926–1927, the Federal Department of Agriculture estimated the average yield per acre in the South at 180.2 pounds. With production of this size, the average cost amounted to approximately 15 cents or 16 cents per pound. The report of the American Cotton Association for 1926 showed that, on several hundred two-acre cotton demonstration farms scattered throughout North Carolina, South Carolina, Georgia, Alabama, and Mississippi, the average yield under intensive cultivation was 913 pounds of lint cotton, and that the average cost of production was $59.88 per acre. This expenditure, however, left an average net revenue of $80.66, since the average amount received for the cotton and the seed was $140.64 per acre. With the problem of joint-cost production of both lint and seed, moreover, the average cost of producing a pound of lint was somewhat arbitrarily reported at 6½ cents. All studies show a wide variation in the cost of producing cotton in different localities and in different seasons; yet in spite of this variation, cotton prices from 1918 until 1931 were high enough to yield a fair net return to a large percentage of those planters who, before the Great War, had been marginal producers.

In recent years, investigations by the United States Department of Agriculture and experiment stations in the Southern States indicated that some methods of increasing cotton yield per acre—such as the adaptation of crops to soil types, the rotation of crops, and the use of improved seed—actually involve in the long run no additional costs to the growers, and that actual losses occurred when no extra expenditures for insect control and for fertilizers were incurred.  In view of this fact, efforts were made, by more effective control of the boll weevil and by the use of commercial fertilizer, to increase the yield of cotton.  From 1910 to 1920, the boll weevil continued to spread across the Cotton Belt and, in 1921, caused an estimated loss of more than 30 per cent of the crop.  Thereafter damages were decreased, especially in dry seasons, by applying control measures, such as hastening the maturity of as much cotton as possible before the weevils became abundant, and by dusting the plants with calcium-arsenate.  Although the use of commercial fertilizer also increased in the Southeastern States, on the majority of farms its application was in too small a quantity to produce the maximum benefit from its use.

In the ante-bellum period the ratio of negroes to whites employed in producing cotton was 8 to 1.  Since the Civil War there has been a great shift in the labor force of the Cotton Belt.  In 1876, nearly 40 per cent of the cotton crop was produced by white farmers; in 1910, 67 per cent.

Immediately after the Civil War, cotton planters, in order to obtain labor, tried a *wage system*.  Since they did not have the cash with which to pay wages weekly or monthly and since the ex-slaves would not wait a year for their pay, this system failed.  Thereafter the practice now known as the *share*, or *cropping, system* developed.  At first its forms were many and various, but soon they became standardized into three kinds: *on halves, third and fourth,* and *standing rent*.  *On halves* meant that the planter furnished everything except the labor, and that the tenant who did the work received one half of the crop. In case of the *third and fourth*, usually, if the planter furnished everything except the labor, the tenant got one fourth of the crop; but, if the planter furnished everything except provisions and labor, the tenant got .one third. In recent years the *standing rent method*—calling for a fixed rent for each acre or farm, to be paid in money or in cotton —has proved more satisfactory than any other methods in securing white tenants.

As a result of social and economic conditions, the percentage of tenancy in the Cotton Belt has been inevitably large. Half the share tenants in the United States are found in the following states, listed in the order of their numbers: Texas, Georgia, Mississippi, North Carolina, Arkansas, Alabama, and Tennessee. In 1900, the census indicated that 67.7 per cent of the farmers who depended on cotton as a chief source of income were tenants. During the first quarter of this century, the percentage of farmers (full owners, part owners, and managers) decreased in each of the leading cotton-growing states, as indicated by the following table: [9]

PERCENTAGE OF FARMERS IN LEADING
COTTON-GROWING STATES

| State | 1900 | 1910 | 1920 | 1925 |
|-------|------|------|------|------|
| North Carolina | 58.6 | 57.7 | 56.5 | 54.8 |
| South Carolina | 38.9 | 37.0 | 35.5 | 34.9 |
| Georgia | 40.1 | 34.4 | 33.4 | 36.2 |
| Alabama | 42.3 | 39.8 | 42.1 | 39.3 |
| Mississippi | 37.6 | 33.9 | 33.9 | 31.7 |
| Arkansas | 54.6 | 50.0 | 58.7 | 43.3 |
| Louisiana | 42.0 | 44.7 | 42.9 | 39.9 |
| Oklahoma | 56.2 | 45.2 | 49.0 | 41.4 |
| Texas | 50.3 | 47.4 | 46.7 | 39.6 |
| UNITED STATES | 64.7 | 63.0 | 61.9 | 61.4 |

The decrease was mainly due to consolidation of farm areas under capitalistic management, with cultivation in the

[9] Compiled from L. C. Gray, "The Trend in Farm Ownership," in the *Annals of the American Academy of Political and Social Science*, Vol. CLII, p. 22.

hands of tenants, and it was partly due to abandonment of farms.

Tenancy in the Southern States does not necessarily mean inefficiency in land utilization; on the contrary, it has long been true that the combination of an ignorant class of negro and white tenants on plantations closely supervised by capable landlords has proved more efficient than the same class working as owners without supervision. Tenants who pay standing rent are not as a rule closely supervised, and as a result, especially in the less prosperous parts of the Cotton Belt, they till their acres in an uninterested and shiftless manner. As H. Snyder points out:[10] "Very frequently do they fail to pay for their 'furnish,' as they call their supply of provisions, and are forced to give up their mules and cows." The chief objection to tenancy in the Cotton Belt is that the tenant's income has generally been inadequate to supply his needs for maintaining a normal standard of living and, at the same time, to permit him to save a sufficient sum to purchase a farm home. The condition has been due in a large measure to the credit system, which frequently has been a great burden on, rather than a boon to, the farm owners.

The breaking up of the plantation system following the abolition of slavery brought about new methods in financing cotton production. In place of the large cotton factors, upon whom the ante-bellum planters relied for credit, there arose small local agents known as *supply*, or *lien, merchants*. These dealers in the interior, instead of the factors at the ports or principal market towns, became cotton buyers and assumed the pivotal position in supplying credit. Before the Civil War, large cotton factors made advances to the planters if their crop, land, and slaves were put up as security. After the war, cotton alone had to be the basis for credit, because temporarily land was almost

---

[10] See H. Snyder, "Negro Migration and the Cotton Crop," in the *North American Review*, January 1924, for a vivid description of tenancy in the Cotton Belt.

valueless, and negroes were no longer property. This situation localized credit in the hands of merchants who knew the financial standing and business habits of the planters. These merchants advanced food and supplies to landowners and tenants and, at times, required a certain number of acres to be planted. In nearly all of the cotton-growing states, *lien laws* were enacted to permit the planters to give their creditors a prior lien on present or future crops. When a crop was picked, the lien merchant took it, making deductions for all advances during the year, plus interest.

During more recent years, country merchants and many of the planters have been carried from one season to another by local country banks. In most communities the creditor demands the indorsement of the landlord on all notes for advances to tenant farmers. In effect, the credit system in the Cotton Belt compelled the planters and the tenants to buy from the *creditor-merchant* only the kind and the quantity of goods that he decided to furnish, for no other merchant would extend credit until the crop mortgages were paid.

Moreover, the local country banks, not being able to make a profit from the sale of goods, as the merchants were accustomed to do, usually exacted an exorbitant rate of interest. In 1921, a survey made by the United States Department of Agriculture found that the average rates of interest charged farmers in the leading cotton-growing states on personal and collateral loans were as follows:

AVERAGE INTEREST RATES IN
LEADING COTTON STATES, 1921

| State | Per Cent |
|---|---|
| North Carolina | 6.23 |
| South Carolina | 8.06 |
| Mississippi | 8.11 |
| Louisiana | 8.34 |
| Alabama | 8.40 |
| Georgia | 8.94 |
| Texas | 9.68 |
| Oklahoma | 9.84 |
| Arkansas | 9.70 |

The interest was always collected in advance, and in many instances the borrowers were required to maintain a certain percentage of the loan as a deposit at the bank. In a few communities, during the decade following 1921, local country banks, under the guise of attorneys' fees for drawing up contracts and other legal forms, resorted to exacting commissions for making loans. On account of fluctuations in crop prices, however, neither the creditor-merchants nor the local country banks became wealthy, and many of them, since 1929, have had to go out of business.

The price fluctuations following 1920 convinced many planters that some measure of grower control of the cotton market was essential for their protection. Numerous cotton coöperatives were set up, but for the most part these actually accomplished little, except to stimulate interest in improving the quality of grade and staple cottons. In accordance with the provision of the Agricultural Marketing Act, passed in June 1929, the *Federal Farm Board* was established to promote the effective merchandising of agricultural commodities. This Board in turn promoted, among other national coöperatives for major commodities, the *American Cotton Coöperative Association,* which was incorporated in January 1930 and has its main office at New Orleans. It has an authorized capital of $30,000,000, distributed among nine Southern States, and also two regional associations, representing more than 150,000 growers. The American Cotton Coöperative Association was effected to improve the quality of cotton produced in the South and, in coöperation with the United States Department of Agriculture, to undertake a campaign to bring about "one-variety cotton communities" throughout the Cotton Belt. This organization and the Staple Cotton Coöperative Association, of Greenwood, Mississippi, handled about one fifth of the South's cotton crop marketed in 1930.

Soon after its formation, however, the American Cotton Coöperative Association found itself unable to cope with the cotton situation. Hence, as an emergency measure, the

Federal Farm Board, in January 1930, formed the *Cotton Stabilization Corporation*. In an attempt to stabilize the price of cotton, this corporation lent to thirteen short-staple coöperative associations for cotton held off the market, approximately $18,500,000, or an average price of 16 cents per pound. As would be expected in any attempt to control supply without regard to demand and to the general decrease in all commodity prices, the cotton price could not be regulated in this manner, and by the end of November 1930, cotton at New York was selling for 6.75 cents per pound.

## TOBACCO

In recent decades, increased consumption at home and abroad has greatly stimulated the production of tobacco. In 1880, the total crop in the United States was 472,661,000 pounds; in 1910, 807,991,000 pounds; and in 1929, 1,500,-000,000 pounds. Although tobacco is a product common to limited regions in both Northern and Southern States, 87 per cent of the product of the country in 1929 came from the South, and North Carolina alone produced nearly five times as much as all the Northern States combined.

Until 1860, Virginia continued to be the leading tobacco state; then, one of the striking changes effected by the Civil War was the permanent shifting of production into the newer fields of Kentucky, Tennessee, and North Carolina—Kentucky quickly assuming the leadership for tobacco production and holding it until 1927. Since then, North Carolina has been producing annually more tobacco than Kentucky and Virginia together. After the Great War, entirely new fields were opened to tobacco production. In south Georgia, where it became necessary on account of the boll weevil to find some other crop to replace cotton, climate and soil conditions were found ideal for the growing of a high grade of tobacco. As a result, in this region where not a pound had been grown a few years ago, production increased from year to year until the yield reached 30,000,000 pounds annually.  Moreover, in every Southeastern State after the coming of the boll weevil, some farms, with soil so adapted, were turned from cotton to tobacco production.

The production of tobacco has increased most rapidly in North Carolina, because that state produces mainly the cigarette types ("bright flue-cured"), for which demand since 1910 has increased more than 600 per cent.  Kentucky produces chiefly Burley, which is especially suitable for the manufacture of pipe and chewing tobaccos.  Whether a region produces export leaf, cigarette tobacco, or Burley, is not a matter of choice, but depends upon the soil type available.

Tobacco requires intensive cultivation and much labor in harvesting and curing; the value per acre is therefore high. The following table indicates the average value of the yield per acre in the leading tobacco states of the South in 1929: [11]

#### AVERAGE YIELD PER ACRE IN LEADING TOBACCO STATES, 1929

| State | Value of Yield per Acre |
|---|---|
| Virginia | $121.80 |
| North Carolina | 123.00 |
| Kentucky | 139.23 |
| Tennessee | 138.36 |

Tobacco has become chiefly a product of the small farm, and only a few acres on a farm are devoted to it.  Its cultivation is often carried on only by the members of the family, and one family of average size is able to work from five to ten acres.  In North Carolina and Kentucky, the average size of tobacco fields is less than five acres, while on a few large farms as many as twenty or thirty acres are planted.  The acreage that each farmer can grow is limited by the amount that he can properly house and cure during the short time in which this must be done to

---

[11] Compiled from U. S. Department of Agriculture, *Yearbook* (1930), Table 170.

insure high quality in the leaf. Therefore tobacco growing, since it is limited to small patches, has worked in advantageously with diversified farming, especially with the "cow, hog and hen program" which has been urged upon the farmers by every state agricultural experiment station in the South.

The old method of selling tobacco at open auction is still used in the South. In order to attract buyers from the outside, each district has one or more warehouses centrally located. When bought, the tobacco is shipped to manufacturing centers, the most important of which are: St. Louis, Louisville, Winston-Salem, and Durham.

Ordinarily the United States has exported about two fifths of her tobacco crop. Such exports have been principally in raw form, not only because each importing country preferred its own methods of manufacture, but also because preferential import duties were levied by those countries on prepared tobacco, such as cigarette, pipe, and chewing tobaccos. Since the demand for tobacco is highly inelastic, because tobacco using is a habit and since the demand for tobacco has increased on account of its growing use both by males and females, its price, during the five years from 1924 to 1929, remained approximately 20 cents per pound. In recent years both growers and manufacturers have been able to reap large profits from tobacco, especially in the region of North Carolina known as the *Golden Belt*.

### Fruits, Nuts, and Vegetables

Prior to 1865, commercial fruit, nut, and vegetable growing received practically no attention as an agricultural industry in the South. There were no large Southern cities to serve as markets, and transportation facilities were so inadequate that distant markets could not be reached. The value of fruits and vegetables as foods was not appreciated, and refrigeration was unknown until 1875. Furthermore, labor was needed for the production of the staple crops—

cotton, tobacco, rice, and corn. In subsequent decades there has been an increasing demand for greenstuffs in the daily diet of American families. Modern refrigeration, railroads, and motor trucks have made it possible to ship fruits and vegetables to distant markets. As a result, commercial fruit and vegetable growing in the South has assumed large proportions.

In 1929, the value of truck crops produced in the South amounted to 43 per cent of the total value of the Nation's truck crops. With the exception of New York and Washington, Virginia produces more apples for sale than any other state. Georgia grows more peaches than any other state except California; and Florida, more oranges than any other state except California. Arkansas and Missouri ordinarily produce more than 25,000,000 tons of grapes.

The South is the only section in which pecans can be grown. In 1929, the estimated crop was 38,000,000 pounds, and the quantity sold amounted to $5,889,000. However, the pecan has not entirely justified the hopes that have been entertained concerning its production, because production costs have been higher than anticipated when the groves were planted.

In the South the principal commercial groves of orange and grapefruit trees have been confined to the portion of Florida lying below Tampa and Daytona Beach. However, citrus fruits have been grown in various localities along the Gulf coast from Pensacola to the Rio Grande. Florida is the chief producer of grapefruit in the United States. Most of the crop is marketed by the Florida Citrus Exchange, a coöperative with numerous local organizations. In recent years the growing of satsumas has expanded rapidly in western Florida and southern Alabama. Peaches have been grown commercially not only in Georgia, but also in the Carolinas and in Tennessee. Many other fruits, including pears, plums, cherries, figs, pineapples, bananas, guavas, and dates, have been grown to some extent commercially in a few regions along the Southern coast.

Since truck and garden crops do not require the long-time investment necessary in orchard culture, their production has increased more rapidly than fruit growing. The most important commercial vegetables produced in the South are: Irish potatoes, sweet potatoes, peanuts, strawberries, watermelons, cabbages, tomatoes, cantaloupes, lettuce, onions, and celery. The Southern fruit and vegetable industry has capitalized mainly upon the earliness of the producing season in the South as compared with that of Northern areas. Agriculture in the Florida Peninsula, outside of the citrus industry, has been developed almost solely upon this basis. Railroad and fast steamship lines to Northern markets have been an important factor in localizing truck farming for early vegetables. Thus, south central Mississippi, southern Louisiana, Savannah, Charleston, and the Coastal Plain of Virginia and Maryland have become important centers for the production of early vegetables. From remote areas of the South, the Illinois Central, the Southern Railroad, and the Atlantic Coast Line carry fruits and vegetables to city markets of the North.

Fruits, nuts, and vegetables have consequently become important money crops in the South. The income derived from these crops has enabled the farmers engaged in orchard culture and truck growing to raise their standard of living, to build new homes, to buy automobiles, and, in many instances, to educate their children in colleges and universities.

## SUGAR

In the South the growing of sugar cane for commercial purposes is confined to Louisiana. In the so-called *Sugar-Bowl*—from St. Martinsville, the alleged tomb of Evangeline, to New Orleans, and especially, along the banks of the beautiful and historic Bayou Teche—thousands of acres are devoted almost exclusively to the growing of sugar cane. Since 1880, the quantity of sugar produced annually in Louisiana has fluctuated widely. In 1908, production reached a maximum of 355,000 short tons, and in 1926, it fell to a minimum of 47,000 short tons.

Usually, production from one year to the next has either risen or fallen approximately 50,000 to 100,000 short tons. These variations have been due to many unfavorable conditions, such as adverse climate, the so-called "mosaic disease" of sugar cane, and changing tariffs. In Louisiana, frosts occur annually, and the pieces of cane to be used for planting must be protected from frosts so that a new crop can be started with them the next spring. In 1919, the Louisiana sugar industry met with disaster on account of "mosaic disease." However, with the development of a new variety of cane, introduced by the United States Department of Agriculture, the sugar industry since 1927 has been rapidly recovering.

As a result of natural handicaps, the production of sugar in Louisiana is largely dependent upon a protective sugar tariff, to offset the high cost of production in competition with imported sugar from places like Cuba, where the climatic conditions are more favorable and the cropping methods are less expensive. Louisiana sugar planters have insisted upon a protective tariff in spite of the fact that their output is only about one per cent of the total quantity of sugar consumed by the United States. From 1873 to 1890, the Government imposed a duty of 2½ cents per pound on unrefined sugar. This protection gave a healthy impetus to the sugar industry in Louisiana.

However, in 1890, all tariff on unrefined sugar was removed and a bounty of 1¾ cents and 2 cents per pound was paid to every producer of domestic sugar. In 1894, the bounty was abolished and an ad valorem duty of 40 per cent substituted. This change came at a time when the world's markets were heavily stocked with sugar from tropical countries where the price had fallen to 1¼ cents per pound. As a result Louisiana planters could not meet

the competition and some went into involuntary bankruptcy. In 1897, the duty was raised. Then, three years
later, Porto Rican sugars were admitted free; and two
years after that, Philippine sugars were admitted free. In
1903, there was made with Cuba a reciprocity treaty admitting Cuban sugar at a 20 per cent preferential.

These acts proved extremely harmful to Louisiana sugar
planters, but in 1913, when sugar was put on the free list
in the tariff bill, the industry was threatened with extinc-
tion. Every preparation was made by the planters to close
out their businesses. Stubbles were plowed up, and factories offered for sale either to junk dealers or to foreign
sugar producers for removal abroad. In fact, no Louisiana
sugar producer thought of continuing in business; but,
before the "free sugar" clause went into effect, it was repealed. The Great War stimulated production, and the
domestic planters recovered their losses. In 1921, a duty
of 2 cents per pound was put on "96 test sugar," and since
that time, the industry has enjoyed a certain amount of
protection from imported sugars.

### RICE

In the colonial period, rice production was confined almost exclusively to South Carolina. Later it was cultivated, though not extensively, in Georgia and Florida, and
a small amount was grown in Louisiana shortly before the
Civil War. During the war, the rice industry in these states
was almost destroyed. Planters either enlisted in the Army
or migrated to the interior, and thus left the fields and
canals neglected. In 1890, the growing of rice was reëstablished in South Carolina and Georgia, but by that time
rice had begun to be grown by more extensive methods in
the west Gulf region. In 1889, Louisiana became the leading rice-producing state in the country. Later the United
States Department of Agriculture, at an expense of $18,000,
introduced in Louisiana and Texas a Japanese rice of the

Kiushu variety, and a tremendous increase resulted in the crop.

In these circumstances—extensive methods of production and high yield—the rice-growing region of the South Atlantic States could no longer compete with the newer region. By 1929, the leading states in rice production were: Louisiana, producing 19,000,000 bushels; Texas, 7,500,000 bushels; and Arkansas, 7,000,000 bushels. Missouri has been producing about 35,000 bushels. Since 1926, South Carolina, Georgia, and Mississippi have produced only negligible quantities. Because the American people do not consume rice in large quantities, about 10 per cent of the South's annual crop has to be exported.

## OTHER PRODUCTS

As in ante-bellum days, the South since 1880 has grown corn, wheat, oats, barley, hay, and forage largely as supply crops and rarely on a commercial scale.

While the total output of cereals in the South has increased during the seventy years between 1859 and 1929, the largest part of the increase has occurred in the states west of the Mississippi River. In 1859, Missouri, Arkansas, Louisiana, and Texas, together, were growing about 137,-000,000 bushels of cereals; in 1929, those states, together with Oklahoma, produced over 514,000,000 bushels, or one half of the total cereal production of the South.

Wheat raising has almost ceased in Georgia, Florida, Alabama, Mississippi, and Louisiana. In 1879, Alabama was raising over 1,500,000 bushels; Mississippi, about 218,-000 bushels; and Florida and Louisiana, lesser quantities. In 1929, Alabama raised only 40,000 bushels; Mississippi, only 68,000 bushels; and Florida and Louisiana, a negligible quantity. During the fifty years between 1879 and 1929, wheat raising in West Virginia, Missouri, Kentucky, and Tennessee has decreased, and in Maryland, Virginia, and Texas, it has increased. The crop, however, has reached its greatest development in the South in Oklahoma and Texas.

This fact is likewise true of barley and rye, which have never been grown extensively in the other Southern States. Corn is grown on nearly every Southern farm and is in part of the South almost the exclusive cereal. In the fifty years from 1879 to 1929, corn production has increased from 573,000,000 bushels to 695,000,000 bushels. During the last two decades, its production in Missouri declined. In the Cotton Belt, when cotton prices fall, the planters usually decrease their cotton acreage and raise more corn; then, when cotton prices rise, they decrease their corn acreage and raise more cotton. In the South, especially in the Cotton Belt, much corn is consumed as food, the per capita consumption being much greater than that in the North.

Among the grasses and forage plants which have been of economic importance in large areas of the South are: Bermuda grass, Johnson grass, crab grass, Texas blue grass, and, in the northern portion of the South, Kentucky blue grass. Cowpeas, Lespedeza, sweet clover, vetch, velvet beans, millet, and other forage crops have been grown more or less extensively in some of the Southern States. The production of these crops has been closely related to livestock raising, and they have been for sale only in minor instances.

### LIVESTOCK

Agriculture in the South has been notably affected by the tendency of livestock production in the United States to shift to areas where conditions are most favorable. During the five years from 1920 to 1925, the number of cattle, other than milk cows, on Southern farms decreased in every Southern State except in Kentucky, where there has been a slight increase, and in Oklahoma, where there has been no change. Since 1920, the number of hogs on Southern farms has also decreased. In Tennessee, this decrease reached a maximum of 52 per cent, and in North Carolina and Oklahoma, 31 per cent and 23 per cent, respectively.

However, the value of Southern livestock still amounts to 28 per cent of the total for the United States.

In the South there developed three distinct varieties of livestock: the razorback hogs, the "piney woods" cattle, and the Texas longhorns. These "scrubs" all thrived well in their environment; for that reason, until recent decades, little attention was paid to raising special-purpose stock— except in the border states, where a few farmers were interested themselves in raising pedigreed horses and cattle.

Large herds of "piney woods" cattle still exist, and a few razorback hogs may be found in the Highland region, but the Texas longhorns practically all disappeared in 1885. In the last two decades, various agencies, such as state agricultural colleges, county organizations, and the press, undertook to educate Southern farmers to the value of improved quality stock. State and county fairs have stimulated interest in blooded or special-purpose farm animals. In 1903, the first public sale of pure-bred cattle in the South was held in Oklahoma City; in 1904, the second took place at Auburn, Alabama; and in subsequent years, similar sales have been held at various other agricultural centers throughout the Southern States. Packing houses have been established at Fort Worth, Nashville, Macon, and other Southern cities. By 1920, the South was producing nearly one fifth of the blooded cattle raised in the United States. Since that time, with the aid of various agencies and because of increased demand, almost every community has been aroused to improve its livestock.

### DAIRY PRODUCTS

Since 1913, dairying has become a strong commercial factor in the South. Kentucky probably is the leading Southern State in dairy development, but nearly every state in the section has to some extent attempted to establish this industry. The official report of the United States Department of Agriculture for 1928 shows cheese production in Arkansas, Georgia, Kentucky, Mississippi, and

Texas, where previously it was of no importance. Production of cheese in Mississippi in 1928 was 2,333,000 pounds, as compared with 15,000 pounds for the previous year; and in Texas, it was nearly 1,000,000 pounds, as compared with none the year before. Obviously the extent of the market will tend to limit such expansion. Dairying has frequently been urged upon Southern farmers in localities too remote from markets to make the industry profitable. The result has meant heavy losses to those farmers who coöperated in such enterprises, and the abandonment of creameries and cheese factories, and the sale of cows at losses were the natural outcome.

### AGRICULTURAL ORGANIZATIONS

As indicated by the above material, the period since 1880 has been for the South one of agricultural expansion. Nevertheless there were years of uncertainty and discontent. In the spring of 1887, the *Progressive Farmer*, a journal published at Raleigh, North Carolina, succinctly described the situation as follows: [12] "There is something radically wrong in our industrial system. There is a screw loose. The wheels have dropped out of balance. The railroads have never been so prosperous, and yet agriculture languishes. The banks have never done a better or more profitable business, and yet agriculture languishes. . . . Towns and cities flourish and 'boom' and grow and 'boom,' and yet agriculture languishes."

This disequilibrium was due largely to external factors operating in outside markets upon which the Southern farmers were dependent both as sellers of produce and as buyers of many articles of consumption and farm implements. However, there were also causes peculiar to the South. As compared to his status in 1860, the status of the Southern farmer in 1890 was relatively low. The large plantations had been broken up, the labor force disor-

---

[12] *Progressive Farmer*, April 28, 1887.

ganized, and the political control of government shifted in many instances into the hands of an urban population. The lien law system impinged more and more on Southern farmers during the periodical declines in commodity prices. In these circumstances, many farmers joined organizations in which they might give effective expression to their discontent.

As early as 1874, a group of frontier farmers in Lampasas County, Texas, formed an organization for the purpose of catching horse thieves, rounding up stray cattle, and purchasing supplies. From this humble beginning the organization by 1878 had become the *Grand State Alliance.* Political dissensions, however, caused its disintegration. The next effort to form a similar organization was made in Parker County, Texas, by a man who had been a member of the old Lampasas County society. This organization proved more successful and became known as the *Farmers' Alliance of Texas.* Although for a considerable time it posed primarily as a social organization, it eventually demanded the adoption of certain economic policies favorable to the agrarian group.

In the meantime the *Farmers' Union of Louisiana* had been established for similar purposes. Seeing an opportunity for extending the alliance scheme of organization, established in northwest Texas, C. W. Macune, an enthusiastic promoter, with evangelistic fervor hastened to unite the Farmers' Alliance of Texas and the Farmers' Union of Louisiana, and to extend the order throughout the South.

In Arkansas, there was in existence a farm order nearly as old as the Farmers' Alliance. In 1882, seven farmers had formed a debating society in Prairie County; this group soon became a state organization, known as the "*Wheel.*" In 1885, the order absorbed another Arkansas farm order known as the *Brothers of Freedom.* A year later, the membership of the "Wheel" had grown to 50,000, in 1887, its 500,000 members included residents of eight states.

The next move was to combine the Farmers' Alliance and the "Wheel" into a Southern organization. This step was effected in 1889, and the old orders gave way to the new *Farmers' and Laborers' Union of America.* Later there were efforts to combine this order—known popularly as the *"Southern Alliance"*—with the northwestern alliance. These organizations promised much for the membership fee, but accomplished little. In fact, the so-called "Southern Alliance," which apparently was a coöperative scheme to help farmers, was actually only a fad used by its promoters in many instances to exploit the credulous farmers who were hopeful of finding in it the promised panaceas. Eventually the organization became enmeshed in politics and passed out of existence.

In 1902, Newt Gresham, of Emory, Texas, founded the *Farmers' Educational and Coöperative Union of America.* By 1914, this organization, built in part upon the ruins of the former alliance, was established in twenty states of the South and Midwest; it promised to accomplish a great deal of good, especially in the marketing of grain and livestock. However, its work in the South has been somewhat superseded by the *American Farm Bureau Federation,* which is national in scope.

As is well known, the South has six of the land banks and joint-stock land banks of the Federal Government, in addition to other national agencies for aiding agriculture. The South likewise receives its share of Federal aid in the various efforts to stabilize the price of farm products. Yet, in spite of these and other agencies, and the efforts of state agricultural colleges, the major part of the farm industry in the South has been in sore distress since the postwar depression in the fall of 1920. The farmer in the Cotton Belt is still close to the peasant level of existence. According to a study of the National Bureau of Economic Research, 52 per cent of the total farm population of the Nation is found in fourteen Southern States, and even in 1918, the per capita current income of the farm population in the South was only $260, as compared with $470 for the rest of the United States. Moreover, in certain agricultural regions of the South there is a growing amount of squalor and poverty, as well as an excessive rate of pellagra.

Professor Wilson Gee has said with much truth: [13] "Our eyes in the past decade have been strained towards Washington, and hands to our ears we have listened to hear of reforms fundamental and substantial enough to give approximate equality between agriculture and industry. Two tariff acts have been enacted, the more recent of them with the avowed intention of aiding agriculture, and both of them have laid a heavier additional burden upon the farmer than they have given him increased income to bear. Some help has been provided in the intermediate credit situation, but this has been of limited usefulness. A commission of agricultural inquiry and a national agricultural conference have met and reported. A committee of the Land-Grant Colleges Association and a business men's commission representing the United States Chamber of Commerce and the National Industrial Conference Board have analyzed the situation and made the results available. Much has been heard about the McNary-Haugen plan, such things as export debentures and ways of applying domestic allotments. Great hopefulness has been stirred in the farmers' hearts by the magic word of stabilization corporations, and other provisions of the Agricultural Marketing Act. The results confessedly are disappointing, and any substantial aid which the Federal Farm Board may bring to American agriculture must come about over a long period of years of somewhat gradual strengthening of coöperative activities."

### Industrialization

Industrial development in the South proceeded rapidly after 1880, and at a greatly accelerated pace for nearly three decades after 1900.

---

[13] *Proceedings of the Southeastern Economic Association* (1930), p. 95. Reprinted by permission of the author.

MANUFACTURING

The capital invested in manufacturing enterprises from 1900 to 1920 increased 390 per cent; the value of the product (to 1925) increased 460 per cent; and the wages paid (to 1925) increased 323 per cent.[14] However, at the present time the South occupies about the same position relative to the Nation as a whole that it did in 1860; for, while there have been gratifying developments in manufacturing in the South, the same progress has been made in other portions of the United States.

GROWTH OF SOUTHERN MANUFACTURING, 1880–1925

|  | 1880 | 1900 | Per Cent of Change in Period |
|---|---|---|---|
| Number of Establishments.. | 53,248 | 113,984 | 114.0 |
| Capital.................. | $329,752,408 | $1,402,890,000 | 325.4 |
| Persons Engaged.......... | 369,462 | 982,528 | 165.9 |
| Value of Material......... | $396,473,202 | $1,043,431,000 | 163.1 |
| Value of Product.......... | $622,840,976 | $1,849,137,000 | 196.8 |
| Wages (Total)............ | $100,227,187 | $366,594,000 | 265.7 |

|  | 1900 | 1925 | Per Cent of Change in Period |
|---|---|---|---|
| Number of Establishments.. | 113,984 | 37,238 | −67.5 |
| Capital.................. | $1,402,890,000 | $6,883,171,000 | 390.6 |
| Persons Engaged.......... | 982,528 | 1,866,000 | 90.0 |
| Value of Material......... | $1,043,431,000 | $6,228,000,000 | 496.8 |
| Value of Product.......... | $1,849,137,000 | $10,371,000,000 | 460.8 |
| Wages (Total)............ | $366,594,000 | $1,553,218,000 | 323.6 |

Cotton. Of the different types of Southern manufacturing enterprises, none is more important than cotton milling. In 1880, there were in the Southern States 184 cotton mills, or 24 per cent of the total for the United States. In 1925, there were 814 mills, or 59 per cent of the total. In 1880, the South had only 6 per cent of the

[14] The 1925 decrease in number of establishments was due to the definition given the term "Manufacturing Establishments," as defined by the United States Census. In 1900, the term included only those establishments having an annual product of $5,000 or more. Statistics compiled from UNITED STATES CENSUS, Reports.

spindles and 6 per cent of the looms, but in 1927, Southern mills had 52 per cent of the spindles and 46 per cent of the looms. In 1880, only 11 per cent of the capital invested in cotton milling was employed in the South, but in 1920, 43 per cent was invested in Southern mills. In recent decades the most extensive construction of cotton mills has been in three states: North Carolina, South Carolina, and Georgia. Important mills were established also in Alabama, Tennessee, Oklahoma, and Texas. The section, moreover, has two rather distinct cotton mill centers: the Piedmont, making medium-grade yarns and goods; and the Southwest, making coarse grades.

The rapid rise of cotton manufacturing in the South has been due to a change in the attitude of the Southern people themselves toward industrialization, and to an effort on the part of cotton manufacturers to reduce their costs of production. In the ante-bellum period, leading Southern thinkers chafed under the section's dependence on the outside world for various manufactures, and as the period drew to a close, significant changes were under way. Then came the Civil War, which was temporarily disastrous for Southern industry; yet, from another point of view, the Civil War released the Southern people from a system under which practically all their savings had to be invested in slaves.

After reconstruction, when the South had reëstablished self-government in the states and cotton culture had been reorganized to meet new conditions, some Southern men with Southern capital began to establish cotton mills. Other Southerners, though not building mills themselves, exerted their influence through the press and aroused Southern people to undertake cotton manufacturing. F. W. Dawson, of the *News and Courier,* of Charleston, South Carolina, until his death in 1889, continually presented to his readers arguments for industrialization, and plans for financing and operating new factories. Other Southern editors, following his lead, became protagonists for industrialization. The Cotton Exposition of 1881, at Atlanta, by displaying machinery for manufacturing cotton, attracted many interested observers, and led in the South to the immediate purchase of $2,000,000 worth of machinery. Later, other expositions, like the North Carolina Industrial Exhibit, at Raleigh in 1884, and the fair in New Orleans in 1895, engendered enthusiasm in cotton manufacturing.

The first mills established in the South after the Civil War were relatively small. The capital was seldom more than $50,000 or $100,000, and in communities unable to raise funds, the machinery was paid for in mill securities or stock certificates issued to the Northern manufacturers of the machinery. In some instances mills were built in communities by selling mill stock upon installment payments ranging from 25 cents to $2 a week. During recent years, outside capital has flowed into the South. A table showing the loss or gain in the number of spindles in the leading cotton-manufacturing states of the Union shows that a large percentage of the spindlage lost in New England reappeared in the South.[15] From 1924 to 1929, the South gained about 2,800,000 spindles, and half of this spindlage gain in the South represented second-hand spindles removed from defunct New England mills and erected in the Southern States.[16]

Apparently the shifting of cotton manufacturing southward has been due largely to an effort to reduce the cost of production by establishing mills near cotton fields and power sources, by employing cheap and complacent labor, and by escaping restrictive factory codes. However, Professor M. T. Copeland, after examining the several alleged advantages, concludes that most of them, except the supply of cheap labor, are offset by more favorable factors in

---

[15] U. S. Department of Commerce, *Cotton Production and Distribution,* Bulletin 167.

[16] "The Coming of Industry to the South," in the *Annals of the American Academy of Political and Social Science,* Vol. 153, p. 30.

Northern industry.[17] Other studies tend to substantiate his conclusions; in fact, it appears that cheap labor is about the only important advantage any of the Southern mills have in competing with the New England mills on a cost of production basis. Most of the labor for the Southern cotton mills has been obtained from two classes, the tenant farmers and the mountaineers, as well as from the lowest class, known as *poor whites.*

The employment of this kind of labor in cotton manufacturing has created one of the South's most difficult industrial problems; this situation is further discussed in Chapter XVII. In 1929 and 1930, strikes broke out in several small mill towns in Virginia and North Carolina. These combats seem to indicate that the cotton mill employers have contributed very little to the economic security of their employees. Indeed, the episodes at Gastonia and Marion, which received national attention, seem to forecast a course of industrial development in the South similar to that which New England experienced before collective bargaining by employees became effective in dealing with absentee owners of mills.

**Other textiles.** In recent years one of the greatest revolutions in the textile world has been the rapid development of "artificial silk," or rayon. This industry has been confined, thus far, mainly to the Southern States, because it has used cotton linters as raw material. Plants have been established in Maryland, North Carolina, Virginia, Tennessee, West Virginia, and Georgia. The greatest manufacturer of rayon yarn was the Viscose Company, with plants at Roanoke, Virginia, and Parkersburg, West Virginia. Up to the present time, rayon has supplemented the other textile fibers—cotton, wool, and silk—but on account of its increasing use, it may adversely affect the cotton-manufacturing industry.

**Power plants.** In the South, forward steps have also been made in the development and use of hydroelectric

---

[17] *Cotton Manufacturing Industry of the United States,* Chapter III.

energy.   The first development in the section was begun by James B. Duke and W. S. Lee, of the Southern Power Company, about thirty years ago.   Since 1908, the South has more than trebled its developed water power, and hundreds of miles of copper strands form a great network of lines carrying to consumers billions of kilowatt-hours of electric energy.[18]

NUMBER OF CONSUMERS OF ELECTRIC
POWER IN SOUTHERN STATES, 1931

| State | Number of Consumers |
|---|---|
| Maryland | 323,712 |
| Virginia | 271,575 |
| West Virginia | 206,416 |
| North Carolina | 252,945 |
| South Carolina | 124,896 |
| Georgia | 208,345 |
| Florida | 242,715 |
| Kentucky | 284,717 |
| Tennessee | 250,240 |
| Alabama | 194,657 |
| Mississippi | 104,842 |
| Missouri | 669,115 |
| Arkansas | 129,930 |
| Louisiana | 195,730 |
| Oklahoma | 297,184 |
| Texas | 701,072 |
| TOTAL | 4,458,091 |

The Southeastern Power System, one of the most important in the United States, is composed of the transmission lines and stations of the following companies:

Southern Power Company of North and South Carolina.
Carolina Power & Light Company of North Carolina.
Georgia Railway & Power Company.
Central Georgia Power Company.
Columbus (Georgia) Power Company.
Alabama Power Company.
Tennessee Power Company.

[18] Compiled from data furnished by the Statistical Department of the National Electric Light Association.

The system has over 3,000 miles of high-voltage lines and serves an area of 120,000 square miles.

Besides this system, there are important, isolated power developments scattered widely throughout the South. Some of these are found in regions where water sites are available; others, where coal is abundant; and a few, where their dependence upon inadequate fuel or water supply makes them almost negligible in contribution to the region's power demand.

Reference must also be made to Muscle Shoals. From Florence, Alabama, to a point within ten miles of Decatur, the Tennessee River flows over a series of rapids for a distance of about forty miles. The most important of these rapids is Muscle Shoals. Soon after the United States entered the Great War, the Government, at a cost of $90,000,000, constructed two nitrate plants in the vicinity of these shoals and began the construction of Dam No. 2, or Wilson Dam. Construction work on this dam was suspended after the close of the war.[19]

Since 1929, the attitude of the Southern people toward power companies has in many instances become more critical on account of the decline in the value of the securities of certain companies while the cost of electricity to the consumer has remained constant. Each Southern State, except Florida, Kentucky, Mississippi, and Texas, has some form of public utility commission for the purpose of regulating all utilities. Whether or not regulation by these commissions has been satisfactory is a matter of opinion, depending upon whether the viewpoint is that of the consumer or that of the power company.

### PRODUCTION OF MINERALS

In recent years the exploitation and the manufacture of Southern minerals, both metallic and non-metallic, have

---

[19] Walter H. Voskuil, in Chapter X of *Economics of Water Power Development*, has briefly and clearly stated the real issues involved in the proposals.

developed at an accelerated pace because of the greatly increased demand both in the South and in outside markets for essential minerals, such as iron, petroleum, and sulphur.

Iron. In 1854, the South produced 12 per cent of the total iron output of the United States. At the close of the Civil War, production had practically ceased; twenty-five years later, it had reached only 6 per cent of the Nation's total output. In 1896, production reached a maximum of 19 per cent, but relative to the unprecedented increase in iron output of the entire United States, Southern production since that date has steadily declined. For a five-year average beginning with 1910, the South produced 11.72 per cent of the iron ore of the Nation; for the five-year average ending with 1926, 11.68. In the production of pig iron, the South produced 13.20 per cent of the total for the Nation during the former period, while during the later period, it produced only 8.3 per cent. In short, while the Southern iron output has shown an absolute increase for the section, production has shown a relative decline as compared with the Nation's total increase. However, in the production of finished rolled iron and steel, the South showed a gain: although producing only 2.65 per cent of the total for the United States in 1901, it produced 4.86 per cent in 1926.

Birmingham, Alabama, is the chief iron and steel center of the South. In 1876, the first coke furnace in Alabama was built at Oxmoor, in the Birmingham region. Three years later, another furnace was built at Birmingham. These pioneers demonstrated the possibilities for making iron at a low cost; consequently, during the decade 1880–1890, coke furnace construction was active in the Appalachian Valley from Alabama to Virginia. During the decade, the Southern iron industry became localized in three regions: the territory between the Blue Ridge Mountains and the Cumberland Plateau, in Virginia, southwestward to Johnson City, Tennessee; the stretch from Big Stone Gap, Virginia, southwestward through Tennessee and

Georgia to the Birmingham district, in Alabama; and a belt lying east of the Tennessee River and extending from northern Alabama through Tennessee and Kentucky. Since that time, the iron industry of the South has been slowly concentrating in two or three of the most favorable localities within these regions, of which Birmingham is by far the most important.

Steel making on a large scale in the South was first undertaken about thirty years ago by the Tennessee Coal, Iron & Railroad Company. In 1899, this company—originally started in Tennessee by Southern men with Southern capital—opened at Birmingham a plant of ten 50-ton, basic open-hearth furnaces. Because of the scarcity of capital and competition from the iron industry in the Lake Superior district, the company experienced many difficulties, a history of which would be highly dramatic. Its stock was for years a football of Wall Street speculators, and successive owners of the company put new capital into it; but every expansion showed the need for further expansion. During the panic of 1907, the company was purchased by the United States Steel Corporation, through special permission of President Theodore Roosevelt and largely for the purpose of stabilizing one or two banking houses in New York which were endangered by the fact that they held as collateral large blocks of the Tennessee Coal, Iron & Railroad Company's stock. Soon after the purchase, several millions of dollars were appropriated by the United States Steel Corporation for the reorganization and development of the plant on scientific lines. However, a suit for dissolution entered against the United States Steel Corporation by the Federal Government, on the claim that the corporation exercised a monopoly through its ownership of the Tennessee Coal, Iron & Railroad Company, delayed further large expenditures, until the Federal Supreme Court decided in favor of the corporation. On account of the extraordinary demand for steel during the Great War, the United States Steel Corporation rapidly expanded its plant in the Birmingham district. After the war, expansion did not stop until 1929, since the enlargement of railroad facilities in the South and the construction of new buildings, as well as orders from foreign markets, constantly demanded an increased output of steel. Birmingham has become not alone the iron and steel center of the South, but also the center of the iron-pipe manufacturing interests of the United States, whose product is shipped to every part of the Nation and to many foreign lands.

At Sparrows Point, Maryland, near Baltimore, a great enterprise was developed to use ore imported from Cuba, Spain, and Africa. The plant's property, acquired by the Bethlehem Steel Corporation in 1916, was greatly expanded during the war. Another large iron and steel interest in the South is the Gulf States Steel Company, in Alabama; but the outstanding plant is that of the Tennessee Coal, Iron & Steel Corporation.

**Petroleum and natural gas.** In recent years the petroleum industry in the South has grown by leaps and bounds. From 1859 to 1875, practically all the oil produced in the United States came from Pennsylvania. The center of production then began to move west and south. West Virginia entered the production column in 1876; Kentucky, Tennessee, and Missouri, soon after. In Texas, commercial production began with the opening of the Corsicana field in 1896; development on the Gulf coast began with the discovery of the Spindle Top pool in 1901. The following year, Oklahoma began production, and, with the discovery of pools in the Bartesville area in 1904 and the Glenn pool in 1906, this state's production rose rapidly. Louisiana became an active producer in 1902. Arkansas, with the discovery of the El Dorado field in 1921, entered the list of oil producers that year.

Omitting Missouri, which has never been an important factor in the petroleum industry, statistics show that, during 1930, seven Southern States—Texas, Oklahoma,

Louisiana, Arkansas, Kentucky, West Virginia, and Tennessee—produced 560,418,000 barrels of crude oil, or 62.5 per cent of the total 1930 production in the United States. The history of production in these Southern States has been varied. In Texas, Oklahoma, Louisiana, and Arkansas, production has been marked by the discovery of *gusher fields*. In contrast, the oil fields of West Virginia, Kentucky, and Tennessee are similar to those in Pennsylvania: they produce oil of high grade, are shallow in depth, and are of long life.

While the total investment in the petroleum industry of the South cannot be determined, the investment in drilling alone has been closely estimated.[20] According to the statistics for the eight oil-producing states in the South, from the date when each began commercial production to 1929, it appears that the total number of wells drilled in the South was 321,893—of which, 21,969 were *wildcat wells*, and 299,924, *proved-area wells*—and that the total investment in drilling amounted to $5,192,245,000, of which $546,369,000, or 10.5 per cent, was spent on wildcat wells. While the industry was of great importance in the development of the regions concerned, it has nevertheless been characterized in many instances by ruthless promotion schemes and by wasteful competitive methods of production.

Since the location of refineries is controlled by proximity to the supply of crude oil and by the location and nature of the consuming market, a group of refineries has been established about the mouth of the Mississippi River between New Orleans and Baton Rouge, and another group has been established around the towns of Beaumont, Port Arthur, and Houston. Tulsa and Dallas, because of proximity to supplies of crude oil and transportation facilities, are important refining centers. St. Louis is a

---

[20] For a comprehensive study of the petroleum industry, see Ralph Arnold and William J. Kemnitzer, *Petroleum in the United States and Possessions*.

prominent center where there is a large market and where oil is brought to the refineries by pipe lines from the so-called *midcontinent fields*.

In recent years the utilization of natural gas has been of similar significance to the South. In 1929, the natural gas production of the section amounted to 1,299,247,000,000 cubic feet, or over 67 per cent of the national output. Texas, Oklahoma, Louisiana, and West Virginia—named in the order of their importance—together dominated the industry. In 1929, the estimated length of natural gas trunk lines in Texas was 7,800 miles; in West Virginia, 4,000 miles; in Oklahoma, 3,700 miles; in Louisiana, 1,800 miles; and in Arkansas and Kentucky, over 1,000 miles each. Since that date, however, the Southern Natural Gas Company, completing a $25,000,000 line from the Monroe-Richland fields in Louisiana, across Mississippi and Alabama, to Georgia, has thus brought natural gas into the industrial Southeast.

**Sulphur.** Since 1906, the South has had a monopoly in the world's sulphur production. Sicily furnished practically all the sulphur consumed prior to that time and governed the market. Although sulphur was discovered in Louisiana in the early sixties, all efforts to mine it at that time by shaft mining methods were futile, for a barrier of quicksand lay between it and the surface. In 1904, Herman Frasch succeeded, by the use of superheated steam, in forcing sulphur up through pipes, in which it ran out on the ground and, a few hours later, returned to its crystal form. As a result of this method, sulphur has been produced at so low a cost in the Gulf area that only a trade agreement between Italy and the American companies has made it possible for Sicilian sulphur to be disposed of, even in European markets. In 1930, Texas produced all of the country's output of 2,558,981 tons of sulphur. In 1925, when the sulphur mine in Louisiana was practically exhausted, Texas alone was left to dominate the market. The Texas Gulf Sulphur Company operates plants at Gulf, New Gulf, and Long

Point; the Freeport Sulphur Company, at Freeport, Texas; and the Duval Texas Sulphur Company, at Benavides. The total value of sulphur produced in the Texas region in 1928 was over $35,000,000.

## MINOR INDUSTRIES

In 1927, the United States Census Bureau listed more than two hundred classifications of manufactures in the Southern States. This long list—which includes, for example, machine shops; planing mills; furniture and shoe factories; tanneries; paper, flour, and grain mills; meat packing plants and potteries—strikingly illustrates the scope and diversity of industry in the South. However, many of these industries have long existed on a small scale in the section, and have in recent years merely increased their output.

**Lumbering.** Southern timber resources are the basis of an extensive sawmill industry and of a less important woodworking industry. As the depletion of the virgin timber of the North continued, the lumber industry turned its attention to the yellow pine forests of the South, and by the last decade of the nineteenth century, lumbering in the section became a large-scale industrial enterprise. The industry was first developed in the Southeast at ports nearest the great Northern market—Virginia and North Carolina; then it gradually extended down the Atlantic coast and along the Gulf. It was operating to full capacity in Georgia during the eighties. About that time, the term *Georgia pine* became well known in the Northeastern market. Meanwhile there was also a development in the Southwest, beginning in Missouri and later extending down into Arkansas, Louisiana, and Texas. Development of the industry both east and west of the Mississippi River ran concurrently. In the earlier part of the twentieth century, many of the most important Southern mills were located in Mississippi, Louisiana, and Texas. This development was largely due to the capital of Northern lumbermen looking for new sources of timber to exploit. Of the Nation's total lumber production in 1900, the South produced 41 per cent; in 1910, 53 per cent; and in 1929, 46 per cent. Since 1929, the low price of lumber has sent several Southern mills into bankruptcy, and has brought the industry almost to a standstill.

The production of naval stores is one of America's oldest industries, and in the Southeastern States it is surpassed in importance only by agriculture and lumbering. The United States produces about 66 per cent of the world's supply of naval stores, and practically all of this amount is obtained from the long-leaf and slash pine forests in the Coastal Plains region from South Carolina to Texas. Nearly 56 per cent of the South's annual production is exported to foreign consumers. Because of this fact, the industry since the Great War has been greatly disturbed by price fluctuations, especially since Russia has disappeared as a buyer of American rosin and is now producing adequate naval stores for her needs.

As a furniture-manufacturing center, High Point, North Carolina, is second only to Grand Rapids, Michigan. The High Point furniture industry was started by local men and developed with local capital, and is probably the most thoroughly localized business management among the large industries in the South. The man who founded the enterprise is said to have been influenced to remain in High Point through hearing the celebrated lecture "Acres of Diamonds," delivered by Russel H. Conwell, of Philadelphia.

In 1927, there were 47 paper mills and 19 pulp mills in the South; in 1930, 60 paper mills and 36 pulp mills. Apparently the trend of the paper industry is toward the South. However, most of the product is coarse wrapping paper; the manufacture of newsprint and high grades of white book paper from Southern pine must await the development of processes which are practical from a commercial standpoint.

In recent years there has been a marked increase in the number and capacity of flour and grain mills, meat packing establishments, and boot and shoe factories. The production of coal has greatly increased, as well as that of various minor minerals, such as manganese, lead, zinc, carbon black, asbestos, and rock asphalt. Much has been said about the development of the ceramic industry, but its possibilities in the South have never been tested to any great extent. During recent times the South has paid more attention to the development of the fertilizer interest and also to the production of Portland cement.

**Fisheries.** For the supply of food fish, in addition to fish for industrial use, the South furnishes about one third of the Nation's catch. The development of an oyster industry of commercial importance in the South was at first confined to Maryland and Virginia; then, after 1885, when the annual yield of oysters from the Chesapeake gradually declined, packing houses in Baltimore established branches in North Carolina and Louisiana. About 1895, pearl fishing in the Southern States developed as an industry, and subsequently almost every river and creek throughout the South was examined. Pearl fishing, however, is no longer of commercial importance in the section.

All this industrial development since 1880 has brought about an increased urbanization of the South. Cities and towns have risen and flourished like the green bay tree. Roanoke, Virginia; Birmingham, Alabama; and Tulsa, Oklahoma, have expanded into important industrial cities; and Atlanta, Georgia, as described by its chamber of commerce, has risen "from the ashes" to be the "Queen of the South." Such urbanization has brought together both uneducated and undereducated wage-earners and the leaders of commercial and social life. Whether this contact daily has stimulated thought and improved the standards of living in the South has become a question for academic discussion; yet the fact remains that a given area when best utilized by a combination of industry and diversified agriculture can sustain in comfort a far larger population than it otherwise could.

## Transportation, Communication, and Commerce

### TRANSPORTATION

**Railroads.** Immediately after the Civil War, every railroad company in the South was confronted with the difficult problem of rehabilitating roadbeds, tracks, and equipment. At first some of the roads were aided by the Adams Express Company, acting through its controlled branch, the Southern Express Company. Other roads were aided to a limited extent by certain Southern cities. The favorite practice of reconstruction was for "carpetbaggers," financed by Wall Street brokers, to buy up simultaneously the stocks of the railroad companies and the members of the state legislatures. The legislatures would then vote millions of dollars in bonds or endorsements to the railroad companies, and the political officials would divert most of the proceeds into their own and their confederates' pockets. This practice continued until the panic of 1873 made such securities unmarketable.

In 1875, a Southern pool, composed of twenty-five railroad companies and managed by a central board, was formed. The purposes of this pool, were: to adjust rate differentials, to enforce agreements, and to apportion net earnings among the companies. For more than a decade, it functioned remarkably well, especially in preventing rate competition. After it passed out of existence under the provision of the Interstate Commerce Act of 1887, prohibiting pooling associations, there followed a short period of rate wars and instability of rates among the Southern railroads.

In 1879 and 1880, important combinations and consolidations of Southern railroads were effected, and new roads were projected and constructed. The whole tendency was toward the establishment of independent trunk lines from the Northwest to the south Atlantic seaboard, with a view to lessening "the vast preponderance of railroad vitality and influence in the North over the South." The panic of 1893 bankrupted numerous Southern railroad companies and promoted still further consolidations.[21] Since 1880, over 65,000 miles of new tracks have been laid in the South, and in 1930, the section had 36 per cent of the total railway mileage in the United States.

The following table shows the main-line trackage in the South and in the United States for 1880, 1900, 1920, and 1930:

### RAILROAD MAIN-LINE TRACKAGE

|  | 1880[a] | 1900[1] | 1920 | 1930 |
|---|---|---|---|---|
| South | 24,866 miles | 61,701 miles | 90,887 miles | 90,333 miles |
| United States | 93,267 miles | 193,346 miles | 252,845 miles | 249,794 miles |

[a] Includes a few miles of some switching and terminal companies.

Since 1916, railroads in the South, as in the Nation, have experienced a period of varied management: Government operation during the Great War, the subsequent return of the roads to their owners, and later attempts at regulation by the Interstate Commerce Commission.

**Roads.** In the South, agitation for improved highways began during the last decade of the nineteenth century. Numerous road conventions were held, including the Virginia Good Roads Convention at Richmond, Virginia, in 1894; the National Road Parliament at Atlanta, Georgia, in 1895; and the Roads Convention at Houston, Texas, in 1895. However, the actual building of good roads in the South since the Civil War has been undertaken mainly by individual counties; in fact, the chief characteristic of the road-building period from 1899 to 1910 was the granting, to counties or road districts, of authority to issue bonds for

---

[21] The largest systems now operating are: in the South, the Chesapeake & Ohio, the Norfolk & Western, the Southern Railway, the Atlantic Coast Line; and in the Southwest, the Southern Pacific, the Union Pacific, and the Atchison, Topeka & Sante Fe.

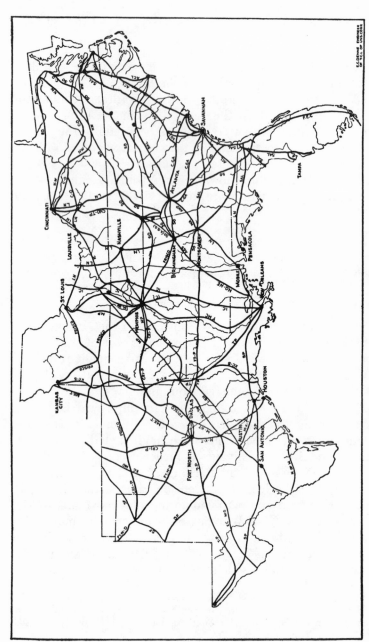

Important Railroads of the South, 1934

the purpose of financing road construction. Such general legislation was provided in all of the Southern States except Maryland and South Carolina, where each county has to be empowered by a special act of the legislature in order to issue bonds.

Concurrently with the increasing use of motor vehicles, the building of good roads progressed in nearly every Southern State. During the first decade of the twentieth century, a number of the Southern States—including Maryland, Virginia, North Carolina, Tennessee, West Virginia, Kentucky, Louisiana, and Texas—created state highway departments and established funds for state aid in highway construction.

Federal aid also has been available. In 1921, Congress passed the Federal Highway Act, which provided that each state should lay out a system of roads—not exceeding 7 per cent of the total national public road mileage—on which Federal aid was to be expended. In selecting the Federal aid system for the South, attention was given to laying out routes which would connect the Southern States with one another, and the entire section with the North, the East, and the West.

During recent years nearly every Southern State has coördinated its road-building program to include county, state, and Federal aid. The method of financing, outside of Federal aid, has in most instances been the issuance of bonds, and the revenue derived from gasoline taxes and license fees. There are, however, vast areas—as in Mississippi, Alabama, and Georgia—which still have clay and sand roads that are practically impassable for motor vehicles in rainy weather. A comparative study of expenditures for road building and of roads actually built in each of the Southern States seems to indicate that upon the administrative personnel of the respective state governments has depended whether or not the taxpayers have received the best possible roads at the least possible expense. In 1930, the state and local (rural) highway systems of the South totaled 1,383,864 miles, of which 221,745 miles, or about one sixth, may be classed as *surfaced roads*.

In 1904, the South spent, including state and county funds, $12,636,000 for building roads; in 1928, including state, county, and Federal aid funds, $459,231,768. As a result of the increasing annual expenditures to construct a system of good roads, several Southern States have, since 1929, been struggling under a burden of bonded indebtedness that is enormous in proportion to their taxable capacity.

**Waterways.** Interest in the development of water transportation in the South since the Civil War has centered in the belief that carriage by such means was cheaper than transportation by rail. Southern advocates of water transportation have consistently worked for governmental appropriations needed to give the waterways unobstructed and dependable channels; until 1924, the amount expended on Southern rivers and harbors was approximately $643,-000,000.

Since that time additional sums have been spent on river and harbor improvements, notably on the lower Mississippi River. After the Government made a deep-water harbor of the port at Houston, Texas, that city recently has become a rapidly growing competitor of Galveston for the export trade from the Southwest. The Government, since the passage of the Federal Control Act of 1917, has also provided large sums for levee building on the Mississippi. As a result of Federal, state, and local expenditures, the total navigable length of waterways—rivers, bayous, and canals—in the South, by 1930, had reached approximately 21,000 miles.

**Airways.** During the last decade, the airplane, as the fastest known means of transportation, has been increasingly used by Southern business men. In 1900, the first successful flight of a "heavier-than-air" machine was made at Kitty Hawk, North Carolina. Since that time air transport routes have been established to connect 48 Southern cities, and in 1929, the first important foreign air-transport service from the United States was inaugurated between Southern cities and South and Central American countries. In 1931, of the $115,068,000 invested in the 1,113 airports established by American cities, business corporations and individuals, $20,200,000, or nearly 18 per cent, was spent in the South. The practical adaptability of this method of transportation to the South augurs well for a profitable future development.

## COMMUNICATION

As a logical accompaniment of trade and transportation, telegraph and telephone companies have covered the South with a network of lines. South Carolina and West Virginia, in 1885, had the first permanent commercial telephone systems. At present, telegraphic communication in the South is furnished by the Western Union and the Postal Telegraph Company; and telephonic communication, by the American Telephone & Telegraph Company and by various smaller independent companies. The South has in time acquired adequate transportation and communication facilities to meet its commercial requirements.

## COMMERCE

Along with the agricultural and industrial development of the South since 1880, there has taken place a great increase in interstate commerce and in foreign trade through Southern ports.

**Foreign trade.** The total annual foreign trade—exports and imports—of the Southern seaboard custom districts from Baltimore to Galveston, together with the districts along the Mexican border, increased nearly 290 per cent from 1900 to 1929. During the same period, exports through Southern ports increased 227 per cent, while imports increased 854 per cent. This increase in imports through Southern ports was due, in part, to the increased consuming power of the South itself, and in part to the growing importance of the trade between the United States and tropical countries, especially the Latin-American countries.

Since trade between the United States and these countries rests largely upon the principle of *absolute advantage* —a difference in climate causing a permanent difference in products—some convenient Southern ports, New Orleans, Mobile, Tampa, and Savannah, have become and will continue to be important gateways of American commerce. Moreover, within recent years the South has greatly increased the number of its foreign markets. Southern products have been sent, not only to every country of South America and Europe that has a seaport, but also to Japan and other Oriental countries, including the British and Dutch possessions in the East. Whether or not the markets can be maintained where trade now rests upon the principle of *comparative,*[22] rather than absolute, *advantage,* will be contingent upon such factors as tariffs, new processes of production, and credit arrangements—all of which affect the cost of production and the marketing of goods.

## A Playground of the Nation

The South has immeasurable recreational assets. The mild climate, coupled with scenic beauty and historic interest, has in recent years attracted an increasing number of health and pleasure seekers from all parts of the United States east of the Rocky Mountains, especially from the North Atlantic States. Although a few Southern health resorts—such as Old Point Comfort, Virginia, and White Sulphur Springs, in West Virginia—antedate the Civil War, the lack of satisfactory transportation facilities, in addition to sectional prejudices, limited their economic importance in that day. Since 1880, the utilization of Southern recreational assets has progressed rapidly, has reached imposing

---

[22] A satisfactory explanation of the principle of *comparative advantage* may be found in John D. Black's *Production Economics,* Chapter V.

proportions, and now has distinct economic significance. Along the Atlantic seaboard from Old Point Comfort to Key West, around the Gulf coast from Tampa to Corpus Christi, and inland at such centers as Asheville and Augusta, many places have become definite tourist resorts, and the large areas contiguous to them—as in Virginia, North and South Carolina, Georgia, and especially Florida —have become dotted with winter homes of persons from other sections.

Many interests have been engaged in encouraging the development of travel in the South. Several states have contributed to this movement by making expenditures for the maintenance of parks and reservations, for the erection of historic monuments, and for similar activities. Several state and regional organizations have been actively engaged in advertising the recreational facilities of their respective areas. To be mentioned as notable examples are: the Virginia State Conservation and Development Commission, the Mississippi Coast Club, the Oklahoma Chamber of Commerce, the Ozark Playgrounds Association of Missouri, and the Kentucky Progress Commission.

Of the numerous business organizations promoting tourist travel, the railroads have been the most active. The Southern Railway issues a magnificent folder describing the scenic beauty of the "Land of the Sky" in western North Carolina. Nor have steamship lines, en route from New York to Florida, failed to point out the restful comfort of travel, the fascination of watching gulls fly over the blue waters, and the charm of the "golden lightening of the sunken sun."

Although the development of Southern recreational facilities has come mainly in recent years, its effect is already evident: the growing number of visitors has not only been of great economic significance to the South, but has had an important influence in counteracting bigotry, parochialism, and intolerance—characteristics of isolation. Through a spirit of sympathy and mutual understanding between the sections, this development has contributed largely to national solidarity of purpose and action.

### Bibliographical Note

There exists a voluminous amount of printed matter dealing with the economic development of the South since 1880, but much of it is prejudiced. The best material available on many economic problems in the South may be found in publications of the Federal Government and those issued by the Southern States themselves.

### GENERAL

The *Blue Book of Southern Progress*, published by the *Manufacturers Record* (Baltimore), particularly the ·volumes for 1924 and 1927, contains valuable data, although the interpretations are frequently biased. Philip Alexander Bruce's *Rise of the New South* (Philadelphia, 1905) is an excellent discussion of the population, agriculture, and financial status of the South after the Civil War; the material does not extend beyond the first of the twentieth century. The *Proceedings of the Southeastern Economic Association* (1930) contains a group of authoritative papers on the South. Howard W. Odum's *American Epic* (New York, 1930) is a reliable and realistic description of the South, with emphasis on the sociological rather than the economic problems. Although not up-to-date, THE SOUTH IN THE BUILDING OF THE NATION, Volume VI (Richmond, 1909), edited by James C. Ballagh, contains a series of articles on different economic aspects of the section for about forty years after the Civil War.

### SPECIFIC

There are a few scholarly treatments of specific problems. To be mentioned are: U. B. Phillips, "The Decadence of the Plantation," in the *Annals of the American Academy of Political and Social Science*, January 1910, pages 37–41; C. O. Brannen, *Relation of Land Tenure to Plantation Organization Since 1920* (Fayetteville, Ark., 1928); Wilson P. Gee and John J. Corson, *Rural Depopulation in Certain Tidewater and Piedmont Areas of Virginia* (Charlottesville, Va., 1929), a publication of the Institute for Research in the Social Sciences, University of

Virginia; R. M. Harper, "Development of Agriculture in the Pine-Barrens of the Southeastern United States," in the *Journal of Geography*, October 1916, pages 42–48, and "Development of Agriculture in Lower Georgia from 1890 to 1920, with a summary for the whole state, 1850 to 1920," in the *Georgia Historical Quarterly*, December 1922, pages 323–354, and "Agricultural Conditions in Florida in 1925," in *Economic Geography*, July 1927, pages 340–353; W. B. Bizzel, *Rural Texas* (New York, 1924); and S. M. Jordan, "Farming as it used to be, and as it is in Missouri," in the *Missouri Historical Review*, October 1927, pages 13–29.

### AGRICULTURE

Cotton has in recent years received more attention perhaps than any other subject connected with the economic system of the South. Among the numerous volumes of a general nature, the most accurately descriptive is H. B. Brown, *Cotton: History, Species, Varieties, Morphology, Breeding, Culture, Disease, Marketing and Uses* (New York, 1927). An illuminating article is that by M. B. Hammond, "The Southern Farmer and the Cotton Question," in the *Political Science Quarterly*, September 1897, pages 450–475. The westward shifting of cotton culture is discussed by A. B. Cox, "New Cotton Areas for Old," in the *Southwest Political and Social Science Quarterly*, June 1927, pages 49–60. See also L. P. Gabbard, "Effect of Large Scale Production of Cotton Growing in Texas," in the *Journal of Farm Economics*, April 1928, pages 211–224; Rupert B. Vance, *Human Factors in Cotton Culture* (Chapel Hill, N. C., 1929); and A. B. Cox, "American Cotton and World Affairs," in the *Southwest Political and Social Science Quarterly*, March 1926, pages 305–317. The marketing of cotton has received an increasing amount of attention during the past decade; instructive works include: "Organized Commodity Markets," in the *Annals of the American Academy of Political and Social Science*, May 1931; R. H. Montgomery, *Coöperative Pattern in Cotton* (New York, 1929); Harry Barth, "Six Years of Coöperation in Oklahoma," in the *Southwest Political and Social Science Quarterly*, June 1928, pages 76–86; and in the same quarterly for December 1928, pages 311–337, "Marketing Arkansas Farm Products," by J. A. Dickey.

The problems connected with the marketing of tobacco have been given slight attention by Anna Youngman, "The Tobacco Pools of Kentucky and Tennessee," in the *Journal of Political Economy*, January 1910, pages 34–49. For a discussion of rice growing in recent years, see Arthur H. Cole, "The American Industry: A Study in Comparative Advantage," in the *Quarterly Journal of Economics*, August 1927, pages 594–643. Of some interest is V. V. Parr and G. S. Klemmedson, "An Economic Study of the Costs and Methods of Range Cattle Production of Forty Ranches in North Central Texas," in the *Cattleman*, September 1925, pages 9–25.

Because the agrarian discontent in the South has been associated with politics, it has received an unusual amount of treatment. The scholarly works dealing with this subject are: John D. Hicks, *Populist Revolt* (New York, 1931), which is a general treatment and includes also a chapter on Southern agriculture, and "The Farmers Alliance in North Carolina," in the *Annual Report of the American Historical Association* (1922), pages 331–332; Benjamin B. Kendrick, "Agrarian Discontent in the South: 1880–1900," in the *Annual Report of the American Historical Association* (1920), pages 267–272; S. A. Delap, "The Populist Party in North Carolina," in the *Trinity College Historical Society Papers* (1922), pages 40–74; and F. B. Sumpkins, *Tillman Movement in South Carolina* (Durham, N. C., 1926). The most searching study yet made of the agricultural problems which have confronted any Southern State is R. P. Brooks, *Agrarian Revolution in Georgia, 1865–1912* (Madison, Wis., 1914). A. M. Arnett, *Populist Movement in Georgia; a View of the Agrarian Crusade in the Solid-South Politics* (New York, 1922), as its title implies, puts the emphasis mainly on the political aspects and only incidentally on the economic. John Bunyan Clark, *Populism in Alabama* (New York, 1927), is a Ph.D. thesis done at New York University.

Written in a more popular style is J. O. Knauss, "The Farmers Alliance in Florida," in the *South Atlantic Quarterly*, July 1926, pages 300–315. Also see M. J. White, "The Influence of Agricultural Conditions Upon Louisiana State Politics During the Nineties," in the *Annual Report of the American Historical Association* (1921), p. 222 *et seq.* For a general discussion of more recent efforts of farmers to exert their influence by group action, see Edward Wiest, *Agricultural Organization in the United States* (Lexington, Ky., 1923), which is Volume 2 in the UNIVERSITY·OF KENTUCKY STUDIES IN ECONOMICS AND SOCIOLOGY.

## INDUSTRY

The rise of industry in the South, particularly since 1916, has inspired a great deal of writing on this subject. A delightful little book of generalizations is Holland Thompson's *New South; a Chronicle of Social and Industrial Evolution* (New Haven, Conn., 1919). To be consulted as a reliable source of information is John M. Hager, *Commercial Survey of the Southeast* (Washington, 1927), a study made and published under the authority of the United States Department of Commerce.

Broadus and G. S. Mitchell, *Industrial Revolution in the South* (Baltimore, 1930), puts the main emphasis on the cotton textile industry. A Ph.D. thesis done at the University of Chicago by Earl C. Case, entitled *Valley of East Tennessee, The Adjustment of Industry to Natural Environment* (Nashville, Tenn., 1925), attempts to show how the physiographic factors have inevitably forced industrialization. Some reliable material may be found in "The Coming of Industry to the South," in the *Annals of the American Academy of Political and Social Science,* January 1931.

Broadus Mitchell, *Rise of the Cotton Mills in the South* (Baltimore, 1921), gives a careful analysis of an underlying situation which subsequent events and developments have revealed all too clearly. Another stimulating study is Holland Thompson, *From the Cotton Fields to the Cotton Mill: A Study of the Industrial Transition in North Carolina* (New York, 1906).

The best general history of the cotton textile industry is M. T. Copeland, *Cotton Manufacturing Industry in the United States* (Cambridge, Mass., 1923). Edwin Mims, in *Advancing South* (New York, 1929), touches lightly upon looms and furnaces in the South, and shows the growing spirit of liberalism in the section.

An inadequate but enlightening treatment of the tobacco industry may be found in B. W. Arnold, *History of the Tobacco Industry in Virginia from 1860 to 1894* (Baltimore, 1897). If due allowances are made for eulogy and exaggeration, there still remains a little valuable material in J. W. Jenkins, *James B. Duke, Master Builder* (New York, 1927), which gives some idea of how the tobacco industry developed to great economic importance in North Carolina.

The best source of information on the oil industry is Ralph Arnold and William J. Kemnitzer, *Petroleum in the United States and Possessions* (New York, 1931). M. O. Phillips: "Tung Oil: Florida's Infant Industry," in *Economic Geography*, October 1929, pages 348–357, gives this widely discussed subject a careful appraisal as a potential source of wealth for the South. The economics of oil production have received brilliant and original treatment by G. W. Stocking, *Oil Industry and The Competitive System* (New York, 1925); this book deserves serious study by all students interested in the future development of the South's exhaustible natural resources.

For a brief summary of the power situation in the Southeast, see Walter H. Voskuil, *Economics of Water Power Development* (New York, 1928), especially Chapter V.

The coming of industry to the South apparently has disturbed the peace of mind of several thoughtful men. A most extreme statement of a kind of emotionalism aroused by industrialization may be found in *I'll Take My Stand* (New York, 1931), written by twelve Southerners who have been accustomed to the quiet of academic life in Nashville, Tennessee. The attitude of radical labor may be found in Tom Tippett's *When Southern Labor Stirs* (London, 1931).

## TRANSPORTATION

There is no adequate treatment of transportation in the South since the Civil War. To be noted as available sources of information are: C. A. McCombs, "The Present Status of Navigation on the Lower Mississippi River," in the *Journal of Geography*, January 1925, pages 11–19; and "Great Inland Water-way Projects in the United States," in the *Annals of the American Academy of Political and Social Science*, January 1928.

CHAPTER XVII

# Present Economic Problems of the South

SEVERAL fundamental economic problems, some of which are deep rooted in the past, now confront the Southern people. The most important of these problems require further discussion.

## Population

In 1880, the population of the South was 18,360,716, or 36.5 per cent of the total population of the United States. By 1930, the population of the section had increased to 39,619,094, but had declined relatively to 32.2 per cent of the total population of the Nation. The increase in the South's population has not kept pace with the increase in the Nation's total population, since, in recent decades, relatively fewer immigrants have come into the South than elsewhere in the United States, and the growth of population has been due largely to natural increase.

### FOREIGN-BORN

In 1920, as compared with 13.2 per cent of foreign-born population in the United States as a whole, that percentage in the South was much smaller, ranging from only 0.3 per cent in North Carolina to 7.8 per cent in Texas. When compared with 25.5 per cent of foreign-born population in New England or 27.2 per cent in New York, that percentage in the South appears almost a negligible element in the population.[1]

---

[1] Compiled from UNITED STATES CENSUS (1920), *Population*.

PERCENTAGE OF FOREIGN-BORN POPULATION IN THE
SOUTHERN STATES, 1920

| State | Foreign Born | State | Foreign Born |
|---|---|---|---|
| Alabama | 0.8 | Missouri | 5.5 |
| Arkansas | 0.8 | North Carolina | 0.3 |
| Florida | 5.6 | Oklahoma | 2.0 |
| Georgia | 0.6 | South Carolina | 0.4 |
| Kentucky | 1.3 | Tennessee | 0.7 |
| Louisiana | 2.6 | Texas | 7.8 |
| Maryland | 7.1 | Virginia | 1.4 |
| Mississippi | 0.5 | West Virginia | 4.2 |

## NEGROES

In 1930, the negro population in the South was 23.7 per cent of the total population. Since 1870, negroes in the South have not increased relatively so fast as the white population. This comparison is clearly pictured in the chart on page 505.

There are still some districts and cities in the South where the negro population is around 50 per cent of the total population. In 1930, the negro population of Mississippi was 1,009,718, or 50.2 per cent of the total population of the state. Georgia had 1,071,125 negroes, the largest negro population in any state, but the percentage was only 36.8 per cent of the total state population. Three counties in the South have a predominant percentage of negroes. These are Tuncia County, Mississippi, which has 18,224 negroes, or 85.33 per cent of the total population; Lowndes County, Alabama, which has 19,632 negroes, or 85.81 per cent of the total population; and Green County, Alabama, which has 16,263 negroes, or 82.37 per cent of the total population. The two Southern cities which have the largest number of negroes are Baltimore and New Orleans. In 1930, the former had 142,106 negroes; the latter, 129,632. At Birmingham, Alabama, the negro population comprises about 42 per cent of the total population. In 1910, 50.6 per cent of the population of Montgomery, Alabama, was negro; 51.1 per cent, at Savannah, Georgia; and 52.8 per cent, at Charleston, South Carolina.

That there has been a rapid net loss of negroes from
the South to the North is not supported by census statistics.
As summarized in the *Negro Year Book* (1931):[2] "The
1920 Census shows that the proportion of Southern-born

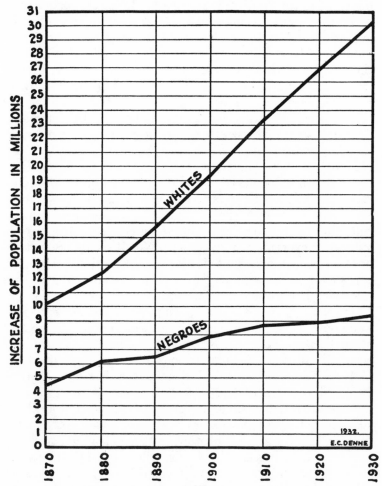

Increase of White and Negro Population in the South, 1870–1930.
Data compiled from UNITED STATES CENSUS, *Reports.*

[2] *Negro Year Book* (1931–1932), p. 340.

Negroes who had migrated to the North or West was 8.1 per cent of the total Negroes born in the South and that this was only about one-fourth larger than the proportion of Negroes who were born in the North or West and had migrated to the South,—6.4 per cent. It is noteworthy that while the migration of Negroes to the North goes on, the migration of Negroes to the South continues and that the number of Negroes from Northern States, 47,223, living in the South in 1920 was 5,734 more than the number, 41,489 from the North or West, who were living in the South in 1910." Since 1890, more negroes have been moving to cities, especially such industrial centers as Birmingham, Alabama; yet, over two thirds of the negroes in the South still live in rural communities.

Many reformers have assumed that the negro population in the South has resulted in a problem based primarily upon racial prejudice. From an economic point of view, however, this opinion is not of supreme importance. As a rule, Southern people are not antagonistic to negroes so long as they remain segregated. Nor does the Southern negro, unless indoctrinated with what the Southerner regards as dangerous propaganda, desire racial equality. In the year 1919, while race riots occurred in Elaine, Arkansas; Charleston, South Carolina; Knoxville, Tennessee; and Longview, Texas, a serious race riot also took place in Chicago, Illinois. The following year, while a race riot occurred in Ocoee, Florida, serious race riots occurred in Duluth, Minnesota, and in Independence, Kansas. During 1921, while only two serious race riots occurred in the South—at Tulsa, Oklahoma, and at Rosewood, Florida— six occurred in the North—at Springfield, Ohio; at Coatsville, Chester, and Johnstown, Pennsylvania; and at Springfield and East St. Louis, Illinois. The so-called "negro problem" of the South is practically the same as the racial problem which the North must face in dealing with many of its foreign immigrants—namely, illiteracy and its concomitant, a low standard of living.

In the South, negroes are concentrated in the rural areas; of all the negroes in the South 6,660,000, or 74.7 per cent, lived in the rural areas in 1920.[3]

PERCENTAGE OF NEGROES LIVING IN RURAL AND
URBAN AREAS OF THE SOUTH

|  | 1920 | 1910 | 1900 |
|---|---|---|---|
| Rural | 74.7 | 78.8 | 82.8 |
| Urban | 25.3 | 21.2 | 17.2 |

In 1925, there were 831,455 negro farmers out of a total of 3,131,418 farmers in the South, or a ratio approximately of one negro to every four white farmers. Of the negro farmers only 23.6 per cent were owners, while 76.5 per cent were tenants. From 1900 to 1925, the number of negro farm tenants increased only 1.9 per cent, while the number of white tenants increased 5.9 per cent.[4]

PERCENTAGE DISTRIBUTION OF FARMERS IN THE
SOUTH, BY TENURE

|  | WHITE | | | | NEGRO | | | |
|---|---|---|---|---|---|---|---|---|
|  | 1925 | 1920 | 1910 | 1900 | 1925 | 1920 | 1910 | 1900 |
| Owners | 57.6 | 60.4 | 60.1 | 63.0 | 23.4 | 23.6 | 24.5 | 25.2 |
| Managers | 0.4 | 0.7 | 0.7 | 0.9 | 0.1 | 0.2 | 0.1 | 0.2 |
| Tenants | 42.0 | 38.9 | 39.2 | 36.1 | 76.5 | 76.2 | 75.4 | 74.6 |
| TOTAL | 100.0 | 100.0 | 100.0 | 100.0 | 100.0 | 100.0 | 100.0 | 100.0 |

The size of negro farms in the South seldom exceeds 30 or 40 acres, and the organization of such farms is simple. The owner usually has a mule, a cow, a few hogs, and some poultry; a ramshackle wagon, a plow, a few hoes, shovels, and axes; and occasionally a model T Ford. The homes of most negro owners and tenants are ill-provided, unpainted, two-or-three-room, box-shaped structures made of boards nailed vertically to a frame and covered with clapboards; or, as in some regions of Georgia, the homes are old-fashioned log cabins with "stick and mud" chimneys.

Few Southern negroes receive more than a subsistence income from agriculture. Although negro tenants as a rule

[3] Compiled from *Ibid.*, p. 127.
[4] Compiled from *Ibid.*, p. 126.

fare about as well as poor white tenants, in a few regions of the South, the negro farmers are reduced *de facto* to a form of serfdom by their credit system, which keeps them continuously obligated to plantation owners who act as their guarantors.  A summary of interviews with 588 negro farmers indicates that a very high percentage of them resort to four types of credit—mortgages, short-time cash, fertilizer, and merchant—and that the costs were excessive and constituted a heavy drain on the negro's income.[5]

#### PROPORTION OF NEGRO FARMERS USING CREDIT, AND COST OF CREDIT

| Types of Credit | Percentage Using Credit | Cost of Credit (Per Cent of Income) |
|---|---|---|
| Mortgages | 51.0 | 6.0 |
| Short-Time Cash | 43.0 | 16.8 |
| Fertilizer | 65.5 | 37.2 |
| Merchant | 52.4 | 26.0 |

As perhaps intended, this system of granting credit to negro tenants has lessened the mobility of such labor.  According to the Federal Census, the number of years that negro tenants had lived on farms which they were renting when the census was taken for 1920 was: less than one year, 15.4 per cent; one year, 24.7 per cent; two to four years, 33.8 per cent; and five years and over, 26 per cent.

During the past decade, a large number of Mexican laborers immigrated into the Southwest.  They constituted a floating supply of labor which was found useful in the cotton fields and in the citrus fruit groves, but their low standard of living allowed their employment at an even lower wage than was paid negro laborers.  Hence they became effective competitors of negro labor.  Whether the Federal Department of Labor, through the exercise of power vested in it by the immigration laws, will continue

---

[5] This is an analytical study based upon interviews with 588 negro farmers, by R. B. Eulster, Institute for Research in the Social Sciences, University of North Carolina.

to restrict such immigration as it has done from 1929 to 1932, remains to be seen.

Since the Civil War, Southern negroes have been migrating cityward. During the Great War and afterwards, when there was on the part of industry an insistent demand for labor because of the virtual stoppage of European immigration, negro migration to cities, especially the industrial centers, was greatly accelerated. During the decade from 1900 to 1920, the negro population of Southern cities increased by approximately 400,000; and during the five-year period from 1920 to 1925, the negro farm population of the South decreased by approximately 800,000. For each Southern State, this decrease in negro farm population and the percentage of decrease from 1920 to 1925 is indicated in the following table: [6]

DECREASE IN NEGRO FARM POPULATION, AND
PERCENTAGE OF DECREASE, 1920–1925

| State | Decrease | Per Cent of Decrease |
|---|---|---|
| Maryland | 14,676 | 23.3 |
| Virginia | 26,096 | 8.4 |
| West Virginia | 422[a] | 10.4 |
| North Carolina | 18,236 | 3.8 |
| South Carolina | 111,270 | 17.4 |
| Georgia | 232,961 | 30.8 |
| Florida | 15,005 | 17.0 |
| Kentucky | 21,093 | 28.7 |
| Tennessee | 35,868 | 17.6 |
| Alabama | 79,576 | 15.4 |
| Mississippi | 73,569 | 10.2 |
| Arkansas | 61,218 | 18.3 |
| Louisiana | 45,990 | 12.7 |
| Oklahoma | 18,306 | 10.4 |
| Texas | 32,821 | 7.8 |

[a] Increase.

While some of the negroes who left the rural areas migrated to Northern cities, the larger percentage concentrated in Southern cities wherever jobs were available.

Negroes have been employed mainly for the heavier

[6] Compiled from *Negro Year Book* (1931–1932), p. 131.

tasks in the building trades; in lumber and furniture mills; in iron and steel plants; in tobacco factories; and in mining, particularly in Alabama and West Virginia. Many negroes, especially negro women, who migrated to the cities became domestic servants. The number of negroes in the various trades and professions has remained relatively small. This has been due in part to white competition and in part to lack of educational opportunity.

Due to the marginal character of negro laborers, their wages have tended to fluctuate widely.[7]    Dr. Snavely found, in a study of negro migration in 1917, that sawmills and turpentine distilleries were willing to pay per day for negro labor $1.50 to $2, and shipbuilding, from $1.75 to $2.[8]    Dr. Pinchbeck's study of negro artisans in Virginia shows that an increase occurred in wages for negro day laborers from $1.13 in 1900 to $3.11 in 1923, and that the peak was reached in 1919 when the rate was $3.56.[9]

The pay of negroes in the South has usually been less than that received by white workers. In Virginia, the average wage for negro carpenters over a period of twenty-three years was 50 per cent less than that for white carpenters. In Georgia industries, according to a study made by the Women's Bureau, the median wage paid negro women was $6.20 per week, while that paid white women was $12.20. Such different wage rates between negro and white laborers in the South have been due to a belief on the part of white employers that negroes can "live on less"; to a lack of bargaining power on the part of negroes themselves; and, in some instances, to a difference in productive efficiency of whites and blacks.

---

[7] For a brief discussion of wage theories, consult Lionel D. Edie, *Economics: Principles and Problems* (2d Edition), Chapter XIV.

[8] Report for the United States Department of Labor: T. R. Snavely, *Negro Migration in 1916–1917*, p. 73 *et seq.*

[9] Raymond Pinchbeck, *Virginia Negro Artisan and Tradesman*, pp. 105–106.

Since 1929, hundreds of negroes in industrial centers of the South have found themselves without employment and solely dependent upon charity for their food, shelter, and clothing. Whether they can return to the rural areas is doubtful, because, as in industry, there is no demand for additional labor in agriculture.

The negro, unlike the Anglo-Saxon, has not yet passed through a long process of evolution in an environment requiring initiative and creative imagination. His habits still tend to ostentatious consumption whenever possible, which, without a system of paternalism on the part of the white population, frequently prevents him from accumulating the necessary capital to improve his economic status. It must be admitted that merchants, salesmen, organizers, and reformers, both in the South and from other sections, have sometimes exploited this economic weakness of the Southern negro. To raise the economic status of the negro population, which comprises practically one fourth of the consumers in the Southern market, is a fundamental problem, however, that involves among other considerations the question of the productive efficiency of negro as compared with white labor.

One of the basic principles of the *New Deal* is that of increasing consumer purchasing power by raising wages of employees to a legal minimum. As embodied in the National Industrial Recovery Act, approved early in June 1933, this principle permits no differential in wages of whites and negroes engaged in the same kind of work. The effect of this legislation indicates already that wherever possible white labor will be substituted for negro labor. How extensive this change may be will depend of course upon the demand for labor, as well as the relative efficiency of negro and white labor. To compel employers to pay the same wage to laborers of unequal efficiency is an arbitrary and impracticable policy. Hence, in so far as there is a difference in the productive efficiency of the two classes of labor in the South, a law equalizing wages in accordance with a single legal minimum will either work a hardship upon those employers who retain their negro employees, or it will add to the great army of unemployed negroes as white employees are substituted for colored laborers. In the long run, perhaps a more satisfactory solution to the problem of raising the negro's economic status in the South will be effected by a general progressive training of the negro through educational facilities including a curriculum made up principally of vocational and business subjects.

## POOR WHITES

The poor whites constitute another element in the population of the South. Before the Civil War, in such areas as east Mississippi and the pine barrens of Georgia, there were poor whites who were characterized by such appellations as "piney woods people," "hill billies," and "clay eaters." As a class distinct from the slaveholders, the small independent farmers, and the artisans, they have been shiftless, ignorant, and degraded. Indeed, Hundley describes them as "the laziest two-legged animals that walk erect on the face of the earth. Even their motions are slow, and their speech is a sickening drawl . . . while their thoughts and ideas seem likewise to creep along at a snail's pace. All they seem to care for is to live from hand to mouth; to get drunk . . . to attend gander pullings; to vote at elections; to eat and sleep; to lounge in the sunshine of a bright summer's day, and to bask in the warmth of a roaring wood fire, when summer days are over." [10]

To this day, in a few areas of the South, there are poor whites whose economic status has never been improved from that of their forbears. During recent years, because of their prejudices and peculiarities, they have frequently been exploited by political demagogues. Certain political candidates, in order to gain the vote of the poor whites,

---

[10] D. R. Hundley, *Social Relations in our Southern States*, pp. 263-264.

have traveled among them in ox-wagons, in model T Fords, or even on foot, and have preached a doctrine of the "forgotten man."

However, it is the hookworm and not the rise of industry nor the concentration of wealth that has been primarily responsible for the existence of this class of economically helpless people in the South. In 1902, Dr. Charles W. Stiles [11] succeeded in demonstrating the prevalence of this malady (*Uncinariasis*) in the sandy, rural districts of the South, the areas in which poor whites have been living for generations. Therefore, since a large part of the proverbial laziness and ignorance of the poor whites can be attributed to a disease, improvement in their welfare may rest upon medical science as well as upon political or economic reform measures.

## Agriculture

Obviously the problems confronting agriculture in the border states of the South are not unlike those of cereal farming and livestock growing areas elsewhere in the United States.

### COTTON PRODUCTION

The Cotton Belt, being one of the most highly specialized agricultural regions of the world, presents problems somewhat peculiar to the South. Cotton producers, as consumers, are largely dependent upon the price they get for cotton; and those sellers who are indirectly dependent upon a market comprised of cotton producers, are affected almost immediately by changes in the price of cotton. This fact has been especially noticeable during the past two years.

Because of the recent precipitous decline in cotton prices, the cotton states of the South are suffering severely

---

[11] C. W. Stiles, *Report upon the Prevalence and Geographic Distribution of Hookworm Disease in the United States,* U. S. Treasury Department, Hygienic Laboratory, Bulletin No. 10.

from the loss of consumer buying power, the decline in property values, and the concomitant falling-off in tax receipts. Cotton planters cannot raise the price of cotton; neither can they, as a rule, effect appreciable reductions in their cost of production. Their taxes are fixed by law to meet the expenditures of government, a great part of which have been incurred through public debts for roads, schools, and the extension of the police powers in the various states. Their expenses for labor and capital appear to be almost at a minimum already.

After the Civil War, cotton planters had to establish a system by which they could more effectively use the freed negroes. As a result the practice now known as the *share*, or *cropping*, *system* was established. According to this system, the landlord furnishes an allotment of land, a house, seeds, implements, and mules. He also gins the cotton, pays for part or all of the fertilizer, and gives the tenant—in practically every case a negro—for planting, cultivating, and picking the crop, a fractional part of it. In the meantime the landlord has usually advanced the tenant supplies for a year, or he may have gone "security" for him at the community store. By this method the negroes are continuously kept in debt, with the result that their status is practically the same as serfdom in the days of the manorial system in England. In other words, the expenses of labor in the cotton fields of the South are already at the subsistence level.

Although there is little mechanized farming in the Cotton Belt, except in the region around Corpus Christi, Texas, cotton planters are compelled to buy many small tools and implements and, in the eastern part of the Cotton Belt, much commercial fertilizer. Under the present system of protective tariff, the sellers of such products are able to hold up their prices for a considerable time after the price of cotton has declined. This practice throws a disproportionate burden not only upon the cotton planters, but upon all farmers who have to buy such articles.

The clamor for relief in the cotton states has brought forth numerous proposed remedies, the most novel of which has been embodied in the *Emergency Farm Relief Act,* approved May 12, 1933. In its declaration of policy, the act states that it aims to establish a balance between production and consumption of agricultural commodities that will restore farm prices to the level of a base period from August 1909 to July 1914—with the exception of the price of tobacco, which is to be restored to the level of a base period from August 1919 to July 1929. The act aims also to correct the inequality of purchasing power between farm products and other commodities. The price increase is to be accomplished through reductions in acreage, or in production for market, of selected, basic agricultural commodities. The revenue necessary for this purpose is to be obtained through taxes assessed against the first domestic processing of the commodity and is to be paid by the processor. However, to provide immediate funds for the administration of the act, as well as for rental and benefit payments to farmers for reduction in acreage, an appropriation of $100,000,000 has been authorized. The Secretary of Agriculture is empowered to administer the act.

In 1933, cotton planters in the South had under cultivation about 39,000,000 acres. The government offered to lease from 25 to 40 per cent of each cotton grower's acreage at a rental of from $6 to $12 an acre, in order to reduce the area under cultivation. Early in July of the same year, President Roosevelt appealed to the cotton growers to coöperate in this program as a "patriotic" duty. Within about two weeks after his message was received, approximately 1,000,000 contracts were signed by cotton planters. In accordance with this program, the 1933 cotton crop has been reduced by more than 4,000,000 bales and cotton planters have received nearly $90,000,000 as acreage rentals. However, in August 1933, after the plowing under of the cotton had been completed, the Government's estimate of the crop showed that production would still include about

1,000,000 bales more than earlier estimates had indicated. This increase occurred in Texas and Oklahoma. As a result, the New York price of cotton dropped below 9 cents per pound, and then tended to fluctuate around that level. The bonus to cotton growers will be recovered by the Government from the processing tax. The rate of this tax, which, according to the law, must be such as will equal the difference between the current average farm price and the fair exchange value, was fixed at 4.2 cents per pound and became effective the first day of August. This tax upon cotton is estimated to yield about $120,000,000.

A somewhat similar program has been used for reducing the tobacco acreage by about 50 per cent. The Georgia and Florida tobacco growers were paid for leaving unharvested an average of four stalk leaves on each tobacco plant grown. The compensation ranged from $15 to $47 per acre. This amount, advanced by the Government, will be raised by a processing tax of about 6 cents per pound.

What effect the New Deal legislation will have upon the agricultural organization of the South will depend upon how long the present administration continues its policy, and to what degree the Government successfully carries out its whole scheme of planned national economy. Clearly, the Emergency Farm Relief Act is not merely a piece of emergency legislation since it does not terminate automatically as do many of the other new laws; however, it may be terminated at any time by the President. Inasmuch, therefore, as farmers are a powerful political pressure group, it may be expected that this act will be continued as a means of granting a direct subsidy to agriculture. It also appears, however, that, if the Government is to carry through successfully the program of the National Industrial Recovery Act, it must use its power to prevent competition of foreign goods in American markets. Such a curtailment of imports might involve a further decline in the volume of exports.

The South produces about 60 per cent of the world's

supply of cotton, and in recent years about one half of the Southern commercial cotton crop has been exported to foreign markets.[12]

EXPORT OF SOUTHERN COTTON, 1925–1930

| Year | Crop (Bales) | Export (Bales) |
|------|-------------|----------------|
| 1925 | 14,698,000 | 8,257,000 |
| 1926 | 15,614,000 | 8,252,000 |
| 1927 | 19,206,000 | 11,243,000 |
| 1928 | 14,444,000 | 7,830,000 |
| 1929 | 15,785,000 | 8,279,000 |
| 1930 | 14,514,000 | 6,852,000 |

The exportable surplus sold in the world market is the fundamental, disturbing factor in the price of the whole cotton crop. If the foreign market price is lower than the domestic price, exports tend to decline and this result, in turn, forces down the price in the domestic market. Since the price of Southern cotton in the world market is largely determined by competition, its price cannot be pegged in this country. Such procedure has already been attempted by the Federal Farm Board, and its efforts to stabilize prices of major agricultural products have been condemned by experience.

Practically the same conditions prevail in the case of tobacco, since in normal times about 30 per cent of the South's crop is exported. Hence, it appears, both cotton planters and tobacco growers are so largely dependent upon foreign markets that a further decline in exports, brought about through an ardent nationalistic program, would mean nothing short of disaster if a large Federal subsidy for the cotton and tobacco regions of the South were not immediately provided.

## DIVERSIFICATION FARMING

Recently much has been said about *diversification* as the ultimate solution for the cotton planters' problem. It has

[12] Compiled from the *Annual Reports of the New Orleans Cotton Exchange.*

been claimed that under a nationalistic program this change would offset the loss of foreign markets.

This method of farming is, however, not new; it was urged upon the Cotton Belt in the period of falling prices before the Civil War. Protagonists of the theory proceed upon the assumption that cotton planters can, at will, substitute mixed farming, or a "cow, hog and hen economy," for a specialized system of agriculture. Yet they overlook the practical consideration that, while this plan would enable the planters to raise enough food for local consumption, it would also produce a supply of cereals and meats in competition with an already abundant supply of those products, with the consequence that prices would probably be driven down to a level as unprofitable as that of present cotton prices.

As a rule, argument by analogy is dangerous in economics. Its results certainly have been most unfortunate when, for example, cheese manufactures were established in Mississippi, simply because they had been successful in similar localities in Pennsylvania. An important difference between the two regions was not considered: Mississippi has no outlet market for dairy products while Pennsylvania has access to metropolitan markets.

The inescapable fact relative to diversification is that the Cotton Belt is more suitable for a specialized agriculture than for any other type, and is, as a result, likely to continue its present practices for a long time. Of course, the economic status of cotton planters will fluctuate with every marked rise and fall in the price of cotton; moreover, on account of the low productivity of land in certain regions of the South, the average per capita income of Southern farmers, notwithstanding subsidies from the Federal Government, may be expected to remain low. Even in 1918, according to a study of the National Bureau of Economic Research, the per capita current income of the farm population in the South was \$260, as compared with \$470 for the rest of the United States.[13]

## Industry

Although in recent years much has been heard about industrialization and the "new industrial revolution" in the South, it will be seen from the map on page 520 that industry in the South is localized mainly within the Highland and the Piedmont regions, principally because of the location of power sites and raw materials. On account of the absence of these factors, there is little industry in the rest of the South, and there probably will be little for a long time to come.

The location of natural resources has made an inevitable division of the economic development of the South into two regions: one more or less industrial, and the other predominantly agrarian.

Apparently the Tennessee River Valley offers the greatest opportunities for future industrial development in the South. By an act of Congress approved May 18, 1933, Muscle Shoals will be completed and operated as a Federal project. Whatever the outcome may be, the development of Muscle Shoals, which was begun in the Wilson administration and subsequently neglected by Republican administrations, is a definite part of the New Deal program. As provided in the 1933 act, a corporation known as the *Tennessee Valley Authority* has been created. This corporation has a board of directors composed of three members, appointed by the President and the Senate for a term of nine years at a salary of \$10,000 annually plus residence in a Government house at Muscle Shoals. The corporation is authorized to construct a huge interconnected system of dams, power houses, and transmission lines to form an entire Tennessee River system; and also

---

[13] See Chapter IX of *Income in the Various States, Its Sources and Distribution, 1919, 1920, 1921,* published by the National Bureau of Economic Research, Inc., New York.

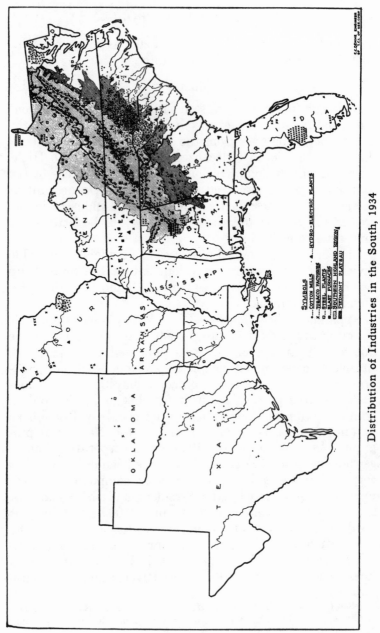

Distribution of Industries in the South, 1934

to improve navigation in the Tennessee River, to control the destructive flood waters in the Tennessee River, and to manufacture and sell at Muscle Shoals fixed nitrogen, fertilizer, and fertilizer ingredients. Surplus electric power is to be sold—preference being given to states, counties, municipalities, and organizations of farmers—for the purpose of supplying electricity to citizens at rates "reasonable, just and fair." For constructing dams, steam plants, or other facilities, the corporation may on the credit of the United States issue serial bonds not exceeding $50,000,000 in amount, having a maturity of not more than 50 years, and bearing interest not to exceed 3½ per cent per annum. In case of war, the Federal Government reserves the right to take over all the property for the manufacture of explosives or for other war purposes.

This project, however, is primarily experimental. Although the board of directors, through dissemination of propaganda, has aroused much enthusiasm for the project, nevertheless the ultimate success of Muscle Shoals is still problematical. Whether or not the loss already incurred by the stockholders of local power companies will be offset by lower kilowatt rates, without a social loss to the communities affected, will depend not only upon the policy of the board of directors itself, but fundamentally upon the fact that a power plant operates according to the principle of diminishing costs. Hence the rate for which the current will be sold, unless a loss is compensated for by means of taxation, will depend upon the extent of the demand for electric power.

The development of industry in the Piedmont and the Highland regions of the South has, in recent years, been rapid and impressive. As Professor Broadus Mitchell says, however: [14] "The present juncture demands not 'political arithmetic' but economic theory."

---

[14] Broadus Mitchell, "Growth of Manufacturers in the South," in the *Annals of the American Academy*, Vol. 153, p. 22.

### The Entrepreneur

From the viewpoint of the industrial entrepreneur, the most fundamental problem in the South is that of finding a sufficiently wide market for his product. The Northern market for many goods is already adequately supplied by Northern factories. Such a condition, in turn, limits the Southern entrepreneur to production for the Southern market or for foreign export. This situation is not true of the tobacco industry, the Texas sulphur industry, and a few other Southern industries that have absolute advantages. In the case of those industries which have been developed on the assumption of comparative advantage, the limitation of their market is the chief factor in determining their size and business profits. The market for steel produced in the Birmingham district is limited almost solely to the South and to the export trade. Mainly because of transportation charges, no steel from this district is used in the automobile industry. Therefore, when the export demand declines, as at present, the Birmingham steel industry becomes wholly dependent upon the needs of the Southern market itself.

For certain products another limitation of the Southern market is the low purchasing power of the negroes, who constitute nearly one fourth of the Southern population. Indeed, the protagonists for the so-called "agrarian movement," who are afraid that industry will ultimately destroy "Southern culture," may calm their fears somewhat by a careful analysis of those fundamental factors which limit industrial expansion.

### The Wage-Earner

In 1929, the number of employees in manufacturing plants in the South was 1,754,907. During the period of industrial expansion, many of these, hoping to improve their economic status and to enjoy an urban environment, left the farm for the factory. In many instances they have been ruthlessly disillusioned. Even in the days of prosperity their money wages were lower than those of factory workers in the North and the West. Nor has it been established that their real wages were so high as those in other sections. According to Dr. Starnes: [15] "In any attempt to compare real wages North and South, the payments in kind which are received by workers in some industries must be taken into consideration. In the textile industry, for instance, cheap house rent, fuel at cost, aid to the sick, and other welfare activities are factors which must be taken into account in making a comparison of real wages North and South. The American Cotton Manufacturers Association has estimated that the value of nominal charges for rent, water, light, fuel, and welfare work is $4.36 a week. Even if we admit that these figures are correct, money wages in the textile plants of the South are still considerably lower than in New England. On the other hand, low wages in the South are not confined to the textile industry. The average per capita income of all wage earners is much lower than in other sections of the country. It is probably true that, taking the South as a whole, the cost of living is lower in this section than in other parts of the United States, but it is not sufficient to account for the noticeable difference in wages."

According to a study of wages and living conditions in the South, made under the direction of the Institute for Research in the Social Sciences, at the University of Virginia, a comparison of wages in the cotton textile industry of the South with those of New England mills, in 1928, shows that the average difference in weekly earnings of the several occupations within the mills was $6.71 in favor of the New England mills. A comparison of wages for

---

[15] G. T. Starnes, "Effects of Industrialization on Labor," in the *Proceedings of the Southeastern Economic Association* (1930), pp. 146–147. Reprinted by permission of the author.

certain of these occupations will be found in the following table: [16]

COMPARISON OF WEEKLY EARNINGS IN
COTTON TEXTILE INDUSTRY, 1928

| Occupation | Average South | Average North | Actual Difference |
|---|---|---|---|
| Card tenders and strippers (male)..... | $10.28 | $17.93 | $ 7.65 |
| Drawing-frame tenders (male)........ | 9.91 | 15.68 | 5.77 |
| Drawing-frame tenders (female)....... | 8.13 | 12.89 | 4.76 |
| Speeder tenders (male)............... | 13.65 | 21.12 | 7.47 |
| Speeder tenders (females) ........... | 11.48 | 15.59 | 4.11 |
| Loom fixers (male)................... | 18.38 | 28.43 | 10.05 |
| Slasher tenders (male)............... | 14.57 | 23.69 | 9.12 |
| Frame spinners (male).............. | 6.76 | 17.51 | 10.75 |
| Frame spinners (female)............. | 8.49 | 14.91 | 6.42 |
| Trimmers or inspectors (female)....... | 9.30 | 12.07 | 2.77 |
| Weavers (male).................... | 13.57 | 19.60 | 6.03 |
| Weavers (female).................. | 12.05 | 17.71 | 5.66 |
| AVERAGE DIFFERENCE.......... | | | 6.713 |

Wages for unskilled labor in the iron and steel industry in the Birmingham district, in 1928, were higher than those in the Southern cotton textile industry; but they were lower than those for the same type of industry in the Pittsburgh district. Wages for skilled labor were not much different from wages paid for similar labor in the North, because most of the skilled labor had to be brought into the Birmingham district from other sections.

Wage rates and earnings varied among different jobs, industries, and states in the South. In practically every industry they were below the level of wages paid in the rest of the United States for similar employment. Relatively the cotton textile and the woodworking industries paid the lowest wages, while the railroad repair shops, the machine shops, and the printing companies paid the highest. Thus, in 1927, the average annual wage for employees in the knit-goods industry in ten industrial states of the South was $655, which was only 59.6 per cent of the aver-

[16] Compiled from Berglund, Starnes, De Vyver, Labor in the Industrial South, p. 99.

age wage paid that industry in the rest of the United States.[17]

According to Mercer G. Evans, of Emory University:[18] "The average wage for the cotton-goods industry in the South was $671, which was 66.3 per cent of the average for the other states. The average wage for the woodworking industries was $748, which was 62.5 per cent. On the other hand, the average wage for foundries and machine shops was $1,230, or 80.4 per cent of the average for the rest of the country; for railroad repair shops, $1,376, or 89.5 per cent, and for printing, $1,570, or 88.5 per cent of the wages in the printing industry in the United States."

The hours of labor in the Southern cotton mills in 1927, have been described by Blanchard as follows:[19] "While Henry Ford has inaugurated the 5-day week, many of the Southern cotton mills retain the 11-hour day and the 12-hour night. They have the longest nominal working week of any considerable manufacturing industry in the United States. The 8-hour day is virtually unknown.

"Legally, North Carolina and Georgia have the 60-hour week, South Carolina the 55-hour week, and Alabama no limit. All of the Southern States allow night work for women. When they work 12 hours a night, they have Saturday night and Sunday night for vacation.

"These are cold statistical statements. What do they mean?

"A man working 11 hours a day in a cotton mill rises at 5:30, bolts a hasty breakfast, and hurries off to reach the mill before the last whistle at 6 o'clock. Probably he stands up all day at the machine, has one hour off for lunch, and leaves the factory at 6:00 P.M. His wife may

---

[17] See Clarence Heer, *Income and Wages in the South.*

[18] Mercer G. Evans, "Southern Labor and Working Conditions in Industry," in the *Annals of the American Academy,* Vol. 153, p. 161. Reprinted by permission of the author.

[19] P. Blanchard, "Labor in Southern Cotton Mills," quoted in the *American Labor Legislative Review* (March 1928), p. 48. Reprinted by permission of the American Association for Labor Legislation.

work with him and go home to prepare the family supper after work.

"The 12-hour night means in practice that a sixteen-year-old girl may stand at the machines from 6 P.M. to 6:15 A.M., with a 15-minute recess for lunch about midnight. I found one mill in Athens, Georgia, which gave no lunch period to its night workers, except to weavers. The other workers ate a midnight sandwich while standing at the machines.

"Night work is particularly gruelling and in most mills there is no extra pay for it. It is not always easy to fill the night force. When there is a shortage of work the employers may give jobs to day workers only on condition that some members of the family work at night."

It should be added that there are some exceptions to these generalizations. Here and there appears an instance of paternalism, as for example in one group of mills in Alabama. Nor is paternalism to be wholly condemned, since many of the factory workers are illiterate and irresponsible. On the other hand, there were in the South a few mills that had exploited women and children even more ruthlessly than Blanchard has described. This practice was made possible, as in Alabama, because there was no legal limit to the hours women might work, and because the state law regarding child labor was not enforced. The excuse for such extreme cases has been due largely to an effort to minimize the cost of production by using cheap labor to operate obsolete machinery which was brought into the South from New England, where higher wages had made the use of such machinery unprofitable.

Generally the wage-earners have been helpless to remedy these conditions. Finally, however, through the interference of the Federal Government, they have found at least temporary protection from exploitation. According to the National Industrial Recovery Act, the President is authorized to approve codes of fair competition submitted to him by industrial and trade groups; and once approved, such a code becomes the standard of fair competition for that group, and will be enforced during a period of two years. Pending the adoption and prescription of codes under this act, the President, on July 21, 1933, announced a Blanket Code to be effective from August 31 to December 31, 1933. By the provisions of this general code, child labor was abolished, and the maximum hours for clerical and mercantile workers limited to a 40-hour week, and for artisans, mechanics, and laborers, to a '35-hour week. Wages were fixed as follows: for clerical and mercantile workers, not less than $15 per week in any city of over 500,000 population; $14.50 in any city of between 250,000 and 500,000 population; $14 in any city between 2,500 and 250,000. The minimum wage fixed for artisans, mechanics, and laborers was 40 cents per hour. The codes subsequently approved for different industrial groups embody, in the main, these general principles.

The code of fair competition for the cotton textile industry, as approved on July 9, 1933, specifically states that the minimum wage which shall be paid by employers to any of their employees—except learners during a six weeks' apprenticeship, cleaners, and outside employees— shall be at the rate of $12 per week when the workers are employed in the Southern section of the industry. This wage, on account of lower living costs in the South, is $1 less per week than the minimum rate fixed for employees in the Northern section of the industry. Employees— except repair shop crews, engineers, electricians, firemen, office and shipping staffs, and outside crews—cannot be employed in excess of 40 hours per week. No minor under 16 years of age may be employed. Codes with somewhat similar provisions have been approved for practically all other industries.

Whether child labor, after the declared national emergency has expired, will again be permitted cannot be predicted. If it may be assumed that labor in the future, as in the past, will strive to hold whatever advantage it has gained, it is reasonable to hope for the ultimate and final abolition of this ancient atrocity—child labor, which, when permitted, has always left in those communities a blight of disease, squalor, and ignorance.

In the South several industries, including the iron and steel industry in the Birmingham district, have refused to employ union labor; as a result, collective bargaining has been impossible. Although unions exist in several skilled trades in the South, the American Federation of Labor has made little headway in the section. Since 1929, strikes in North Carolina and Kentucky have plainly indicated the backwardness of Southern labor in matters of organization. However at the present time, according to the National Industrial Recovery Act, employees are given the right to bargain collectively. This right, no doubt, will enable labor to organize quickly in the South, especially if the policy adopted by the various unions follows that already adopted by the American Federation of Labor: an avowed interest in cost reduction and waste elimination.

The fundamental cause for the helplessness of labor in the South is that there is a surplus supply of labor. Should labor use the strike as a weapon—as it did in the rayon industry at Elizabethton, Tennessee—there is always enough new labor quickly available to replace the old force, especially if the labor is unskilled or semiskilled.

## EXPLOITATION

The problems of industrial development, however, are not confined to entrepreneurs and wage-earners; they affect society as a whole. There is no doubt, of course, that industry has brought great benefits to the South. The statistics of the distribution of electrical energy indicate, on a broad basis, the higher standard of living realized through the use of electric lights, electrical refrigeration, radios, and other electrical conveniences.[20]

---

[20] See pages 479–481 of this text.

On account of the rapid development of industry in the South, not only has progress been realized in the education and tastes of the people, but there has been made available a greater variety of consumers' goods, by means of which many of the higher-salaried wage-earners have enjoyed practically a luxury standard of living.  Since 1929, however, the depression has wiped out many of the gains which industry brought to the South, and several industrial communities are now faced with the grave economic problems of financial ruin and unemployment.

In some localities there is arising a dangerous class consciousness, due primarily to absentee ownership.  During the last three decades, much capital has flowed into the South from other sections.  Most of the iron and steel industry is owned by Northern corporations.  The electric power plants, though many of them were originally built by local capital, have nearly all passed into the control of holding companies with headquarters located usually in New York City.  In the cotton industry, companies in New England operate mills in the Piedmont region; and the rayon industry is controlled by absentee owners.  Retail chain stores, with Northern control, have driven out of existence many of the local, independent dealers.  Much watered stock in such corporations as public utility holding companies, investment trusts, and oil companies, has been sold to Southern people.  The South unfortunately has been a land of "suckers" for smooth stock salesmen, mainly because Southern people, being predominantly agrarian in their experiences, are too often unfamiliar with the intricate financial structure of large corporations and the involved methods of investment analysis.  In short, the South's resources—raw materials, labor, and savings—have been exploited.  The profits derived from Southern industry have gone elsewhere, or have been returned to the South only in the form of loans.

As soon as the depression impinges upon such absentee owners, they curtail production or close their plants completely, and a great army of unemployed are thrown upon the respective communities to be supported by charity. In this situation are the seeds for eventual disaster. "To prevent this disaster," says Professor T. N. Carver, of Harvard University, "the South should take active measures to build up savings institutions and to encourage rich and poor alike to invest their savings wisely, to the end that, so far as possible, resident ownership should displace absentee ownership." [21]

## Banking

The South has the lowest per capita savings, and demand and time deposits of all sections of the United States. In 1931, the average per capita savings deposit of the sixteen Southern States was only $58.47, and the average per capita demand and time deposits was only $149.62.[22] At the same time, the average per capita savings deposit of the New England States was $593.02, and the average demand and time deposits was $797.86.

### BANKING LEGISLATION

From the close of the Civil War until the beginning of the twentieth century, the increase in the number and deposits of banks in the South was slow. Throughout the Cotton Belt, the destruction of the plantation system was followed by the establishment of the cropping system. To supply the tenants with food and clothing during the growing season, the local merchants assumed the role of "banker" by advancing the necessary supplies and allowing the debtors to pay at the end of the season, when enough cotton was to be presented to satisfy each account. In

[21] T. N. Carver, "The Economic Effects of the Growth of Manufacturing," in the *Proceedings of the Southeastern Economic Association* (1930), p. 156.

[22] See U. S. Comptroller of the Currency, *Annual Report* (December 1931). Although this report lists Maryland, Missouri, and Oklahoma as "Eastern," "Middle Western" and "Western," respectively, the above calculation has been made to include these states as "Southern."

other regions of the South, merchants accepted agricultural produce in direct exchange for goods or in payment of accounts. This practice was adopted mainly as a makeshift in the absence of money and bank credit in the rural communities. In the towns and cities, state banks predominated.

Under the National Bank Act of 1863, no bank could be chartered with a capital of less than $50,000, an amount too large for many small towns to provide. The rates of interest in the South were too high to make it profitable to invest capital in Government bonds, in order to put into circulation bank notes limited to 90 per cent of the par value of such bonds. Furthermore, national banks were prohibited from making loans on real estate, but this was the chief collateral in the South after the Civil War. Finally, the act prohibited a national bank from lending more than 10 per cent of its capital to any one person. This restriction was impractical, because frequently the cotton business of an entire community was concentrated in the hands of one person.

In 1900, the Gold Standard Act modified the National Bank Act by authorizing the establishment of national banks with a minimum capital of $25,000 in places of less than 3,000 inhabitants. This provision met the needs of the South, and the number of national banks nearly doubled within the next five years. During the first quarter of the twentieth century, not only did the number of national banks increase at an accelerated rate, but state banks sprang up in the South almost like mushrooms.

With rising prices after 1914, there was a great demand for credit, in order to expand agriculture and business in general. To meet this demand, the state bank was the most easily organized and operated institution, because in most Southern States its authorization was very loosely circumscribed by law. In 1928, the South had 6,185 state bank and trust companies, and 2,251 national banks. The growth of banking for specified years from 1876 to 1930 is indicated in the table below: [23]

### NUMBER OF BANKS IN THE SOUTH AND AMOUNT OF INDIVIDUAL DEPOSITS

| Year | Amount of Individual Deposits | Number of Banks |
|------|------------------------------:|----------------:|
| 1876 | $ 160,187,000 | 1,127 |
| 1881 | 221,759,000 | 1,007 |
| 1909 | 1,728,037,000 | 7,391 |
| 1914 | 2,372,031,000 | 9,207 |
| 1919 | 4,958,956,000 | 9,459 |
| 1923 | 5,958,175,000 | 9,854 |
| 1930 | 6,971,096,000 | 7,411 |

### BANK FAILURES

Although the increase of banks, particularly state banks, in the South has been phenomenal, at the same time no section of the United States has had so many bank failures. During the ten and a half years prior to June 30, 1931, there were in the South 2,667 suspensions of state and private banks, and 344 suspensions of national banks—a total of 3,011 bank suspensions, or 39.1 per cent of all the bank failures in the United States during that period.[24] For the New England States, the total number of bank suspensions during the same period was only 30, of which 26 were state and private banks, and only 4 were national banks. (For further statistical detail, see table, page 533.)

In a general way the enormous number of bank failures in the South may be attributed to three causes: adverse economic conditions in local communities; incompetent management; and laxity of state laws regulating banking.

Obviously, if a small bank has made its loans mainly to local business men without collateral, whenever the com-

---

[23] Compiled from D. R. Crissinger, "Fifty Years of Banking in the South," in the *Manufacturers Record*, Pt. II, pp. 133–134. See also *Federal Reserve Bulletin* for October 1930.

[24] Statistics compiled from U. S. Comptroller of the Currency, *Annual Report* (1931), p. 37.

NUMBER OF BANK SUSPENSIONS IN THE SOUTH
JANUARY 1, 1920 TO JUNE 30, 1931

| State | State and Private Banks | National Banks | Total |
|---|---|---|---|
| Alabama | 63 | 18 | 81 |
| Arkansas | 217 | 25 | 242 |
| Florida | 215 | 22 | 237 |
| Georgia | 347 | 21 | 368 |
| Kentucky | 74 | 4 | 78 |
| Louisiana | 45 | 2 | 47 |
| Maryland | 11 | 2 | 13 |
| Mississippi | 112 | 13 | 125 |
| Missouri | 415 | 17 | 432 |
| North Carolina | 212 | 26 | 238 |
| Oklahoma | 224 | 70 | 294 |
| South Carolina | 237 | 28 | 265 |
| Tennessee | 104 | 6 | 110 |
| Texas | 282 | 70 | 352 |
| Virginia | 69 | 8 | 77 |
| West Virginia | 40 | 12 | 52 |
| TOTAL SOUTH | 2,667 | 344 | 3,011 |
| TOTAL UNITED STATES | 6,628 | 1,044 | 7,672 |

munity collapses on account of a severe business depression
or on account of a crop failure, or for some other general
cause, the bank itself cannot escape failure. In discussing
this problem before the Banking and Currency Committee
of the House of Representatives, in April 1930, John K.
Ottley, of the First National Association of Atlanta, said: [25]
"When strongly adverse economic conditions strike a local
community in which there is a bank which serves that community alone, it is next to impossible to prevent such a
bank from failing. Successive periods of drought, the activity of a fruit pest or of a plant disease, the adverse conditions of the market for a local product—such causes as
these have brought about the downfall of hundreds of banks
in our [Atlanta Federal Reserve] District. Such banks by
virtue of their limited size and influence cannot possibly
secure the type of management which modern banking de-

[25] *Banking and Currency Committee Hearings,* H. Res. 141, 71st Cong.,
2d sess.

mands, but even with good management the local bank under [these] conditions . . . would be virtually helpless. . . . Many of these banks failed because the community in which they operated failed."

As court records show, a few bank failures in the South have been due to the dishonesty of bank officials. By and large, however, cases of malfeasance have been very few in proportion to cases of misfeasance. In the South it has been too frequently assumed by well-to-do farmers, merchants, and mechanics, that they can become successful bankers because they have been reasonably successful in their original vocation. After entering the banking profession, they usually do well as long as prices are rising and there is general prosperity in the community; but, when prices fall and city correspondents begin to call for curtailment of loans, these self-appointed bankers become panicky and adopt a policy of being "hard-boiled," or they assume a wise dignity in the hope that their bank will escape failure. Although such men usually master the technique and understand the internal economies of banking, they seldom know anything about those external economies which fundamentally affect banking.

As a rule, in the South, laws regulating the organization, supervision, and operation of state banks are not so strict as those in New England.[26] According to Southern state statutes, banks are permitted to organize under general laws and with a small amount of capital. In South Carolina, there is no provision for the amount of capital required to establish a bank, and any bank may have trust powers if it has a capital of $25,000. In Alabama, Ar-

---

[26] The data for the laws governing state banking in the South has been compiled from the last banking laws and amendments of the Southern States as follows: Alabama, 1928; Arkansas, 1925; Florida, 1926; Georgia, 1919, and amendments to 1927; Kentucky, 1926; Louisiana, 1923; Maryland, 1927; Mississippi, 1925, amended to 1927; Missouri, 1919; North Carolina, 1927; Oklahoma, 1926; South Carolina, 1923; Tennessee, 1927; Texas, 1927; Virginia, 1926; West Virginia, 1927.

kansas, Mississippi, Missouri, Oklahoma, and Tennessee, banks can be established with a capitalization of only $10,000 in communities having a population below a specified number, which ranges from 500 in Oklahoma to 1,000 in Alabama, Mississippi, and Tennessee, or to 2,500 in Arkansas, or to 3,000 in Missouri. In Florida, the required capitalization is from $15,000 to $50,000, according to the population of the town; in Virginia, $15,000 to $25,000; in Kentucky and Louisiana, from $15,000 to $100,000; in Texas, from $17,500 to $100,-000, and in no case is the amount to exceed $10,000,000; in Georgia, from $25,000 to $50,000; in Maryland, $25,000 to $200,000; and in North Carolina, $25,000 to $100,000. In West Virginia, the law governing the capitalization of state banks is identical with the Federal law governing the capitalization of national banks.   Five of the Southern States—Alabama, Louisiana, Missouri, South Carolina, and Virginia—do not require double liability of stockholders. For example, in Alabama, in a community having a population of less than 1,000, a bank can be established with a capital of only $10,000 and without double liability of stockholders.   Such small, unit banks cannot command trained managers, nor do they have the necessary financial connections to offset severe losses caused by a prolonged depression.

In each of the Southern States there is provided by law a special banking official, whose duty is to supervise, by means of periodical examinations, the operations of all banks authorized by the state.   The efficiency of these departments depends upon the ability of their personnel, and how far removed they are from political control.   The banks are required to publish in a local newspaper, once or twice a year, statements of their condition.

In every Southern State there are laws requiring state banks to keep certain reserves.   These reserve requirements are summarized in the following table:

## RESERVE REQUIREMENTS UNDER STATE BANKING LAWS IN THE SOUTH

| State | Aggregate Deposits | Demand Deposits | Time Deposits |
|---|---|---|---|
| Alabama | ------- | 15% | ----- |
| Arkansas | 20% | -------- | ----- |
| Florida | 20% | -------- | ----- |
| Georgia | -------- | 15% | 5% |
| Kentucky | -------- | 13% | 3% (Same as National Banks) |
| Louisiana | -------- | 20% | ----- |
| Maryland | -------- | 15% | ----- |
| Mississippi | -------- | 15% | 7% |
| Missouri | -------- | 15% | ----- |
| North Carolina | -------- | 15% | ----- |
| Oklahoma | 20% | -------- | ----- |
| South Carolina | -------- | 7% | 3% |
| Tennessee | -------- | 10% | ----- |
| Texas | -------- | 15% | ----- |
| Virginia | -------- | 10% | 3% |
| West Virginia | -------- | 15% | ----- |

Although these reserves, ranging from 10 to 20 per cent, are apparently high, yet this amount usually includes what is due from other banks, and thus the actual cash reserve requirements are reduced probably by one half.

State banks which are members of the Federal Reserve System, like national banks, are subject to the Federal law. In 1928, only 333 state banks and trust companies, or about 5 per cent of all the state banks and trust companies in the South, were members of the Federal Reserve System.

The banking laws of the Southern States have made possible the existence of entirely too many small, independent, unit banks. Perhaps a step in the right direction would be the establishment of branch banking—that is, large urban banks with branches located in the smaller communities. So far, only eight Southern States—Kentucky, Louisiana, Maryland, Mississippi, North Carolina, South Carolina, Tennessee, and Virginia—authorize branch banking; seven Southern States—Alabama, Arkansas, Florida, Georgia,

Missouri, Texas, and West Virginia—prohibit it; and Oklahoma has no specific provision relating to it.[27]

The National Banking Holiday in March 1933 completely disclosed the underlying weaknesses in the South's banking structure. Upon an examination of the national banks and the state banks by Federal authorities and state bank examiners, respectively, it was found that practically one fourth of the banks in the South which had been closed during the holiday were not sufficiently liquid to function as banks. After the investigation many small communities and a few cities—for example, Greensboro, North Carolina —were temporarily without banking facilities. Since that date definite action has been taken to remedy the situation.

Under the *Emergency Banking Act,* approved March 9, 1933, national banks and state banks that are members of the Federal Reserve System, have been able, where necessary, to increase their capital by selling preferred stock to the Reconstruction Finance Corporation and to their own common stock holders. Also, bank *conservators,* appointed by the Federal Comptroller of the Currency, have been busily engaged throughout the section in liquidating or reorganizing wrecked banks.

Although at the present writing, accurate statistics are not available to show the total amount of losses to depositors, indications describe the bank situation rather clearly. Perhaps nothing short of complete nationalization of the banking system of the states will again bring back public confidence and permit the South to have a normally functioning banking system; for those bankers of "the old order" who have survived have been so terrified by past experiences that they will be overcautious in extending credit to support even ordinary business transactions, much less business expansions.

---

[27] *Federal Reserve Bulletin,* December 1929.

## Public Finance

Of the difficult economic problems confronting the Southern people, few are as complex as those of public finance. Because of the rise of industry and trade within the past three decades; the increase in population, especially in the industrial centers; and the more general diffusion of knowledge, persistent demands arose for roads, schools, and the extension of police powers in the states to promote public health and safety. At the same time the South had a comparatively low per capita wealth and income, partly because of the impoverished negro element of the population. To meet these demands, nearly all of the Southern States have been compelled to resort to heavy borrowing and to revising their tax systems in order to make them yield increasing amounts of revenue.

### STATE INDEBTEDNESS

In 1927, the per capita net debt of each Southern State, exclusive of county and municipal debts, was as follows: [28]

#### PER CAPITA NET DEBT OF SOUTHERN STATES, 1927

| State | Amount |
|---|---|
| Alabama | $16.34 |
| Arkansas | 1.58 |
| Florida | No state debt[a] |
| Georgia | 2.92 |
| Kentucky | 0.99 |
| Louisiana | 8.51 |
| Maryland | 14.99 |
| Mississippi | 9.57 |
| Missouri | 19.93 |
| North Carolina | 51.44 |
| Oklahoma | 1.30 |
| South Carolina | 16.03 |
| Tennessee | 6.96 |
| Texas | 0.81 |
| Virginia | 10.52 |
| West Virginia | 30.62 |

[a] The constitution of the state of Florida prohibits indebtedness by the state as a state. The local debt in 1927 was $465,138,000.

[28] Compiled from U. S. Department of Commerce, *Financial Statistics of States* (1927).

At the same time, the per capita debt of local state debts in the United States was $12.32. North Carolina had the highest per capita debt of all the states in the Nation, and no state in New England had so high a per capita debt as West Virginia. Mississippi had a higher per capita debt than the average per capita debt of the New England States; and Alabama, slightly higher than the average per capita debt of the Middle Atlantic States, including New York, New Jersey, and Pennsylvania.

In 1927, the total state debt in the South amounted to $2,749,487,000, and made a total public debt of $3,162,759,-000. This amount was 4.2 per cent of the estimated true value of property in the Southern States at that time.

Since 1927, a few Southern States have increased their indebtedness. In 1927, the state debt of Alabama was $36,871,000; by the end of 1930, it was $62,511,000. In Missouri, the state debt was increased from $65,559,000 in 1927 to $100,180,000 by the end of 1931; and in South Carolina and Tennessee, it was increased from $5,004,000 and $14,695,000, respectively, in 1927 to $41,745,060 and $21,923,000, respectively, by the end of 1931. Thus, it is evident that nearly all the Southern States, with the possible exceptions of Georgia, Kentucky, and Virginia, are burdened, in proportion to their present wealth, with a heavy bonded indebtedness, since property values have shrunk enormously since 1929.

Along with the increasing bonded indebtedness, the Southern States have been confronted with the problems of constantly tapping new sources of revenue and of increasing, when possible, existing taxes, in order to meet increases in current expenditures, to set up sinking funds, and to meet the interest requirements of their bonds. At the same time the state governments have had to expand the fiscal machinery and make it more efficient from an administrative point of view.

## TAX SYSTEMS AND NEW TAXES

In the Southern States, fundamental changes in the tax systems have occurred very slowly and have come primarily as a result of general economic evolution.  From colonial beginnings, these tax systems have advanced step by step, not only by the modification of old tax forms, but also by the inclusion of new taxes.  In nearly every Southern State the earlier specific taxes on land and on particular classes of movables were, by the middle of the nineteenth century, swept together, by a constitutional rule of uniformity, into a *general property tax*.  At present, ten Southern States—Alabama, Arkansas, Georgia, Mississippi, Missouri, North Carolina, South Carolina, Tennessee, Texas, and West Virginia—on account of this original mandatory provision of their constitutions, still have to rely upon the general property tax as the hub of the entire tax system.  In these states this tax is clearly regressive.  Almost invariably it imposes an unequal burden on rich and poor, on the farmer and the city property owner.  Indeed, the modest and comparatively inexpensive homes of laborers can be, and usually are, assessed at more nearly the real market value than the costly residences of the well-to-do.  Furthermore, there is undoubtedly underassessment in the rural sections; yet in the cities, only a small amount of the tangible wealth—costly household furnishings, and diamonds and other precious jewels—is ever assessed.  In other words, from the standpoint of justice, the chief characteristics of the general property tax in the South, as elsewhere, are undervaluation, evasion, and discrimination.

In view of these facts, Florida, Louisiana, Maryland, Oklahoma, and Virginia have adopted a *classified property tax;* that is to say, property is taxable at different rates, according to a system of classification.  Usually the rates on intangibles are lower than those upon real property, the assumption being that such discrimination will tend to lessen evasion in listing intangibles.

The administration of property taxes in the South is very simple. In every state, except Arkansas, Mississippi, North Carolina, Oklahoma, South Carolina, and Virginia, real estate is assessed annually. In Arkansas, Mississippi, and Oklahoma it is assessed every two years; in North and South Carolina, every four years; and in Virginia, every four years in cities. Personal property is assessed annually in every Southern State; and all property, except in two states, is assessed at "fair market value." In Arkansas, property is assessed at 50 per cent of its market value, and in Alabama, at 60 per cent.

Coming down from the old tax forms of a past generation are *license taxes* and *poll taxes*. Extensive use is made of license taxes, because they are easily administered and because tax officials as a rule believe that the numerous occupations and small businesses have a tax ability which, by its very nature, cannot be reached by the general property tax or the classified property tax. Poll taxes in the South yield relatively little revenue. Each Southern State, however, except Maryland, levies a poll tax. In most of these states the payment of the poll tax is a prerequisite to voting in political elections, and is often used as a device for social or class discrimination.

Increasing fiscal needs have brought into use in the Southern States several supplementary taxes. The most careful analysis that has been made of these new developments in taxation in the South is that by James W. Martin, director of the Bureau of Business Research, University of Kentucky. He explains the effort to attract industry into the South by tax exemptions, and presents a possible correlation of the new tax forms with the change in the type of taxable property and source of income, particularly in the so-called industrial region of the South.[29]

In order to induce the establishment of manufacturing plants, fourteen Southern States have enacted more tax

[29] "Industrial Changes and Taxation Problems in Southern States," in the *Annals of the American Academy*, Vol. 153, pp. 224–237.

statutes than all the remaining thirty-four states. Indeed, during the past decade, various Southern States which formerly had exempted new factories from taxation for a period of five years, increased the time of exemption to seven or ten years. Kentucky even adopted a measure providing for the taxation of machinery and inventory of manufactures at only the state rate, and thereby providing for permanent exemption from local taxes. Such tax exemptions, however, cannot be defended from any sound, long-run point of view. At most, they tend to subsidize one competitor at the expense of another, and seldom have they been the cause for locating factories in any Southern State.

Martin's study shows that in recent years the Southern States have attempted to avoid a breakdown of the general property tax by adopting supplementary taxes—such as, special excises, general sales taxes, motor license and gasoline taxes, and income taxes. As early as 1922, special excises, particularly on tobacco, began to be of considerable importance in the South; by 1930, six of the Southern States were collecting such imposts. There has also been a tendency to tax commodities in general, but such legislation in the South has thus far been confined to Georgia, Kentucky, Mississippi, and West Virginia.

By 1929, every Southern State had a *liquid-fuels tax*. The rate ranged from 2 cents to 6 cents per gallon. Although the *motor-tax* movement has become national in scope, the Southern States have gone farther than others in the use of these revenue devices. While none of the Southern States has an extremely high-average *registration-tax* rate for motor vehicles, none of them has a rate so low as that in Arizona or in California. Furthermore, no state outside of the South imposes a 7-cent rate for its gasoline tax. Indeed, the special motor-tax revenues constitute a larger percentage of total state revenue receipts in the Southern than in the other states. However, the expenditures for highways, in proportion to the number of motor vehicles, are higher in the South than elsewhere.

In 1923, six of the Southern States had passed income tax laws. The amount of revenue produced by state income taxes in the South has always been very much less than that derived from income taxes in the Northern and Western States, not because the rates have generally been lower in the Southern States, but because the initial exemptions were more generous and the administration was less efficient. The following table includes a comparison of the four most important special-tax revenues in the South with the total state revenue receipts.[30]

#### TOTAL STATE REVENUE RECEIPTS COMPARED WITH SPECIFIED CLASSES OF TAX REVENUES, 1928

(Thousands of Dollars)

| | I | II | III | IV | V | VI | VII | VIII | IX |
|---|---|---|---|---|---|---|---|---|---|
| Aggregate of | Total State Revenues | Special Excises | Ratio of II to I (Per Cent) | Gross Sales Taxes | Ratio of IV to I (Per Cent) | Motor License and Gas Taxes | Ratio of VI to I (Per Cent) | Income Taxes | Ratio of VIII to I (Per Cent) |
| Southern States... | 466,591 | 8,917 | 1.9 | 5,173 | 1.1 | 180,930 | 38.8 | 18,995 | 4.1 |
| Outside Southern States... | 1,468,841 | 3,466 | 0.2 | 3,777 | 0.3 | 466,572 | 30.4 | 151,006 | 10.3 |

The South has shown tenacious determination to escape the complete breakdown of its fiscal systems by too rigid adherence to the general property tax as a primary source of revenue. In order to achieve that purpose, the Southern States have adopted supplementary taxes: some are distinctly questionable, as the *general sales taxes;* some are poorly coördinated with the tax system, as many of the *special excises;* and a few are wholly commendable, as the *income taxes.*

As a result of the prolonged depression, the fiscal systems of several of the Southern States have virtually collapsed. Burdened with debts contracted during the period of prosperity when tax receipts were adequate to meet sinking

---

[30] *Ibid.,* p. 229. Reprinted by permission of the author.

fund and interest requirements, many municipalities in the South have recently, on account of delinquent taxes, found it impossible to meet these requirements. In most of the Southern States, school teachers and state and county employees either have not been paid at all or have had their salaries drastically reduced. In these circumstances it has become necessary to seek new sources of revenue. A few of the Southern States—for example, Mississippi and North Carolina—have resorted to the general sales tax as an emergency measure. Others have relied upon the revenue from the production and sale of beer. As a consequence of the repeal of the Eighteenth Amendment, a few of the Southern States—Kentucky particularly—will increase their revenue from special taxes on liquor.

Although it is difficult at present to predict the future of taxation in the South, it is nevertheless reasonable to expect necessary changes to meet new demands. For example, the burden of the ad valorem tax, if the exchange value of real property continues to decline, will strike more and more disproportionately the property owners as a class. Such taxpayers, in these circumstances, presumably will become a pressure group in legislative matters and will, therefore, demand some consideration. Moreover, if the present decline in the general price level continues for a considerable length of time, still other of the Southern States will eventually be faced with the problem of raising, by means of their present tax systems, sufficient revenue to meet, without a deficit, not only the interest and sinking-fund requirements of their bonded debts, but at the same time the ordinary current expenditures of government.

### The South's Future

During the past the population in the South has made a constant effort to utilize to advantage the physical environment afforded by nature, and the progress of each generation has been conditioned by, and at the same time has more or less modified, the given environment. Grave economic problems, such as those just discussed, now cast a shadow over the Southern people.· Apparently the New Deal offers at least temporary relief from some of these problems. But if the South in the long run is to utilize its abundant natural resources to the best possible advantage for its economic and social development, fundamental changes must be inaugurated in the banking and the fiscal systems of the Southern States; barriers now checking the free flow of foreign trade must be removed; and an adequate educational system must be maintained for the training of the rising generation.

### Bibliographical Note

For the various topics in this chapter, primary materials may be obtained from publications of Federal Government bureaus; official documents of the states, such as bank laws, tax laws, and special reports; and statistical reports of industrial corporations.

A specialized treatment of one element of the South's population may be found in John C. Campbell's *Southern Highlander and His Homeland* (New York, 1921).

Of the hundreds of books on the Southern negroes, perhaps the most disinterested general approach is Charles S. Johnson, *Negro in American Civilization* (New York, 1930). A great deal of information may be found in the *Negro Year Book, An Annual Encyclopedia of the Negro* (1931–1932), edited by Monroe N. Work (Tuskegee Institute, Ala.). To be mentioned also are: S. D. Spero and A. L. Harris, *Black Worker: The Negro and the Labor Movement* (New York, 1931); "The American Negro," in the *Annals of the American Academy of Political and Social Science*, Volume 130, November 1928; W. H. Brown, *Education and Economic Development of the Negro in Virginia* (Charlottesville, Va.,·1932).

While several studies have been made of taxation in the South, only a few are available in published form. *Report of the Tax Commission of North Carolina* (Raleigh, N. C., 1928) is by far the most comprehensive tax survey yet made in any of the Southern States. See also *Taxation in Virginia* (New York, 1931), by Harry Stauffer; and *Taxation in Alabama*, by E. Q. Hawk in the BULLETIN OF BIRMINGHAM-SOUTHERN COLLEGE

(Birmingham, Ala., 1931). Besides a brief survey made by James B. Trant, "More Effective Regulation of State Banks," in the *Southern Banker,* November 1931, practically no studies of importance have been made of the present banking situation in the South.

Numerous surveys have been made of the agricultural system in the South. The most important of these include: E. C. Branson, "Farm Tenancy in the South," in the *Journal of Social Forces,* March and May 1923; and W. B. Bizzel, *Farm Tenancy in the United States* (College Station, Tex., 1921).

There are two excellent works on the labor situation in Southern industry: Berglund, Starnes, and De Vyver, *Labor in the Industrial South* (Charlottesville, Va., 1930), a study authorized by the Institute for Research in the Social Sciences, at the University of Virginia; and Clarence Heer, *Income and Wages in the South* (Chapel Hill, N. C., 1930). An illuminating interpretation may be found in G. T. Starnes, "Effects of Industrialization on Labor," in the *Proceedings of the Southeastern Economic Association* (1930), pp. 140–151. A careful analysis from the viewpoint of the cost of production in the cotton textile industry may be found in Claudius T. Murchison, *King Cotton is Sick* (Chapel Hill, N. C., 1930). Also of interest are: J. J. Rhyne, *Some Southern Cotton Mill Workers and Their Villages* (Chapel Hill, N. C., 1930); Lois McDonald, *Southern Mill Hills* (New York, 1929); Marjorie Potwin, *Cotton Mill People of the Piedmont* (New York, 1927); Paul Blanchard, *Labor in Southern Cotton Mills* (New York, 1927); Dexter M. Keezer, "Low Wages in the South," in the *Survey,* November 15, 1926; M. N. Work, "The South's Labor Problem," in the *South Atlantic Quarterly,* January 1920, pp. 1–8; and W. H. Glasson, "Economic Needs of the South," in the *Annals of the American Academy of Political and Social Science,* January 1910, pp. 167–171. See also George Sinclair Mitchell, *Textile Unionism and the South* (Chapel Hill, N. C., 1931).

Howard W. Odum, *American Epoch,* contains not only valuable chapters on the present social and economic status of the South, but also an excellent bibliography.

# Index

# DATE DUE